SHAMANISM, DISCOURSE, MODERNITY

VITALITY OF INDIGENOUS RELIGIONS

Series Editors
Graham Harvey, Open University, UK
Afeosemime Adogame, The University of Edinburgh, UK
Inés Talamantez, University of California–Santa Barbara, USA

Ashgate's *Vitality of Indigenous Religions* series offers an exciting new cluster of research monographs, drawing together volumes from leading international scholars across a wide range of disciplinary perspectives. Indigenous religions are vital and empowering for many thousands of indigenous peoples globally, and dialogue with, and consideration of, these diverse religious lifeways promises to challenge and refine the methodologies of a number of academic disciplines, whilst greatly enhancing understandings of the world.

This series explores the development of contemporary indigenous religions from traditional, ancestral precursors, but the characteristic contribution of the series is its focus on their living and current manifestations. Devoted to the contemporary expression, experience and understanding of particular indigenous peoples and their religions, books address key issues which include: the sacredness of land, exile from lands, diasporic survival and diversification, the indigenization of Christianity and other missionary religions, sacred language, and revitalization movements. Proving of particular value to academics, graduates, postgraduates and higher level undergraduate readers worldwide, this series holds obvious attraction to scholars of Native American studies, Maori studies, African studies and offers invaluable contributions to religious studies, sociology, anthropology, geography and other related subject areas.

OTHER TITLES IN THE SERIES

Anishinaabe Ways of Knowing and Being
Lawrence W. Gross
ISBN 978-1-4724-1734-3

Progress and Its Impact on the Nagas
A Clash of Worldviews
Tezenlo Thong
ISBN 978 1 4094 6820 2

Religious Change and Indigenous Peoples
The Making of Religious Identities
Helena Onnudottir, Adam Possamai and Bryan S. Turner
ISBN 978 1 4724 0297 4

Shamanism, Discourse, Modernity

THOMAS KARL ALBERTS
University of Cape Town, South Africa

Routledge
Taylor & Francis Group

LONDON AND NEW YORK

First published 2015 by Ashgate Publishing

Published 2016 by Routledge
2 Park Square, Milton Park, Abingdon, Oxon OX14 4RN
711 Third Avenue, New York, NY 10017, USA

First issued in paperback 2018

Routledge is an imprint of the Taylor & Francis Group, an informa business

British Library Cataloguing in Publication Data
A catalogue record for this book is available from the British Library

The Library of Congress has cataloged the printed edition as follows:
Alberts, Thomas Karl.
  Shamanism, discourse, modernity / by Thomas Karl Alberts.
      pages cm. – (Vitality of indigenous religions)
  Includes bibliographical references and index.
    ISBN 978-1-4724-3984-0 (hardcover)
  1. Shamanism. 2. Indigenous peoples – Religion.
  3. Civilization, Modern. 4. Religion and culture. I. Title.
  BF1621.A43 2015
  201'44–dc23

                                                      2014037350

ISBN 13: 978-1-138-54881-7 (pbk)
ISBN 13: 978-1-4724-3984-0 (hbk)

for Ushka

in memory of Paul Alberts

Contents

List of Figures and Table

Acknowledgements

All writing is autobiographical. Each chapter, discussion and idea printed in the following pages corresponds with a time and place where it developed and conversations and experiences through which it was thought, so that reading these pages reminds me of the people with whom I shared the writing of this book. They are written into these pages too. I acknowledge with thanks Jama Bernard, Meritt Buyer, Melissa Chatton, David Chidester, Ben Cope-Kasten, Chris Davies, Martino Dibeltulo, Emily Douglas, Jim Faherty, Masha Falina, Aslam Farouk-Ali, Jonathan Faull, Brian Gannon, Helene Greiche, Derek Gripper, Anton Gruter, Anel Hammersma, Renée Holleman, Sajid Iqbal, Maryam Ishani, Jonathan Japha, Sherry Japha, Paul Johnson, Raghav Kishore, Jonathan Kop, Samantha Langsdale, Emily Leys, Kim Levine, Desné Masie, Tomoko Masuzawa, Kathleen McDougall, Arthur Minnaar, Kimberly Powers, Anthony Rickards, Margot Saffer, Sandra Sahyouni, Maxim Sansour, Maggie Schmidt, Alexis Scholtz, Mandy Schreiber, Henrietta Settler, Akiko Shinya, Jacqueline Shoen, Christin Spradley, Natalie Sternberg, Fawaz Taj, Paul Tremlett, Michael Whiting, and Grace Yukich. I thank my family, Anne-Louise Alberts, Paul and Charmaine Alberts, Adrian, Marcus and Dewald Alberts, Graham Rabbitts, Barbara and John Wright, Neil and Ming Colquhoun, John, Alex and Leesa Campbell-Colquhoun, and Jo Gurney.

This book would not have been possible without the support of a few special people: I thank Sian Hawthorne for her passion, careful criticism and friendship. I thank Cosimo Zene, for welcoming me to SOAS, his patience and kindness. I am grateful to Guy Meyer for generously putting options on the table when there were none and continuing a chain of events that scarcely anyone could have dreamed of all those years ago. I thank Federico Settler for his subversive instinct, inspiring friendship, and loyalty. Finally, I am deeply thankful to my beautiful partner and wife Anna, for her patient support and encouragement, her amazing ability to find just the right perspective and words to express it, and for her love.

Thomas Colquhoun-Alberts
London, 17 July 2014

List of Abbreviations

Unless indicated otherwise, all quotations are reproduced verbatim. Use of italics and upper-case reproduce the emphases in the cited original. The Bibliography includes all cited works. Where cited sources include abbreviations of institutional or corporate authors, these are listed in the Bibliography by the abbreviated name. A complete list of abbreviations used in this research is listed below.

Anon.   Anonymous author
CERD   Committee on the Elimination of Racial Discrimination
CIPR   Commission on Intellectual Property Rights
COICA   Coordinadora de las Organizaciones Indígenas de la
            Cuenca Amazónica
CSIR   Council for Scientific and Industrial Research (South Africa)
DOH   Department of Health (South Africa)
DST   Department of Science and Technology (South Africa)
FSS   Foundation for Shamanic Studies
GAIA   The Gaia Foundation
IOL   Independent Online
IA   Internet Archive
IACHR   Inter-American Commission on Human Rights
IACrtHR   Inter-American Court of Human Rights
ICCPR   International Covenant on Civil and Political Rights
ICERD   International Covenant on the Elimination of Racial Discrimination
ICTSD   International Centre for Trade and Sustainable Development
IFC   International Finance Corporation
IKS   Indigenous Knowledge Systems
ILO   International Labour Organization
ILO169   International Labour Organization Convention Concerning
            Indigenous and Tribal Peoples in Independent Countries (No. 169)
IUCN   International Union for Conservation of Nature
n.d.   no date
NGO   Non-governmental Organisation

NPC	National Planning Commission of South Africa
PCTD	patents, copyright, trademarks and designs
RAFI	Rural Advancement Foundation International
RRF	Ringing Rocks Foundation
SME	Shamanism and Medicine for the Earth
SSC	shamanic state of consciousness
SSN	Sacred Sites Network
SSP	Society for Shamanic Practitioners
SSSHT	Society for the Study of Shamanism, Healing and Transformation
THO	Traditional Healers Organisation
THPA	Traditional Health Practitioners Act
TKDL	Traditional Knowledge Digital Library
UN	United Nations Organisation
UNCHR	United Nations Commission on Human Rights
UNEP	United Nations Environment Programme
UNHRC	United Nations Human Rights Committee
WCC	World Council of Churches
WCED	World Commission on Environment and Development
WCIP	World Council of Indigenous Peoples
WGIP	Working Group on Indigenous Populations
WHO	World Health Organization
WWF	World Wildlife Fund

Chapter 1

Introduction

The Problem

During the three centuries since the earliest reports about someone called a 'shaman' were authored by European travellers to Siberia's southern steppes, shamans have been identified in cultures and locations increasingly removed in space and time from North Asia. Varieties of globally distributed local religiosities have been assimilated into a globalised shamanic idiom, prompting proposals that 'shamanism' is a 'new world religion' (for example, Cox 2003, 2010). At the same time, the notion that shamanic practices are better conceived as techniques and therefore available to anyone, rather than confined only to the called has prompted their even wider embrace. In its temporal dimension, shamans have been identified in the early histories of Judeo-Christianity (for example, Craffert 2008, Keeney 2006 and Money 2001), in ancient Greece (discussed in Chapter 2) and even implicated with the very beginning of human cognitive evolution some 40,000 to 60,000 years ago (for example, Winkelman, discussed below). Today, shamans are widely imputed to exist in all places and at all times throughout human history. A key question therefore arises: how did a kind of ritual specialist first reported in Siberia in the seventeenth century become an eponymous category of a universal religiosity? The many interrelated answers to this question have in common that figurations of shamans are useful and represent value for an assortment of advocates and proponents of shamanic religiosities, as well as for their detractors.

This observation, although hardly novel, is nevertheless important to state at the outset, because it helps account for the significant and wide-ranging transformations in shamanism discourse in recent decades. This suggestion adumbrates a second range of questions: for whom has shamanism become important, and why? What does this discourse do? What are its uses, effects, implications and consequences? How have these interventions and applications contributed to elaborating shamanism in the twenty-first century? Here the problem shifts orientation from shamanism's historical conditions of possibility towards considering how this discourse is effective in the contemporary world.

Since the 1970s, several constellations of interests and values have given a new prominence to shamanic religiosities, stimulated new proliferations and intensifications of shamanism discourse, and variously deepened and extended shamanism's entanglements in domains of knowledge and practice in which it was previously less prominent. I consider these developments with reference to three practical domains. First, since the 1970s, a transnational indigenous peoples' movement has articulated a sophisticated critique of the universal right of all peoples to self-determination in relation to their lands, territories and resources, and has challenged human rights jurisprudence to find durable solutions without compromising the sovereignty of states or the nation-state system of international law. Solutions emerging from recent court judgments place great store in the 'intertemporal dimension' of indigenous 'cosmovisions', and utilise an established transnational discourse on shamanism to argue and articulate their key provisions; in doing so, they have consolidated shamanism discourse in new practical domains by adding legal precedent and citation to shamanism's discursive regularities.

Second, since the late 1970s and early 1980s, concern about degradation of the Earth's biosphere have prompted distinctions between sustainable and unsustainable forms of human development. Conservationists turned to indigenous peoples believing they could derive models from indigenous examples of sustainable use of natural resources. Indigenists in turn saw growing anxiety about destruction of natural environments as another vehicle for drawing attention to indigenous peoples' grievances. However, by promoting the notion that indigenous peoples are inherently disposed towards living in harmony with nature, the indigenist-environmentalist alliance revised the primitivist trope of the noble savage with the notion of the 'ecological Indian', who is more of nature than in it (Nadasdy 2005: 292). Ecocentric disposition became a measure of ontological difference and indigenous ontology became the embodiment of a critique of anthropocentric mastery of natural environments. Again, shamanism supplied both discursive language with which to articulate ecocentric disposition as ontological difference and the critique this difference implied with respect to the unsustainability of anthropocentric models of development.

Finally, the emergence in recent decades of a specifically neoliberal *homo economicus* has transformed some shamans into spiritual entrepreneurs whose investments in their embodied human capital – in their skills and experience, social and spiritual networks and related qualities of their corporeal being – render their shamanic practice as a form of economic self-conduct. However, as the correlate of a neoliberal art of government, neoliberal subjects, including shamans, are also increasingly targeted by sovereign power, even as the principle of economy in self-conduct increasingly undermines the juridical form of the sovereign's authority and reduces the domain in which sovereign power can be exercised effectively. Amid transformations of culture into commodity, knowledge into property, tradition into patent, identity into asset and shamanic practice into human capital, shamanic religiosities are increasingly drawn into the ambit of things arranged by governments as much as by professional shamans to optimise desirable ends.

The problem I want to draw out of these discussions is how these domains of knowledge and practice – I term them 'indigenism', 'environmentalism' and 'neoliberalism' – contribute to relaying and extending shamanism as a discursive formation by adjusting and consolidating the principles of its unity, its mechanisms of assimilation and exclusion, its strategies for accumulating and deploying authority and the range of its effects.

In the background of this book is a concern with time, which is to say the temporalisation of a relation between past, present and future; but also *our* time, which is to say a relation between a structure of time represented in shamanism discourse and a subjectivity for whom this temporal relation is important. This problem adumbrates the third area of inquiry with which this book is concerned. Europeans authored reports about shamans for European audiences beginning at the height of the European Enlightenment; the story of shamans' emigration from Siberia to populate the world and human history is a European story that closely shadows the moods and predilections of European modernity. Of course, this is not to say people who are today known as shamans did not exist before European observers testified to the fact. But the discourse about this kind of person and its elaboration and extension to other places and times is inseparable from conditions of possibility brought about by modernity. There may have been shamans before the eighteenth century, but without modernity there is no shaman*ism*. Following Michel Foucault, this research understands modernity as the structure of a relation between the time of the present and past, one that produces a form of subjectivity marked by a tendency to exalt the present by seeking its limits. As I explain below, this modern subjectivity is double-hinged, with one arm establishing a form of relationship with knowledge of the world and another establishing a form of relationship with the knowing self. This double-hinged subjectivity is instantiated in a practical limit attitude in epistemological and ontological dimensions, in turn establishing a self-perpetuating dialectic that animates and innervates modern history. The simultaneously particularising and universalising tendencies of statements about shamans are part and parcel of modernity's practical limit attitude and account for the proliferations and intensifications of shamanism discourse in general since the eighteenth century.

In summary, the argument developed in the course of the following chapters is as follows: the emergence of modern subjectivity inaugurated, among many consequences, a discourse oriented by ideas and practices attached to a particular kind of person, that is, a shaman. Over the following centuries, this discourse was elaborated in considerable detail via the perpetual motion of the modern limit attitude that oscillates between epistemological labour, figured in a tendency towards universalism, and ontological labour, oriented toward contingency. This elaboration was part of a globalising European modernity such that by the twenty-first century, its constituting terms, categories and ideas were authoritatively available, if not already applied, to virtually all times and places in human history and supplied discursive language to a diverse array of concerns and interests. These concerns have in turn facilitated proliferations and intensifications of shamanism discourse in new practical domains and at increasing scales of complexity and transnational distribution. I argue that these can best be seen in shamanism's imbrications with indigenism, environmentalism and neoliberalism.

To be clear then, this is not an ethnographic study; I am less interested in particular shamans in particular places except in so far as such examples illustrate the larger argument about transnational shamanism discourse. When I refer to spiritual or shamanic traditions, I prefer the sociological emphasis of 'shamanic religiosity', by which I mean practices and beliefs related to a person who, while in an altered state of consciousness, engages with spirits with the intention of influencing events and fortunes impacting others, whether individuals or collective groups. This definition is deliberately broad and is intended more as a positive rubric than a normative definition. This rubric is adapted from common definitions of the classic Siberian shaman, which generally emphasise three elements: a shaman is someone who 1) enters a trance-state in which they 2) journey into a spirit world 3) on behalf of or in service to a community (for example, Eliade 1964, Hoppál 2004, Hultkrantz 1973, Siikala 2004). This definition tends to narrow what counts as shamanic and I have toned down the emphasis on shamans' out-of-body journeys in recognition that the terms 'shaman' and 'shamanic' increasingly designate spirit mediums and possession states too. I also de-emphasise shamans' communal role to include New Age or neo-shamanic adaptations which tend to be more individualistic (although not necessarily so). Possession states are often also not communal, particularly as spirit mediums' practices, like neo-shamans', become increasingly entrepreneurial. Finally, I prefer the sociological emphasis on situated social practices over shamans' experience as emphasised by phenomenologists like Eliade and Hultkrantz.

As for shaman*ism*, I use this term to designate a discourse. My approach draws on Foucauldian archaeology and pays attention to the regularities, unities, modalities and strategies that link statements about shamans into a knowledge structure. However, I supplement this approach with attention to the accidents and contingencies that have shaped the emergence in history of a discourse about shamans. Thus, a genealogical account of shamanism precedes the more archaeological orientation of discussions of indigenism, environmentalism and neoliberalism. Furthermore, I take seriously Arjun Appadurai's recommendation that the study of discursive forms ought to broaden what counts as discourse (Appadurai 1996: 159). Key sources include scholarly sources, including many published a century or more ago, as well as popular books and magazines written for general audiences; reports and legal instruments produced by transnational organisations, particularly agencies of the United Nations Organisation (hereafter UN), but also activist and professional organisations of various kinds; legal documents, including court judgments, national legislation and international conventions and declarations; documents published by or on behalf of national governments, including policy directives, statements by statutory agencies and submissions to regulatory authorities; as well as a variety of digital sources, including promotional material published by shamanic practitioners and practitioner organisations on personal websites and via digital social media. All these sources are cited in the bibliography. Before considering methodological and theoretical questions, however, a brief sketch of the ways in which shamanism, indigenism, environmentalism and neoliberalism are imbricated will help set the scene. Then follows an explanation of modern subjectivity's limit-seeking labours along with consideration of this book as another instantiation of this practical limit attitude. The remainder of the chapter considers a range of representations of shamans along with recent trends in thinking about and representing shamanism. That discussion helps situate this work in relation to shamanism discourse, of which it is also a part, as well as offering a contrast between contemporary formations of shamanism discourse and the genealogy of shamanism that is the focus of Chapter 2.

The Terrain

Credo Mutwa is well known to a generation of South Africans as a folklorist, traditional healer and shaman. Beginning in the 1950s, Mutwa promoted himself as an authority on African folklore and tradition and during the 1960s published several collections of southern African folklore (Mutwa 1969, 1966,

1964). Although Mutwa's elaborate and evocative accounts of southern African culture and religion bore virtually no resemblance to recorded ethnographic data, either then or since (Chidester 2004: 72; Rose 1965: 471), his renditions of African primitivity and unassimilable difference from white-settler culture gained him favour with the apartheid regime and permission to build a 'cultural village' in Soweto, the sprawling township south-west of Johannesburg reserved for black South Africans by segregation laws. The village depicted rural 'tribal' scenes corresponding to the different ethnic profiles at the centre of the apartheid policy of separate development. It was torched during the 1976 Soweto Student Uprising. Despite re-establishing his village in the 1980s as an artists' retreat and tourist attraction conveniently close to the gambling and tourist resort of Sun City in the Boputhatswana Bantustan, by the 1990s Mutwa was widely regarded as an eccentric whose rambled musings on 'things African' were derisively dismissed by black South Africans and increasingly ignored by whites.

During the 1990s, however, Mutwa's fortunes changed. In 1997, he addressed a meeting of the World Health Organisation in Kampala, Uganda, on traditional healers and 'Indigenous Knowledge Systems' (Chidester 2004: 76–7) and in 1999 addressed the 'Living Lakes' conference in California, where he received a Best Conservation Practice Award from the Global Nature Fund. His books were brought back into print and he supplemented them with new titles (Mutwa 2003, 1999, 1996). He received visits from international authors and luminaries of the global New Age circuit, including Stephen Larsen of the Joseph Campbell Foundation, family therapist, cybernetician and 'all-American shaman' Bradford Keeney, and British conspiracy theorist David Icke. The gist of Icke's six-hour interview with 'Zulu shaman Credo Mutwa' is that Mutwa confirms Icke's claim that Planet Earth is controlled by a cabal of extraterrestrial, shape-shifting reptiles, with the juicy addition that these reptiles have been known to Africans for millennia as the Chitauri and are supposedly mentioned frequently in African folklore. Less outlandish but similarly celebratory is the volume of Mutwa's 'dreams, prophecies and mysteries' titled *Zulu Shaman* and edited by Larsen (Mutwa 2003), while Keeney was so enamoured with Mutwa that he included in his 'Profiles of Healing' series a book-length feature on Mutwa, 'the most famous African traditional healer of the 20th century' (Keeney 2001, RRF 2010b). Published by the Ringing Rocks Foundation (hereafter RRF), an organisation founded in 1995 'to explore, document, and preserve indigenous cultures and their healing practices', RRF bestowed on Mutwa the honorific 'Distinguished Artist and Teacher of African Traditional Culture' and awarded him a lifetime stipend that would 'allow this treasure to live out his days free to create as he chooses' (RRF, quoted in Chidester 2004: 77).

Mutwa is neither unique nor an anomaly. A small but popular publishing industry translates local southern African religiosity into a globalising shamanic idiom, and spiritual, self-help and pop-psychology shelves of popular bookstores feature several collaborations between proponents of Euro-American 'New Age spirituality' and African 'shamans' (discussed in Chapter 5). And not only in Africa: the Foundation for Shamanic Studies (hereafter FSS) is a quasi-scholarly not-for-profit organisation based in Mill Valley, north of San Francisco. The FSS was founded in 1979 by Michael Harner, a retired anthropologist whose interest in shamanic religiosities was catalysed by his fieldwork among Jívaro and Conibo communities in the Ecuadorian and Peruvian Amazon respectively during the 1950s and early 1960s. Harner's interest in shamanic religiosities culminated in his theory of 'core shamanism', his distillation of shamanism's essential elements. Core shamanism is the organising principle of the FSS's '[dedication] to the preservation, study and teaching of shamanic knowledge for the welfare of the Planet and its inhabitants' (FSS 2012a). Towards this end, during the 1990s the FSS led several 'expeditions' to the Republic of Tuva to assist Tuvans recover their shamanic heritage after decades of Soviet domination (Brunton 1994, Uccusic 2000). Like the RRF with Credo Mutwa, the FSS awarded 'founding father of Tuvan shamanism' Mongush Barakhovich Kenin-Lopsan the honorific 'Living Treasure of Shamanism' along with a lifelong stipend. Similar outreach and recovery projects based on core shamanism have been pursued in other parts of the world, most recently among a Baniwa community in the north-west Amazon basin (see Chapter 4). Over the years, the FSS has grown into an international operation, with 'faculty members' and affiliate organisations spread across North America and Europe and several in Australia, South East and East Asia and South America.

The labours of the FSS and RRF are complemented and supported by professional shamans such as the several hundred registered members of the Society for Shamanic Practitioners. Largely based in North America, these professional shamanic practitioners are determined to establish shamanic practice as a credible profession and viable career option. They host regular conferences, publish industry journals (as opposed to scholarly ones) and extensively utilise online resources, such as the professional networking website Linked-In, where membership of the Shamanism group had grown to over 2,000 members by May 2014. These and similar efforts have contributed significantly towards establishing the transnational template of shamans-as-healers/counsellors/therapists tapped by Credo Mutwa, the FSS and the RRF, among many similar examples. Consider the RRF's ten-volume 'Profiles of Healing' series: described as an 'encyclopedia of the world's healing practices', the ten volumes aim to 'evoke the experience of being with traditional healers, shamans and medicine people as they teach their cultural ways' and credits series author Bradford Keeney with undertaking 'the broadest and most intense field studies of global shamanism in history' (RRF 2010a, 2010c). Although Keeney is not featured in the series, he is the subject of *American Shaman: An Odyssey of Global Healing Traditions* (Kottler et al. 2004), which was awarded Best Spiritual Book of 2004 by *Spirituality and Health* magazine in the 'Shamanism' category, according to Keeney's website (Mojo Doctors 2012).

But such apparently New Age circuits are not isolated from the societies in which they are embedded and with which they connect, even if their discourses tend to represent them as autonomous from the conditions of their own possibility. For example, 'indigenous knowledge', such as promoted internationally by Credo Mutwa and celebrated by both popular and specialist literature, has been an important plank in successive post-apartheid governments' strategies to modernise South Africa's economy in accord with former president Thabo Mbeki's version of a developmental state. A cornerstone of Mbeki's vision of an African Renaissance (Odora Hoppers 2002), this strategic prioritising of 'indigenous knowledge' has also transformed local traditional healers into 'African traditional health practitioners', targeted them with an ensemble of legislative, policy and regulatory interventions and brought them into the ambit of things disposed by government towards desired ends. The South African example is hardly unique. In Brazil during the 1990s, alliances between local indigenous tribes and international environmental advocacy groups shifted the locus of tribes' indigenous identity from historical dispossession of valuable land to contemporary possession of valuable local knowledge about environmental resources, plant and animal species and biodiversity conservation. This reworking of indigenous peoples' public image from 'combative warriors' to 'stewards of the forest' generated new representations of shamans as privileged keepers and protectors of valuable indigenous knowledge and elevated shamans to new prominence in Brazilian public life (Conklin 2002). As political power flowed from tribal chiefs to shamans, new alliances emerged between central government and indigenous groups, now represented by shamans, to resist international biopiracy by foreign corporations and regulate bioprospecting in the national interest.[1] These developments not only reversed indigenous

---

[1]   Robinson's distinction between bioprospecting and biopiracy, adapted from the ETC Group (previously the Rural Advancement Foundation International) is useful here. Bioprospecting refers to 'the exploration of biodiversity for commercially valuable genetic and biochemical resources'; biopiracy refers to 'the appropriation of the knowledge and genetic resources of farming and indigenous communities by individuals or institutions

tribes' exclusion from Brazilian national imaginaries, they also anchored these imaginaries in indigenous knowledge. As Beth Conklin has argued, these transformations have distilled an increasingly generic image of shamanic religiosity that, firstly, singles out medicinal plant use as the core of shamanic practice and expertise, and secondly, separates shamans from images of conflict, killing and death (see Chapter 4).

This rendering of a generic shaman therefore is not simply a faddish enthusiasm for certain circuits of New Age discourse. It is a consequence of a convergence of interests that have restructured practical fields, implicated categories of people increasingly identified as shamans and inflected shamanism discourse with symbolic capital cached in notions of indigenous knowledge and identity, sustainable development and spiritual, as much as physical, health. For example, pharmaceutical companies have been prominent among corporate interests currying favour with local indigenous healers. Pharmaceutical companies have long appreciated that indigenous healers offered valuable research leads, but were restrained from pursuing these leads by a combination of logistical difficulties inherent in collaborating with often remote and relatively inaccessible indigenous communities, as well as difficulties inherent in scientifically isolating medicinal properties of plants identified from folk traditions. During the 1980s, however, indigenist activism and the indigenist-environmentalist alliance increased visibility of and access to indigenous communities while advances in genetic science improved efficiencies in scientific research. The combination of these factors meant that collaborating with shamans and other kinds of traditional healers became both viable and desirable. At least one transnational corporation, Shaman Pharmaceuticals, made data collection from indigenous communities and traditional healers a cornerstone of their research and development strategy, as it sought a foothold in the lucrative and highly competitive phytomedicines market. However, as that market has grown – in 2006 its global worth was estimated at nearly $43 billion and up to $60 billion with a 7 per cent annual growth rate (Okigbo and Mmeka 2006: 88, World Bank 2006: 2) – public-sector interests have also become increasingly prominent. So great have been concerns in India, particularly following several high-profile cases of biopiracy, that India's government established the Traditional Knowledge Digital Library, a government-funded project to 'safeguard the sovereignty of [India's] traditional knowledge' (TKDL 2012). The archive conforms to international patent classification specifications, while agreements with Japan, the European

---

seeking exclusive monopoly control (usually patents or plant breeders' rights) over these resources and knowledge' (see Robinson 2010: 11–18).

Union, United Kingdom, United States and the World Intellectual Property Organisation grant confidential access to their respective patent offices to prevent intellectual property theft.

While governments of developing countries such as Brazil, India and South Africa are increasingly alert to the threats to their economies posed by biopirates,[2] they are also increasingly alert to the benefits and opportunities of bioprospecting. For example, the South African government is working hard to position South Africa as an important player in the international pharmaceutical industry. The 'supportive policy environment' the government has gradually devised identifies 'indigenous knowledge' as a critical element in 'the "farmer-to-pharma" value chain' (alongside 'biotechnology ... infrastructure' and 'biodiversity heritage exploitation') (DST 2008: 10), and is coordinated with legislative reforms, institutional bodies, regulatory authorities, state agencies, private-sector interests and traditional healers' organisations and associations. Sovereign power is increasingly entangled with the discursive regularities and embodied practices authorising generic representations of shamanic religiosities as modes of health practice and sources of practical knowledge.

This then is the terrain on which the following chapters are situated and the intersections with which they are concerned. I argue that imbrications between the practical domains I refer to as 'indigenism', 'environmentalism' and 'neoliberalism' have facilitated proliferations and intensifications of shamanism discourse at increasing scales of complexity and transnational distribution. More than this, discursive and embodied practices imbricating these domains are extending shamanism into domains in which previously it has been less prominent. International human rights law, sustainable economic development, intellectual property, and neoliberal governmentality are a few of the examples I consider.

With the exception of Chapter 2, this analysis almost entirely draws on data from Africa, the Americas and Europe. There are historical reasons for this selection. Transnational indigenism coalesced in the Americas where a succession of meetings and conferences attended by indigenous delegates from across the region during the 1970s sustained the nascent movement until an indigenous agenda was formally institutionalised at the UN in 1982. Similarly, the Amazon Basin was the crucible in which the indigenist-environmentalist alliance was forged in the late 1980s, while Europe and North America were regions where ecocentrism as indigenous ontological difference found the widest appeal. My focus on transatlantic exchanges between North American and African

---

2   See McGown and Burrows (2006) for forty case studies from Africa.

shamanic practitioners reflects how African shamanic religiosities increasingly appeal to North American audiences in much the same way that South American shamanic religiosities appealed a generation ago, although today these audiences are arguably more usefully construed as markets. As the correlate of neoliberal entrepreneurialism, neoliberal governmentality is also an important problem for this research. I illustrate this problematic with reference to post-apartheid South Africa, where the government's implementation of a raft of policies, legislation and regulatory authorities designed to bring 'African traditional healers' into the ambit of things coordinated towards desired ends is an instructive example of the implications for shamanism of neoliberalism's statecraft. The implications of these historical developments have been felt around the world and my analysis touches on impacts in other regions too, including Australia and Asia. However, restrictions on length, coupled with the necessities of a focused discussion, have precluded considerations of further examples.

Modernity's Double-hinge

The tendency to think of modernity as an epoch with a definite beginning and trajectory of development is as important to the concept of 'modernity' as it is problematic. It is important because the sense of a rupture between 'the present' and an era preceding it has given the present a quality of urgency, with a sense of purpose and mission. This tendency has been instrumental in supplying a temporal vision with a teleological connection imposed between past, present and future projecting a more or less consistent line of development and progress. It is problematic because the notion of a sudden rupture is empirically false and a teleology of progress is easily contested. However, more problematic than the veracity of the claim is the claim's effect. If modernity can be distinguished from other periods of human history, it is not simply because, as Habermas (1990) suggests, 'moderns' wish to express a consciousness of their present as the culmination of a transition in time. This is hardly novel, as usages of 'modern' since the fifth century attest (Benavides 1998: 187). Rather, it is because this consciousness inheres in a contradiction, one that introduces ambivalence into moderns' relation with the present time of modernity such that the present appears activated and becomes animated in a mode easily given to personification of temporality, as if time itself were conscious with purpose, intention and obligation.

Capturing and arresting this problem for long enough to illustrate its workings has been an enduring preoccupation for a range of historians, philosophers and cultural critics, and more often than not, Friedrich Nietzsche has featured prominently in their accounts. For example, Paul de Man credits Nietzsche with recognising that the impulse behind all 'genuine modernity' is the hope of reaching a true present unencumbered by past mistakes and false knowledge. This true present will be a new point of origin marking a new departure. The problem, de Man argues, is that as a principle of origination, modernity turns into a generative power that is itself historical because it cannot but engender history; he illustrates his point by recalling Nietzsche's frequent resort to the image of a chain (de Man 1970: 390). Bruno Latour similarly acknowledges Nietzsche when he points to the 'illness of historicism' that afflicts moderns: 'They want to keep everything, date everything, because they think they have definitively broken with their past' (Latour 1993: 69). Breaking with the past requires a past to break with, so that affirmations of modernity become as many iterations and painstaking reconstitutions of a past that avowedly is not in the present. Except that it is, because of moderns' 'incapacity to eliminate what they nevertheless have to eliminate in order to retain the impression that time passes' (ibid.). Coming into focus here is a sensitivity shared by De Man and Latour to a paradox at the centre of the idea of modernity: to the importance of desire in the labour of being modern and to the usefulness of a relational approach to critiquing modernity. De Man's deconstructive approach and Latour's method of leveraging critique from disjunctures between nature, politics and discourse both indicated helpful and important options. However, I find Michel Foucault's account of modern subjectivity particularly useful in relation to modern shamanism. For all the criticisms levelled at Foucault's work – and there are many, of which the most serious and devastating surely is Derrida's (discussed below) – Foucault's critique of modern subjectivity remains compelling, because it draws out the relation between desire and paradox in a way that succinctly illustrates their mutuality and co-determination, and therewith describes a mechanism or a motive force that is also (misrecognised as) the sense of modern progress and development and easily given to personification of temporality.

Foucault's reflections on 'modernity' in his essay 'What is Enlightenment?' were prompted by his close reading of Immanuel Kant's 1784 essay *An Answer to the Question: What Is Enlightenment?* (Foucault 2003, Kant 2009). Foucault saw in Kant's essay a novel approach to thinking about the present and therewith a way into the problem of characterising modernity. Foucault begins by noting that Kant's portrayal of Enlightenment as 'exit' or 'way out' departed from conventional forms of philosophical reflection on the present by characterising the present as historical difference. This difference is not the same as distinction, in the sense of belonging to a present distinguished by certain inherent characteristics. Rather, it is a relational difference, along the lines of the difference 'today' introduces with respect to 'yesterday' (45).[3] Kant's definition of Enlightenment as 'man's emergence from his self-incurred immaturity' suggests the locus of this difference is an emergent subjectivity, one more mature with respect to yesterday's youth. Foucault is also interested in the formation and constitution of this new subjectivity. His interpretation of Kant's understanding of Enlightenment – simultaneously a collective process and an act of personal courage that, taken together, superimpose the universal, the free and the public uses of reason – stresses the modifications of pre-existing relations between will, authority and the use of reason through which this subjectivity is formed.

Although Foucault discounts Kant's essay as minor within Kant's larger body of work, he is drawn to it because, Foucault suggests, it stands at the crossroads of critical reflection and reflection on history (48). On the one hand, Kant's essay is concerned with the overall passage of human history towards maturity and on the other hand seeks to show how each individual, in their own way at every moment, is responsible for that process. Written three years after publication of *Critique of Pure Reason* and four years prior to *Critique of Practical Reason*, Kant's essay represents Kant's reflections on the status of his own enterprise. This juncture is where Foucault thinks Kant's essay is most significant. It is also where Foucault takes his leave. Although Kant's relational approach to the Enlightenment as event appeals to Foucault, Foucault is more interested in developing the proposal that the Enlightenment as event inaugurates a subject position marked by a relation to time and therewith to itself in time. Foucault is looking for a way to represent the modern self-understanding instantiated by this relation with the present such that the dynamo of history set in motion by this relation, along with its implications for modern self-understanding, is emphatic. Rather than speaking of modernity in temporal terms as an epoch or historical period that can be distinguished from pre- or post-modern, Foucault proposes regarding modernity as an attitude, one that struggles with attitudes of 'countermodernity'. His exemplar is Charles Baudelaire, for whom being modern, according to Foucault, was less about 'consciousness of the discontinuity of the passing moment' and more about an attitude, one that 'consists in recapturing something eternal that is not beyond the present instant, nor behind it, but within it' (49). In contradistinction to the spectator's posture of the *flaneur*, the man of modernity is distinguished by a will to exalt the present:

---

3   Unless otherwise indicated, page citations in this discussion refer to Foucault (2003).

> For the attitude of modernity, the high value of the present is indissociable from a
> desperate eagerness to imagine it, to imagine it otherwise than it is, and to transform
> it not by destroying it but by grasping it in what it is. Baudelairian modernity is an
> exercise in which extreme attention to what is real is confronted with the practice of
> liberty that simultaneously respects this reality and violates it. (50)

In this way, Foucault develops his characterisation of modernity as a limit attitude: a way of thinking and feeling, acting and behaving that 'marks a relation of belonging and presents itself as a task' (48). Foucault's characterisation of the modern philosophical ethos as a limit-attitude turns the Kantian question back on itself: whereas Kant drew attention to the limits of what is knowable, but in the form of a necessary limitation ('limits knowledge must renounce exceeding'), the modern philosophical ethos directs us to query 'whatever is singular, contingent, and the product of arbitrary constraints' within what is given to us as universal (53). This limit attitude, practiced in the form of a possible crossing-over, neither takes universal structures as its objects, nor is transcendental or aimed at making metaphysics possible. Instead, it is critical and directed at the historical events that have constituted selves as doing, thinking, saying subjects. No longer does enlightened inquiry deduce from the form of what we are the limits of what we can do and know. Instead, the modern critical attitude separates out from the contingencies that have made us the possibilities for saying, thinking and doing differently: 'It is not seeking to make possible a metaphysics that has finally become a science; it is seeking to give new impetus, as far and wide as possible, to the undefined work of freedom' (53–4). For this reason, the modern critical attitude is both practical and experiential; this work 'at the limits of ourselves' constantly 'puts itself to the test ... of contemporary reality' such that it grasps both where change is possible and desirable, and the form this change should take.

From this perspective, being modern refers to a practical attitude informed by a philosophical ethos rooted in a mode of interrogation that is modernity's Enlightenment heritage. The impetus towards critique is a consequence of this attitude's structure and effectiveness, each in a co-dependent relation and mutually inclusive identity. This attitude accomplishes its effects because its form as historical ontological examination interrogates its own contingencies and acts on these contingencies as the limits crossing of which will satisfy the will to freedom. But such satisfaction is as temporary as the crossing, for every action has its contingencies and temporalities, and so new limits enable new practices in the ceaseless critique of being modern: 'we are always in the position of beginning again' (54). Being modern, the *being* of being modern, means that the task of practical critique cannot be refused. But neither can the freedom it desires be achieved, because freedom that is identical with desire is always restricted by the transiency of desire's fulfilment. And so the historical time of modernity is characterised by an enormous proliferation and intensification as the limits of knowledge are pushed outwards and the limits of the desiring self are elaborated with ever-growing complexity and refinement.[4] For Foucault, as for Baudelaire, the modern limit attitude is double-hinged, with an epistemological arm establishing a form of relationship with the present and an ontological arm establishing a form of relationship with one's self: 'To be modern ... is to take oneself as an object of a complex and difficult elaboration' (50). Epistemological labour adds to what is already known, by questioning and discovering, testing and elaborating, rejecting and correcting, modifying and adjusting and similar procedures for submitting data to methodical analysis, thereby expanding the limits of knowledge at a given point in time and therewith one's relationship with the present. Ontological labour references work at the limits of the self by identifying the contingent in everything given as universal and thereby multiplying the surfaces of appearance of the knowing self. Ontological labour draws attention towards embodiment, towards particularities of bodies and differences between particular bodies. The simultaneity of epistemological practice that tends to produce universal structures, and ontological practice that tends to deconstruct universals into embodied contingencies, establishes a self-perpetuating dynamic, a perpetual motion dynamo that animates and innervates modern history. If this summation merely resembles atemporal human cognition, recall that since the seventeenth century this double-hinged labour has been put to work in the services of a practical attitude that, firstly, desires to grasp the present to transform both the present and the knowing self; secondly, is equated, conflated, or otherwise regarded as identical with an exercise of personal liberty and freedom, and therefore, thirdly, presents itself as a task and indeed an obligation that may not be refused.

This is all good and well, but it remains to explain how modernity as limit attitude is related to shamanism's proliferations and intensifications. And why shamanism – why this evident desire for shamans and for what shamans are variously taken to represent? The implication of Foucault's theory of modernity, that we should see the modern limit attitude at work in shamanism discourse, is confirmed by the heterogeneous proliferations of claims about shamans and pertaining to something like 'shamanic religion'. Today, there are more claims

---

4   Foucault's analysis of 'the historical moment of the disciplines' and their practice upon the body illustrates this kind of elaboration (Foucault 1977a: 137–8, cf. 135–69).

about an objective shamanic religiosity oriented around agentive spirits and 'non-ordinary reality' than ever before and they are increasing; and yet every claim represents another surface of appearance, not of an objective shamanic religiosity, but of a desiring self. Shamanism as discourse illustrates well the alternating dynamic between modern epistemological and ontological practices. This brings us to the second question. Eighteenth-century European reports about shamans recounted shamans' claims to knowledge beyond reason's limits, claims that effectively renounced the limits of Enlightened reason. No wonder then the century of denunciation that followed: shamans were dismissed as so many charlatans, tricksters and frauds. But where there are claims to a knowledge beyond reason's limits, to a kind of practice that doesn't merely labour at the limits but actually transcends them, these have strongly appealed to some moderns for precisely the same reason they have appealed to moderns who reject them. An aesthetic critique of modernity relies too on the modern limit attitude, even if only to renounce it (Tremlett 2008, cf. Asad 2003: 45–52).

One implication of Foucault's thesis is that this kind of labour by and large is inescapable. Yet if every critique is merely another staging in the reproduction and elaboration of its respective object of knowledge and subject of desire, then there cannot be an Archimedean point from which to articulate a critique. Foucault was aware of this problem and recommended the method of historico-ontological critique to address it, although it is doubtful that his recommendations to steer clear of 'all projects that claim to be global or radical', or to confine one's critique to 'very specific transformations' – perceptions of sexuality or insanity are his examples – either escapes totalising systems of representation ('... more general structures of which we may well not be conscious and over which we may have no control') or diminishes reliance on the same discursive structures the modern attitude takes as its object of critique. This is Jacques Derrida's well-known criticism of Foucault's *Folie et déraison*:[5] Foucault's attempt to write a history of madness, 'of madness *itself*', is unfeasible because such a history must rely on the language of reason, 'the language of psychiatry *on* madness', on madness already constituted as 'an object and exiled as the other of a language and a historical meaning which have been confused with logos itself' (Derrida 2005a: 33–4). Foucault did not satisfactorily address Derrida's critique, although he accedes to it in his essay on the Enlightenment. Without mentioning Derrida, Foucault writes, 'It is true that we have to give up

---

[5]   An abridged English translation was published in 1967 titled *Madness and Civilization: A History of Insanity in the Age of Reason*; an unabridged translation was published in 2006 titled *History of Madness* (see Foucault 2006, 1967).

hope of ever acceding to a point of view that could give us access to any complete and definitive knowledge [*connaissance*] of what may constitute our historical limits' (Foucault 2003: 54).

That said, Foucault's shift towards genealogy was partly a response to criticisms of the archaeological method of his earlier studies, including Derrida's and Foucault's own self-critique (for example, Foucault 2002: 183–4).[6] The development of Foucault's methodology from archaeology to genealogy is well known: Foucault's earlier studies tended to place greater emphasis on the appearance of objects (asylums, madness, prisons) and gave less attention to their transformation in time. Or, more precisely, less attention to how discourse produces identity between non-identical objects via a range of discursive regularities that appropriate, transform, incorporate and assimilate disparate and heterogeneous social forms and thereby gives shape, structure, regularity and unity to a discursive formation in time. Foucault himself was aware of this limitation and acknowledged that archaeology is 'a sort of motionless thought' that 'seems to treat history only to freeze it' (ibid.: 183). Taking Nietzsche as his point of departure, Foucault argued that his genealogical method opposes the search for origins with a historical sensibility, one that opens a way towards critiquing suprahistorical perspectives and a view of history as the unfolding of a long and continuous series of events in accord with the destiny of a people. This historical sense Foucault thought capable of avoiding the domination of a suprahistorical perspective 'if it refuses the certainty of absolutes' and cultivates 'a dissociating view' that perceives divergence and discontinuity, includes

---

6   Considerations of Derrida's deconstructive critique have progressed considerably since Carlo Ginzberg claimed that Derrida transformed Foucault's project 'into silence pure and simple – perhaps accompanied by mute contemplation of an aesthetic kind' (Ginzberg 1992: xviii). Like Derrida, Gayatri Spivak, Derrida's most loyal and consistent interpreter, is also acutely sensitive to the structures of language that ensure the Other as Subject is not accessible to Foucault, whose subject position is unalterably not-Other (Spivak 1999: 268; cf. 1988). *Contra* Ginzberg, who reads Derrida's 'facile, nihilistic objections' as the cessation of speech, Spivak considers the problem from the subject-position of an Other constituted by a language that is not their own. In questioning whether the subaltern can speak, she asks of the conditions conducive to their speech act. Spivak's question is foreshadowed by Derrida's shifting interests away from prioritising the impossibility of an answer to the question posed by *différance* towards placing greater emphasis on ethics and therewith the political. Referencing Derrida as much as Emmanuel Levinas, Spivak suggests 'life is lived as the call of the wholly other, which must necessarily be answered … by a responsibility bound by accountable reason'. Thus Derrida outlines the 'deconstructive embrace' of justice and law, ethics and politics, gift and responsibility, and the aporia that links the undeconstructible first term of each pair with the calculus of the second term which supplies, via the supplement 'and', the imperative for responsible action (Spivak 1999: 425–8; cf. Derrida 2005b, 1999).

marginal elements and is 'capable of shattering the unity of man's being through which it was thought that he could extend his sovereignty to the events of his past' (Foucault 1977b: 153).

The problem of course is the genealogical method does precisely that. That is to say, for all its improvements on the archaeological method, to the extent that genealogical critique adds a temporal dimension, it does stake a claim in the present on elucidating events of the past. Derrida's critique stands. At a methodological level, genealogy works against the tide of *différance*. The trace of a finite pattern of descent works in the opposite direction to the trace of infinite deferrals halted only by the instantiation of a metaphysics of presence or an originary violence, such as that which establishes law. Against the always already of deconstruction stands the intending will of the genealogist, whose objective is not to deconstruct so much as to reconstruct differently. Genealogy operates within the calculus of law, politics and responsibility; it is not interested in aporias that disclose justice, ethics and the gift of life as a supplement supplies a lack and adds an excess. Indeed, genealogy instantiates the modern limit attitude; its commitment to critique via a methodological refusal of the certainty of absolutes arguably is emblematic of the alternation of epistemological and ontological labour. Foucault noted that 'History becomes effective to the extent that it introduces discontinuity into our very being', commenting in a later passage that 'Through this historical sense, knowledge is allowed to create its own genealogy in the act of cognition' (Foucault 1977b: 153, 157). Moreover, Foucault's suggestion that genealogical critique is motivated by a kind of personal liberation from 'the meta-historical deployment of ideal significations and indefinite teleologies' (ibid.: 140) anticipates his subsequent observation in his essay on Kant – that the modern limit attitude makes a practical task of liberty, one that may not be refused.

This acknowledgement relates to another arguably more fundamental problem. As Derrida noted, Foucault's study of madness relied on a language *about* madness to represent and convey its critique, one that was inevitable, inescapable and undermined Foucault's own aspirations to write a history from within. In doing so, Foucault's study became an influential and enduring part of the structuration of a discourse about 'madness'. A similar issue confronts this study, to the extent that it too is situated as external to 'shamanism' and relies on a vocabulary generated by scientific and literary discourses about shamans to critique that same discourse. The corollary to these respective observations is important. Foucault's study of madness simultaneously reinforced a distinction between 'madness' and 'sanity' and privileged the latter over the former because the alignment of his study with sanity (that is, reason) is embedded in the very structure of language articulating his analysis. Similarly, this study of shamanism reinforces a distinction between 'religious' and 'secular' and privileges the latter over the former because its practice of 'secular' scholarship and alignment with secularity is embedded in the language articulating my analysis. Formulated in these terms, the difficulty here exceeds the terms of a debate about methodology that has occupied scholars working in the academic field of the study of religions for several decades. That debate has grappled with the implications of the fact that 'religion' is a category of specifically European provenance and part of what we might name, after Heidegger, as the onto-theological tradition (in which 'secularism' is equally embedded), that cannot be universalised without perpetrating epistemic violence against those non-European cultures and traditions to which it is applied. That debate has progressed through critiques of phenomenological approaches to studying 'religion' (J. Smith 1987, 1982, 1978), the *sui generis* status of 'religion' (McCutcheon 1997; cf. 1999), ideological labours implicit in utilising 'religion' as a universal category (Fitzgerald 2000, Masuzawa 2005) and has acknowledged the field's indebtedness to imperial conquest and colonial administration for providing data in the form of 'religious' Others (Chidester 1996, King 1999, Lopez 1995). However, in recent years, this debate has rubbed up against the problem that the notion of 'secular', as in 'secular' academic research and writing, is a category of similarly questionable provenance and universality, although one that, compared with 'religion', remained mostly unquestioned until relatively recently (for example, Asad 2003, Dressler and Mandair 2011). The methodological problem coming into focus is that far from two independent universal categories, differentiation between 'secular' and 'religious' is historically contingent upon a phase of human history, albeit only the last few centuries, in which European ways of knowing have dominated. More than that, this dichotomous differentiation has been an important and highly instrumental tool in that domination. By exporting religion to its colonies, 'religion' became a marker of difference from a European centre empowered by its mastery of 'secular' technologies – notably science, democracy and capitalism – along with a self-serving monopoly of the 'virtues' it attached to them. This European self-understanding *qua* 'secular' nevertheless has required the reality and universality of 'religion' for its own coherence, now modulated by a legislated differentiation between public and private domains. The academic study of 'religion' has of course been an important forum for constituting and perpetuating the normativity of this peculiarly Western dichotomy and modulation. The difficulty for scholars of 'religion' is therefore particularly acute: not only is the universality of 'religion' questionable, but the practice of 'secular' scholarship about 'religion' turns out to be problematic too. With some exasperation, scholars of religion increasingly ask whether it is possible, at a methodological level, to write about 'religion', 'religious' practices, 'shamanic religiosity', or indeed neoliberal economics or human rights law as 'secular' projects, in ways that do not perpetuate an assumption that these terms signify two distinct and universal categories, when in fact they are mutually imbricated, co-determining and provisional.

The problem, as Derrida noted, is that when we speak of 'religion', we are confronted with the problem of Latin, which is to say the globalisation of a language, but also the irresistible hegemony of a culture that is not Latin but Anglo-American:

> For everything that touches religion in particular, for everything that speaks 'religion', for whoever speaks religiously or about religion, Anglo-American remains Latin. Religion circulates in the world, one might say, like an *English word <comme un mot anglais>* that has been to Rome and taken a detour to the United States. Well beyond its strictly capitalist or politico-military figures, a hyper-imperialist appropriation has been underway now for centuries. It imposes itself in a particularly palpable manner within the conceptual apparatus of international law and of global political rhetoric. Wherever this apparatus dominates, it articulates itself through a discourse on religion. From here on, the word 'religion' is calmly (and violently) applied to things which have always been and remain foreign to what this word names and arrests in its history. (Derrida 2002a: 66–7)

Derrida noted further that the same can be said for the entire 'religious vocabulary', including 'cult', 'faith', belief', 'sacred', 'holy' and similar terms, to which we might add 'ancestor spirits', 'spirit possession', 'trance' and similar terms from the 'shamanic' vocabulary. The co-extensiveness of 'religion' and worldwide Latinisation 'marks the dimensions of what henceforth cannot be reduced to a question of language, culture, semantics, nor even, without doubt, to one of anthropology or history':

> *Globalatinization* (essentially Christian, to be sure), this word names a unique event to which a meta-language seems incapable of acceding, although such a language remains, all the same, of the greatest necessity here. For at the same time that we no longer perceive its limits, we know that such globalization is finite and only projected. What is involved here is a Latinization and, rather than globality, a globalization that is running out of breath *<essoufflée>*, however irresistible and imperial it still may be. (Derrida 2002a: 67)

From this perspective, comparative studies of religions in postcolonial contexts are particularly important and instructive, because they bring into sharp relief the Eurocentric, theological and secularist presuppositions of the academy. Richard King has suggested postcolonial studies of religions are better conceived as a kind of 'foreign body' or 'point of infiltration' within the university that indicate opportunities to interrogate and debate the academy's preconceptions (King 2011: 54). Or as David Chidester has put it, religion is not the object of analysis, but its occasion (Chidester 1996: 259). That is one response to the problem of religion. Mandair and Dressler argue that a genealogical approach to studying 'religions' 'helps to release the space of the political from the grasp of the secularization doctrine' by 'bringing to light the often hidden function of secularism in religion-making'. Nevertheless, on its own, genealogical critique fails to grasp the nettle of 'the circular relationship among history, secular critique, and the liberal imaginary', whence the aporia at the heart of the religion/ secular problematic. Indeed, Mandair and Dressler argue all three strands of post-secular scholarship, namely liberal secularist socio-political philosophy, 'postmodernist critiques' of ontotheology (the quote marks are theirs) and genealogies of power, '[reify] the dialectic of the religio-secular construct and the politics in which it is embedded'. Instead, they call for a meta-perspective that is both post-secular and post-religious, 'and, to the extent that the religious and the secular are epistemologically and semantically linked, for a perspective that is *post-secular-religious*' (Mandair and Dressler 2011: 19). Developing and testing the adequacy of such a perspective is the task set the eleven contributors to Dressler and Mandair's edited volume *Secularism and Religion-Making* (Dressler and Mandair 2011).

These critiques of methodology in the study of religions are important, productive and highly stimulating. That said, at a methodological level, my ambitions are considerably more modest. While I shine a critical light on constructions of 'religious' objects, from 'shamans' and 'shamanic practitioners' to 'sacred sites' and '*sangomas*', I do not exercise the same degree of critical engagement with the 'secular' status of, for example, 'human rights' or 'neoliberal governmentality', or indeed this book as a form of 'secular' writing. For purposes of answering the questions informing it, I acknowledge but do not engage the 'impossible inheritance' of globalatinised vocabularies nor the task of 'un-inheriting' them via the kinds of metaperspectives proposed by Mandair and Dressler (on 'un-inheriting', see Mandair and Dressler 2011: 18–19). Although bracketing this problem arguably perpetuates this reification, sustaining a metacritique of globalatinisation at the same time as advancing a systematic critique of shamanism's imbrications with indigenism, environmentalism and neoliberalism would confuse the focus.

To summarise then, 'modern' in the following chapters means a kind of subjectivity that emerged via developments and transformations in European culture and society between the sixteenth and eighteenth centuries and then proceeded. Modernity as epoch refers to the temporalisation of this mode of subjectivity and its indexing by instantiation of a range of preferred political, social and economic arrangements. This characterisation specifically rejects the historicist suggestion that modernity is the leading edge of universal human history unfolding, or that it signposts the telos of human development, universalised and periodised. The approach here is precisely the opposite. The notion of 'modern' and its preferences for certain social arrangements is historically a peculiarly European idea, while the project of extending it to all corners of the world has been animated by the logic of modern subjectivity itself. That is to say, the modern limit attitude has given rise to a range of ideas about a modern self, notably pertaining to individual autonomy and personal liberty, such that preferred arrangements, for example, secular liberal democracy, monogamous marriage, or capitalist economies, appear virtuous and the best possible 'order of things'. To the extent that this study operates within this framework, this analysis could be said to participate in the project of 'provincialising Europe' (Chakrabarty 2000; cf. 2002), but only to a limited extent. Although this study shares a similar critical orientation towards European modernity, the history told here does not narrate subaltern histories or aspire to mediate subaltern voices. This study is not about shamans or shamanic religiosities, although obviously it does implicate them. This study is about shaman*ism*, a structure of knowledge produced of modern subjectivity and one of many modes of discursive practice by which modern subjects are formed and historically European concerns with interpolating the self into preferred socio-political arrangements and dispositions have spread around the world. Neither does this study assume an Archimedean vantage beyond modern limits. Rather, it is undertaken in the mode of a 'critical ontology of the present' (Foucault 2003: 56) that inevitably also instantiates the modern limit attitude that pivots modern subjectivity.

This account of modernity may be read to imply a subjectivity and temporality that is pre-modern or non-modern, or at least an attitude that is counter-modern. An implication that can only ever be a gesture of the powerful (Chakrabarty 2002: xix), this is why modern selves, at least initially, were European selves and why liberty, equality and fraternity were denied non-European populations in Africa, Asia, Australasia and the South Pacific and the Americas, and indeed Europeans who were not male, landed and monied. A few centuries later, however, we are all in various ways products of European modernity, albeit differently affected and shaped by globalised modern institutions and mechanisms for achieving certain social arrangements. Globalised modernity has brought us into altogether new conditions of neighbourliness and therewith transformed putative difference *from* into difference *within* (Appadurai 1996: 29). By this I mean to draw attention to how modernity encounters itself in similitudes and disjunctures, in difference that circles back on itself to be (re)presented as familiar but not the same, as different but not too much. To wit, as Piers Vitebsky has argued, an organising trope of shamanism discourse has been that shamanic religiosity belongs in the past of remote tribes and the present of modern subcultures. Since the 1990s, however, a shamanic revival has appeared in the present of some of those tribes, who today are neither remote nor tribal and who now, along with modern subcultures and often in the same ceremonies, practice something called 'shamanism' (Vitebsky 1995). The FSS's report of its expedition to Tuva illustrates this problem. FSS Field Associates Director Bill Brunton conceived of the expedition to emulate the Dalai Lama's 1992 visit to Tuva and celebration of Tuva's Buddhist tradition that ensued. Brunton hoped to do the same for local shamanic traditions (Brunton 1994). Towards this end, Brunton enlisted the apparently enthusiastic support of Tuva's then-President Sherig-Ool Oorzhak whose personal involvement elevated the FSS group's successive meetings and joint public performances with prominent Tuvan shamans to national event. During the first of four FSS expeditions to 'the Land of Eagles', core shamanism, an example par excellence of modern shamanism discourse, became a model for rehabilitating 'their [Tuvans'] shamanism', while this rehabilitation, undertaken in the mode of an authentic recovery of a pre-Russian past, formed a crucial part of Tuva's project of post-Soviet nation formation and nationalist development. In this way, shamanism and nationalism, two quintessentially modern discursive modes, converge under the sign of primordial and pre-modern, and modernity circles back to confront its products as if for the first time. Similar patterns of resemblance and differentiation are evident in indigenism, environmentalism and neoliberalism.

A last point to note here is the importance of bodies in shamanism discourse and the double-hinged labour shamanism exemplifies. Early reports from Siberia recounted tales of shamans who slashed their bodies and miraculously survived, while Enlightenment scientists took delight in unmasking these slashed bodies as concealed substitutes and repositioning shamans' allegedly extraordinary bodies within ordinary limits. Theorists of neurosis focused on hysterical bodies to account for disordered minds, while romantics through the years have idealised shamans' capacities to exit their bodies and undertake extraordinary journeys in disembodied worlds or alternatively to manifest disembodied spirits in ordinary worlds. Still other accounts have been variously awed and fearful of shamans' shape-shifting bodies, or shamans' powers to impinge other bodies, whether by cure or affliction. We see this focus on shamans bodies in relation to indigenism, environmentalism and neoliberalism too: shamans embody a bond that binds people with place, such that place articulates collective identity and founds the right claimed by all 'peoples' and particularly indigenous peoples, to collective self-determination in relation to their lands, territories and resources; shamans' bodies supply valuable symbolic capital to a critique of anthropocentric mastery of nature and embody a subject position from which to articulate that critique; shamans' bodies are distinguished by relatively rare skills and abilities that offer shamans a competitive advantage amid neoliberal emphases on entrepreneurialism of the self, but for roughly the same reason also marks shamans' bodies as targets for biopower. If shamans' bodies have been a focal point for shamanism discourse, the labours associated with directing that focus, regarding that perception and representing and sometimes sharing that consideration inheres in another body, one that gives practical effect to double-hinged labour via practices of representation. In Chapter 2, I address the relationship between these two bodies, between the shamans' body as a knowledge object and the body of a knowing subject who embodies and gives practical effect to the modern limit attitude. For the remainder of this chapter, however, I want to consider a range of these effects by considering representations of shamans along with trends in thinking about and representing shamanism.

Representing Shamans

Early writings about shamans tended to be concerned with the origins of a religio-cultural institution apparently prevalent among indigenous populations of Central and North Asia. Opinion was divided between whether shamanic religiosity originated in Siberia or came from elsewhere, India and China being favourite sources. In some versions of the former view, 'shamanism' was regarded as the original religion from which all other religions have emerged (I consider a version of this hypothesis in Chapter 2); in the latter view 'shamanism' was regarded as a degeneration of 'Brahmanism' or 'Lamaism'. Both accounts sought evidence for their respective hypothesis in philological analyses of the term 'shaman', with the Sanskrit term *sramana*, Pali term *samana* and Manchu term *saman* being favourites among orientalists. The Polish anthropologist Maria Czaplicka provides a useful summary of these philological arguments in her 1914 monograph *Aboriginal Siberia*: 'In Sanskrit *śram* = to be tired, to become weary; *śramana* = work, religious mendicant. In the Pali language the word *samana* has the same meaning. These two latter words have been adopted by the Buddhists as names for their priests.' Alternatively, '*samam* is a Manchu word, meaning 'one who is excited, moved, raised'; *samman* (pronounced *shaman*) and *hamman* in Tungus have the same meaning. *Samdambi* is Manchu: 'I shamanize', i.e. "I call the spirits dancing before the charm"' (Czaplicka 1914: 197–8; see also Mironov and Shirokogorov 1924). Linguistic morphology invited cultural and historical comparisons. For example, based on philological analysis, F. Max Müller concluded: 'Shamanism found its way from India to Siberia via Tibet, China, and Mongolia. Rules on the formation of magic figures, on the treatment of diseases by charms, on the worship of evil spirits, on the acquisition of the supernatural powers, on charms, incantations, and other branches of Shaman witchcraft, are found in the Tanjur, or the second part of the Tibetan canon, and in some of the late Tantras of the Nepalese collection' (Max Müller 1868: 233–4). Many Russian observers were of the same opinion (Znamenski 2004a, 2003a).

However, some observers were unconvinced by either the Sanskrit or Pali evidence. American anthropologist Berthold Laufer thought the debate amounted to little more that the history of an error. After weighing the evidence he concluded 'Tungusian *saman*, *šaman*, *xaman*, etc., Mongol *šaman*, Turkish *kam* and *xam*, are close and inseparable allies grown and nourished on the soil of northern Asia – live witnesses for the great antiquity of the shamanistic form of religion' (Laufer 1917: 371). Indeed, Laufer was dismissive of 'pan-Indianism, which held the minds of scholars enthralled ... and the germs of which are not yet entirely extirpated' (ibid.: 364). Turning inside out the question of Indic philological diffusion into central and north Asia, Laufer argued that the word 'shaman' found its way into both Indo-European and Uralic (Finnish; Hungarian) languages 'as a scientific term' and cited the noted Assyriologist A.H. Sayce to demonstrate the point. In the second volume of his *Introduction to the Science of Language*, Sayce wrote: 'In Shamanism, so called from the Shaman or Siberian sorcerer, who is himself but a transformed *śrâmana* or Bhuddhist missionary priest, we rise to a higher conception of religion' (Sayce 1880: 293). Sayce's evolutionary theory of religion posited a succession of transformations beginning with ancestor-worship and fetishism into the 'higher conception' Sayce identified with shamanism, then totemism and eventually polytheism which 'gives birth to its own destroyer' in the form of a 'Godhead' '(who) becomes more abstract, more worthy' as the generations pass (ibid.: 288–99). The transformation of 'shaman' into a type and 'shamanism' into a category accelerated as Anglo-American writings about north Asian cultures and societies proliferated during the nineteenth and early twentieth centuries, a topic I explore in greater detail in Chapter 2 with reference to North American anthropology.

Another forum for scientific applications of 'shaman' and 'shamanism' concerned shaman's mental states. Explanations of shaman's strange behaviour in terms of the sciences of physiology and psychology were frequent from the end of the nineteenth century. Znamenski gives the early example of Russian physician M.F. Krivoshapkin who in 1865 compared shamanism with hysteria and named the condition 'hysterical demonomania' (Znamenski 2004: xxxvi). Taking up the theme, Bogoras wrote in 1910 that in 'Studying shamanism, we encounter, first of all entire categories of men and women who either suffer from nervous agitation or who are obviously not in right mind or completely insane', suggesting that this nervous agitation is especially noticeable among women because they are more prone to neurosis (Bogoras, quoted in ibid.: xxxvii). By the turn of the twentieth century, shamanism was also seen as a psychiatric condition linked with the environment and was described in theoretical terms as arctic hysteria. Maria Czaplicka and Swedish scholar of religion Åke Ohlmarks were particularly influential in popularising this explanation of shamans' mental states, basing their observations on earlier fieldwork by Bogoras, Jochelson, Sieroszewski and others (discussed in Chapter 2). For example, Czaplicka claimed 'the essential characteristic of a shaman is a liability to nervous ecstasy and trances' and thought the notion of being called by spirits to the shaman's vocation 'generally equivalent to being afflicted with hysteria' (Czaplicka 1914: 198, 172). Czaplicka directly attributed this 'pathology' to Siberia's harsh environment:

> Shamanism seems to be such a natural product of the Continental climate with its extremes of cold and heat, of the violent *burgas* and *burans* [snow and wind storms], of the hunger and fear which attend the long winters, that not only the Palaeo-Siberians and the more highly cultivated Neo-Siberians, but even Europeans, have sometimes fallen under the influence of certain shamanistic superstitions. (Ibid.: 168)

That passage appears in Czaplicka's *Aboriginal Siberia*, in the section titled Pathology which also consisted in a single chapter titled Arctic Hysteria. In his Preface to *Aboriginal Siberia*, the anthropologist of religion R.R. Marett praised Czaplicka's discussion 'of those remarkable facts of mental pathology summed up in the convenient term "Arctic Hysteria"'. He continued, 'This side of her work is all the more important because, apart from these facts, it is difficult or impossible to appreciate justly the religious life of these Siberian tribes; and to say the religious life of a primitive people is almost to say their social life as a whole' (Marret, in ibid.: vii–viii). In similar terms, Ohlmarks also emphasised the unique nexus of shamanism, hysteria and arctic weather. He described Siberian 'shamanism' as 'the great hysterical attack which ends with cataleptic collapse, partly the arctic delirium of persecution and spirit hallucination' (Ohlmarks, quoted in Znamenski 2007: 99; cf. Ohlmarks 1939: 352). Novakovsky agreed: 'this scourge of the northern tribes is the product of that media in which they are forced to live and lead a difficult struggle for existence' (Novakovsky 1924: 113). Although the theory of arctic hysteria did not endure, the relationship between 'shamanism' and psyche remained a preoccupation well into the twentieth century. For example, the French-trained Russian anthropologist Sergei Shirokogorov devoted several chapters of his 'Psychomental Complex of the Tungus' to the subject of shamans and the 'psychomental conditions of shamanism' (Shirokogorov 1935; cf. Mitriani 1992). Psychiatry and psychology were important vehicles through which 'shaman' as type and 'shamanism' as category were universalised and applied to an ever-widening range of ethnographic data. By mid-century, however, psychiatric approaches, which tended to emphasise shamans' personality, were losing favour to psychoanalytic approaches, which tended towards more sympathetic interpretations of shamans' mental states in relation to their role and function within their community (for example, Boyer 1962, Devereaux 1969, Kraus 1972, Silverman 1967). Claude Lévi-Strauss called psychoanalysis 'the modern version of shamanistic techniques' and 'shamans and sorcerers' precursors to psychoanalysts (Levi-Strauss 1963: 204). Increasingly 'shamanism' was represented as a social institution in 'primitive', 'pre-modern', or 'traditional' societies that channelled symbolically the fears and anxieties of local communities.

Soon, however, medico-scientific representations of 'shamans' and reductionist explanations of 'shamanism' in terms of pathology or social role and function were challenged by non-reductionist accounts that saw in shamans' experiences the essence of religion. Probably no scholar has been more influential in popularising interest in shamans in the West and expanding the application of the term 'shamanism' than Romanian scholar Mircea Eliade. Eliade's book *Shamanism: Archaic Techniques of Ecstasy* was originally published in French in 1951, when Eliade was living a self-imposed exile in Paris. An aspiring scholar of religion, Eliade taught briefly at the École Pratique des Hautes Études and used his appointment there to position himself in an international network of scholars of religion, which included the Italian historian of religion Raffaela Pettazzoni, Dutch phenomenologist Gerardus van der Leeuw and German scholar of religion Joachim Wach. Eliade would eventually succeed Wach as Professor of the History of Religions at the University of Chicago's School of Divinity in 1958, a position he held until his death in 1986. Eliade's achievements are considerable. He transformed the study of religions at American universities and beyond, deeply influenced a generation of students and scholars and through this expanding range of influence established 'history of religion' as a disciplinary field. Still, his ideas and his early political allegiances were heavily criticised even in his lifetime and especially since his death. His legacy has been a point of sometimes-vociferous debate among scholars of religion and a lightning rod for wider debates about theory and method in scholarship about religion, particularly the validity and usefulness of phenomenological approaches to studying religion and the enduring impact of Eliadian phenomenology in the field of study of religions. It is not necessary to repeat those debates, these have been exhaustively addressed elsewhere (representative examples include Allen 1988; Alles 1988; Corless 1993; McCutcheon 2003, 1997; Rennie 2006, 2001; J. Smith 2004: 61–100, 1987: 1–23). Instead, I want to restrict this discussion to Eliade's book on 'archaic techniques of ecstasy' and its relation to shamanism discourse. It was only after *Le Chamanisme et les Techniques Archaïques de l'Extase* was expanded and published in English translation in 1964 that Eliade's book became widely, although not unanimously, regarded as the authoritative study of shamanic religion and practice. This perception was doubtlessly aided by Eliade's growing authority as the pre-eminent scholar of religion in North America, symbolic capital he used to establish the reputation of both his book and that also contributed to *Shamanism* becoming the 'turntable' between intellectual discourses of the nineteenth century and popular appropriations of shamanism in the twentieth century (Boekhoeven 2011: 128, 138–9; Von Stuckrad 2002: 173–4). Shamans occupy an important place in Eliade's overarching intellectual project and his study of shamanic 'techniques of ecstasy' is presented as evidence of his theory of religion and illustrative of the appropriateness and usefulness of his comparative method. It is therefore useful to very briefly sketch Eliade's account of religion before considering his representations of shamans.

Eliade rejected reductionist explanations of religion in terms of physiology, psychology, sociology, economics, linguistics, or art as simply false because they omit 'the one unique and irreducible element in it – the element of the sacred' (Eliade 1958a: xvii). This element 'which belongs to [religion] alone and can be explained in no other terms' was the key term and organising principle of Eliade's theory of religion. In *The Sacred and the Profane* Eliade argued that the world comprises two fundamental and irreconcilable domains and therewith planes of existence, 'the sacred' and 'the profane'. Whereas profane space is experienced as 'homogenous and neutral', sacred space is reality, it is 'the only *real* and *real-ly* existing space'. Eliade named the experience of the 'nonhomogeneity of space' 'religious experience' and claimed it is a 'primordial experience, homologizable to a founding of the world':

> For it is the break effected in space that allows the world to be constituted, because it reveals the fixed point, the central axis for all future orientation. When the sacred manifests itself in any hierophany, there is not only a break in the homogeneity of space; there is also revelation of an absolute reality, opposed to the nonreality of the vast surrounding expanse. The manifestation of the sacred ontologically founds the world. ... the heirophany reveals an absolute fixed point, a centre. (Eliade 1959a: 21)

The notion of 'hierophany' occupies a central place in Eliade's work. Constructed of the Greek *phaino* (to appear; to manifest/be manifested; cf. kratophany, theophany, epiphany, ontophany), hierophanies are manifestations of the sacred that, as such, rupture the homogeneity of profane space and therewith reveal absolute reality. Since any object is capable of transfiguration into an hierophany, hierophanies are intensely paradoxical: 'A *sacred* stone remains a *stone*; apparently (or, more precisely from a profane point of view), nothing distinguishes it from all other stones. But for those to whom a stone reveals itself as sacred, its immediate reality is transmuted into a supernatural reality' (ibid.: 12). Contrasted with sacred space manifested or revealed in hierophanies, in profane space, '*true*' orientation is impossible, 'for the fixed point no longer enjoys a unique ontological status; it appears and disappears in accordance with the needs of the day.' In place of a world, 'there are only fragments of a shattered universe' in which man is 'governed and driven by the obligations of an existence incorporated into an industrial society'. To live in a profane world is ontologically disorienting, whereas '[t]he sacred is saturated with *being*' (ibid.: 12, 23–4).

This desire to live in a real and effective world, 'a sanctified world', Eliade claimed was the motive reason for elaborating 'techniques of *orientation* which, properly speaking, are techniques for the *construction* of sacred space'. Not to be confused with human labour, 'in reality the ritual by which he constructs a sacred space is efficacious in the measure in which *it reproduces the work of the gods*' (ibid.: 29). Eliade thought this labour of 'making the world sacred' and orienting one's ontological being around a sacred centre was a primordial impulse, which is to say, a universal generative principle, that inseparably connected 'religious conceptions' and 'cosmological images' to form 'the system of the world':

> *(a)* a sacred place constitutes a break in the homogeneity of space; *(b)* this break is symbolized by an opening by which passage from one cosmic region to another is made possible (from heaven to earth and vice versa; from earth to the underworld); *(c)* communication with heaven is expressed by one or another of certain images, all of which refer to the *axis mundi*: pillar (cf. the *universalis columna*), ladder (cf. Jacob's ladder), mountain, tree, vine, etc.; *(d)* around this cosmic axis lies the world (=our world), hence the axis is located "in the middle," at "the navel of the earth"; it is the Centre of the World. (Ibid.: 37)

Eliade thought this orienting 'cosmic pillar', an *axis mundi* equivalent to 'the centre of the world' that connects 'cosmic levels' grounds ontological being and founds our shared world. For Eliade, this 'system of the world' is the archetypal cosmogony reproduced in specific techniques of constructing sacred space, techniques that replicate 'the paradigmatic universe created and inhabited by the gods' (ibid.: 34). In *Patterns in Comparative Religion*, Eliade clarified that his notion of the 'Centre' is not necessarily a cosmological idea. Repeating the same point in *Shamanism*, Eliade explained that the Centre refers to the scene of any hierophany that 'manifested realities ... not of our world, that came from elsewhere and primarily from the sky' (Eliade 1964: 259–60). It is pre-eminently a shaman's mastery of techniques of ecstasy that enables him, alone among 'magicians and medicine men of primitive societies', to journey between cosmic levels (ibid.: 259; cf. 5, 107). Although the morphology of shamanic techniques may vary, the 'essential schema' is everywhere the same: the shamans' trance enables him to pass through an 'opening' or 'hole', the same hole through which passes the central pillar of the world and through which gods descend to Earth and the dead descend to the underworld; 'it is through this same hole that the soul of the shaman in ecstasy can fly up or down in the course of his celestial or infernal journeys' (ibid.: 259). Mastery of 'archaic techniques of ecstasy' that enable shamans to journey between cosmic levels differentiates shamans from other members of their clan as much as this ability distinguishes 'shamans' as a type of magico-religious person (ibid.: 107). Eliade organised *Shamanism* around illustrating this thesis. The book begins with general comments related to 'shamanism and mystical vocation', followed by four chapters on initiation into the shamanic vocation. Eliade used the encyclopaedic method he associated with history of religions as an academic discipline to present ethnographic evidence illustrating the universality of the 'cosmic pillar' and the shaman's 'celestial ascent' and descent to the underworld. The only continents from where Eliade does not draw examples are Antarctica and Africa, explaining in a footnote that identifying shamanic elements in African religions 'would lead us too far' (ibid.: 374, n. 116).

Critical evaluations of *Shamanism* tend to repeat a common range of criticisms directed at all Eliade's works, including that his approach is ahistorical, crypto-theological and motivated by a politics of nostalgia. Indeed, Eliade argued in his short 'Forward' to *Shamanism* that 'all history is in some measure a fall of the sacred, a limitation and diminution. But the sacred does not cease to manifest itself and with each new manifestation it resumes its original tendency to reveal itself wholly'. Continuing this line of thought, he wrote, 'The shamanic phenomenon itself' is of greater importance than the specificity of 'various historical and cultural aspects', for with shamanism 'we are dealing with a complete spiritual world', knowledge of which 'is a necessity for every true humanist; for it has been some time since humanism has ceased to be identified with the spiritual tradition of the west, great and fertile though that it is' (ibid.: xxv–xxvi). I do not want to repeat well-known criticisms of Eliade's work. Readers can consult the critiques cited above. More useful for present purposes is to note the door Eliade opened towards representations of shamans that are more literary than conventionally academic. Indeed, for anthropologist Michael Taussig, *Shamanism* 'epitomises' how 'anthropology and the comparative history of religion established the "shaman" as an Object of Study', by identifying a 'type' found in the Siberian wilderness, 'now everywhere from New York City to Ethnopoetics'. In Taussig's view, the trope of the shaman's magical flight between celestial realms by means of archaic techniques of ecstasy, 'generally and mightily mysteriously male', is a potent example of both 'the mystifying of Otherness as a transcendent force' and the 'reciprocating dependence on narrative' this stress on mystery entails. If Eliade's classic work on 'shamanism' illustrates anything, Taussig suggests, it is that 'a certain sort of anthropology and social science, geared to particular notions of the primitive, of story-telling, of boundaries, coherence, and heroism … has … recruited "shamanism" for the heady task of ur-narrativity' (Taussig 1992: 159–60; cf. Taussig 1989: 40–45, Taussig 1986).

In similar vein, several of Eliade's critics have drawn attention to his fiction-writing, including Daniel C. Noel whose discussion of literary sources for contemporary shamanism writing includes the observation that in 1949 Eliade took a break from writing *Le Chamanisme* to pen *The Forbidden Forrest*, in which the main character Stefan discovers 'a great and terrible secret': 'I understood that here on earth, near at hand and yet invisible, inaccessible to the uninitiated, a privileged space exists, a place like a paradise, one you could never forget in your whole life once you had the good fortune to know it' (Eliade, quoted in Noel 1997: 30). Jeroen Boekhoven's commentary on Eliade's legacy contextualises his fiction-writing in relation to the Eranos network, a collection of primarily European scholars of religion, anthropologists, philologists, mythologists and other intellectuals who shared a common commitment to mysticism, esotericism and privileging 'the hidden and mystical side of religion'. Carl Jung was influential from the beginning and gradually his idea of the archetype became a focal point and organising idea for wide ranging discussions about the transcendent unity of all religions and a universal primordial tradition (Boekhoven 2011: 142–3). The network developed its American roots with the establishment in 1940 of the American Bollingen Foundation. Named after Jung's residence on the shore of Lake Zurich and funded by the wealthy philanthropists Paul and Mary Mellon, the Foundation sponsored publishing the Bollingen Series for the specific purpose of propagating Jungian ideas, particularly concerning archetypes, symbolism, mythology and a universal collective unconscious. Boekhoven's discussion attributes the success of the English translation of *Shamanism* to the growing influence in North America of ideas generated by this network concerning shamans, particularly in the work of Joseph Campbell and Eliade, both of whom were published in the Bollingen Series on several occasions (ibid.: 129–61; cf. McQuire 1989).

Certainly, the 'Bollingen Connection' suggests something of the genealogy of 'a certain sort of anthropology and social science' Taussig blames for mystifying otherness as a transcendent force. Boekhoven's Bourdieusian analysis of mid-century representations of shamans in European and North American mysticism and esotericism illustrates some of the ways the key terms of shamanism discourse had diffused into European languages via the 'scientific' languages of psychiatry, anthropology, psychology and increasingly the aesthetic inclinations of religious studies. In the latter case, these inclinations were aligned with an established notion that shamans were essentially similar to 'ancient ecstatics and artists' (Von Stuckrad 2002: 773; cf. Flaherty 1992), in turn supplying scholarly authority to subsequent iterations of similar claims. Indeed, the notion that something like 'shamanic consciousness' is the origin of poetry and art has been a prevalent theme in much shamanism discourse, from the performance-installations of Joseph Beuys and Marcus Coats, to Allen Ginsberg's likening Bob Dylan to a shaman, to the curators of a 2008 Jackson Pollock retrospective in Paris doing the same with the famous abstract expressionist (Klein et al. 2008, Rothenberg 1967, Walters 2010).

As well as enabling wider circulations in Anglo-American discourse of representations of shamans that were increasingly more literary and popular than scientific and scholarly, these representations also increasingly displaced the reality of contemporary 'real flesh-and-blood' shamans, to borrow a phrase from Alcida Ramos, with a Baudrillardian simulation of indigenous religiosity bordering on hyperreality (see Chapter 4). With Baudrillard in mind, Taussig (1992: 79) wonders whether the signifier 'shaman' is empty or whether this emptiness is capable of being filled by innumerable meaning-makers, in which case are we faced with 'a world of anarchist semioticians striking back at the emptiness of postmodern life?'

Consider Hungarian anthropologist and linguist Felicitas Goodman's monograph *Where the Spirits Ride the Wind: Trance Journeys and Other Ecstatic Experiences* (Goodman 1990). Presenting findings from her experiential research into thirty bodily postures, Goodman claims to have discovered these induce specific kinds of trance states and visions that are neither temporally nor culturally contingent, but in fact universal. Frequently referring to shamans and drawing on Campbell and Eliade ('the venerable father of shamanic studies'), Goodman suggested that 'the secret of the postures was revealed by design' and is of considerable importance:

> Like 'other new movements ... going in the same direction toward "the strange inward sun of life" [Goodman is quoting from D.H. Lawrence's *The Hopi Snake Dance*] ...[the postures] take us to strange and beautiful worlds. They teach us to divine, to heal, and to celebrate. They comfort us and soothe our fears, better than any of our scientific achievements. And they thrill us with ever-renewed, never-predictable adventure, adding the very stuff of miracles to a modern existence that all to often is drab and unappealing. (Ibid.: 66)

Goodman makes a similar complaint in her previous book *Ecstasy, Ritual and Alternate Reality: Religion in a Pluralistic World*, on that occasion against the hostility to 'religion' allegedly shown by urbanites of 'the modern industrial city'. As against the antagonism of modern 'city-dwellers', Goodman celebrates 'the hunter-gathers', 'the horticulturalists', 'the agriculturalists' and 'the nomadic pastoralists' whose community life is constructed around 'emotionality, spiritual ecstasy and mysticism, and strident supernaturalism' which she claims is the 'core of religion worldwide' (Goodman 1988: 170, Geertz 1993: 370–71).

Noel has coined the neologism 'shamanthropology' to describe this kind of research (Noel 1997). A contraction of 'shaman' and 'anthropology', Noel's term foregrounds the farce or 'sham' he suggests is propounded by 'anarchist semioticians' (Taussig's phrase) like Goodman, Carlos Castaneda, Joan Halifax and Michael Harner. These latter three writers Noel claims have been the leading figures in popularising a style of writing about and representing 'shamans' in terms of trance journeys and techniques of ecstasy. Noel focuses on the period between 1968 and 1982, years bookended by Castaneda's *The Teaching of Don Juan* and Halifax's *Shaman: The Wounded Healer*. This temporal framing includes Harner's *The Way of the Shaman*, which confirmed the transformation of the genre from Castaneda's blend of evocative ethnographic fiction into popular and readily accessible techniques that, like Goodman's postures, can be cultivated through appropriate training and practice (Castaneda 1968; Halifax 1979, 1982; Harner 1980; cf. Nicholson 1987; on 'mainstreaming' 'native spirituality' in North America, see P. Jenkins 2004). Noel's temporal frame is perhaps better regarded as a convenient signpost of intensifying popular interest in evocative, purportedly ethnographic writing about shamans, since blends of evocative fiction-writing with academic ethnographic-writing about shamans can be traced at least as far back as the late nineteenth-century writings of Waclav Sieroszewski and other exiled critics of Tsarist policies, some of whom I consider in Chapter 2. Nevertheless, by the second half of the twentieth century a range of ideas about and attributions to 'shamans' and their 'religion' had formed a shamanic idiom far-removed from the reality experienced by 'real flesh-and-blood' shamans. Andrei Znamenski alludes to this idea when he writes of the history of shamanism studies as 'the adventures of a metaphor'. It is not only writings *about* shamans by the likes of Castaneda, Harner, or Goodman, or indeed Max Müller, Czaplicka, or Eliade. Also significant here are styles of contemporary shamans' self-representation, whether neo-traditionalist neo-shamans (for example Wallis 2003, 1998) or indigenist shamans whose tactical choices about self-representation hold considerable significance for their cultural and sometimes physical survival, as I consider in Chapter 4.

Imbrications of popular and scholarly discourse on shamanism and the tendencies of this discourse towards citing shamans' journeys in spirit worlds as evidence of the irreducible element of 'the sacred' or the origins of a timeless and unchanging universal ur-religion have posed considerable difficulty to researchers interested in studying historically situated 'shamanic traditions' or the contemporary contingencies of persons described by themselves or others as 'shamans'. 'The pure products have gone crazy in the plasticity of flow', Paul Johnson has suggested, adapting James Clifford's influential observations about the cultural politics of ethnographic research and writing to Johnson's work on the category of 'indigenous religions' formed amid global circulations of bodies and signs (P. Johnson 2002: 301, Clifford 1988). Michael Taussig's *Shamanism, Colonialism, and the Wild Man: A Study in Terror and Healing* is an excellent example of the fraught politics of ethnographic research and challenges of ethnographic writings in (post-) colonial societies (Colombia in Taussig's case). As well as bearing very little resemblance to anything published by shamanthropologists or scholars working in the Eliadian mode of historians of religion, Taussig argues his field research suggests 'a type of modernism' that seems to atomise parts and destabilise the imputed whole. In place of a 'centralizing cathartic force ... there exists an array of distancing techniques involving and disinvolving the reader or spectator and thus, potentially at least, dismantling all fixed and fixing notions of identity'. Taussig recalls Roger Dunsmore's commentary on the visions of Black Elk, famously told to Joseph Epes Brown and John Neihardt. Taking Black Elk 'as a sort of paradigm of what it means to be a man of vision', Dunsmore thought that Black Elk 'overturned our *expectation* that the holy man arrives somewhere at the truth'. Instead, Dunsmore thought Black Elk 'deeply involved in not *knowing*, and in the risk that when he gives his vision away it will be ignored, misunderstood, or misused' (Dunsmore, quoted in Taussig 1992: 160–61). 'It is to that *not knowing,* and to that *risk,* that we must, I feel, refer shamanic discourse', writes Taussig, before inviting his readers to pause and contemplate the violence entailed both in the relationship between coloniser and colonised and appropriations of indigenous cultures by 'White mysticism'. Considered from the perspective of 'a man of vision' who is also a subject of colonial violence and violently dispossessed of his identity,

> the risk involved in giving the vision away looms very high indeed, and we then
> begin to realise what is incumbent upon us who receive the vision as members
> of a colonial institution – Anthropology, Comparative Religion, or whatever
> names and ciphers are here relevant. ... What we do with that radical uncertainty
> is the measure not only of our ability to resist the appeal for closure, but also
> of our ability to prise open history's closure with the lever of its utterly terrible
> incompleteness. (Ibid.: 161)

Since the 1980s, the field of shamanism studies has expanded and diversified dramatically. Although several avenues of inquiry do not resist the appeal of closure and inductive theories of 'shamanism' endure, whether a common feature of human societies, a crucial stage in humans' evolution (whether 'religious' or cognitive), or a universal technique for transcending given reality, a range of research interests are also markedly more critical of previous scholarship and reflexive in their studies of shamans and shamanism. They demonstrate a willingness and commitment to prise open history's closure, as Taussig puts it. In the course of the past two decades, three significant literature reviews have mapped much of the interests, problems and developments of shamanism scholarship since the 1980s. Read together, they illustrate remarkable proliferations, intensifications and dispersions of interests related to shamanism in the Anglophone academy, along with changing representations of shamans. Monig Atkinson's widely cited review references approximately 250 publications mostly from the 1970s and 1980s (Atkinson 1992). A bit more than a decade later, Adlam and Holyoak surveyed over 600 publications up to 2003, all but four published after 1990 and 100 after 1999 (Adlam and Holyoak 2005). Thomas DuBois's review of trends in shamanism research since Atkinson includes nearly 150 publications since 2000 (DuBois 2011). A comparison of these reviews shows remarkable developments. In 1992 Atkinson's discussion of two decades of research noted thematic interests in psychology and therapy, contextual analyses of politics, gender and text/performance, along with a postscript on neo-shamanism and New Age religiosities. Although her postscript was the shortest of her discussions, she regarded neo-shamanism as the most significant development for the field, wondered whether it would be sustained beyond another decade or two and advised more reflexivity in scholarship because anthropologists, whose writings are a key source for neo-shamanists, are deeply implicated in these developments (Atkinson 1992: 322–3). By 2005, this research direction had yielded a range of inquiries probing methodology, identity politics, psychology, syncretism, bricolage, authenticity and neo-shamanism's imbrications with related developments, from modern paganism to environmentalism (Adlam and Holyoak 2005: 530–34). Similarly, Atkinson observed that attention to 'non-verbal dimensions of shamanic ritual' was encouraging consideration of relations between shamans and their audiences (as opposed to relations with spirits). A decade later, Adlam and Holyoak reviewed scholarship of the intervening years on methodological and theoretical considerations in shamanic performance and applications in studies of shamanic performance in South Korea and post-Soviet Russia, to argue for the importance of interdisciplinary approaches to performance as social phenomena of social scientific interest (ibid.: 519–27; Atkinson 1992: 320–21). Adlam and Holyoak's survey also showed proliferations of archaeological approaches to studies of material culture, with consequences for historical reconstructions of past shamanic religiosities and implications for contemporary revivals of shamanic traditions and identities. This challenging and diverse research addresses shamans' roles mediating between personal, social and political contexts in local, national and international forums and the complex relations and circulations that result.

Thomas DuBois's review steps back from the prolific output of shamanism research to take in trends since Atkinson's review. DuBois suggests the most significant trend has been towards particularisation of research in subfield specialisations and ethnographic studies, the latter particularly in Asia (2011: 102; cf. Ma and Meng 2011). Although DuBois does not mention Adlam and Holyoak, their review bears this out. Extending Atkinson's and Adlam and Holyoak's respective discussions, DuBois identifies particularisation with increasingly nuanced interests in shamanic material culture, entheogens and gender and sexuality research, along with ground shifts in approaches to older interests that have revisited longstanding inquiries and enabled wholly new research interests and agendas. DuBois's example of the latter is the shift in shamanic healing research away from scepticism towards credulity and curiosity. Although this shift was well underway during the 1980s, interests in shamanic healing as a function of socially-negotiated processes within a wider community have only more recently been addressed in related fields, including medical anthropology and performance studies (DuBois 2011:104). Similarly, long established lines of inquiry concerning gender and sexuality in shamanic traditions are being reassessed, resulting in new researches into, for example, sexualised relations between shamans and spirits and spiritual marriage (ibid.: 106; see also citations in Adlam and Holyoak 2005: 528).

A second major trend in shamanism research DuBois labels 'transcendent and cognitive approaches'. These approaches rely on inductively derived cross-cultural models and advance evolutionary approaches to the study of religions, either via history of religions or cognitive science of religion. A good example is Michael Winkelman's (2010) theory of shamanism as 'biopsychosocial paradigm of consciousness and healing'. Winkelman developed his theory over the course of nearly three decades of researching and writing about shamans in cross-cultural perspective, beginning with his hypothesis that pre-historic shamans adapted universal psychophysiological potentials of all human beings (trance, ecstasy, altered states of consciousness, and so on) to the needs and contingencies of hunter-gatherer societies. Winkelman claims this adaptation began an evolution of religion in a succession of magico-religious practitioner types he gives as Shamans, Shaman/Healers, Healers, Malevolent Practitioners, Mediums and finally Priests. Although Winkelman's theory is not much different from similar proposals a century ago (for example, Dixon 1908, McGee 1901, Ward 1909) and his claims about the 'universals' of shamanic religiosity echo Mircea Eliade, Åke Hultkrantz and Michael Harner, Winkelman elaborated and refined these earlier ideas in two ways. Firstly, at a methodological level, Winkelman's initial study compared 47 societies selected from the Standard Cross-Cultural Sample using cluster analysis of 98 analytical variables condensed from 200 descriptive variables in ten variable areas (Winkelman

1992, 1990, 1986). Secondly, at a theoretical level, Winkelman elaborated his quantitative evolutionary approach by combining it with emerging interests in neuroscience and evolutionary psychology to argue that 'neurognostic structures' are innate to human physiology and that 'shamanism plays a central role in elucidating neurotheology' (Winkelman 2002a: 73, 2002b: 1873–4, 2004: 197–8). Winkelman's combination of statistical, cross-cultural analysis with 'neurognostic or neurophenomenological perspectives' (Winkelman 2000: 58) forms the basis of his argument that 'shamanism' is a universal evolutionary adaptation of hunter-gatherer societies, 'the foundations of human cognitive evolution and spiritual experience' and 'the biological origins of religiosity' (Winkelman 2004: 194, 2006: 89).

The third and last significant trend reported by DuBois is 'rhetorical approaches' to studying shamans. These approaches conceive of shamanism along Foucauldian lines as a construct, idea, notion, or metaphor. Historicising studies, such as by Marjorie Balzer, Jeroen Boekhoven, Gloria Flaherty, Roberte Hamayon, Caroline Humphrey, Ronald Hutton, Alice Beck Kehoe, Michael Taussig and Andrei Znamenski, have turned their temporalising critiques towards the accidents, contingencies and interests that have produced a modern discourse on shamanism. Hamayon and Flaherty have both been previously mentioned; Hamayon links a historicised account of shamanism with contemporary theoretical and methodological questions and Flaherty examines the eighteenth-century conditions of possibility for later imaginings of shamanism. Kocku von Stuckrad's research on nineteenth-century idealisations of nature in shamanism discourse echoes Flaherty, although his argument is in the form of a genealogy of contemporary Western esotericism (Von Stuckrad 2003, 2002). More recently, Znamenski has written widely on shamanism in nineteenth-century Russia, paying close attention to Orthodox Christianity (2003b, 1999), the Siberian regionalist movement (2005, 2004) and Russian sources for historiography (2003a). In terms similar to Boekhoven and Noel, Znamenski's *The Beauty of the Primitive* situates these historical analyses in relation to 'the Western imagination' (Znamenski 2007). Although not normally a historian of Russian history, Ronald Hutton (2001) has similarly considered the historical sources for scholarship about shamans and Siberia and finds considerably more contingency, inconsistency and outright invention than much contemporary confidence admits. In similar critical vein is Alice Beck Kehoe's critique of what she terms the primitivist tradition in European studies of shamanism (Kehoe 2000). Michael Taussig's *Shamanism, Colonialism and the Wild Man* places similar emphasis on representations of shamans in discourses about non-European Others, although Taussig's approach is also considerably different from and even unique among rhetorical approaches. To begin with, Taussig's critique of 'shamanism' is firmly grounded in thick ethnographic description based on his years of fieldwork in Colombia. Writing thick description is particularly challenging in post-colonial societies like Colombia because colonial hegemony is mediated by 'cultures of terror'. Cultures of terror are eminently mysterious, Taussig suggests, because they flourish by means of rumour, are nourished by an intermingling of silence and myth and produce 'conditions of truth-making and culture-making' that resist interpretation: 'With European conquest and colonization, these spaces of death blend into a common pool of key signifiers binding the transforming culture of the conqueror with that of the conquered' (Taussig 1986: 5). Gesturing to the politics of 'writing culture', Taussig suggests that the reality of cultures of terror makes a mockery of understanding and derides rationality. He pointedly asks what sort of speech, writing and construction of meaning can manage and subvert it (ibid.: 8–9; Marcus's criticism of Taussig's earlier work *The Devil and Commodity Fetishism in South America* is perhaps also relevant here, see Marcus 1986: 176–80). Taussig has responded to these challenges by developing a highly idiosyncratic rhetorical style distinguished by emphases on thresholds, mystery and performance which owes more to Benjamin than Foucault, notwithstanding his Foucauldian emphasis on the 'truth effects' of discourses that are themselves neither true nor false (Taussig 1986: 288). All that said, the discourses that interest Taussig are the discourses of colonial terror in South America (of which shamans in Colombia are a part), not shamanism discourse *per se*. Taussig hardly refers to the history of European discourses (philological, medical, esoteric and so on) about shamans in his 'study in terror and healing', saving those criticisms for his subsequent work on 'the nervous system' (I use quotation marks to flag that, as with much of Taussig's writing, the obvious meaning is usually the beginning of a much more elaborate and surprising unfolding). Even here, as we saw earlier, his criticisms are restricted to a perfunctory demonstration of the utter uselessness of the Eliadian account for ethnographic studies of cultures of terror and spaces of death (Taussig 1992: 159–61, 165; cf. Taussig 1989: 40–41). Although Taussig also conceives of shamanism as a discourse and 'shamans' appear fairly frequently in his writings (see also Taussig 1999, 1993), his approach does not engage shamanism in these terms. In this sense at least, his writing style offers a useful counterpoint that teases out some of the limitations of conceiving of shamanism as an idea or construct that can be critiqued via Foucauldian genealogy.

This kind of historicising of representations of shamans is closest to the approach I develop in the following chapters. However, as well as emphasising the contingencies of previous scholarship and the historical circumstances of researchers, I am also interested in how this knowledge is effective in the contemporary world. I am interested in how circulating knowledge about shamans encounters related discursive fields and how these imbrications stimulate and generate new inflections, articulations and representations, thereby further proliferating and disseminating shamanism discourse to new practical contexts. I am particularly interested in how shamanism discourse multiplies, fragments and circles back to encounter itself in unfamiliar forms. More than that, I am interested in how three centuries of shamanism discourse establish the conditions of possibility for feedback loops that tap earlier formations of the discourse for practical purposes in the present time. This is where I hope this study of shamanism in relation to indigenism, environmentalism and neoliberalism offers new insights. The essay by Piers Vitebsky briefly mentioned earlier is a good example of what I have in mind. Vitebsky's interest in how shamanic knowledge mediates global historical processes led him to compare declining shamanic religiosity among the Sora, a scheduled tribe in eastern India, with the shamanic revival among Sakha communities of the Sakha Republic, a semi-autonomous state in the Russian Federation. For the Sora, historically an individual's sense of self was linked with ancestors, a relationship mediated by agricultural production and consumption via appropriate rituals on particular plots of land attached to particular ancestors. However, as market economics transformed Sora subsistence, this mediation became increasingly inappropriate. Agricultural production was sold and consumption became detached from the particularity of plots. With deterritorialisation, grain became merely food and was no longer a carrier of one's parents' spirit or soul. Shamanic religiosity declined. Whereas the Sora had many shamans but not shamanism, the Sakha had few shamans but were becoming increasingly attentive to something called 'shamanism'. Vitebsky noted that the Sakha shamanic revival responded to the break-up of the Soviet Union and therewith new opportunities to assert autonomy for the indigenous Sakha people, stimulated to a considerable extent by the region's valuable gold and diamond deposits. However, this revival was less inclined towards a religious sensibility attached to the local environment and more towards an abstract sense of ethnicity: 'they know their knowledge about shamanic ideas, not as habitus but as facts', remarks Vitebsky, facts packaged with proprietary copyright and trademark (Vitebsky 1995: 286). Amid federal devolution, shamanic knowledge distinguished Sakha land, national identity and knowledge from other kinds of identities and knowledges in other places. The Sakha's hitching of local shamanic knowledge to global environmental concerns in the form of their possession of indigenous knowledge valued elsewhere instrumentalised the global idiom of environmental concern to legitimate ethnic claims. The Sakha succeeded where the Sora failed because, as Vitebsky puts it, the exchange rate for converting local knowledge into global currency favoured the Sakha: gold and diamonds below and a political vacuum above.

But what happens when emphasis shifts from local knowledge to global setting? Vitebsky notes that for New Age enthusiasts, shamanic religion has never been indigenous. As with the Sakha shamanic revival, New Age shamanic knowledge also advances a critique of here and now and relies on notions of time and place other than here and now to do so. But if shamanic knowledge is a kind of re-localisation, in the hands of New Agers it is on a transnational scale, while that 'local elsewhere' is 'avowedly foreign' – native America, Amazon basin, southern Africa, Siberia, ancient Europe and so on. In a global setting, New Age shamanic knowledge is cosmopolitan and universalist, not nationalist or accommodated to the desires of sovereign power, and for the same reason is stripped of much that would distinguish a local character. Michael Harner's 'core-shamanism', discussed in Chapter 4, is paradigmatic of this tendency. If shamanic religiosity is becoming a kind of world religion as Cox (2003) suggests, Vitebsky argues it is in a globalised form in which local elements that don't travel well are stripped away, as in the Sora example, while those that do are adjusted and assimilated to the discursive regularities of global idioms and interests, as in the Sakha example (Vitebsky 1995: 196).

Since 'watertight distinctions' between 'traditional shamanistic societies' and New Age shamanic movements are no longer plausible (ibid.: 188), the challenge is how to theorise imbrications and mediations between and among traditional and neo-shamanic religiosities and articulate their effects. There is irony in this effort. Not long ago, modern discourse aligned so-called 'traditional shamanistic religion' with pre- or non-modern societies, while New Age religiosities were identified with modern industrial subcultures. Yet when one considers that struggles to elaborate such quintessentially modern ideas as human rights have been fought hardest by indigenous and colonised societies; that the lesson of modernisation (that development requires a nation and a state) is nowhere more appreciated than among those for whom nationalism is both a response to systematic underdevelopment and a delivery vehicle for the promise of progress; that the penetration of the commodity form into previously less commoditised domains of identity, knowledge and culture is felt most acutely in so-called traditional societies, then it appears that postcolonial, underdeveloped and traditional societies are in the vanguard of contemporary history. Arguing this point, Jean and John Comaroff suggest that 'the signposts of history unfolding' are in the south not the north. Postcolonies around the world are harbingers of the future rather than legacies of failed imperialisms and arguably reverse 'the taken-for-granted telos of modernity' (J.L. Comaroff and Comaroff 2006: 40).

The case studies presented in the following chapters tend to support this view. Whether indigenist critiques of human rights law and jurisprudence, symbolic economies of indigenous authenticity, or neoliberal entrepreneurialism and statecraft, these examples show how discursive and embodied practices of formerly (and arguably still) colonised peoples implicate shamanism in several of the most significant global processes and developments transforming how people live together in the world today. But not only formerly (or still) colonised people or in postcolonial states. A key concern for all these case studies is demonstrating the political economy of historical processes and social change. This perspective extends Adlam and Holyoak's predictions for the future of shamanism studies. Writing in 2005, they suggested future research would increasingly give attention to 'considerations of consumerism, the effects of late capitalism, commodification, the impact of new technologies and the changing profiles of cultures in circulation' (Adlam and Holyoak 2005: 535). Certainly these problems are receiving attention in shamanism research, as Adlam and Holyoak's and Dubois's respective reviews suggest. I would add to this list the role and place of the state. The state has become an important problem for research on shamanic religiosities. Prominent among these have been shamanic revivals in North Asia following the dissolution of the Soviet Union. Marjorie Balzer has been consistently attentive to how these revivals imbricate indigenous identity, state power and economic reproduction, particularly although not exclusively in Sakha Republic (for example, Balzer 2008, 2003, 1999, 1996; Balzer and Vinokurova 1996). Related research has considered revivals in relation to neotraditionalism and nationalism and the shamanic market place amid social anxiety and societal disorder (Buyandelgeriyn 2007; Humphrey 1999, 1994; Laruelle 2007; Lindquist 2005; Pika and Grant 1999). A different arena for considering imbrications of shamanism and the state is South Korea, where shamanism has been instrumental in alternately legitimating state hegemony and challenging political authority. Several researchers have written on instrumentalisations of shamanism alternatively by Park Chung-hee's government following his 1961 *coup d'état* and by the student-led reform movement (for example, Choi 1997, Hogarth 1999, Janelli 1986, Sorensen 1995). Korean shamanic religiosity usefully illustrates another important issue for a historical contextual critique of shamanism. Since Mircea Eliade popularised mystical ascent and heroic journey into spirit worlds as the essence of shamanic religiosity, scholars have debated whether 'spirit medium' traditions and 'possession states' can be considered shamanic. Noting the problem of agency and control, several scholars have noted that traditions emphasising soul flight broadly corresponds with traditionally nomadic societies where shamans tend to be male, whereas in traditions predicated on spirit possession mediums tend to be women and the household the site of ritual activity (for contributions to this debate, see Atkinson 1992: 317). Some scholars have argued that a decline in the soul flight type and rise in the possession type in East Asia corresponds with the expansion of state authoritarianism and consequent loss of shamans' charismatic authority (Anagnost 1987: 59). In South Korea the vast majority of shamans are women and a disproportionate number of their clients are too (Kim 2005: 296; cf. Kendall 1998, 1985). Undoubtedly gendered aspects of shamanism discourse raise important question for shamanism studies although this is not a lens I focus on the examples considered here. Weaving feminist perspectives into the theoretical framing introduced above would add too many layers of complexity and ultimately detract from the focused discussions I pursue in respective chapters. On questions of the state, I discuss examples from Central and South America in Chapter 4, while South Africa is a focus of Chapter 5.

Shamanism. Indigenism. Environmentalism. Neoliberalism. Each signifies a practical domain where the shifting meanings and relative importance of people identified as 'shamans' have been argued over and worked out. They are imbricated too, so that shifts in one domain contribute to shifts in another. At the same time, all these shifting meanings and associated representations are products of a practical limit attitude. As a task identical with personal liberty and therefore one that may not be refused, this limit-seeking attitude innervates and animates discourse about shamans and accounts for the proliferations, intensifications and dispersals of diverse representations of shamans in recent decades. This in short is the argument I hope to illustrate in the following chapters.

Chapter 2

Shamanism

This chapter presents an historical overview of a discourse about shamans that emerged from imperial Russia during the eighteenth and nineteenth centuries. It is historical in the sense that it recapitulates a fairly well-known story about changing reports about shamans, who they were, what they did, their roles, social status, techniques, experiences, mental states, and so on. Most scholars emphasise the determinative role of the European Enlightenment and Russian imperialism in establishing the 'paradigms of permissibility' for representing shamans (Flaherty 1992). This discussion will echo those assessments. As such, I revisit well-tilled ground, some of it extensively and some of it less so. At any rate, it is not my intention to revise (much less overhaul) this genealogy of shamanism that with some variations has been well-documented and tested against available sources. (See, for example, Flaherty 1992, 1988; Francfort and Hamayon 2001; Hutton 2001; Thomas and Humphrey 1996; Znamenski 2007, 2004b, 2003a, 2003b, 1999.)

My intention is slightly different. At one level, I recount this history so that the reader may be more familiar with the provenance of that category of person we today call a shaman. It is, after all, the key category of the discourse that is our central object. At a more reflexive level, however, I also want to demonstrate the operations of modernity's double-hinge in the articulation of epistemological circumscription and ontological contingency. This is perhaps where the historical account I present here acquires a genealogical quality. The following discussion pays close attention to the chance accidents, idiosyncratic appraisals, false understandings and innumerable related contingencies that inflected a range of interests and inquiries pertaining to shamans and in turn shaped and sustained this discourse during these two centuries and since. Is this attention to the contingent limits within the circumscribed unity of knowledge about shamans sufficient to disrupt that imputed unity? I hope so. But it too relies on a dialectic between labour that on the one hand tends to proliferate and disperse statements about shamans and on the other tends to multiply and condense the surfaces of appearance of a knowing self; the genealogy I present here does not (because it cannot) escape the double-hinged articulation of epistemological and ontological labour. Seen from this perspective, this genealogy has a performative aspect that involves the (body of the) reader in elaborating this discourse and reproducing a specifically modern subjectivity. I revisit this problem in this chapter's conclusion, but flag it now so that the reader may be alert to where this discussion is heading.

Some clarifications are necessary at the outset. The timeframe I have chosen happens to coincide with the periodisation of centuries. Although records mention persons resembling people subsequently known as 'shamans' prior to the eighteenth century, the modern discourse on shamanism emerged with the ambitious project of Tsar Peter the Great (1662–1725) to reform Russian state and society. Peter's Grand Embassy tour of Europe in 1697–98 instilled in the young Tsar a vision of a modern, developed Russia on a par with the highest European civilisations. Peter became convinced that Russia needed closer alignment with European culture and society and set about transforming Russia from a backward, feudal principality on the margins of Europe into a civilised, enlightened, modern imperial power. Accordingly, he embarked on a programme of social, educational and government reforms, adopted an expansionist foreign policy backed by a modern military, founded an Imperial Academy of Sciences to rival the Royal Society and the French Academy of Sciences and in 1721, just three years before his death, he proclaimed as the Russian Empire all the territory from St Petersburg to the Pacific. The Academy sponsored expeditions across Siberia and their reports about Siberia's indigenous plant and animal life, climate, topography, geology, astronomical observations and cartography also included some of the earliest reports about shamans. A discourse about shamans grew in step with Russia's settlement of and changing attitudes towards its Asian possession. On the other end of this frame is the turn of the twentieth century, when the term 'shaman' was systematically applied to indigenous ritual specialists and ceremonial officiates beyond Siberia. I discuss this development with reference to the notion of shamans' 'emigration' to the Americas and the gradual supplementing and then supplanting of terms such as 'priest', 'conjurer' and 'medicine-man' with 'shaman', so that by 1908 the president of the American Folk-lore Society could deliver as his presidential address a paper on 'Some Aspects of the American Shaman' in which he remarked on 'the general uniformity' of shamans from the Arctic North to Patagonia (Dixon 1908: 12).

As for my distinction between Russia and Siberia, usually 'Russia' refers to a political entity and 'Siberia' to the geographical region of North Asia. However, I use the terms to distinguish between imperial centre and colonial possession that in geographical terms loosely corresponds respectively to the regions west and east of the Ural Mountains. As the Urals were regarded as the natural boundary between Europe and Asia, it is fair to say that in the eighteenth and nineteenth centuries, Siberia was regarded as Russia's Asian possession. Early in the seventeenth century, Russian Cossacks had reached the Pacific coast and by mid-century there were scattered Russian settlements as far eastward as the Chukchi Peninsula and along the Amur River. However, Peter's proclamation of the Empire rapidly accelerated Russian conquest and settlement. Shamans were among the most exotic and unfathomable aspects of native life encountered by Russians and from this imperial context emerged a discourse on shamanism.

Discovering Shamans

Reports by European adventurers and explorers of their encounters with indigenous ritual specialists in Siberia first piqued the curiosity of Europeans in the late seventeenth century. Nicolaas Witsen's account of his travels in parts of Siberia during 1664–65 provided the first significant account of shamans. A former mayor of Amsterdam, Witsen (1641–1717) described a person he calls a 'schaman' and accompanied his description with a drawing of a person with clawed hands and feet, wearing a hooded fur coat and antlers, holding a flat drum. The illustration was captioned 'Tungusschaman; or, The Priest of the Devil' (Znamenski 2007: 5–6). The Swede Philip Johann von Strahlenberg (1667–1747) provided the next significant account of shamans. An officer in the Swedish Army exiled for thirteen years in Siberia following his capture by Russian forces at the Battle of Pultawa in June 1709, Strahlenberg subsequently accompanied German physician Daniel Messerschmidt on the latter's journeys into the Siberian hinterland during the early 1720s. Strahlenberg's account, published in German in 1726 and in English translation in 1738, was the first to deal extensively with the shaman's drum and included a detailed drawing and favourable comparison with the drums of the Saami of northern Scandinavia. Strahlenberg's was also the first account of Siberian shamans that reported the hallucinogenic properties of the fly agaric mushroom, although his text mentions nothing of the mushroom's ritual use (Von Strahlenberg 1970: 397). As for Messerschmidt, the Imperial Academy of Sciences had him surrender his notes, although they were later made available to scholars working under the auspices of the academy. The notes make clear that Messerschmidt saw shamans as tricksters and frauds (Flaherty 1992: 48).

The first scientific expedition across Siberia took place 1733–43 and was directed towards the Kamchatka Peninsula, on the north Pacific Rim between the Okhotsk Sea in the west and the Bering Sea in the east. Under the leadership of Captain Vitus Bering (1681–1741), the Great Northern Expedition (or First Kamchatka Expedition) led to a proliferation of new information about shamans, as each of the expedition's more prominent participants published their notes and memoirs in the years following. As their writings make clear, many of these enlightened explorers regarded it their responsibility to expose shamans' fraudulence. For example, the Russian naturalist Stephan Krascheninnikow took great satisfaction in exposing the tricks of the Itel'man shaman Karyml'acha. He claimed Karyml'acha's trick of slashing a seal's bladder filled with blood and concealed under his clothes while claiming to be slashing himself was so cheap and poorly executed, 'I could not help laughing at the simplicity of the trick, which the poorest player of legerdemain would have been ashamed of' (quoted in Flaherty 1992: 48). German historian Gerhardt Friedrich Müller was similarly scathing. On one occasion, he insisted a Sakha shaman perform for a specially selected audience. After the audience exposed her tricks, Müller forced her to sign a confession of her fraud. He later wrote:

> It suffices to say that all of them [séances] are basically similar. Nothing miraculous happens. The shaman emits an unpleasant howling, while jumping about senselessly and beating a flat drum which has iron bells attached inside to intensify the din … It does not take long, however, to be convinced of the futility of the farce, of the deceit by those earning their living in this way. (Quoted in Znamenski 2007: 8)

Still, Müller was on the whole more careful in his descriptions of indigenous rituals and customs than his colleague the botanist and chemist Johan Georg Gmelin, whom Müller chided for representing the religious ceremonies of the Tartars 'in some details, but almost too comically' (quoted in Black 1989: 46). Gmelin wrote of a shaman's performance he witnessed:

> At length, after a lot of hocus pocus and sweating, he would have us believe that the devils were there. He asked us what we wanted to know. We put a question to him. He started his conjuring tricks while two others assisted him. In the end we were confirmed in our opinion that it was all humbug, and we wished in our hearts that we could take him and his companions to the Urgurian silver mine, so that they might spend the rest of their days in perpetual labour. (Quoted in Narby and Huxley 2001: 28)

The Second Kamchatka Expedition (1768–74) continued the reporting strategies of the first. Johann Gottlieb Georgi, a German scientist, explorer and expedition member, admitted to his readers that he had shortened his account of shamanic 'magic and conjuring tricks due to their obvious foolishness' (quoted in Znamenski 2004a: xxii). If shamans were still fools and frauds, reporting strategies also developed new themes with modified, though no less contemptuous, conclusions. Petrus Simon Pallas, a German botanist and zoologist who led the Second Expedition, reported: 'Usually these shamans are the most cunning people. Through skilful interpretation of their own dreams and other tall tales they achieve a respected status' (quoted in Znamenski 2007: 7). Both foolish and cunning, towards the second half of the eighteenth century still another characterisation was added. Georgi, for example, noted that shamans are 'partly barefaced impostors, partly deceived fanatics' (quoted in Hutton 2001: 33). In other words, shamans were simultaneously deceivers (whether foolish or clever) and madmen who 'shout', 'twist their mouths' and 'produce pranks characteristic of the insane and behave as madmen' (Znamenski 2007: 7).

As the century drew to a close, reporting on shamans centred on their psychological makeup, particularly the shamans' supposed hypersensitivity and excitability. Georgi connected these traits with the climate, topography and general environment. Vasilii Zuev, Pallas's 18-year-old research assistant, was particularly intrigued by shamans' mental states, going so far as to name madness and fear as defining qualities of shamans' vocation: 'When you irritate the shaman too much, he becomes wildly insane. He gallops, rolls on the ground, and hoots. In such moments, the shaman is ready to hit people around him with what he holds in his hands.' Speculating on the cause of the shaman's 'insanity', Zuev is confounded: 'I do not know how to explain this. It could be their general weakness, gullibility, or simple stupidity', adding, 'To be honest, I would rather classify his behaviour as a sort of illness' (Zuev, quoted in Znamenski 2007: 10). In the course of a century, the figure of the shaman had been a satanic agent in league with the devil, a foolish impostor, a clever charlatan and a lunatic suffering from mental illness.

At the same time that Enlightenment explorers and scholars were preoccupied with the mental states of shamans, many also became preoccupied with the origins of shamans' rituals and traditions. Gerhardt Müller, for example, in his *History of Siberia*, wondered whether shamanic religiosity originated spontaneously among Siberian natives or whether it migrated to Siberia from elsewhere. Deciding upon the latter, Müller proposed India, from where it spread across northern Asia and into Scandinavia. For Müller, shamanism was a degenerative version of Hinduism. His contemporary, Georgi, agreed with the degenerative thesis: 'Because of wars, rebellions, population movements, wanderings, the lack of education, and the misinterpretation of tales by stupid and deceiving priestly people, this order [shamanism] was turned into disgusting idol worshipping and blind superstition' (Georgi, quoted in Znamenski 2007: 12–13). For both Müller and Georgi, the imputed polytheism of shamanic belief was evidence of its degenerate character. These twin concerns with origins and mental states have been enduring preoccupations for scholars ever since. In the nineteenth century, however, these concerns were increasingly tied with and perceived through the prism of Russia's relationship with Europe and its imperial aspirations.

By the beginning of the nineteenth century, Russia held dominion over all the territory from the Urals to the Bering Sea, the Arctic Ocean to the southern steppes and now set about populating its empire with Slavs and extracting Siberia's natural wealth. These imperial strategies were fraught with difficulties, not least the sudden and precipitous decline of the fur trade and the harsh environment that seemed to preclude settlement and productive exploitation of the land. Thus the imperial vision of 'our Peru', 'our Brazil', 'our East India' and 'our Nile' gave way to a pervasive cynicism about Siberia's value as a colonial asset and activated anew Russia's ambivalence regarding its relationship to and status in Europe (Bassin 1991: 771). As ambivalence towards Europe took hold of Russian political discourse and intellectual life, attitudes towards Siberia mirrored anxieties and aspirations at the imperial centre in St Petersburg. For some, barren, primitive, backward Siberia confirmed Russians' worst anxieties about Russia's lowly status among European states. For others, however, Siberia was an Eden that would satisfy Russia's search for positive qualities and virtues to seed a new, authentic Russian identity. This latter aspiration was reflected in the shifting terms of shamanism discourse, away from concerns with priestcraft, cunning fraud and madness and towards interests in native culture, mythology and religiosity.

Between Occident and Orient

The first half of the nineteenth century was a time of crisis and introspection for Russia. The advent of romanticism re-oriented the intellectual and creative environment of Europe and challenged Russia to recalibrate its standing and status. At the same time, invasion by Napoleon's armies prompted Russians to doubt whether they would or could be part of the European community of nations, a question that seemed definitively answered by the Crimean War at mid-century. Russia responded with mournful introspection that gradually developed into a national debate about the nature and substance of Russian identity and the positive values and virtues that distinguished the Russian people (cf. Bassin 1999: 37–8). Certainly, many thought that none existed. Peter Chaadaev famously captured this sentiment in his 'Philosophical Letter', published in 1833, in which he lamented the emptiness of Russian history:

> We do not belong to any of the great families of the human race; we are neither of the West nor of the East, and we have not the traditions of either. Placed, as it were, outside of time, we have not been touched by the universal education of mankind ... Among us there is no internal development, no natural progress; new ideas sweep out the old, because they are not derived from the old but tumble down upon us from who knows where. We absorb all our ideas ready-made, and therefore the indelible trace left in the mind by a progressive movement of ideas, which gives it strength, does not shape our intellect. We grow, but we do not mature; we move, but along a crooked path, that is, one that does not lead to the desired goal. We are like children who have not been taught to think for themselves ... . (Chaadaev 1978: 162–8)

Since the Petrine era, Russia had moulded itself in the image of European nation-states. But as pride gave way to abjection and the terms of Russia's unique contribution to modernity and unique worth as a (European) people remained illusive, Russian enthusiasm for Europe gave way to antipathy and deep ambivalence, notwithstanding Russia's intellectual debt to German intellectuals. Indeed, this ambivalence was underlined by Russian experiments with nationalism that aped the German example (Bassin 1999: 38, Saunders 1982: 58, cf. Greenfeld 1992).

Several historians of Russian imperialism have argued that this ambivalence stimulated among some influential Russian intellectuals a 'messianic sensibility', a sense of Russia's calling that was held to supersede the conflicts and disputes between westernisers and slavophiles or moderate liberals and opposition radicals (Bassin 1999, Duncan 2000, Rowley 1999). Alexander Herzen captured the sentiment:

> We shared a common love ... From early childhood, a single strong, instinctive, physiologically passionate feeling was imprinted on us as it was on them ... And, like Janus or the two-headed eagle, we looked in different directions, but at the same time a *single heart was beating within us*. (Quoted in Bassin 1999: 45)

Messianism represented more than an ideal. As a special virtue and unifying force of Russian identity, messianic thinking identified action towards fulfilling its messianic calling with a moral obligation. As demands grew to extend Russia's political influence (regardless of practical possibilities or political implications), messianic nationalism became 'the cradle of an unbridled imperialism: the nation, the chosen vehicle of God's designs, sees in its political triumph the march of God in history' (Hans Kohn 1939: 13). Much of this energy was naturally directed towards south-eastern Europe and the fostering of pan-Slavic unity. But from the 1840s and 1850s, this energy was also directed eastwards as the messianic mission engaged transformations in Russian Orientalism.

During the late eighteenth and early nineteenth centuries, Russia's intellectual elite shared in the 'oriental renaissance' that swept Europe (Schwab 1984). Russia saw in Asia, particularly China, the realisation of civilisation's most exalted qualities – high moral principles, veneration of tradition and intellectual enlightenment – all qualities Russians thought were not (yet) sufficiently realised in their own society. This vision of the Orient particularly appealed to Tsar Nicholas (1796–1855), because it accorded closely, he thought, with his own vision of autocratic rule. His Minister of Education Sergey Uvarov agreed and established an Oriental Academy in St Petersberg.[1] From the 1830s, however, ideas about the Orient began to change. Fairly rapidly, the idea developed that the Orient had fallen into decay and stagnation. As Bassin (1999: 51) succinctly puts it:

> Fascination and veneration gave way with surprising ease to condescension and disgust, and rather than spiritual enlightenment, lofty aesthetic accomplishment, and virtuous and wise social principles, the East now came to epitomise precisely the opposite: social degeneracy and intellectual and spiritual inanition.

Russia's estimations of the Orient were related directly to competition between Nicholas's Official Nationality and the popular messianic nationalism of the likes of Alexander Herzen. The ease and rapidity with which Russian Orientalism reversed its attitude towards the Orient is a measure of how quickly the messianic sentiment was catching on. Russian Orientalism thus became an increasingly important element in the Russian national discourse as competing interpretations of the Orient refracted the political contest.

Writings about shamans and shamanism in the nineteenth century should be understood against this backdrop. By and large, later scholars of 'shamanic

---

[1]   Studies of Russian Orientalism have become a highly productive area of scholarship in the post-Soviet era. See, for example, David-Fox et al. (2006), Tolz (2009) and Van der Oye (2010).

religion' did not situate their analyses with due reference to this context, certainly not the range of prominent scholars whose work established an a-historical canon of what 'shamanic religion' is and what shamans do. While it has become almost passé to critique Eliadian phenomenology or Joseph Campbell's deistic naturalism,[2] for the most part critiques of these scholars' works have addressed questions about how we ought to approach the study of religions and less often the consequences and implications of how we have already studied religions. This problem can be illustrated with reference to the Altai deity Ülgen and the researches of the Siberian regionalist movement.

Wilhelm Radloff and Bai-Ülgen

Russian ambivalence towards Europe stimulated new appraisals of Siberia and more positive interests in the region's native inhabitants, including shamans. Although Wilhelm Radlof's influence was only felt in the last decades of the century, the sympathetic turn between the 1840s and 1860s created enabling conditions for Radlof's later contributions. Two scholars were particularly important in this regard. Dordji Banzaroff (1822–55), an ethnic Buryat educated at Russian universities and therefore in a unique position regarding Russian attitudes to indigenous religiosity, argued forcefully against the Enlightenment position that shamanism was a degeneration of some other tradition that had migrated north from India or China:

> Careful study of the subject shows that the Shamanistic religion ... did not arise out of Buddhism or any other religion, but originated among the Mongolic nations, and consists not only in superstitious and shamanistic ceremonies ... but in a certain primitive way of observing the outer world – Nature – and the inner world – the soul. (Quoted in Czaplicka 1914: 167; cf. Czaplicka 1999)

It is perhaps significant that Banzaroff was inspired by the *Naturphilosophie* of Alexander von Humboldt, particularly von Humboldt's insistence, inspired by Herder, on the influence of natural environments in shaping human societies (Znamenski 2007: 18). For present purposes, it is enough to recognise that for

---

2   See, for example, Campbell's four-volume *Masks of God*. Consisting of *Primitive Mythology* (1959), *Oriental Mythology* (1962), *Occidental Mythology* (1964) and *Creative Mythology* (1968), Campbell intended to write 'the first sketch of a natural history of the gods and heroes ...' (J. Campbell 2000: 5).

the first time shamans and their beliefs and rituals were represented as authentic, indigenous, and worthy of serious scholarship.

The second scholar is Matthias Alexander Castren (1813–53). A Finnish philologist and folkore enthusiast, Castren was probably the first and, in the 1840s certainly the most significant, individual to explicitly relate shamanism with nationalism, in his case Finnish nationalism. Castren, as he put it himself, 'could not pause before finding a connection that links the Finnish tribe with some other larger or smaller groups in the rest of the world' (quoted in Znamenski 2004a: xxvii). That connection Castren found via comparative philology. In the course of his studies, however, Castren also speculated on similarities between Siberian shamans and indigenous ritual specialists among the Saami and stressed the positive role of shamans in their communities (see Musi 1997: 79–85). In Castren's view, shamans were heroic figures who 'conquer nature not only through vigorous bodily movements and incomprehensible words', but through their sheer force of will (quoted in Znamenski 2004a: xxvii).[3] Contrary to the Enlightenment view of shamans as passive recipients of the commands of superior supernatural forces, Castren regarded shamans as active social agents.

Banzaroff's and Castren's work indicated how attitudes towards shamans were changing. They took seriously shamans' roles as social actors, the former by arguing for the authentic indigeneity of shamanic beliefs and rituals and the later by situating indigenous peoples within a network of genetic, philological and cultural relations that extended from northern Europe to the Caspian Sea. In doing so, they asked new questions about the origins and development of shamanic institutions and their relation to the myths, beliefs and ritual practices of traditions from which shamans were previously thought to be particularly vile aberrations. Banzaroff's and Castren's more positive views of shamans modified the discursive field to an extent that enabled Radloff's enduring contribution – enduring because Radloff was a key source for Mircea Eliade's account of shamanism and because it was on Radloff's recommendation that Franz Boas contracted Waldemar Bogoras, Waldemar Jochelson and others to the Jesup North Pacific Expedition (see below).

---

[3]   Castren was not the first to connect Siberian indigenous religiosity with the Saami people of Lapland. As early as 1726, Strahlenberg commented about the 'Czeremissi, or Scheremissi', 'a pagan people under the Government of Casan' in the Volga River basin: 'There is a great Affinity between their Tongue and that of the Finlandians; But it is now very much mix'd both with the Russian and Tartarian.' About the 'Barabintzi', 'A Heathen nation, between the Cities of *Tara* ad *Tomskoi*', he says '... they and the *Finnlandians* were formerly one Nation.' Besides linguistic similarities, he notes that 'They make Use of such Drums as the *Laplanders* do' (Von Strahlenberg 1970: 334–5, 354–5).

Radloff is well-known as an orientalist and his contributions to Turkic philology are widely documented (see Hatto's Introduction in Radlov and Hatto 1990), although his role in shaping shamanism discourse by and large has not been taken up by shamanism scholars, despite his considerable influence. Znamenski credits Radloff with breaking the speculative tradition of shamanism scholarship and notes that until the twentieth century, Radloff's work, along with Castren's, remained the principle works on shamanism in the West and Radloff's rendering of shamans was the basis of many European encyclopaedias' entries on shamanism. Radloff also played an inspiring role in the ethnographic researches of the Siberian regionalists in the last decades of the century and his influence can be traced via the regionalists and exile ethnographers of the late nineteenth century into the heart of the shamanism discourse as it was formulated in North America in the early decades of the twentieth century.

A German by birth, Wilhelm Radloff (1837–1918) was educated at the University of Berlin. Upon graduating in 1858, Radloff and his new wife relocated to Siberia where he took a post as a schoolteacher at Barnaul, in the Altai region of Siberia's southern borderlands. While at Barnaul, he undertook philological investigations in local languages and recorded and collected local heroic myths. Using his adopted name Vasilii Vasilievich Radlov, he gradually rose to prominence among Russia's educated elite. Among his offices, Radloff was a founder of the International Association for the Exploration of Central Asia, director of the Asian Museum in St. Petersburg and, as one of the deans of Russian anthropology, a prominent collector and publisher of folklore texts comparable to some extent with the stature of Franz Boas in North America. Educated in the German romantic tradition, Radloff was influenced by von Ritter's and von Humboldt's *Naturphilosophie* as well as romantic Orientalism's emphasis on comparative linguistics and philology. He brought with him to Russia a sympathetic approach to indigenous religiosity, lamenting that 'the poor shamans are not as bad as they are usually perceived.' Noting that shamans 'are carriers of the ethical ideals of their people' and 'no worse than clerics of other religions', he placed shamanism on a par with Buddhism, Christianity and Islam (Radloff, quoted in Znamenski 2007: 36). He continued Banzaroff's argument that shamanism was indigenous to the region and not a distortion or degeneration of 'Brahamism' or 'Lamaism'. He also continued the philological studies begun by Castren and it is for this work that he is most remembered. Still, his letters of the 1860s were an ethnographic classic for later scholars of shamanism and formed the basis of his two-volume work *Aüs Sibirien* [From Siberia] (Radlov 1884).

Probably Radloff's most enduring contribution to the discourse on shamanism is regarding the Altaic spirit Ülgen. Radloff introduced to shamanism discourse what has been termed 'the Ülgen séance', which thereafter rapidly gained pre-eminent status in ethnographic representations of Central Asian shamanism. The Ülgen séance became a key topic in Eliade's work on shamanism, where Ülgen is a centrepiece of Eliade's discussion of shamanic cosmology, the shaman's election by spirits and his celestial ascent (Eliade 1964: 190–204; see also pp. 77–8, 275–8; 1958: 105–6). The Ülgen séance refers to a transcript of an Altaian ritual addressed to the spirit Ülgen and includes prayers, supplications and the shaman's utterances. As such, it is apparently the first complete textual record of a shaman's ritual invocation of spirits and the focus of the first part of the second volume of Radloff's classic work (Radlov 1884: 19–50). However, Radloff neither recorded the transcript of the ritual nor did he witness it. It is not even clear that there was an event to witness. The provenance of the text is between the 1840s and 1850s in the Altai region of southern Siberia from an unidentified Russian orthodox missionary who recorded it in the Altaian language from an Altai native. It is unclear whether or not this person was a shaman. As the text consists only of a ritual invocation and does not mention the ritual setting, it seems likely the missionary did not witness a particular séance and simply recorded what was told to him. There are no surviving clues as to the nature of their relationship, the scene in which it unfolded, or the specific purpose of making the record. All we have is the anonymous manuscript, which was stored in the archives of the Altaian Orthodox mission, where the missionary and ethnographer Vasilii Verbitskii discovered it. Verbitskii published the text in its entirety in a Siberian newspaper in the 1870s, where Radloff read it for the first time.[4] Radloff then translated parts of the text into German and published them in 1884 in *Aus Sibirien*, from where it was picked up by the burgeoning field of Siberian regionalist ethnographers in the last decades of the century, as well by as a new generation of North American anthropologists and mythologists in the early decades of the twentieth century. On the Ülgen seance's path to canonisation, in 1895, Mikhailovskii (1895: 74) called Ülgen 'the celestial deity ... who dwells on the golden mountain in the sixteenth heaven'; in 1925, Leo Sternberg (2004: 139) called him 'the Lord of Heaven', and in 1936 Nora Chadwick named him 'the highest god of the Heavens'. Elaborating on the séance, she wrote: 'The ceremony is, in fact, not merely, not even primarily, a dramatic spectacle, but a piece of religious communion, shared by the whole tribe, and a kind of public sermon', adding in a footnote, 'We may compare Moses and the giving of the Law at Mount Sinai' (Chadwick 1936a: 95).

---

[4]   Eliade (1964: 190, n. 37) gives the place and date of this publication as Tomsk in 1870. The missionary ethnographer Verbitskii republished the entire text, as he found it in the archive, in 1893 in the original Altaian accompanied by his translation in Russian.

Chadwick thought the 'minute observations of the traveller and field worker' insufficient for '[coming] to any kind of just estimate of the phenomenon known as shamanism'. That estimation requires 'the synthetic work of the arm-chair anthropologist', who must 'essay to reconstruct history' by examining the oral traditions among the people concerned. These may then be compared with reports of fieldworkers concerning 'shamans' dress, dance, general technique with sculpture, paintings and any inscriptions of the past which have been preserved in more civilised neighbouring countries'. Thus she qualified her lengthy study 'Shamanism among the Tartars of Central Asia': 'These considerations must be my excuse for offering some observations on a class of people of whom I have no first-hand knowledge. Like many others who have written on this subject I have never seen a shaman and am ignorant of their languages' (Chadwick 1936a: 76–7). A specialist in Turkic epic poetry, Chadwick's armchair synthesis began with the observation that Turkic 'oral literature' is closely related to Turkic spiritual ideas and concepts (ibid.: 98; Chadwick 1936b: 291). One of the main spiritual ideas and concepts known to Siberian observers via Radloff was Ülgen, and Ülgen came to feature prominently in Chadwick's work. Thus, in her work on oral epics of Central Asia, she divided the cosmology of the 'Turkic religion' into 'two spiritual environments which are mutually hostile', 'the highest one ... ruled by ... Bai Ülgen' and a second one, in which 'The personnel live underground, and their ruler is Erlik Khan' (Chadwick and Zhirmunsky 1969: 98). This dualistic rendering of Ülgen, who is ruler of Heaven and giver of the law and 'wicked Erlik', who is ruler of the underworld and associated with illness and harm, is found in earlier accounts by orthodox missionaries (Znamenski 2007: 37; cf. Znamenski 2003b), as well as early ethnographers, for example, Mikhailovskii (1895: 77, 72–3). On another occasion, she inserted Ülgen into narratives in which he is not mentioned. For example, upon reading an account of a healing ritual among the Yukut of northern Siberia (present-day Sakha Republic) recorded by Sierozsewski probably in the 1880s and reproduced in Mikhailovskii (1895: 92–5) and Czaplicka (1914: 233–9), Chadwick noted that 'The invocation concludes ... with a prayer to the "Greybeard" that the shaman's thoughts may be approved, and his requests granted.' Grey-beard, she insisted ('I have no doubt') refers to 'Kydyr or Ülgön, the highest god in heaven'. She attributed her confidence to 'the oral literature of the Tartars' wherein Ülgen 'is generally represented ... with a grey beard so long that he treads on it as he walks – a sufficiently striking description of a god of the beardless Tartars' (Chadwick 1936a: 96). Though Chadwick does not cite her sources for this claim, throughout her work she cites the authority of Radloff's fieldwork and acknowledges that her knowledge, or as she puts it, 'our knowledge', of Tartar 'oral poetry', 'is derived chiefly from the great collection ... of Radlov' (Chadwick 1936b: 291–2).

Besides rendering Ülgen as equivalent of the Abrahamic god, the path to canonisation also established the Ülgen séance as a kind of liturgical text, increasingly rigid and inflexible. Eliade, for example, insists that 'its structure is always the same' and therefore 'It has not been thought necessary to mention all these differences, which chiefly affect details' (Eliade 1964: 190). Significantly, successive generations of scholars not only cited Radloff, but recognised the text's obscure origins in Altaic mission records and acknowledged the role of the missionary ethnographer Verbitskii in bringing it to Radloff's attention. However, having obliged the conventions of good scholarship, these scholars went on to elaborate their arguments, apparently convinced that having identified the source of their data, they enhanced the authority of their narrative rather than call attention to the reliability of their sources. Thus Ülgen entered the discourse on shamanism via a translation in German of a partial reproduction of a record retrieved from a missionary archive and produced several decades earlier by an unknown missionary, of an event he did not witness, from the testimony of an unknown informant (Znamenski 2007: 37; 2003a: 281–2).[5]

The Ülgen séance is an instructive example of the workings of the discourse around shamanism and the homogenising universalism that has brought into being the figure of the shaman as a key trope in western discourses on indigenous religiosity. It demonstrates a tendency towards transforming a particular event or narrative account into a universal structure based on particulars that are operationalised as universal features. This movement in thought necessitates silencing or ignoring the situatedness of that particular element and obscuring the production of that universalism in discourse. The particularities of the Ülgen séance that have been most widely universalised relate especially to shamanic cosmology and the notion of the shaman's ascent to heaven via the various

---

[5]   The obscure provenance of the Ülgen séance and its subsequent canonisation in shamanism discourse recalls other occasions when indigenous cultural artefacts, both material and intangible, have been proclaimed to have an importance disproportionate to their status in the culture from which they were elevated. Examples include Spencer and Gillen's recollection of the Tjilpa cosmogonic myth about Numbakulla, recorded in 1896, republished with substantial revisions in 1927, and recounted by Eliade to evidence his theory of a cosmic axis orienting sacred space (Eliade 1973: 5–3; 1959a: 32–5; cf. J. Smith 1987). Another example is *The Tibetan Book of the Dead*. Collected quite randomly by Walter Evans-Wentz and published by him in 1927, it became a mainstay of esoteric and spiritualist literature. As Lopez wryly notes, 'One wonders how the course of Western history might have changed had Major Campbell, the British officer, given Evans-Wentz a monastic textbook on Buddhist logic, for example' (Lopez 1998: 52; cf. Lopez 2011).

celestial levels of the Cosmic Tree/Pole/Pillar of the World. Eliade's writings on shamanic cosmology are foundational to his work in comparative mythology and morphology of religions, and he consistently evidences these writings with reference to Radloff's rendering of Ülgen. Sometimes he relies on additional sources, but they too rely on Radloff (for example, Eliade 1958: 105–6). And yet, as Znamenski (2007: 36) has noted, Ülgen was only one of the chief spirits for a few Altaian clans; some clans never mentioned Ülgen and others did not consider him a major deity.

Radloff's ethnographic research was extremely limited, as Radloff himself admitted when he acknowledged that his information was primarily derived from 'hints' and 'legends, fairy tales, stories, and songs' (Radloff, quoted in Znamenski 2003: 10). Not only did Radloff not undertake ethnographic research among the Yakut of northern Siberia, he did not have an opportunity to witness the shaman's dramatic ritual performance he had read about in the memoirs and reports of travellers. He relied on second-hand accounts, and sometimes third- and fourth-hand accounts, as the Ülgen example demonstrates: 'Shamans, who could become our sole reliable source in this matter, usually are afraid to expose their secrets. They always surround themselves with an air of mystery, which is so important in their vocation' (Radloff, quoted in Znamenski 2004a: xxix). Radloff did, however, have several close encounters. On one occasion, he met two former shamans, both converts to Christianity, who refused to divulge their secrets on account of their new faith. In a telling example of the circumstances of ethnographic fieldwork in the imperial borderlands of southern Siberia, Radloff recounted their refusal:

> Our former god is already furious at us for betraying him. You can imagine what he can do if he learns that we, on top of everything else, betray him. We are even afraid more that the Russian God might find out how we talk about the old faith. What will save us then? (Ibid.)

We may reasonably assume that Radloff's account is less a verbatim report than a representation of their dilemma meant to explain his difficulty in obtaining their cooperation. The closest Radloff came to witnessing the fabled shaman's 'gothic-like' séance was the ritual cleansing of a dwelling following a death in the family, a ceremony Radloff noted included elements of the classic shamanic performance. Reflecting on the experience, Radloff wrote:

> This wild scene, magically illuminated by fire, produced in me such a strong impression that for a while I watched only the shaman and forgot about all those

who were present here. The Altaians were also shocked by this wild scene. They pulled out their pipes from their mouths and for a quarter of hour there was a dead silence. (Ibid.)

Besides this performance and a short thanksgiving prayer shared with him by a Teleut shaman, Radlov reconstructed a picture of shamanism from, as he put it, 'fragmentary utterances of adherents of shamanism and shamans themselves' (quoted in Znamenski 2003: 10).

Whatever the reliability or otherwise of Radloff's ethnographic fieldwork, the bigger issue at stake here is the ways in which the field of research into Siberian shamans pioneered by Radloff in the last decades of the nineteenth century came to produce an archive of ethnographic texts that in turn became the bedrock of subsequent scholarship on shamans. The challenge is to articulate in history the emergence of this new field. Some clues have already been suggested with reference to Russia's ambivalent relationship with Europe. I want to flesh these out by considering the Siberian regionalists and political exiles that conducted this research and authored this scholarship. Their intellectual project was intimately entwined with this ambivalence, and their scholarship, its range, approach to data, research methods, language, tone and style of its analyses, selections, omissions, motives and purposes all contributed to shaping and structuring a discourse about shamans that sustained a research agenda that arguably endures today.

Regionalists in Eden

From the late 1850s, a group of intellectuals and activists formed around a common interest in promoting Siberia's development and its role in Russian national life. All were Russian and educated in European Russia, though most were born in Siberia and many were exiled there on account of their political activities. They were nationalist in orientation, in a pan-Russian rather than pan-Slavic or Siberian-separatist sense. In other words, theirs was a multicultural approach and they agitated for recognition of indigenous peoples' rights and a withdrawal of the paternalism that marked the Russian state's orientation to 'aliens' (that is, Siberian indigenes). They saw themselves as a variant of the Great Russian People, 'grounded in territorial, social, and historical differences' (Watrous 1993: 117). Politically, the regionalists advocated a federalist Russian state, with different regions granted considerable autonomy to manage their affairs. They saw models for emulation in British Canada, Australia and especially the federal constitutionalism of the United States of America. As federalists, they saw their future with Russia but nevertheless wanted greater autonomy for Siberia to direct its own policies of modernisation and development. The best-known proponents of regionalism were Grigorii Nikolaevich Potanin (1835–1920) and Nikolai Mikhailovich Iadrintsev (1842–94) and the movement reached the height of its influence in the 1880s with the publication of Iadrintsev's *Siberia as a Colony*. However, from this pinnacle, the movement declined, particularly following the opening-up of Siberia to the forces of modernisation and class formation, increased Russian immigration following the inception of the Trans-Siberian railway project, as well as shifting government policies aimed at Russifying indigenous populations. With Iadrintsev's death in 1894, the 'golden age' of Siberian regionalism passed, though regionalist advocates continued agitating under the leadership of Potanin until his death in 1920, by which time the Romanov dynasty had ended and the dawn of the Soviet era had fundamentally altered the nature of Russian domination in North Asia.[6] From the perspective of a genealogy of shamanism, the significant issue is that the intellectual project initiated by the regionalists to create a new Siberian imaginary and elevate Siberia's status in the eyes of Russians significantly impacted representations of shamans in late nineteenth-century Siberian historiography, played an instrumental role in facilitating shamanism's expansion into North American scholarship and had deep and long-lasting influences on the shape of shamanism discourse well into the twentieth century.

The messianic-inclined Russia intelligentsia, of which the regionalists were a part, in some instances prominently so, sought virtues and values that would distinguish Russians as a distinct people, along with a sphere of influence in which to project Russia's destiny as redeemer of the project of modernity. Siberian indigenous myths, rituals, symbols and culture more generally offered valuable resources to Russian messianic nationalism. Consequently, the image of the shaman that emerged during this period is deeply inflected with this history and characterised by its contradictions, notably the ambivalent tensions

---

[6]   Stephen Watrous summarises the regionalists' political aspirations: ' … their views stressed a mix of equal rights and self-determination for Siberia, reflecting a perceived absence of both throughout the three centuries of Siberia's inclusion within the Russian empire. Regionalists sought, on the one hand, to gain for Siberia whatever liberties, rights, and opportunities Russians west of the Urals enjoyed; on the other, they wished the central government to assure a more open and autonomous development for Siberia – to be less like Russia, if so desired' (Watrous 1993: 113; also see Bassin 1999, Diment 1993, Forsyth 1992, Grant 1997, Kovalaschina 2007 and Slezkine 1994). For a discussion of dissident and regionalist attitudes to the United States during the nineteenth century, see Bassin 1991: 776–9, Slezkine 1994: 114 and Watrous 1993: 120–21.

between antipathy towards Europe and mimicry of European norms and values. Iadrintsev, for example, wrote of the 'unforgettable impression' left on him by a shaman's ritual performance he witnessed:

> I remember that night when I had to stop at that place. That mysterious beautiful night with thousands of bright stars spread over the awesome mountains full of savage beauty and poetic charm. I saw the shaman in a fantastic costume decorated with rattles and snake-like plaits. Feathers were sticking from his helmet, and in his hands he held a mysterious drum. At first, the shaman circled around the fire. Then he jumped out of the shelter to bark to the open air. My ears still can hear his magnificent howling, his call for spirits, and the wild mountain echo that responded to his invocations. (Quoted in Znamenski 2003: 12)

That impression was published in 1885, five years after Iadrintsev first visited the Altai. During his first visit, he noticed what he perceived as striking similarities between Siberia and ancient Greece. Writing in 1880 to a friend in Switzerland, Iadrintsev enthused:

> Mores and customs of local savages are extremely interesting. Their religion is shamanism. But what is shamanism? This is Pantheism. In a nutshell, the Altai is Greece, where everything is animated: rivers, mountains, stones; here one can hear thousands of legends and what legends they are! (Quoted in Znamenski 2003: 12)[7]

Such comparisons between Siberian shamans and ancient Grecian pantheism were recorded frequently in Iadrintsev's travel notes (Znamenski 2004b: 148). His friend and colleague Grigorii Potanin went further to argue that shamanism was the wellspring of Christianity. Reversing the degenerative thesis favoured by Enlightenment scholars, Potanin's 'oriental hypothesis' drew parallels between southern Siberian and Central Asian shamanic legends on the one hand and Hebrew, Russian, early Christian and European mediaeval mythologies on the other. Drawing on Castren's philological studies, Potanin announced:

---

[7]   Similarly, Chadwick saw parallels between the 'oral poetry of the Tartars' and the 'early epic poetry of Europe': '... the types of characters depicted, and the action of the poems are closely analogous to those of the Homeric poems and of *Beowulf*.' The main difference in her view was that Central Asian poetry relates 'not to the actual, but to the spiritual experiences of their heroes ... and heroines ... in sharp contrast to most of the oral poetry of Europe', with the exception of the Homeric and early Norse epics: 'Odysseus would have found himself in a perfectly familiar milieu among the heroes of the Kara-Kirghiz' (Chadwick 1936b: 291).

Now I am inclined to think more than ever that Christianity originated from the Finnish tribes in Southern Siberia. That Mongol Nestorian vision according to which Christ was called Erke was not a sect brought from the West but it was the origin of Christianity. The legends of the mission, of God's son, appeared in Siberia. (Quoted in Kovalaschina 2007: 116, n. 39, cf. 96–8)

He concluded:

We clearly see that it is the central Asian shamanic legend that lies at the foundation of the legend about Christ, and that the image of Christ himself was shaped according to the image that had existed many centuries earlier in inner Asia. (Quoted in Znamenski 2007: 46)

The regionalists shared Castren's and Radloff's romantic sentiments, but employed these for different ideological purposes: to demonstrate that Siberian culture was on a par with, if not superior to, European culture. Both Iadrintsev and Potanin advanced strategies to suggest that Siberian shamanism was at the roots of European civilisation, though in this effort Potanin arguably surpassed Iadrintsev in boldness. By postulating the origins of Christianity in Siberian shamanism, Potanin's oriental hypothesis argued for an alternative to romantic Orientalism's claim that the roots of western civilisation were in India: '[Southern Siberia] is the genuine motherland of humankind. It was here that the first seeds of Christian legends were planted. Now I am quite sure that the Eden of Adam and Eve was located at the sources of the Irtysh River on the banks of which I was born' (quoted in Znamenski 2003: 45–6).

Andrei Anokhin, another regionalist scholar and contemporary and colleague of Iadrintsev and Potanin, was similarly moved: 'Shamanism represents the peak of expressive skills of the Altaian singing, people with weak nerves are not able to withstand the power of the feelings which are transmitted through a shaman.' An ethnomusicologist particularly interested in Ostiak and Altaian shamanism in western and southern Siberia respectively, Anokhin compared the 'shamanic mystery plays' with the Hebrew psalms, finding in them 'the same incorruptible sincerity that reflects a simple, but deeply sensitive soul, the same metaphors, the same magnificent pictures of surrounding nature' (Anokhin, quoted in Znamenski 2004b: 150; cf. 2003: 50–54). As with Radloff, Potanin and Gavriil Ksenofontov (Potanin's student and another advocate of the Judaeo-Christian debt to shamanism), Anokhin's work was a key source for contemporary and later participants in the discourse on shamanism, including Campbell, Eliade and Sternberg (for example, J. Campbell 2000: 251–2; Eliade 1964: 36–44, 200–201; Sternberg 2004: 104).

Yet for all their efforts to elevate shamans' image in the eyes of the Russian public, Siberian indigenous cultures presented a dilemma to the regionalists. On the one hand, the regionalists regarded Siberia's indigenous peoples as signposting a new pan-Russian identity oriented eastward and away from Europe. Under the intellectual leadership of Potanin and Iadrintsev, the regionalists celebrated natives' close-knit communities and the value natives supposedly placed on equality and independence. Potanin remarked on 'their phenomenal honesty and the heavenly [*raiskie*] rules of their social life' (quoted in Slezkine 1994: 116). In regionalists' eyes, Siberia's natives demonstrated a model of social organisation that stressed values and virtues the regionalists thought lacking in Europe, including European Russia (that is, west of the Urals). On the other hand, Siberia's indigenes were a potent symbol of Siberia's backwardness and lack of development. 'The moral lives of the aliens', wrote S.S. Shashkov, 'is a bizarre mixture of repulsive vices and patriarchal virtues' (quoted in Slezkine 1994: 115). In addition to disgust at filthy natives who feasted on raw meat, by the latter decades of the nineteenth century a new theme was emerging that lamented how natives were corrupted by Russian lifestyles. For example, N.V. Latkin complained:

> Drunkenness, knavery, laziness, apathy, and a feebleness caused by various sicknesses, smallpox, and especially venereal diseases ... have changed the character of this people, which used to be known for its courage, valor, agility, kindness, and truthfulness. (Quoted in Slezkine 1994: 116)

The regionalists' dilemma was of course a product of their contradictory desire to reject European identity and simultaneously identify with European values and aspirations. This ambivalent impulse suggests something of the regionalists' attitude towards European Russia and it is significant that the regionalists were dissidents, exiles and outspoken critics of Tsarist autocracy. Setting aside for the moment the ideological articulations of backward, primitive and savage natives, certainly indigenous populations were in dire straits, both physically and economically. However, the regionalists were astute enough to recognise that the extreme penury in which many natives survived was a consequence of Tsarist exploitation, abuse and neglect (Forsyth 1992: 158–63). The regionalists felt a moral responsibility for Siberia's indigenous peoples, much as the Russian intelligentsia accepted moral responsibility for the Russian peasantry. As Iadrintsev put it, 'Every time we hear about their predicament, we should experience pangs of conscience' (quoted in Slezkine 1994: 117). However, in Siberia's colonial context, the predicament that concerned the regionalists was not merely the decline in the condition of natives; regionalists were very concerned that indigenous peoples faced extinction, a circumstance that were it to come to pass, would confirm Russia and its imperial ambitions as comparably dishonourable and unconscionable as the English, French, or Spanish.

The regionalists' solution to the dilemma of honest natives brought low by Russian vices was to advocate a civilising mission to indigenous populations. For regionalists anxious to avoid comparison with the European imperial powers' treatment of indigenous populations, this civilising mission was more than a matter of conscience, it was a matter of pride. Reflecting a general transformation in Russian elite politics, the regionalists' strategy redefined savagery as poverty and backwardness as indigence, largely attributable to unjust imperial policies towards Russia's colonial possession. Yet this was not a revolutionary reformulation away from the evolutionary schema that underpinned imperial attitudes to native populations in Africa, the Americas and India no less than Siberia; parallels with paternalist notions of the 'white man's burden' are clear. This civilising mission called on new administrators to humanise government, merchants and traders to stop unfair practices and missionaries to devote themselves to educational work. This was, as Iadrintsev put it, 'the obligation of the superior race engaged in spreading civilization' (quoted in Slezkine 1994: 117). Potanin agreed. Referencing Siberia's far eastern region, he wrote in 1861, 'the role of further developing civilization [in the Amur region] has fallen to Russia' (Potanin, quoted in Bassin 1999: 197). Slezkine suggests these transformations in how natives should be treated stemmed from a transformation in how natives were understood. Now natives were regarded as having rights: 'The preservation of alien tribes, the spread of education among them, as well as their involvement in civic and educational life, is as much the historic right of aliens for human existence as it is the historic duty of the Russian people in the East' (Iadrintsev, quoted in Slezkine 1994: 117). In this way, Russia's civilising mission was promoted as according with natives' rights on grounds of their humanity rather than their citizenship, while the civilising mission in practice amounted to the Russification of Siberian native populations (Forsyth 1992: 154–62, Slezkine 1994: 116–17).

An important plank in the regionalists' strategy to civilise Siberia was educating Russians about indigenous cultures, a task the regionalist scholars saw as their unique role and obligation as members of the superior race engaged in spreading civilisation. They achieved this by several means, including books, pamphlets and ethnographic exhibitions. Znamenski recounts such a staging in 1909 in the city of Tomsk (Znamenski 2004b: 153–5, 2003: 15–16). Organised by Potanin, Anokhin and the archaeologist and ethnographer

V.A. Adrianov, this performance transformed Tomsk's 'hall for public gatherings' (*domobshchestvennogo*) into a Siberian 'house of culture', complete with animal skins, depictions of a polar night and a huge block of ice. Before crowding spectators, native actors dressed in the traditional garb of Altaians, Buryats, Tartars and Khanty performed live ethnography by playing musical instruments, reciting excerpts from their epic legends and displaying scenes from native life with household items, sacred altars and replicas of native dwellings. The centre of attention for much of the evening was Mampyi, an Altaian shaman. Mampyi collaborated closely with Potanin and his colleagues, by contributing to devising the structure of this ethnographic theatre and promoting the regionalists' project to recover indigenous cultural identity.

According to Znamenski, a contemporary account published in the journal *Etnograficheskoe Obozrenie* describes how Mampyi divided the evening's shamanic performance into several acts. First, Mampyi described the meaning of the ritual he was about to perform, before donning his costume and addressing a fire. Then he addressed several ancestral spirits in a 'whirling dancing manner' before finally concluding his performance by removing his costume and in 'a singing manner' explained the meaning of the ceremony he had just performed. Six days later, Mampyi performed as a living illustration accompanying a scholarly paper read by Adrianov on the basics of Siberian shamanism. That evening, at the Tomsk Technological Institute, the paper was read again and Mampyi repeated his performance for a third time. Znamenski reports that Potanin and his colleagues were so inspired by the success of their ethnographic showcase that they sought and found other shamans with whom they staged similar ethnographic performances in several other cities, including Barnaul and Irkutsk (Znamenski 2007: 51). It is perhaps also worth noting here that Mampyi, a key source and collaborator of Anokhin's, is also a key source for Eliade's discussion of Altaic shamans' descent to the underworld and is the only shaman for whom Eliade had specific ethnographic data, recorded by Anokin (Eliade 1964: 200–204).

The regionalists mobilised Siberian indigenous cultures in their efforts to formulate and articulate a distinct and worthy pan-Russian identity. Siberia's most exotic and well-known emblem of indigenous religiosity offered a vitalising element and so featured in their writings and their broader project to stimulate a new vision of Siberia that could form the basis of that pan-Russian identity. Yet for all their ambition, the regionalists tended to confine their research and writings to southern and western Siberia, particularly the Altai region, which was also a favourite holiday destination for Potanin and his colleagues. The situation was somewhat different in northern and eastern Siberia. Economic and industrial development had hardly touched most parts of the north and east, unlike the southern steppes where Russian settlement, manufacturing and merchant trading were rapidly transforming Siberian society. More generally, policies of Russification had not had nearly as much impact in the north-east as in the south-west, to a large degree because few Russian administrators and missionaries were willing to tolerate the harsh, inhospitable climate. The climate similarly ensured Russian settlers stayed away on account of the immense difficulty of productively settling the land. As a result, the north-east remained largely unchanged, or certainly far less changed by Russian imperialism than the south. In terms of the discourse on shamanism, this fact held two implications. First, many indigenous communities were still nomadic and relied on hunting and fishing as well as their reindeer herds for survival, unlike in the south where natives increasingly adopted sedentary lifestyles and Russian customs. The second implication is that the north-east remained a favourite destination to which to banish political dissidents and troublemakers. These two implications converged when political exiles from Tsarist Russia turned to ethnography in a bid to occupy themselves in the long, lonely years of their banishment. Some, like Vladimir G. Bogoraz (Waldemar Bogoras) and Vladimir Ilych Jochelson (Waldemar Jochelson) went on to establish successful academic careers on the basis of their involuntary Siberian exile.

Although not as easily given to the romantic musings of the regionalists, exiles and regionalists were familiar with one another's work and in some cases were on personal terms. Yet the exiles identified first and foremost as Europeans. In this respect, their self-understanding distinguished them from the regionalists. They were also more scientifically inclined and brought distinctly European epistemological orientations to bear on their research. This distinction is demonstrated in sharpest relief with reference to exiles' writings and ideas about shaman's mental states, a theme the exiles gathered under a heading that was as much a diagnostic designation as a rubric for all manner of strange behaviours exhibited by natives.[8]

---

8   A second distinction is the exiles' tendency to blend fictive writing with scientific research. Waclav Sieroszewski is a notable example (Manouelian 2006, Theodoratus 1977; more generally, see Knight 2000). Although an interesting discussion could be had with reference to experimental styles of 'writing culture' (Clifford and Marcus 1986), I have omitted this theme owing to constraints of length weighed against the value this theme would contribute to the problem, as I have framed it in terms of exiles' representations, of arctic hysteria.

Arctic Hysteria

The subject of shamans' mental states is as old as the discourse itself. Russian and European observers interpreted shamans' bizarre behaviour while in trance as evidence of an abnormal and deficient mind. Generally, the question of shamans' apparently strange and abnormal behaviour was approached by successive travellers, authors and scholars within the paradigms of permissibility of their period. Up to the early eighteenth century, shamans' behaviour was attributed to possession by devils. During the eighteenth-century Enlightenment, shamans were seen as stupid and mad, or alternatively as clever charlatans engaged in a performance for duplicitous ends. During the nineteenth century, romantic nationalists such as Iadrintsev and Potanin, though still committed to rational demystification, were nevertheless moved by shamans' professed ability to commune with spirits and impressed by the respect accorded them by their fellow natives. Yet since at least the Second Kamchatka Expedition, when Zuev classified shamans' bizarre behaviour as a variety of illness, observers had sought to pathologise shamans as a means to gaining explanatory control over what otherwise escaped their comprehension, if not rational explanation. In the last years of the nineteenth century and the early decades of the twentieth, this pathology went by the name 'arctic hysteria', a term, when applied to shamans, that proposed a causal relation between geography, climate and mental states. This approach to apprehending shamans was another strategy to bring shamans under normative control by submitting the cultural institution of shamanic religiosity to scientific disciplinary power.

Although the history of describing shamans as mentally ill begins more than a century before, the nineteenth-century discourse on female hysteria offered a widely accepted 'scientific' explanation for shamans' behaviour, and the prevalence of arctic hysteria among native populations was a common feature in reports and writings by exiles. Stanislaus Novakovsky summarised exiles' accounts of arctic hysteria in a 1924 article. He reported 'all travelers are unanimous that women are especially susceptible to hysterical disorders' and quoted Sieroszewski to support his claim: 'Girls are also subject to this disease, but it is women who are especially susceptible and more so after marriage or after unfortunate child birth' (Novakovsky 1924: 119). Similarly, Waldemar Jochelson reported that arctic hysteria was widely prevalent among women, indeed, in up to half the female population. He reasoned, 'As these fits develop mostly in grown-up girls or young women, it may be inferred that they are in some way connected with the sexual functions' (Jochelson 1975b: 31). Nineteenth-century medicine's preoccupation with female hysteria was familiar to the exiles and they were quick to interpret shamans' behaviour in terms of hysteria. They saw in the shaman's leaps, shouts, screams, mimicry, contortions, sweating, shivering, shaking, twitching and similar physiological signs indicators of a deranged mind, nervous disorder and neurosis. While the exiles reported that arctic hysteria was an affliction common in women, they noted 'nervous attacks' afflicted men too, 'shamans in particular' (Jochelson 1975a: 416–17). Similarly, in *The Chukchee*, Bogoras (1974: 426) introduced his discussion of 'the psychology of shamans' by noting, 'shamans are very nervous, highly excitable persons, often almost on the verge of insanity'. Jochelson (1975a: 47) too emphasised shamans' nervous disposition: 'Those that become shamans are usually nervous young men subject to hysterical fits, by means of which the spirits express their demand that the young man should consecrate himself in the service of shamanism.'

The suggestion that men were also prone to hysteria seemed to undermine the contention that this 'nervous disease' had something to do with female 'sexual functions'. To some extent, this problem was obscured (and thereby resolved) by its attribution to male shamans, rather than men in general, because this attribution invoked long-standing suspicions about shamans' mental states. This was one strategy to deal with the problem of men afflicted by a condition supposedly prevalent among women.[9] A different strategy accounted for the affliction in terms of causal factors independent of differences between the sexes. In contrast with the first strategy, that relied on popular medical discourses of the time, the second strategy drew on geographical determinism and posited the arctic climate as the main causal factor. In general, a combination of both strategies was deployed, depending on the category of person under consideration and the extent of Russification at their location. The less Russified and more 'savage' the area, the stronger the preference for arctic hysteria; the inverse accounted for a preference for female hysteria (see Worobec 2001). Thus Novakovsky (1924: 113) could say of arctic hysteria, 'this scourge of the northern tribes is the product of that media in which they are forced to live and lead a difficult struggle for existence.'

Among these northern tribes, Jochelson (1975a: 416) reported that arctic hysteria is 'widely prevalent among the Yukagir, Tungus [Evenki], Yakut, and also among the Russian immigrants', although he thought the Yukaghir of the

---

9   It is worth noting the circularity of this argument. Shamans are not like normal men; they are particularly prone to nervousness and thus are more like women, in which case their neurotic behaviour can be explained because, being more like women, they are more prone to neurosis and hysteria.

Kolyma River basin were the worst afflicted.[10] Jochelson distinguished two forms of arctic hysteria. *Menerik*, he suggested, is indistinguishable from 'fits of hysteria in civilised countries'. He continued:

> As these fits develop mostly in grown-up girls and young women, it may be inferred that they are in some way connected with the sexual functions. Among the young male population, hysterical fits are principally due to the influence of religious imagination. They are observed in the nervously strained youths who are inclined to become shamans. (Jochelson 1975b: 30–34)

Menerik is female hysteria manifested in shamans. The *menerik* episode begins with the afflicted person singing 'the wishes of the spirit that tortures him'. They are usually in a seated position and this stage may continue for a day or more. In the next stage of the *menerik*,

> ... suddenly the patient looks like a savage, or, with an air of exaltation, begins to sing, first gently, then louder, waving his arms and swinging his body ... the future shaman complains, in the song, of the spirits that compel him to start the shaman's career, strangle him, and threaten death if he does not consent to follow their call. Sometimes it is apparently the spirit himself, that has entered into the patient, who sings ... Often the singing is followed by cramps, contractions, or an attack of epilepsy. (Ibid.)

Jochelson described another form of arctic hysteria with reference to the Yakut term *meriak*. He admitted this condition is stranger and more complicated than *menerik*, but suggested that in general it consisted in 'extreme impressionableness ... fright and timidity'. With this form of arctic hysteria, the afflicted person is easily given to shock and fear at the slightest suggestion, following which they shout obscenities, often referencing genitals, usually female but on occasion male as well, and apparently involuntarily. Jochelson reported this condition usually afflicted women and estimated that half the population of women aged 30 or 40 years and older was afflicted, giving several examples. A variation of this form of hysteria, also classified under the term *meriak*, consisted in extreme imitation, which Jochelson compared with hypnosis:

---

[10] *The Koryak* mentions arctic hysteria only briefly and refers readers to his report *The Yukaghir and the Yukaghirized Tungus* because 'all the forms of this disease occur developed to the highest degree' among the Yukaghir of the Upper Kolyma river region (Jochelson 1975b: 31; cf. 1975a: 416, n. 2).

The effects of the hypnotist are produced while setting in motion, by words or by postures, certain ideas in the subconscious mind of the subject. In arctic hysteria, suggestions like hypnotic ones take place with the full consciousness of the person, when he is awake. The auditory and visual impressions (the latter are absent in suggestions of artificial sleep) act on the mind of the patient in evoking certain actions not only with his full consciousness, but even against his wish. He has no power to restrain himself. Besides, the suggestion may be intentional or unintentional on the part of the person who makes it. Even animals or natural forces may bring about hypnotic states. Everything uncommon, everything that strikes the mind of the patient through the organs of sight or hearing, evokes in him repetitions. The patient repeats the sounds of animals and the words of men, which he has heard; he imitates certain postures of grimaces, and does everything which he is told to do, even the most absurd, ridiculous, indecent, or dangerous things. (Ibid.)

This kind of uncontrollable imitation renders the afflicted person vulnerable to abuse and Jochelson cites examples of Yukaghirs abused in this way both by their fellow clanspeople as well as Russians.[11]

As one might expect, doing ethnographic research in a society afflicted by this kind of pathology can be difficult. Jochelson (1975b: 35–6) recalled an incident regarding a woman he wished to photograph. Having positioned her by a screen, he instructed her to look at the top of the camera and not move. '... her face became as if petrified, and her eyes motionless. Fearing that such a state might end in a fit, I hastened to tell her to get up. She at once got up and went away.' However, it could also be dangerous too, not only for the person afflicted with *meriak*, but also for the person suggesting behaviour to imitate or abusing the person thus afflicted. Jochelson explained this in terms of contradictory brain functions. At the moment of suggestion, two brain functions activate independently and contradictorily. While a 'reflectory half' submitted without control, a 'conscious half, although suppressed, and powerless to counteract the automatic action', initiated resistance by attacking the 'supposed hypnotizer' with a knife, axe, or any improvised weapon at hand. Bearing in mind that persons afflicted with *meriak* are susceptible to suggestion regardless of the intention of a suggester, conceivably anyone can find themselves under attack at any moment

---

11   The manner in which mimicry, when abused in this way, becomes obedience is intriguing. Jochelson recounts the incident of a woman who seized a horse by the tail upon instruction of a young man standing nearby. She was about to be dragged away, when he instructed her to let go. What is being abused here is not the woman's capacity for imitation, but her obedience to instruction.

for any innocuous suggestion. Aware of these dangers, Jochelson thought it dangerous to experiment with 'patients' when there was no-one around to restrain 'their outbursts of resentment', although he adds that 'in the eyes of the natives, I was too important a man to be assaulted or struck with impunity.' By way of demonstrating this point, he recounted an incident in which a Yukaghir woman, 'being frightened at the crack of the shutter of my camera, rushed not at me, but at my Cossack, who was standing by, at the same time exclaiming the names of the male sexual organs, and trying to take hold of his'. Accounting for this incident in terms of his model of simultaneous, contrary brain impulses, Jochelson adds to his model a capacity for strategic discrimination: 'She must, then, have consciously transferred her anger from me, who was the cause of her fright, to another person, who could be assaulted' (Jochelson 1975b: 37).

Jochelson described a curious society. A sizeable portion of the population – half of all women over 30 years, the majority of younger women and all shamans – was supposedly susceptible to uncontrollable behaviour, ranging from soft singing for several hours to seizures, profanity, undressing in public, disappearing for hours into the Arctic tundra, day or night, wearing nothing but light clothes or even sometimes naked, and given to committing violence against themselves and others at apparently inoffensive suggestions. At the same time, people in this state sometimes displayed an uncanny capacity for reasoning, such as the woman who substituted for Jochelson his Cossack companion. In another of Jochelson's examples, we may infer a degree of strategic reasoning was involved when the spirits that had caused a teenage girl to suffer hysterical fits released her upon her parents' acquiescence to their demand to give their daughter a new dress (1975b: 31–2). There is a sense of perplexity in these and other ethnographers' observations about Arctic hysteria, a sense that they are not quite confident they have understood or adequately explained this strange affliction. They seem ambivalent and their tone alternates between dissatisfaction with the extent of explanatory control asserted with theories of contradictory brain functions and distinctions between hysteria types, determination to explain this phenomenon in terms of mental impairment, and resignation that the phenomenon in question possibly escapes their explanatory powers. Dissatisfied but lacking alternative explanations, Bogoras, Jochelson, Sieroszewski and their exiled peers settled for reporting and describing in the style of the mildly perplexed (cf. Miller 1999).

This episode is reminiscent of Taussig's discussion of the strange coexistence of faith and scepticism reported by Boas about Kwakiutl attitudes towards the efficacy of shamans' healing techniques, a problem Taussig contrasts with Evans-Pritchard's efforts to uncover Zande witchdoctors' 'tricks of the trade'. Likening Kwakiutl shamanism to a slippery fish ('the more you try to pin it down, the more it wriggles'), Taussig notes Evans-Pritchard's faith in ethnography: 'In the long run, however ... an ethnographer is bound to triumph. Armed with preliminary knowledge nothing can prevent him from driving a deeper and deeper wedge if he is interested and persistent' (quoted in Taussig 1998: 242). The resemblance with the exiles' reports about Arctic hysteria is simply that, like the tricks of Kwakiutl shamans and Zande witchdoctors, the phenomenon of Arctic hysteria seemed to elude arrest at the hands of ethnographers' wedge of scientific reason. I don't want to push the comparison too far and I recognise that interest in shamans' mental states is a somewhat different inquiry from interest in the tricks and techniques of indigenous healers. However, I think these two images – the slippery fish and the driving wedge – suggest something of the troubled relationship between what shamans are and their representation in language. By merging the theory of female hysteria with a putative relationship between mental states and 'that media in which they are forced to live', the theory of Arctic hysteria drove the wedge a little deeper. Yet still the slippery fish of shamans' mental states eluded circumscription and epistemological containment. In the final section of this chapter, I want to draw out this problem more explicitly by considering the importance of language in the emigration of the term 'shaman' to North America. Thereafter I will return to these images of the driving wedge and the slippery fish by way of conclusion.

Emigration

Since the late seventeenth century, an indigenous term 'shaman' had been translated as 'juggler', 'conjurer', 'sorcerer', 'priest', 'wizard', and so on. During the second half of the nineteenth century, however, 'shaman' was proffered as the equivalent term in English for different native terms. I want to consider this problem in relation to North America. The important backdrop for this development was the emergence in the North American context of ethnography and anthropology as scholarly disciplines, particularly Franz Boas's influential studies of indigenous communities on Baffin Island and along the continent's north-west coast. The particularist and relativist method developed by Boas and the generation of peers and students he influenced had to manage a dilemma, one inherent in modernity's double-hinged articulation of ontology and epistemology: ethnographic particularism must work with cross-cultural categories if it is to establish a science of anthropology founded on comparative analysis. Not only that, but the familiar available terms – 'sorcerer', 'conjurer', 'priest', 'medicine-man' and the like – belonged to a discourse the Boasians' new particularist methods intended to repudiate. During the 1880s, while Boas was still experimenting with his method, these terms were gradually being supplemented and gradually supplanted by the term 'shaman'. During the 1890s, when the Boasian methodological emphasis on ethnographic particularism was growing in influence and the theory of cultural diffusion was growing in popularity, 'shaman' was embraced for providing a cross-cultural comparative category that was acceptable because of its native provenance, a claim sustained in turn by ethnographic research from Alaska and the North-west that supported the diffusion theory in relation to North-east Asia.

The notion that North American medicine men were similar to Siberian shamans was already suggested in the eighteenth-century writings of American adventurer and explorer John Ledyard. Well known as the chronicler of Captain Cook's last voyage, Ledyard's accounts of his travels in Siberia included favourable comparisons between 'the Shamant' and 'Priests' of 'savage' Asia and America, 'and collaterally of every other untutored being' (Ledyard 1966: 191–2; cf. Carver 1781: 384–7). Jared Spark's 1828 biography of Ledyard was republished several times during the nineteenth century and contributed to elevating Ledyard's status. By the mid-nineteenth century, the term 'shaman' was becoming more familiar to American audiences, for example, through articles like 'Description of a Siberian Shaman', published in at least three US newspapers.[12] In 1854, Randolph Marcy gave 'shamans' as a synonym for 'medicine-men' in his *Exploration of the Red River of Louisiana in the year 1852*. The passage related to a Comanche 'medicine-lodge' and Marcy, who also authored the well-known *Prairie Traveler* handbook, reproduced it in his 1863 book *Thirty Years of Army Life on the Border* (Marcy and McClellan 1854: 107, Marcy 1863: 60). Both titles were republished on several occasions. 'Medicine man', 'conjurer', or less commonly 'priest' were still widely preferred, particularly since most ethnographic research was still collected by serving or retired military personnel schooled in the social evolutionary ideas of the era. However, with moves towards professionalising ethnographic research during the 1870s and particularly after the founding of the Bureau of Ethnology in 1879, this language began to change.

Consider, for example, Albert Gatschet. Born in Switzerland and trained as a linguist at Bern and Berlin, Gatschet travelled to North America to study

---

[12]   Originally published in *Sharpe's London Magazine* in November 1846, 'Description of a Siberian Shaman' was reprinted in *Sartain's Union Magazine of Literature and Art*, 10 (January–June 1852), pp. 250–51; *The National Magazine*, 1 (July–December 1852), pp. 250–52; and *The Crayon* 2(12) (19 September 1855), p. 182.

native languages. He was soon working for the United States Geological Survey and Bureau of Ethnology. In April 1877, Gatchet presented a paper to the American Philosophical Society on the language of the Timucuan people of the Florida peninsula. Gatschet's paper included English translations of Timucuan words; for the Timucuan '*itufa*' Gatschet gave 'sorcerer, wizard, medicine-man', and for '*ituhu*' Gatschet offered 'to pray, conjure, invoke, charm, bewitch' (Gatschet 1877: 640). By 1880, Gatschet had subtly modified his translation. In another paper read before the Society, Gatschet abandoned his earlier translation of *itufa* and instead formed a noun from his earlier translation of '*ituhu*', so '*itufa*' was now translated simply as 'conjurer' and '*ituhu*' became 'to charm, bewitch' (Gatschet 1880: 486). He also introduced another Timucuan word, '*iarua*', translated as 'sorcerer, conjurer'. Gaschet obtained the new term from Rene de Laudonniere's reports of his travels in Florida and credits the translation to de Laudonnierre, but adds his own explanatory note: 'This epithet given to the Timucua shamans refers to their prophetic power and the convulsions affected by them to obtain oracles of war; from yuru to tremble, to be shaken or contorted' (ibid.: 500). Gatschet's note references his introductory comments where he recalled observations by the seventeenth-century Franciscan Padre Francesco Pareja about the 'incantations' of Timucuan 'conjurers', who 'after contorting himself in the most terrific manner for about twenty minutes' advised the chief (these are Gatschet's terms). Pareja's reports, which Gatschet thought to be among 'the most precious relics of Floridian antiquity' (Gatschet 1877: 628–9) prompted him to note: 'In a people which believes in the power of conjurers over ghosts and spirits, the influence of the bewitcher or shaman must be necessarily immense' (Gatschet 1880: 473). This appears to be the first occasion Gatschet uses 'shaman' in his writings; by 1883, he was using 'shaman' as an English equivalent term, giving 'conjurer, Shaman' as the English translation for '*Ka'tchmish*' in a paper on the Shetimasha Indians of southern Louisiana (Gatschet 1883: 156–7).

W.J. Hoffman provides another illustration. Two weeks before Gatschet read his Shetimasha Indians paper before the Anthropological Society of Washington, Hoffman read to the Society a paper comparing pictographs he studied in California in 1882 with similar examples collected in Alaska. Hoffman described each pictograph individually and then interpreted the series as a narrative. Hoffman's choice of language suggests his individual descriptions were already interpretations. For example, his description of engravings on an ivory bow included the following (numbers correspond to the pictograph sequence):

... 8. The hunter, or narrator, sitting on the ground in an attitude of supplication. He is asking the Shaman for success in the chase. 9. The Shaman. Incantations are performed by making short circular movements with the hands, above and on either side of the head. A Shaman is always drawn with one or both hands elevated, and the gesture for this personage is made as if he were performing such ceremonies. In the present instance the left arm is still raised, while the right is extended toward the supplicant, signifying that the request has been granted. 10. The Shaman's winter lodge. 11. Trees surrounding the habitations of this individual. I2. The Shaman's summer habitation. (Hoffman 1883: 140)

This style of using 'shaman', in which Hoffman assumed his readers' familiarity with the term so that further description or explanation was unnecessary, is typical of his paper (see also ibid.: 143, 146). For example, Hoffman stated of a pictograph showing 'an ornamented head, with body and legs having an indefinite termination': 'The only interpretation that can be offered is that it represents a Shaman'; he says no more (Hoffman 1883: 131). The only description of 'shaman' I have found in Hoffman's work is a footnote to an article published in 1881: 'The term "medicine" is usually applied to anything partaking of the nature of a charm or fetish, and is prepared with attendant ceremonies by a "medicine chief" or shaman' (Hoffman 1881: 240n). His paper on pictographs also offered 'shaman' as the single English translation of several indigenous words, a preference he repeated in subsequent articles. However, his later articles swapped the order of presentation by giving English words followed by their indigenous translation. So, for example, in the Waitshum'ni dialect, Hoffman gives '*Ang'tru*' as the indigenous word for 'Shaman' (Hoffman 1886b: 374). Another article published in the same issue of *Proceedings of the American Philosophical Society* gave Selish translations for approximately 360 English words, including 'Chief', 'Friend', 'Indian', 'Whiteman', 'Frenchman' and 'Shaman' (Hoffman 1886a: 363). In 1888, Hoffman published 'Pictography and Shamanistic Rites of the Ojibwa', a prelude to his lengthy 1891 study of Ojibwa Midē, 'or shamans' (Hoffman 1891, 1888), which was submitted to the Secretary of the Smithsonian Institution for inclusion in the Seventh Annual Report of the Bureau of Ethnology. Hoffman's article on Ojibwa 'shamanistic rites' in the third issue of *American Anthropologist's* inaugural volume was not the first in the volume to allude to shamanism in its title; the previous issue included 'The Prayer of a Navajo Shaman' by Washington Matthews (1888). Another example of an anthropologist who embraced the term 'shaman' during the last two decades of the nineteenth century, the entry for 'priest' and 'medicine-men' in the index of Matthews' monograph on Navaho legends referred readers to the entry for 'Shaman' (Matthews 1897; cf. Matthews 1894, 1888, 1886, 1885).

James Mooney also belongs in this survey. Mooney seems to have first used 'shaman' in a 1889 article titled 'Cherokee and Iroquois Parallels', a one-page commentary in Issue 4 of *The Journal of American Folklore* (Mooney 1889a). Mooney's favourable comparison of a Huron cosmogonic myth described by Horatio Hale in Issue 3, with his account of a Cherokee mythological hero named Tawiskalû published in Issue 2, makes the point that 'Tawiskalû is invoked by the Cherokee shamans in many of their secret formulas' (ibid.: 67). However, his original discussion in the journal's second issue did not mention shamans and instead consistently refers to 'medicine-men', one of whom is Mooney's informant, and as a category of person are also important characters in Cherokees' myths and legends (Mooney 1888: 98). Mooney was using a term he had not used previously. Similarly, on a different point of comparison regarding ritual use of tobacco among Onondaga described in articles by De Cost Smith and W.M. Beauchamp in Issue 3, in 'Cherokee and Iroquois Parallels', Mooney writes that the same variety of tobacco plant was used by Cherokee 'shamans', although neither Smith nor Beauchamp used that term (Mooney 1889a: 67). A month later Mooney's 'Cherokee Mound-Building' described the 'shamanistic rites' through which the carefully constructed mounds and attached symbols 'were invested with ... fatal magic properties' (Mooney 1889b: 167–8) and a year later Mooney's description of 'Cherokee ball play' (contemporary lacrosse) gives prominence to 'shamanistic ceremonies' and the role of 'shamans' in preparing players for competition (Mooney 1890). By the time Mooney published *The Sacred Formulas of the Cherokee* in 1891, he wrote confidently of the 'shamans of the tribe', 'shamanistic prayers and ceremonies' and the 'opposing forces of Christianity and shamanism' (Mooney 1891).

Franz Boas's writings similarly indicate an emerging preference. His early publications about his research on Baffin Island and among Kwakiutl communities on the Pacific North-west coast do not mention shamans and refer instead to 'medicine-men' (1888: 57, 1887: 400, 1884: 261). For example, in 1887, Boas wrote of the Baffin Island Eskimos: 'By their help [help of spirits] a man may become what is called angakoq, a kind of priest or wizard. The spirits help him to discover the causes of sickness and death and therefore he is the medicine-man' (1887: 400). From 1889, however, he began using 'shaman', writing about the Snanaimuq of British Columbia in Volume 2 of *American Anthropologist*:

Sickness is produced by the touch of the ghosts, who, according to the belief of the Snanaimuq, appear in the shape of owls. The sick are cured by the shamans, who do not use rattles in their incantations. Shamans acquire their art by encounters with spirits, for whose apparition the novice prepares himself by long-continued bathing in lakes and by rubbing the body with cedar twigs 'to remove all bad smell.' (Boas 1889: 326)[13]

Like Hoffman before him, from the early 1890s onward, Boas published vocabulary lists of indigenous translations of English words and settled on 'shaman' as his preferred English term. For example, in 'Vocabularies of the Tlingit, Haida and Tsimshian Languages', Boas gave indigenous terms for 'shaman' (Tlingit: *iqt*; Haida: *sk·ā'g·a*; Tsimshian: *suwa'nsk*), 'hairdress of shaman' (Tlingit: *k'īts*; Haida: *gyiētl*), 'shaman's hat' (Tlingit: *wak*), 'shaman's rattle' (Haida: *dlkumhitaga'n̄gō*), 'dance of shaman' (Tlingit: *iqtdāidē'dē*; Haida: *sk·ā'g·atwīkat-sō*), 'song of shaman' (Tlingit: *iqtk·'acī'reē*) and 'baton of shaman' (Tlingit: *wū·sag·a'*; Haida: *t'ask·'*) (Boas 1891). He published a similar list of Kwakiutl language (1893). When Boas published the Salish story of Wā'walis in 1895, both his line-by-line translations and revised summary edit of the complete English translation used 'shaman' as his English term (Boas 1895: 35–8). When in 1898 he published his collections of Tillamook folklore, gathered among indigenous inhabitants of North America's Oregon coastal region, Boas dispensed with providing the text in the Tillamooks' language and provided instead his summary edit in English, with 'shaman' as his English term. For example, in the story of The Six Travellers, Boas describes how the chief, seeking revenge on the Killer Whale,

> ... hired a powerful shaman ... They had four canoes lashed together and covered with a platform of planks, on which the shaman was dancing. When they approached the rock, the shaman ordered the people to hide their faces and to turn backward. They turned the canoes, and the shaman began his incantations ... (Boas 1898: 34, cf. 32–3)

The gradual displacement of 'medicine-man', 'conjurer', 'sorcerer' and the like by 'shaman' was validated by the Jesup North Pacific Expedition (1897–1902), which treated the north Pacific on both sides of the Bering Strait

---

[13] It is not clear why Boas specifically mention rattles, although it may reference an earlier passage on marriage ceremonies (Boas 1889: 322), or an earlier article in which rattles and drums feature prominently in the story of the cannibal Ham'ats'a (Boas 1888: 59).

as a single cultural area. The expedition's research was conducted under Boas's directorship, who, on Radloff's recommendation, recruited Bogoras, Jochelson and Sternberg for the Siberia part of the research (Znamenski 2007: 65; cf. Kendall and Krupnik 2003). This validation was cemented by 1908 when Roland Dixon used his presidential address to the annual meeting of the American Folk-lore Society to address 'Some Aspects of the American Shaman'. Declaring his intention to 'extend rather than restrict the meaning of the term', Dixon began:

> I ... shall use it as applying to that motley class of persons, found in every savage community, who are supposed to have closer relations with the supernatural than other men, and who, according as they use the advantages of their position in one way or another, are the progenitors alike of the physician and the sorcerer, the prophet, the teacher, and the priest. (Dixon 1908: 1)

Comparing examples from the Arctic to Patagonia, Dixon surveyed how shamans came to their vocation; their roles, status and standing in the community; and specialisation, functional differentiation and typological evolution from 'healer-shaman' in lower stages of development to 'shaman-priest' in higher ones. Noting the 'wide prevalence of the idea of the personal manitou', Dixon argued that the person and position of the shaman indicates 'a significant instance of the unity of race feeling which can be recognized throughout almost the whole of American culture'.

Remarking on the 'prevalence' throughout the Americas of the idea of a personal Manitou, as well as the general weakness of the idea of ancestral worship, Dixon concluded:

> The American shaman thus, in his lack of dependence on ancestral spirits and the greater deities, and in deriving his powers from animals and natural phenomena, exemplifies strikingly the spirit of the American Indian as a race; and in the general uniformity of these characteristics throughout both continents serves as an illustration of the belief that in spite of minor differences as among themselves the culture of the American Indians is fundamentally one in type, influenced perhaps slightly here and there by other cultures, but yet in spite of this autochthonous.

By the beginning of the twentieth century, a discourse about shamans had travelled some ways from imperial Russia, conveyed by language as much as by the interests and proclivities of a new generation of professional scholars.

Genealogy and the Double-hinge

By way of concluding this chapter, I want to revisit the task I set at the beginning when I suggested the analysis I present here would consist in both genealogical and performative aspects, the former relating to a critique of shamanism's emergence in history and the latter relating to the operations of modernity's double-hinge in representing that critique. The presentation of a genealogy of shamanism discourse suggests something of the relationship between epistemological and ontological labour and the alternation between strategies that circumscribe shamans as a category or type and contingencies that escape circumscription and erode the imputed stability of shamanism as a knowledge domain. I want to tease out the operations of this relationship by considering the operations of modernity's double-hinge in the genealogy presented in this chapter. Taussig's contrast between the driving wedge of reason and the slippery fish of Kwakiutl shamans' tricks I think also illustrates the two arms of this hinge. Although I borrow these images from Taussig, I do not use them quite in his enigmatic way. For Taussig, the driving wedge and slippery fish are metaphors for a relationship between the exposure of fraud and the skilled revelation of skilled concealment, an idea Taussig develops in relation to transgression (Taussig 1999). Adapted to illustrate the operations of modernity's double-hinged subjectivity, the driving wedge references epistemological labour that incessantly works at the limits of what is knowable by cleaving one into two and circumscribing anew. The slippery fish in turn references ontological labour in which the possibility of transparent apprehension and arrested circumscription is denied by the very contingencies of the knowing self. The result is endless oscillation between circumscribed unity and embodied contingency on which is erected the fragile edifice of the universal.[14]

I think the chronophotograph is a striking emblem of this relationship. Developed by Étienne-Jules Marey and other early pioneers of photography, Marey photographed moving objects at twelve frames per second for one second and superimposed the photographs to form a single composite image of an object in motion. By dividing objects into sequential elements,

---

[14]   There are echoes of Derrida here, and the driving wedge and slippery fish could be adapted to relate the relationship between logocentrism and *différance*. However, whereas for Derrida deconstruction is intrinsic to the structure of language and necessitates logocentrism to arrest the contagion of endless deferral, in this discussion I am more interested in foregrounding the productivity of this relation by emphasising its dialectic (see Derrida 1976: 49; cf. Derrida 1973)

Figure 2.1 'Pole Vault', chronophotograph by Étienne-Jules Marey, circa 1890
© Etienne Jules Marey/collection Cinémathèque Française.

entirely new observations became possible and the outer limits of what was regarded knowable were defined anew. Yet the corollary of a circumscribed and unified knowledge-object is a knowing subject who sees in twelve different instantiations of a circumscribed knowledge-object, the locomotion of pole-vaulting for example, twelve contingencies on which the unity of pole-vaulting relies (Figure 2.1). These contingencies are established in two dimensions. First, in sequence, so that we see first the tip of the vaulter's pole, and then half its length enter the frame, followed by ten images of the vaulter in different positions between jumping and landing (that is to say, 'read' in the correct sequence). Second, in relation to the photographer-witness, whose body corresponds in time with the scene they are recording and who recognises in this correspondence that the division into twelve is arbitrary and necessarily must be infinitely divisible if it truly corresponds with the whole of their witnessing experience. Regarded in this way, the chronophotograph is emblematic of the relationship between a driving wedge that divides to circumscribe and a slippery fish that recognises in the delimited contingencies of the series the necessary incompleteness of a circumscribed, unified truth about pole-vaulting (or galloping in another famous example).[15]

In the preceding genealogy of a gradual expansion of a domain of knowledge about shamans and shamanic religiosity, I have paid close attention to the contingencies supporting the edifice of a universal shaman. I have tried to pay attention to the strategies, modalities and regularities that circumscribed shamans (who they were, what they did, their roles, status, techniques, experiences, mental states and so on) as well as the accidents, deviations, reversals and idiosyncratic appraisals along the way that sustained a discourse about shamans. To that extent, the discourse on shamanism as represented here is similar to a chronophotograph, with its delimitations, sequence and circumscribed unity. Yet there is still a third dimension that bears some consideration. The relation between a composite image and a viewer is a relation between a representation of the past and the viewer's present. The chronophotograph is both a representation *of time*, of the circumscribed unity of differentiated moments ordered into a composition, and a representation *in time*. Regarded in this historical dimension, the chronophotograph becomes a critical image, or at least acquires critical potential. Certainly the intention of my genealogical study is a critical one – to show the fragile contingencies supporting a structure of knowledge about

---

[15]   Eadweard Muybridge famously settled the question whether all four hooves of a galloping horse are simultaneously off the ground during a single stride. Muybridge displayed his photographs in a moving series rather than a chronophotograph, and his zoopraxiscope was an early experiment in motion pictures.

shamans widely regarded today as coherent, stable, reliable. However, this critical potential only becomes possible or readily apparent when genealogy recognises its limits, which is to say, gives itself over to critique by acknowledging that the divisions and sequencing supporting its circumscription are contingencies too, to say nothing of the details of thematic, stylistic and innumerable other choices. Put another way, a critical genealogy of shamanism must establish a relationship between the dialectical composition of its epistemological and ontological labours on the one hand and a viewer's perception of that composition on the other. This perception is a form of practice, inheres in the body and embodies the modern limit attitude and labour dialectic this limit attitude occasions.[16] We see here the complete operation of modernity's double-hinge and the way it forms a dialectic between epistemological and ontological labour, as well as the way this dialectic becomes data for a new, second-order labour that will in turn occasion a third-order labour and so on, as statements about shamans proliferate and disperse, while embodied instantiations of modern subjectivity multiply and condense. This is what Foucault means by writing 'effective history' and why he recommends genealogy be in the mode of historico-ontological critique: 'Nothing in man – not even his body – is sufficiently stable to serve as the basis for self-recognition or for understanding other men' (Foucault 1977: 153; cf. 153–7, 2003: 53–4).

In the following chapters I hope to develop an effective history of contemporary shamanism by considering the emergence of shamans in legal discourses that have secured rights for indigenous peoples; promotions of shamans as indices of sustainable human development who supply valuable symbolic capital to a critique of anthropocentric mastery of nature; and finally, professional shamans who, by embodying a specifically neoliberal *homo economicus*, are eminently governable, but for the same reason are not reducible to *homo legalis* and therefore resist circumscription by sovereign power. Each of these discussions will consider the operations of modernity's double-hinge in relation to these respective topics. However, they will not explicitly foreground the third dimension relating the chronophotographic image *of time* with the viewer/reader *in time* as I have done here. This chapter has acknowledged this problem by demonstrating its operation and therewith illustrating the full and perpetual turn of the double-hinge. With this acknowledgement, I want to reinstate the circumscription of a first-order dialectic and give this study over to the reader to complete the circuit linking representation with critique.

---

[16] This formulation is adapted from Walter Benjamin's critique of surrealism (Benjamin 1986b; cf. Alberts 2008: 131–3).

Chapter 3

Indigenism

This chapter develops a more oblique perspective on shamanism and the double-hinged technique for which it serves as a metonym than the more direct approach of Chapter 2. This perspective considers the emergence in history of 'indigenous peoples' as a transnational identity discursively distinguished from other kinds of identities by arguing that the terms of this distinction, along with their consistency and coherence, have been formulated only relatively recently and that this identity operates at a transnational level to unite geographically dispersed indigenes in a political project at a scale larger than the cultural or ethnic boundaries of specific indigenous communities. In this sense, 'indigenous' is a political identity and 'indigenism' is its corresponding discourse. The particular focus of this chapter is the notion of a special relationship between collective peoples and their ancestral lands, how this relationship is represented in indigenist discourse in specifically cosmological terms and how this representational strategy in turn has been used to both claim and advance indigenous peoples' collective right to self-determination. To be clear then, this chapter is not concerned with ethnographically defined communities of 'native', 'aboriginal', 'tribal', or 'small peoples', but rather with the discourse that identifies 'indigenous peoples' as political entities along with delineating the concerns that ostensibly unite them.

The crucial category for indigenism is self-determination, by which indigenous rights advocates mean the right of 'all peoples' guaranteed in Article 1 of both the International Covenant on Civil and Political Rights and the International Covenant on Economic, Social and Cultural Rights to 'freely determine their political status and freely pursue their economic, social and cultural development'. For indigenous peoples, exercise of this right is entwined with rights to their 'lands, territories and resources'. This phrase developed gradually. During the 1970s, the United Nations Special Rapporteur's decade-long study of problems facing indigenous populations (discussed below) considered lands and territories separately and hardly mentioned resources. The International Labour Organisation's (hereafter ILO) Convention 169 established in 1989 (also discussed below) specifies that 'the term land ... includes the concept of territories' and that land rights include rights to natural resources on and below the land. The Declaration on the Rights of Indigenous Peoples adopted in 2007 uses the phrase 'lands, territories, and resources' ten times and only once uses any of the three terms in isolation from the others, in Article 31 on indigenous peoples' cultural rights, which includes the right to their 'genetic resources'.[1]

The argument developed below is that the cosmological rendering of a special bond between people and place amounts to practices and agentive processes of bounding space, or 'practices of territoriality' (Penrose 2002: 279). As Penrose shows, the importance of territorial practices is that they are the means by which people harness the latent material and emotional qualities of space. Harnessing these qualities confers power, emblematically represented in the hyphenated bond between nation and state. The ascendancy of the nation-state model has encouraged the notion that territoriality is primarily a geographic expression of power. But although geographic conceptions of territory predominate, the defining characteristic of territory is that it is bounded, not that it is geographic. As Annsi Paasi suggests, 'boundaries may be simultaneously historical, natural, cultural, political, economic or symbolic phenomena and each of these dimensions may be exploited in diverging ways in the construction of territoriality' (in ibid.: 280). So, although territorial practices always take material space as their objective focus, how space is bounded varies, as are the kinds of relational bonds cultivated between people and bounded spaces that in turn transform lands into territories.

Indigenous activists have been adept at mobilising different notions of boundaries to advance their territorial claims in the face of considerable resistance from nation states. Indeed, one of the greatest obstacles to securing rights for indigenous peoples has been the argument made by states that recognising indigenes as *peoples*, as opposed to simply another demographic category of people, confers a collective right to self-determination and therewith a right to secession or statehood, thereby threatening the contiguity of states' geographic territories.[2] It is noteworthy that the 2007 Declaration on the Rights of Indigenous Peoples was adopted by the UN General Assembly only

---

[1] Convention 169 is the only major binding international legal instrument specifically addressing the rights of indigenous peoples. As of February 2012, it has been ratified by 20 countries, mostly in Central and South America, and is the subject of an international campaign to persuade all ILO members to assent to its provisions. The Declaration on Rights of Indigenous Peoples adopted by the UN General Assembly in 2007 is not legally binding. The Declaration was adopted with 143 countries in favour and 11 abstentions. Only Australia, Canada, New Zealand and the US voted against.

[2] For a discussion of 'the battle of the "s"', see Niezen (2003: 60–65).

after indigenous activists accepted the solution that had solved this problem in previous conventions (notably ILO Convention 169) by inserting into the text a specific qualification denying a causal link between a right to self-determination and a right to sovereign independence. Thus, Article 46[1], the last of the Declaration, reads:

> Nothing in this Declaration may be interpreted as implying for any State, people, group or person any right to engage in any activity or to perform any act contrary to the Charter of the United Nations or construed as authorizing or encouraging any action which would dismember or impair, totally or in part, the territorial integrity or political unity of sovereign and independent States.

This concession by indigenous activists would have been difficult to accept in the 1970s or 1980s, when activists were still primarily oriented by an anti-colonial emphasis on self-determination and sovereign independence. However, indigenous territorial practices have shifted over the years and have created a circumstance whereby this denial of 'external self-determination' has become tolerable and even compatible with indigenous claims.

Legal scholar Karen Engle has observed that indigenous claims to self-determination since the 1970s have advanced two different ways of understanding this right. One version equates self-determination with a right to secession and statehood, another with autonomy within a state. The stronger version recalls treaty agreements between settler-colonists and indigenous societies, draws inspiration from anti-colonial struggles in the UN era,[3] and is pursued in terms of a collective right to self-determination guaranteed by the Charter of the United Nations and both International Covenants. The softer version draws inspiration from indigenous self-understanding to formulate a non-separatist form of self-determination. In this version, culture more than geography bounds territory and bonds people with place, and territorial practices are undertaken in terms of an individual, human right to culture. Furthermore, these two competing understandings of self-determination broadly mirror a distinction in indigenous activism between the global North and the global South. During the past decade, Engle argues, the softer version has gradually won the debate as indigenist activists have won greater autonomy

---

3   By 'UN era', I mean the period following the Second World War when the basic architecture of international human rights law comprising the Universal Declaration of Human Rights (1948) and the two International Covenants (1966) were adopted by the UN General Assembly and institutionalised in the UN's structures.

for indigenous peoples at the substate level by advocating their claims in terms of a human right to culture. Indigenists and indigenous communities in Central and South America have been at the forefront of these debates and the inter-American human rights system has functioned like a laboratory where the softer version has been tested against international human rights laws. Several test cases during the first decade of the new century have elaborated the softer version's kernel ideas in terms of applicable laws, have found this legal route to be highly effective at advancing indigenist claims and have in turn conveyed these ideas into global human rights jurisprudence and legal precedent, as we will see later in this chapter.

However, and this is the crux of the problematic developed in this chapter, for substate autonomy to satisfy indigenists' desire for self-determination, it must be recognised and guaranteed by law to be practical, while still retaining its ontological dimension to be meaningful. The ontological requirement has seen the sudden saliency in human rights jurisprudence of indigenous cosmology, but the legal requirement requires universal categories because the realm of law and policy can only operate at the level of epistemology. So the shaman appears, somewhat unexpectedly, in the field of indigenist discursive practice, as that field has been constituted in the Inter-American Court of Human Rights in recent years. The interesting aspect of the solution to indigenous claims to self-determination being developed in the inter-American legal system and carried to other jurisdictions by force of legal precedent is the subtlety of the reliance on shamanism. That is not to suggest this reliance is light or optional. It is quite the opposite. But it is off-hand, as if the shaman was always there, waiting in the wings for a cue, whereupon the operations of modernity's practical limit attitude are set to work interpolating indigenous ontology into the epistemology of human rights law.

This chapter comprises four discussions. The first introduces indigenism, clarifies key terms and considers the conditions of possibility that have been conducive to indigenism's emergence on the global stage since the early 1970s. The second discussion demonstrates the articulation and consolidation of a remarkably consistent transnational indigenous identity that has successfully unified globally distributed indigenous communities into a political project to secure rights for indigenous peoples, of which the most important is the right to self-determination. The third discussion considers the strategic shift away from emphasis on a hard right to self-determination towards a softer right to indigenous autonomy at a substate level. This discussion along with the last, in which I consider several precedent-setting legal judgments emerging from the Inter-American Court of Human Rights in recent years, are where the kinds of territorialising practices that will fulfil a desire for self-determination reconceptualised as autonomy become so important. I argue that indigenists have turned to indigenous cosmology to convey the bond between people and place into law. As a form of territorial practice, the expression of cosmology is no longer supplemented by ritual, but rather by a discursive language, an episteme in the Foucauldian sense, about shamans. In the Inter-American Court of Human Rights, that means speaking about 'the indigenous cosmovision', 'intertemporality', 'shamans', 'shamanic rituals' and 'shamanic knowledge'.

Indigenous, Indigenist, Indigenism

Before proceeding, the term 'indigenous' needs some clarification. Who counts as indigenous is a notoriously thorny question and none of the many definitions proposed over the years have been entirely satisfactory. For their part, indigenous activists have historically deferred defining who is indigenous in favour of a positive right to self-definition, guaranteed by the self-determination provisions of the Universal Declaration on the Rights of Indigenous Peoples. As the term is used here, 'indigenous' is a transnational identity produced during the course of political struggles and accompanying debates since the late 1960s about communities and societies of 'natives', 'aboriginals', 'small peoples' and 'tribal peoples', the nature of the problems confronting them and the range of solutions that will remedy their often, if not always, desperate situation. Indigenous identity, in this view, has been produced discursively and is a product of indigenist discourse, or indigenism. Not to be confused with *indigenismo*,[4] indigenism as I use the term may be understood as a discourse that emerged in the late 1960s and early 1970s oriented by the reinvigorated struggles of indigenous activists and their non-indigenous allies (collectively, indigenists) to combat assimilation policies, protect indigenous communities against further encroachments on their territories and secure collective rights and special protections for indigenous peoples at the international level, particularly through the UN system.

---

[4]   In South America, *indigenismo* was initially a late nineteenth-century mestizo cultural and political movement concerned with vindicating indigenous populations after centuries of abuse (Coronado 2009). By the 1940s, however, the 'Indian problem' was seen mainly in terms of social and economic development; acculturation and Ladinoisation were seen as variably both inevitable and desirable, while *indigenismo* became a policy framework aimed at assimilating indigenous populations to mestizo identity (Sieder 2002b: 191; Stavenhagen 2002: 26).

This approach is similar to Ronald Niezen's, for whom indigenism is an invented tradition and 'indigenous' the corresponding political identity. As such, indigenism has much in common with and much distinguishing it from other kinds of invented traditions, prompting Niezen's attentiveness to similarities and distinctions between indigenism, ethnonationalism and indigenous and ethnic identities (Niezen 2003: 6–11; cf. 2009: 17–43). Niezen's approach is usefully contrasted with Alcida Ramos's. Like Niezen, Ramos is an activist-anthropologist with decades of experience working with indigenous communities in the Amazon basin. Advancing an analysis at once broader and more circumscribed than Niezen's, Ramos sees indigenism in Brazil as 'an elaborate ideological construct about otherness and sameness in the context of ethnicity and nationality' that functions in ways similar to European Orientalism: 'Indigenism is to Brazil what Orientalism is to the West ... just as "the Orient is *Orientalized*," so is the Indian *Indianized*' (Ramos 1998: 6–7; see also 2003: 356–79). Whereas Niezen conceives of indigenism as a rights-based discourse through which a new transnational identity has been produced, Ramos conceives of indigenism more broadly, as a discursive formation linking mass media agencies, creative writers, missionaries, activists, anthropologists, state actors and indigenes themselves. At the same time, whereas Ramos focuses more narrowly on Brazil and beyond that the Amazon basin, Niezen's perspective is global.

As anthropologists and activists, both Niezen and Ramos are personally experienced and invested in the politico-legal struggles that have shaped indigenous identities. Yet the differing emphases of their perspectives have led them to develop their research in different ways. Ramos's analysis of 'the manipulation of primordialities' and the emergence of the 'hyperreal Indian' has led her to propose indigenism as 'an American Orientalism' (Ramos 2003: 356, 373; see also Ramos 1994). Niezen's interest in the gains of indigenous peoples' legal protections in recent decades has led him to consider the role of human rights discourse in forming a new global, transnational identity (Niezen 2003).[5] This chapter develops a narrower view similar to Niezen's legalistic approach (Anaya 2004; Kingsbury 2001, 1998; Tennant 1994). I conceive of indigenous identity as a transnational identity category that has emerged on the global scene largely in response to indigenous peoples' struggles for human rights. As a discursive formation, indigenism also implicates discursive areas besides law.

---

[5]   More recently, Niezen has examined this problematic 'at both ends of the spectrum', which is to say, 'as a transnational phenomenon that is pushing the boundaries of supra-state activism' and 'as a source of legal standards and expectations of social justice that are contributing to ethnic formalism, sharpening the boundaries of belonging, and redefining the cultural reference points of collective identity' (Niezen 2009: xiii).

Along with Ramos and others (for example, Brown 1993, K.B. Warren 1998), I am alert to indigenous activists' instrumentalisations of certain essentialist representations in advancing their human rights agendas and the implications these continue to have for indigenous activism today, issues explored in more detail in Chapter 4. Where my own interest differs from both Ramos's American Orientalism and Niezen's transnational legalism is with regard to the place and role of indigenous cosmology in territorialising practices.

Struggles by indigenous communities to protect their lands and ways of living from encroachment by settler societies are centuries old. However, it is only relatively recently that the legitimacy of these struggles have become widely recognised and the notion of 'indigenous peoples' has become an accepted part of international discourse. Partly this is because the notion of 'peoples' suggests something like 'nation', in which case indigenous peoples ought not be restrained or impeded from determining their social and political future, including exercising territorial sovereignty. Of course, impeding indigenous self-determination is precisely what settler societies have done for centuries. Indeed, among indigenous activists, the potency of broken treaties stems from precisely the point that a treaty is a solemn agreement between nations. Persistent refusal by one nation to honour that agreement amounts to refusal to acknowledge the peoplehood of another nation who have not refused the same. In recent decades, however, this has begun to change, as the notion of 'indigenous peoples' has received wider acceptance. An important question is why this has changed. Why, after centuries of persecution and neglect, have indigenous peoples' grievances come to the fore and enabled the formation and consolidation of a transnational indigenous imaginary?

In short, what changed was the terrain on which indigenous struggles were contested. Several factors and processes intersected over a period of several decades to alter the context of indigenous struggles and create a more enabling political context for indigenous aspirations. Probably the most consequential development was the Allies' rhetoric during the Second World War about the rights of peoples to collective self-determination, notably in the Atlantic Charter of 1941. Notwithstanding the Allied powers' regret and back-pedalling after the war, this rhetoric proved valuable to anti-colonial revolutionaries and intellectuals from Africa to Indochina who demanded independence and eventually dismantled European empires. This rhetoric also led to the establishment of an institutional mechanism – the United Nations Organisation – through which the principle of national self-determination could be advanced, by way of defining, explaining and defending 'the fundamental rights of all peoples'. The rhetoric and politics of self-determination, anti-colonialism and decolonisation undoubtedly helped indigenous representatives and sympathisers draw attention to indigenous peoples' plight and favourably transformed the discursive context of indigenous peoples' struggles (Coates 2004). The failure of assimilation policies, both in terms of socio-economic outcomes and political costs, along with the rise of international non-governmental organisations (hereafter NGOs) and the consolidation of something like an international civil society were also important factors (Niezen 2003). Although broadly correct, these factors tend to be put forward as if they were contemporary with one another, yet fail to explain why it wasn't until the 1970s that indigenous political struggles really took off. During the 1950s and 1960s, the rights that mattered were collective rights, while human rights were largely moribund. In other words, the emergence of the indigenous peoples movement during the 1970s coincided with the rapid proliferation and widespread embrace of the human rights framework on the international scene, despite the anti-colonial claims to collective self-determination that stimulated indigenous activism. Certainly this turn towards human rights created an enabling environment for indigenous activism in recent decades. But it was the internationalisation of the human rights paradigm that achieved this, not an international embrace of self-determination and its institutionalisation via the UN. It is important to keep this distinction in mind, because it has implications for understanding how indigenist discourse proceeds from the 1990s.

Legal scholar and historian Samuel Moyn's revisionist history of human rights (Moyn 2010) does not say much about rights for indigenous peoples, but the historicising lens he focuses on how human rights came to be embraced globally goes a long ways towards explaining why indigenism took off during the 1970s. Moyn argues the human rights born in 1948 only began to show signs of life in the 1970s. Prior to that and as far back as the eighteenth century, the rights that mattered belonged to nations. These rights spoke of collective self-determination rather than protection of individuals and were essentially anti-colonial: 'Human rights simply *were* the struggle for self-determination' (ibid.: 109). By the late 1960s, however, new visions of social change proliferated around the world. Why, Moyn wonders, amid 'the massive infusion of energy to social mobilization' (ibid.: 133), did human rights survive and manage to capture the collective imagination?

Moyn's argument is that the turn to human rights occurred because human rights substituted moral for political utopianism. The vision of a different, better, world premised on human dignity and worth appealed in large part because it enabled actors in diverse contexts to make common cause at the same time that competing alternative utopianisms came to be seen as unviable. More than that, the vision of the universal irreducible worth of individual human beings offered leverage against contending utopianisms by framing the minimalist vision of human rights as a moral critique of the maximalist utopianism of Marxist, socialist, nationalist, pan-African, or pan-Arabian visions, 'a convergence that often began as a strategic retreat from those prior, more grandiose utopianisms' (ibid.: 121). The aspiration towards a moral critique of politics facilitated by human rights appealed because it appeared to transcend politics by restoring to activism the sense of a pure cause once sought in politics itself but now regarded as impossible. As one observer said of Amnesty International: 'Sending a card ... will not change the world very much. But it is surely worth investing a little time and postage to try to help two other individuals to secure justice, or at least find courage' (quoted in ibid.: 147). This imagining of a moral utopia and its substitution for a failed political one is the achievement that enabled the ascendancy of human rights from the 1970s after two decades of failure.

But the appeal of moral utopianism was not in itself sufficient to displace variants of political utopianism. 'What mattered most of all', Moyn argues (ibid.: 132), 'was the competitive forum in which human rights had to win their way. For human rights were only one among other ideologies that could have prospered and did in fact, as absorption of the Cold War contention of social models entered its 1960s decline.' In this competition, human rights were seen as preferable not only because they were strategically valuable and practically feasible, but also because they were seen as morally pure. At the same time, the notion of moral constraints to politics appealed to disparate actors because this fiction insulated their ideas from political sanction, even if their activism made them a target. In this sense, 'the fiction of moral autonomy from politics was a condition of political relevance', because morality could retain its purity 'even where politics had shown itself to be a soiled and impossible domain' (ibid.: 145–6, 170).

The relevant period is the decade following 1968. By 1968, the few NGOs that worked with the concept of human rights envisaged by the Universal Declaration concluded that the UN had failed to become the primary forum for human rights activism promised by the Dumbarton Oaks agreements and envisioned in the Universal Declaration. The 1968 conference in Tehran marking the Universal Declaration's twentieth anniversary made this much clear. Egerton Richardson, Jamaica's ambassador to the UN and in 1963 the first person to propose a UN human rights year, wrote in his contribution to an NGO response to the Tehran conference: 'Tehran was our moment of truth ... when we saw what it means to be promoting the cause of Human Rights by working mainly through governments' (quoted in ibid.: 128). In a similar vein,

British political scientist H.G. Nicholas would later remark on 'the inherent absurdity of an organization of governments dedicating itself to protect human rights when, in all ages and climes, it is governments which have been their principal violators' (quoted in ibid.: 129).

Moyn's impressive discussion of the events, the historical processes and the ideas underpinning them shows the linkages and influences between disparate movements in the decade following 1968. It is too much to summarise them here. It suffices to note that Moyn's analysis alights on East European dissidents who found in human rights a language for conveying their critique of the failings of Marxist utopianism in the wake of the Prague Spring; on Latin American leftists whose alliances with Amnesty International drew international attention to right-wing dictatorships in that region and their links with foreign governments, notably in Washington;[6] on liberation theology's appeal to human rights groups who recognised in liberation theology's notion of moral constraints on politics strong echoes of the explicit framework of human rights activism being developed simultaneously in other parts of the world; on the importance of international NGOs, particularly Amnesty International, as agents linking disparate local movements within an emerging transnational human rights framework; on the adoption of human rights language by liberals in the United States and the embrace of the human rights paradigm by the Democratic Party, culminating during the first year of Jimmy Carter's presidency in 1977; and on dissidence in eastern Europe, particularly the moral philosophy of Václav Havel, whose vision of politics as morality alone received its most coherent and systematic articulation in Havel's essay 'The Power of the Powerless', wherein he tries to show 'the very special political significance of morality in the post-totalitarian system' (Havel 1985: 89).[7] It is not that any one actor or factor explains the proliferation of human rights imagination and rhetoric during the 1970s. Rather, human rights emerged gradually in different contexts and for different reasons, each enabling further preferences for rights rhetoric amid declining

---

[6]   This even as they recognised that 'the success of their denunciations depended on keeping radical claims for social change separated from their human rights activism' (Markarian, quoted in Moyn 2010: 142).

[7]   For Havel, human rights meant more than a moral transcendence of politics; he sought the permanent substitution of morality for politics: 'It is of great importance that the main thing – the everyday, thankless, and never ending struggle of human beings to live more freely, truthfully, and in quiet dignity – never impose any limits on itself, never be half-hearted, inconsistent, never trap itself in political tactics, speculating on the outcome of its actions or entertaining fantasies about the future. The purity of this struggle is the best guarantee of optimum results when it comes to actual interaction with the post-totalitarian structures' (Havel 1985: 89).

alternatives.[8] This series of synergistic and coalescent movements displaced competitors and contributed towards globalising human rights as a discursive paradigm for representing a utopian vision oriented by universal human dignity and anchored in personal morality.

As a novel framework for a utopian re-imagining of the limits of being human, two interrelated aspects of the human rights paradigm are significant. On the one hand, the notion of the universality of human dignity and worth conveys a critique of the contingencies and expediencies of politics. Imagined as issuing from personal and private individual conscience, the notion of natural justice on which it relies can only operate at the ontological level. The notions of 'conscientious objectors' and 'prisoners of conscience' are illustrative. On the other hand, law circumscribes the moral transcendence of politics conveyed in the idea of universal human rights. More specifically, the language of law, the requirements of consistency, the specificity of words and their referents ('self-determination', 'land', 'territory', and so on), places the utopian vision of moral transcendence within epistemological limits. From this perspective, the link between the emergence of indigenism and the new human rights paradigm is significant beyond simply the emergence in history of a political context more conducive to redressing indigenous peoples' longstanding grievances.

Indigenous movements' agitation for self-determination took off at precisely the moment that self-determination as the principle content of human rights was waning and a liberal notion of individual human rights was rising. Prior to the 1970s and at least since 1923 when Cayuga Chief Levi General Deskaheh travelled to Geneva to personally petition the League of Nations,[9] indigenous activism was oriented by the notion that 'nations' have a natural right to self-determination. The UN General Assembly's adoption of the UN Declaration on the Granting of Independence to Colonial Countries and Peoples formally equipped anti-colonial nationalism with this right after 1960 (UN 1960). Article 2 of the Declaration reads: 'All peoples have the right to self-determination; by virtue of that right they freely determine their political status and freely pursue their economic, social and cultural development.' Article 6

---

8   Notable for its absence from Moyn's survey are the various political movements associated with identity politics since the 1960s. Moyn places these movements in the same genealogy as the earlier civil rights and woman's movements, which he interprets as part of much longer struggles over the form of the nation state and the meaning of citizenship (Moyn 2010: 31ff).

9   Chief Deskaheh's petition to the League of Nations was ignored, although his efforts marked one of the earliest attempts by indigenous peoples to seek recourse though international institutions (*Akwesasne Notes* 1991, Niezen 2003: 31–6).

qualified this right, however, by restricting it to 'dependent peoples' in 'Trust and Non-Self-Governing Territories', adding: 'Any attempt aimed at the partial or total disruption of the national unity and the territorial integrity of a country is incompatible with the purposes and principles of the Charter of the United Nations.' The anti-colonial emphasis on self-determination was poorly suited to indigenous activism because it envisaged colonisation by a foreign power rather than domination by a settler society, broken treaties notwithstanding. Although post-war anti-colonialism was crucial in galvanising an indigenous political consciousness, it did not offer much by way of actual gains for indigenous peoples' struggles. Indeed, from the 1940s to the 1960s, laws and policies pertaining to indigenous populations were designed to promote assimilation into dominant societies (Tennant 1994). Gains and advances for indigenous struggles came only much later, after human rights had displaced anti-colonialism and other competing utopian imaginaries and had gained for indigenous movements recognition – on moral grounds – that their grievances might be legitimate and at least merited closer attention. This attention, when it finally came, was framed in terms of discrimination against indigenous populations, rather than self-determination for indigenous peoples.

It may seem trite to suggest that the history of indigenism and indigenist political struggles since the 1970s has been oriented by the challenge to attain collective self-determination within the framework of individual human rights. However, this broad claim and especially the means by which indigenous aspirations have been realised in recent years has been profoundly consequential – and not only for the many indigenous communities around the world who have at last achieved some measure of recognition and protection following centuries of violence, or the many more who today stand a better chance of securing the same. The successes of indigenist political projects have occasioned new assessments of what being modern means, of modernity's limits, and therewith of insertion points for leveraging still more freedom at the limits of prevailing standards of normative justice.

The history of indigenism is a response to two demands. First, indigenist discourse has had to accommodate the concepts of collective self-determination to the conceptual framework of individual human rights, while still retaining 'indigenous' as both a collective identity and irreducible at the ontological level. As indigenous leader George Manuel put it in 1974, 'aboriginal peoples can only argue the morality of their case' (quoted in Wright 1988: 376). Second, indigenist discourse has had to articulate these reformulated concepts in the language of law, but in such a way that this circumscription at the epistemological level of laws and governing policies retains the ontology of 'being indigenous'. This articulation of limitations is modernity's double-hinge at work in indigenism. The fulcrum on which it rests is the problem of territorialisation, of bounding space and bonding it with identity, of welding culture and land and making land into culture. Interpolation of indigenous ontological being into the epistemology of human rights law is territorial practice par excellence.

At this point, we have arrived at the problem of indigenous cosmology, or more precisely, at a perspective on the question of indigenous cosmology. 'Indigenous cosmology', like 'indigenous peoples', is a discursive construct and operates in a similar way. Ronald Niezen's observations about indigenism are apposite of 'indigenous cosmology' too: 'It sets social groups and networks apart from others in a global "we-they" dichotomy. It identifies a boundary of membership and experience that can be crossed only by birth or hard-won international recognition. It links local, primordial sentiments to a universal category' (Niezen 2003: 9)

As a universal category, 'indigenous cosmology' (singular) was brought into being in the course of indigenist struggles. Unlike 'indigenous peoples', however, it took a while longer for this category to gain the kind of power it has today. From the 1970s, indigenous religious practices (they were still represented in discourse in plural terms) were a means of representing an identity between indigenous communities and lands. Through the 1970s and 1980s, indigenous religiosity was increasingly important in underwriting a transnational indigenous identity that could claim rights specifically on behalf of 'indigenous peoples'. More recently, as indigenous self-determination transformed into indigenous autonomy within states, the potential of 'indigenous cosmology' to deliver self-determination for 'indigenous peoples' become clearer. 'Indigenous cosmology' has provided a crucial basis for legal arguments to secure indigenous title to ancestral lands, territories and resources. It is as if a key has been found that solves, for indigenists at least, a significant portion of the problem of territorialisation, of interpolating indigenous being into human rights law. This issue is the subject of this chapter's concluding discussion, where I consider the Awas Tingni case before the Inter-American Court of Human Rights and reintroduce shamanism to the discussion. Indigenism's elevation of cosmology and religiosity as a fundamental dimension of indigenous identity and rights to self-determination emerged into a space conceptually framed by a European discourse about shamans and conveyed via projections of European power/ knowledge. As a universal category, 'shaman' has been an instrumental part of indigenism's double-hinged interpolation of ontological being and legal epistemology. Thus trial testimony and court judgments speak of 'shamans', 'shamanic religion', 'shamanic rituals' and 'shamanic knowledge'. At the same time and as part of the same process, the category's usefulness in elaborating jurisprudence and legal precedent has added the authority of judicial judgments to shamanism discourse, extended shamanism's field of application into the global field of international law and added law's emphasis on consistency, rationality and citation to shamanism's discursive regularities.

Transnational Identity Formation at the UN

It is impossible to summarise all the associations and alliances, themes and issues, challenges, failures and successes involved in the emergence of an indigenous movement from the early 1970s. However, several events during this important decade indicate the nascent and growing indigenism movement, initially mainly in the Americas, although in Australia and New Zealand too. In North America, the nascent American Indian Movement (hereafter AIM) was galvanised politically by a new willingness to challenge the authority of the federal government and intellectually by a critique of Euro-American thought, exemplified by the seminal writings of Vine Deloria (1973, 1969). In the US, this willingness was famously associated with the reoccupation of Wounded Knee in the Pine Ridge reservation in February 1973. Following a 71-day stand-off with the federal government, AIM initiated a campaign for legal mechanisms to protect indigenous peoples' rights. In South and Central America, the situation was quite different. Indigenous peoples who continued to live traditional lifestyles on their ancestral lands faced encroachments on their territories. Suspended between state authoritarianism on the one hand and Marxist revolutionary struggles on the other, indigenous peoples throughout the region, but particularly in Mesoamerica and the central Andean highlands where 85 per cent of Latin America's indigenous populations are concentrated (Sieder 2002a: 2), found it extremely challenging to organise into regional associations. Nevertheless, the new human rights ascendancy enabled their struggles via a growing concern among missionaries and anthropologists working with local indigenous communities, leading to a rapid growth of indigenous federations from the late 1960s (Brown 1993: 316). A conference in 1971 in Barbados was an important moment. Organised by the World Council of Churches as part of its Programme to Combat Racism and attended primarily by anthropologists from the region, the Declaration of Barbados emphasised 'the Indian is an agent of his own destiny', noted 'the beginnings of a pan Latin-American [Indian] movement' and affirmed 'the right of Indian populations to experiment with / and adopt their own self-governing development and defence programmes' (WCC 1971).

The first significant inter-continental meeting of indigenous leaders was in 1975 in British Columbia, Canada. Representatives of indigenous groups from North and South America, Australia, New Zealand and Scandinavia argued forcefully for an international declaration on the rights of indigenous peoples and formed the World Council of Indigenous Peoples (hereafter WCIP) to advance this goal (Coates 2004: 244–5, Dahl 2009: 39–40). At the same time, AIM pushed to establish an International Indian Treaty Council (hereafter IITC) accredited with NGO status at the UN. Accreditation was granted in 1977 and a few months later the IITC organised the Native American Delegation to the International NGO Conference on Discrimination Against Indigenous Populations in the Americas, held in Geneva in September (Niezen 2003: 44–5). The IITC circulated a draft indigenous peoples' rights declaration at the conference (Coulter 2009: 544, Eaglewoman 2009: 560–62, Niezen 2003: 44–5). The UN NGO conference was organised by the UN Sub-Committee on Racism, Racial Discrimination, Apartheid and Decolonization as part of the UN Decade for Action to Combat Racism and Racial Discrimination. The Decade opened a new channel for indigenous activism. Although racism had been a key concern since the UN's founding, it wasn't until the 1970s that racism became a priority issue for the Commission on Human Rights. In 1973, the same year as the siege at Wounded Knee, the UN General Assembly adopted the Convention on the Suppression and Punishment of the Crime of Apartheid and declared the Decade for Action. The UN NGO conference was attended by fifty international NGOs, representatives of sixty indigenous groups from fifteen countries, representatives of UN agencies including the Commission on Human Rights and the Commission on the Status of Women, as well as observers from forty UN member states (Niezen 2003: 44–5). From this impetus, the UN Working Group on Indigenous Populations was established in 1982, giving indigenous peoples around the world a permanent forum at the UN and certifying the 'Fourth World' movement's emergence onto the world stage. As Niezen has noted, the Working Group quickly became the largest UN forum dealing with human rights issues, for the most part directed towards drafting an international declaration on indigenous peoples' rights (ibid.: 45–6).

In the space of a decade, the problems facing indigenous populations had moved from being among the world's most persistently disparaged and ignored issues to being accorded the legitimacy of a dedicated space at the most important organisation for international relations. Although only the beginning of a much more challenging and protracted struggle to 'make place' at the UN

(Muehlebach 2001), by any reckoning this was a significant accomplishment, considerably enabled by the human rights turn of the 1970s. It is telling, for example, that 1977, the crucial year for the new rights ascendancy in Moyn's model, was also a crucial year for global indigenous activism, when arguably the four most important international conferences of indigenous activists during the 1970s took place in as many months.[10] During indigenism's formative decade, something like a transnational indigenous identity began emerging on the world scene. As one might expect, indigenous peoples' relationship with their ancestral lands was a vitalising element of this identity. Indigenous activists and their supporters in multilateral forums like the UN advocated indigenous peoples' unique relationship with their ancestral lands as the basis for securing special measures and protections that would secure indigenous peoples' rights to their land, resources and territories. This unique relationship was framed in terms of cosmology and mediation by spirits and injected a spiritual and religious element into the core of what it meant to be indigenous.

The first major UN report on indigenous populations relied on this framing. By any reckoning, the study by Special Rapporteur José Martínez Cobo of 'the problem of discrimination against indigenous populations' is impressive. Conducted over a decade and comprising nearly 1,500 pages organised into ten thematic areas[11] and published in twenty chapters over three years, the Special Rapporteur's study comprehensively profiled the nature of discrimination faced by indigenous populations in thirty-seven countries and territories (UNCHR 1981b).[12]

---

[10]   These conferences were the inaugural Inuit Circumpolar Conference (Alaska, June), Barbados II (Barbados, July), the Second General Assembly of WCIP (Sweden, August) and the UN NGO conference (Geneva, September). In 1981, when UN Special Rapporteur José Martínez Cobo began reporting on his study of discrimination against indigenous populations, he narrowed his discussion of international action to these four events in 1977 and suggested these meetings were pre-eminent among the innumerable meetings of this period (UNCHR 1981a: para. 114).

[11]   These thematic areas were health, housing, education, language, culture, occupation, employment and vocational training, land, political rights, 'religious rights and practices' and 'equality in the administration of justice and legal assistance'.

[12]   The thirty-seven countries are: Argentina, Australia, Bangladesh, Bolivia, Brazil, Burma, Canada, Chile, Colombia, Costa Rica, Denmark (Greenland), Ecuador, El Salvador, Finland, France (French Guyana), Guatemala, Guyana, Honduras, India, Indonesia, Japan, Laos, Malaysia, Mexico, New Zealand, Nicaragua, Norway, Pakistan, Panama, Paraguay, Peru, the Philippines, Sri Lanka, Surinam, Sweden, the United States of America and Venezuela. Notable exceptions are countries in Africa and the then-Soviet bloc.

Two aspects of Cobo's study are particularly relevant for present purposes. The first is that it is framed entirely in terms of human rights. It is, as its title indicates, a study of *discrimination against* indigenous populations; it says little about indigenous self-determination. The study's methodology proceeded by describing the situation of globally distributed indigenous populations and then assessing this against established legal protections, measures and special provisions. Consequently, the resulting profile of discrimination emphasised limitations and shortcomings in existing human rights instruments. As a historical document, the report illustrates precisely the ascendancy of human rights and ejection of self-determination that marked the transition from post-war self-determination to post-1968 human rights. Secondly, at a discursive level, the report significantly contributed towards formulating indigenous identity as a global, transnational category. Indeed, a substantial part of the Special Rapporteur's work involved defining 'indigenous', 'indigenous population' and 'indigenous peoples', and the various interim reports completed on the way to the final report spent considerable effort making an inventory of the component parts of indigenous identity. Notably, indigenous peoples have a historical continuity with lands subsequently confiscated, they consider themselves distinct from dominant societies, and they wish to continue existing in accord with their own distinct cultures and customs.[13] The Special Rapporteur finally settled on the following definition:

> Indigenous communities, peoples, and nations are those which, having a historical continuity with pre-invasion and pre-colonial societies that developed on their territories, consider themselves distinct from other sectors of the societies now prevailing in those territories, or parts of them. They form at present non-dominant sectors of society and are determined to preserve, develop and transmit to future generations their ancestral territories, and their ethnic identity, as the basis of their continued existence as peoples, in accordance with their own cultural patterns, social institutions and legal systems. (UNCHR 1983b: para. 379)

By using the terms 'indigenous populations' and 'indigenous peoples' interchangeably and across all but one continent, the study lends the authority

---

[13] The question of defining the meaning of indigenous has been a productive, if intractable, problem through the history of the indigenous peoples' movement. For a discussion of the difficulties of establishing positive definitions of 'indigenous peoples', see Niezen (2003: 18–23). For arguments in favour of a constructivist approach, see Kingsbury (1998).

of no less a body than the UN to the legitimacy of indigeneity as a transnational identity. That the Special Rapporteur could refer to 'indigenous peoples' with such apparent ease suggests the extent to which the human rights paradigm had displaced the self-determination one, notwithstanding, on the one hand, the encouragement this usage gave indigenous activists who continued to frame their claims in terms of a hard right to external self-determination (that is, statehood) and on the other hand the deepening intransigence of states to indigenous claims and their subsequent resistance to the work of the UN Working Group on Indigenous Populations.

Be that as it may, an important aspect of this transnational indigenous identity is its articulation in terms of a cosmologically oriented and spiritually mediated relationship between indigenous peoples and their lands. Put another way, if indigenous advocacy for rights to land title indexed indigenous peoples' sameness in the sense of an entitlement already enjoyed by non-indigenous people, indigenous peoples' special and unique relationship with their ancestral lands indexed their alterity from settler, immigrant, or otherwise non-indigenous communities and societies.

The chapter on land deals mainly with indigenous rights of ownership and countries' measures protecting or denying that right, in accordance with the study's human rights orientation. The review makes clear that the range of indigenous grievances pertaining to dispossession of ancestral lands is varied and complex. At 203 pages, almost double the second longest chapter (on education), the chapter's detail and length is hardly surprising, given that land has been arguably the most controversial and most compelling of indigenous claims against settler societies (ibid.: para. 288).[14] Still, the Special Rapporteur's introductory remarks draw together the diverse and complex examples his study reviews under the rubric of indigenous peoples' spiritual and sacred connection with their land:

> Before considering the measures adopted in the various countries, a few brief remarks should be made on the significance and importance which the land has for indigenous populations. It must be stressed that there is a fundamental difference between the relationship which indigenous peoples have with the land and the relationship which other sectors of the population of the countries covered by this study have. It will then be easier to understand why all indigenous peoples throughout the world place so much emphasis on the land and land

---

[14] Unless indicated otherwise, subsequent paragraph citations refer to relevant paragraphs of Chapter 17 on indigenous peoples' relationship with land (UNCHR 1983a).

tenure, to place the problems of land and land tenure in their proper perspective and to have some idea of what indigenous peoples think and feel when land – their land – is at issue. (Para. 50)

Elaborating this 'fundamental difference', the study notes that 'discoverers, conquerors and settlers who invaded erstwhile purely indigenous territory' utilised a secular and individualistic concept of 'absolute ownership' of land, one that rendered land as possession and commodity, gave the landowner rights to make use of their possession as they liked and established the parameters of what is today spoken of in terms of land tenure (para. 55). Contrasted with this concept:

> For indigenous peoples, the concept of land tenure had a very different meaning.
> It belonged to the community; it was sacred; it could not be sold, leased or left
> unused indefinitely. Between man and the land there was a relationship of a
> profoundly spiritual and even religious nature. They spoke of Mother Earth and
> its worship. For all those reasons it was in no way possible to regard it as a mere
> possession or still less as a commodity. (Para. 56)

Subsequent paragraphs sample customary laws regulating indigenous, cooperative communal tenure of property to illustrate and evidence this distinction between indigenous and settler concepts of land. The issue for this discussion is the significance the Special Rapporteur's study attaches to the sacred, spiritual, or religious quality of indigenous concepts of land, along with the importance of this quality in distinguishing indigenous among other kinds of identities. To begin with, the report makes clear that this 'profoundly spiritual and even religious' relationship is foundational: 'The whole range of emotional, cultural, spiritual and religious considerations is present where the relationship with the land is concerned' (para. 51). For indigenous peoples, land is the source of identity and life:

> It is land that defines the group (clan, tribe, people or nation), its culture, its way of
> life, its life style, its cultural and religious ceremonies, its problems of survival and
> its relationships of all kinds within the community and with other groups and,
> above all, its own identity. Land is synonymous with the very life of indigenous
> populations. (Para. 73)

Recalling Penrose's thesis about territorial practices, it is indigenous peoples' active relationship with land that transforms land into territory and activates its generative potential, so that identity and life may flow from it. Contrasting this kind of active relationship with the relationship non-indigenous populations have with land, the report draws attention to the indigenous 'attitude of respect and veneration' for land, an attitude that distinguishes non-indigenous approaches to 'the development of land and its effective use' from indigenous approaches that are, 'in ecological terms, more rational and sound' (para. 65). This convergence between an ecological and a venerative attitude is mentioned again later when the Special Rapporteur writes, 'The religion of indigenous peoples, their culture, self-esteem and respect are today also based largely on a continuing and sacred relationship with ancestral land, certain specific areas of which must remain undisturbed' (para. 72).

There is therefore considerable scope for conflict when non-indigenous groups or state authorities disturb sacred lands, deny indigenous peoples access to sacred lands, or desecrate land regarded as sacred by indigenous communities by using it in ways that violate indigenous laws.

This problem is addressed in Chapter 19 on Religious Rights and Practices (UNCHR 1982).[15] Although most of the chapter's sixty pages are addressed to assessing measures by states to protect the 'religious rights and practices' of 'indigenous populations' (notably, 'to profess and practice their religion of belief', 'not to be compelled to participate in the activities of any religion or belief', 'not to be discriminated against on the ground of religion or belief' and, 'not to be compelled to receive instruction in a religion or belief contrary to their convictions or to the wishes of indigenous parents or legal guardians'), a section on access to and protection of sacred places shifts into the terminology of 'indigenous peoples'. Noting that 'The attachment of indigenous peoples to their land is a fact well noted in history' (para. 172), the Special Rapporteur continues: 'It is also a well-established fact that indigenous peoples all over the world hold certain areas of their ancestral land as holy' (para. 173). Subsequent paragraphs explain that lands may be sacred for indigenous peoples because certain 'sacred places' are 'the dwelling place or embodiment of spiritual beings' or contain burial grounds, architectural structures, sculptural works, 'or other natural features of religious significance'. This sacred character gives rise to 'religious laws governing the sites', including obligations and prohibitions concerning who may or may not visit the site, for what purpose and appropriate rituals and manner of conduct, as well as noting consequences to the individual, group or community if laws are not observed or the physical character of sacred

---

[15] Subsequent paragraph citations refer to relevant paragraphs of Chapter 19 (UNCHR 1982).

lands is altered. These may include 'damages [to] the spiritual nature of the land, [and endangering] the well-being of the indigenous religious practitioners in their roles and religious obligations as guardians and preservers of the natural character of specific land areas' (para. 182).

Notwithstanding these kinds of conflicts, which are the Special Rapporteur's topical concern, the issue for this discussion is the report's emphasis on the sacred quality of indigenous peoples' 'special attachment' to their ancestral land, one that involves 'a combination of aesthetic appreciation, socio-cultural sympathy and deep-seated spiritual and religious feeling' (UNCHR 1983a: para. 71). This point is reiterated in Chapter 22 on Conclusions, Proposals and Recommendations, where the Special Rapporteur prefaces his summary of 'indigenous peoples" 'natural and inalienable right' to their lands, territories and resources by emphasising that 'it is essential to know and understand the deeply spiritual relationship between indigenous peoples and their land as basic to their existence as such and to all their beliefs, customs, traditions and culture':

> For such peoples, the land is not merely a possession and a means of production. The entire relationship between the spiritual life of indigenous peoples and Mother Earth, and their land, has a great many deep-seated implications. Their land is not a commodity that can be acquired, but a material element to be enjoyed freely. (UNCHR 1983b: paras 196–7)

This discursive representation of a sacred, foundational and generative relationship between indigenous peoples and their ancestral lands was and remains the crucial plank in the formulation and articulation of a global transnational indigenous identity, one that is distinguishable from other kinds of global transnational identities and therefore capable in theory of vestment with specially reserved rights and protections. Transforming this capability into actuality was the task of the UN Working Group on Indigenous Populations.

The UN Subcommittee on the Prevention of Discrimination and Protection of Minorities established the Working Group on Indigenous Populations in 1982 (hereafter WGIP or Working Group). 'The first United Nations mechanism on indigenous peoples' issues' (UN 2009:2), the WGIP's mandate was, as the Special Rapporteur put it, 'to deal exclusively with problems concerning the observance of the rights and freedoms of indigenous populations throughout the world'. In practical terms this meant requesting information from states and other sources, reporting on states' compliance with relevant norms and standards, and monitoring and ensuring indigenous participation in the evolution of those standards (UNCHR 1983b: paras 304–5). From only thirty indigenous and non-indigenous participants at the WGIP's first meeting in 1982, within two decades over a thousand participants were attending WGIP's annual meeting, the vast majority of them from indigenous communities (Muehlebach 2001: 420). This growth was consequential to the Working Group's decision in 1983 to permit direct participation by representatives of indigenous communities. Unprecedented in the state-centric UN system, the Special Rapporteur praised the WGIP's 'wide approach' as 'indispensable' to executing its mandate (UNCHR 1983b: para. 306). He also recommended that the WGIP produce a draft declaration on indigenous peoples' rights (para. 312), although the recommendation was hardly necessary, given that indigenous demands for a declaration had been a catalyst for the indigenous peoples movement in the 1970s. These same activists now had an institutional home and voice at the UN. Preparing a declaration was a focus of the Working Group's activities from its inception and significantly contributed to the WGIP becoming the largest UN forum dealing with human rights issues (Niezen 2003: 46), notwithstanding that it took eleven years to produce a draft,[16] and a further fifteen years before the Declaration on the Rights of Indigenous Peoples was agreed and finally adopted in 2007 (UN 2007). Thus, the WGIP was key in consolidating a transnational indigenous identity, united by a common experience of alienation, suffering and powerlessness as much as by a shared project to articulate rights and entitlements and devise legal mechanisms that would, if not remedy, at least improve the situation of indigenous peoples in their different contexts.

Although the WGIP was the only multilateral forum specifically mandated to monitor and promote indigenous issues globally, including developments of applicable norms and standards, it was not the only international forum developing and promoting rights for indigenous peoples. From the late 1980s and through the 1990s, the international legal and policy framework pertaining to indigenous peoples shifted towards mechanisms that would not only recognise the legitimacy of indigenous peoples' grievances but also protect their livelihoods and secure their futures (Anaya 2004, Tennant 1994). These mechanisms were instrumental in consolidating and normalising the notion of a unique cosmologically oriented relationship between people and place as the core of indigenous identity. Notable examples are the ILO's Convention 169 (hereafter ILO169), the World Bank's Operational Directive 4.20 on Indigenous Peoples, the Human Rights Committee's General Comment 23

---

[16] The first draft of the Declaration was presented to the UN at the commencement of the International Year of the World's Indigenous People on international human rights day on 10 December 1992, the same day Rigoberta Menchú of the K'iche' people in Nicaragua was awarded the Nobel Peace Prize.

on interpreting the minority rights provisions of the International Covenant on Civil and Political Rights, and the Committee on the Elimination of Racial Discrimination's General Recommendation 23 affirming that discrimination against indigenous peoples falls within the scope of the International Convention on the Elimination of All Forms of Racial Discrimination.

ILO169 was groundbreaking. Adopted in 1989 after a three-year drafting process, ILO169 was the first international legal instrument to attempt to define who may be considered indigenous and establish their rights within the international legal system (Mato 1997: 177).[17] ILO169 contains several articles relevant to indigenous peoples' land rights, notably Articles 4, 7 and 13–19. For purposes of this discussion, the most important is Article 13(1), which emphasises 'the special importance for the cultures and spiritual values of the peoples concerned of their relationship with the lands or territories ... and in particular the collective aspects of this relationship' (ILO 1989). The Human Rights Committee's General Comment 23 clarified the provisions of Article 27 of the International Covenant on Civil and Political Rights (hereafter ICCPR). The ICCPR, along with the International Covenant on Economic, Social and Cultural Rights and the Universal Declaration on Human Rights, form the pillars of the international human rights system, although unlike the Universal Declaration, the two covenants are binding treaties. Adopted in 1966, they came into force in 1976. The ICCPR's Article 27 recognises the rights of 'ethnic, religious, or linguistic minorities'. By the 1990s, some indigenous peoples, such as the Yanomami of the northern Amazon basin, had enjoyed some success relying on these provisions to persuade the court of the deficiencies of the less specific American Declaration on the Rights and Duties of Man (cf. Wiessner 2011: 204 n. 51, *Coulter et al. v. Brazil*). Recognising the tidal changes in international law, in 1994 the newly established office of the UN High Commissioner for Human Rights issued General Comment 23 on Article 27 property rights. The Comment clarified that 'one or other aspects of the rights' protected by Article 27 'may consist in a way of life which is closely associated with territory and use of its resources', that '[t]his may particularly be true of members of indigenous communities' and that 'the [Human Rights] Committee observes that culture manifests itself in many forms, including a particular way of life associated with the use of land resources, especially in the case of indigenous peoples.' The comment concluded 'The protection of

---

[17] Along with ILO Convention 107, a 1957 document advocating assimilation of indigenous populations that was superseded by ILO169, these two conventions are the only major binding international instruments specifically dealing with indigenous peoples' rights.

[Article 27] rights is directed towards ensuring the survival and continued development of the cultural, religious and social identity of the minorities concerned, thus enriching the fabric of society as a whole' (UNHRC 1994: paras 3.2, 7 and 9). General Comment 23 made it unequivocally clear that Article 27 protections apply to indigenous communities and may be relied on by them (Engle 2010: 115–16), as indeed happened shortly thereafter in a case involving the Ainu of Japan's Hokkaido Island (*Kayano et al. v. Hokkaido Expropriation Committee (Nibutani Dam Decision)*. Then, in 1997, the UN's Committee on the Elimination of Racial Discrimination (hereafter CERD) issued its own General Recommendation 23 clarifying and affirming that the provisions of the International Convention on the Elimination of All Forms of Racial Discrimination (ICERD) apply to indigenous peoples. Like the ICCPR, although in less stringent language than ILO169, General Recommendation 23 also emphasised the connection between indigenous cultural identity and land, and called on signatory states to recognise indigenous peoples' rights to their lands, to restore their title, or provide adequate compensation when this was not possible (CERD 1997: paras 2, 3, 5).

These developments demonstrate the growing salience of indigenous issues in international law and illustrate that the question of a special and unique relationship between people and place remained axiomatic of indigenous peoples' struggles. Special Rapporteur Cobo's report went a long way towards establishing indigeneity as a global, transnational identity category in terms of a cosmologically oriented, spiritually mediated special and unique relationship between people and place. Even if the question of its cosmological orientation and its mediation by other-than-human agents was less emphatically foregrounded in policy and legislation, this dimension remained pivotal to its discursive articulation, particularly at the WGIP.

In the same year that CERD issued its General Recommendation, the UN Commission on Human Rights appointed WGIP Chairperson Erica-Irene Daes to prepare a Special Rapporteur's report on indigenous peoples' relationship to land 'with a view to suggesting practical measures to address ongoing problems in that regard' (UNCHR 2001: para. 1).[18] The bulk of the report, compiled over four years, addressed legal issues related to restoring indigenous peoples' title to their lands and reversing legal doctrines by which they have been dispossessed of their territories.[19] For purposes of this discussion, two aspects of the report

---

[18]   Unless indicated otherwise, citations refer to the relevant paragraphs of the Daes report (UNCHR 2001).

[19]   The 1992 case *Mabo v. Queensland (No. 2)* in the Australian state of Queensland repudiated the colonial doctrine of *terra nullius* and was a high-water mark in these efforts,

are important. The first is the report's reiteration of indigenous peoples' 'relationship with the land and all living things'; it is, as the Special Rapporteur wrote, 'at the core of indigenous societies' (para. 13). The second aspect is the report's integration of indigenist discourse from multiple discursive sites into a coherent analytical framework. Both these aspects succinctly encapsulate the report's second section, titled 'Relationship of indigenous peoples to their lands, territories and resources'. The Special Rapporteur recalled discussions at the WGIP about 'the spiritual, social, cultural, economic and political significance to indigenous societies of their lands, territories and resources for their continued survival and vitality' (para. 12). Citing supporting research and publications, the report reiterated that indigenous peoples' 'unique relationships to their traditional territories' distinguish and sustain 'the spiritual and material foundations of their cultural identities'. The report went on to quote an indigenous lawyer activist to similar effect: 'the Aboriginal vision of property was ecological space that creates our consciousness, not an ideological construct or fungible resource . Their vision is of different realms enfolded into a sacred space. It is fundamental to their identity, personality and humanity' (para. 14).

Thereafter, the report recapitulates the responsiveness of 'the international community' to indigenous claims, beginning with Special Rapporteur Cobo's report. Erica-Irene Daes's report repeats the earlier report's conclusion about the importance of knowing and understanding 'the deeply spiritual special relationship between indigenous peoples and their land as basic to their existence', following that paragraph with this one, also repeated from Cobo's conclusions and recommendations chapter:

> For such peoples, the land is not merely a possession and a means of production. The entire relationship between the spiritual life of indigenous peoples and Mother Earth, and their land, has a great many deep-seated implications. Their land is not a commodity which can be acquired, but a material element to be enjoyed freely. (UNCHR 2001: para. 16; orig. UNCHR 1983b: para. 197)

The Special Rapporteur recalled Article 13 of ILO169, the draft Inter-American Declaration on the Rights of Indigenous Peoples and Article 25 of the Draft Declaration on the Rights of Indigenous Peoples to emphasise that indigenous peoples' 'profound relationship' with their lands, territories and resources comprises collective and intergenerational aspects, as well as social, cultural,

---

although subsequent developments have reversed some of these gains (see Scott and Mulrennan 2010).

spiritual, economic and political dimensions and responsibilities (para. 20). The notion of a 'profound spiritual and material relationship' (para. 121) between peoples and place at the core of indigenous identity recapitulates a quarter-century of indigenist discourse and in a sense frames the analytical framework the report proposed. The framework itself differentiates the kinds of problems indigenous peoples face today in relation to their lands, including states' failures to acknowledge indigenous peoples' relationship with land and to demarcate indigenous titles, along with issues relating to expropriating and returning indigenous lands and relocating indigenous communities.

A comparison between the Daes and Cobo reports suggests the extent of indigenism's gains during the intervening years. One might characterise the older report as centrifugal and the more recent report as centripetal, in the sense of proliferating discursive sites in the case of the Cobo report and integrating diverse and disparate discursive practices into a central organising architecture in the case of the Daes report. Whereas Cobo reported on existing measures (in 1983) that protected indigenous land rights and 'steps taken' to guarantee indigenous interests, Daes summarised key provisions of the most significant legal innovations since the earlier report, including two that were still in draft form and not yet adopted. Whereas the earlier report was framed in terms of an audit of protections, the later report emphasised the subsequent convergence of 'principles' and 'international standards' informing 'the main or most important legal materials' pertaining to indigenous peoples' relationships to their land. A 12-page annex inventoried pertinent articles from the Universal Declaration of Human Rights, the International Convention on the Elimination of All Forms of Racial Discrimination, CERD's Recommendation 23, ICCPR Article 27 and General Comment 23, ILO169, the Rio Earth Summit's Agenda 21, the World Bank's Operational Directive 4.20 and the Draft Declaration on the Rights of Indigenous Peoples. A further annex listed a selection of salient cases from Australia, Canada, International Arbitration Tribunals, the International Court of Justice, the Permanent Court of International Justice and the United States of America.

From the late 1980s, drafting international legal instruments protecting indigenous peoples' rights was a prolific and highly contested site of human rights discourse that drew in a range of indigenous organisations and activists, intellectuals and professionals, particularly lawyers and anthropologists, many of whom were also indigenous (see T. Turner 1997, Warren and Jackson 2002b: 3–13 and Wright 1988). Although progress on the draft Declaration on the Rights of Indigenous Peoples was painfully slow, achievements on other fronts meant that by the end of the twentieth century, a considerable apparatus of legal rights and recourses, standards and norms, monitoring and reporting mechanisms was in place (see Pritchard and Heindow-Dolman 1998). Even if states' compliance was poor, the fact that legal standards were being elaborated and refined and that non-compliant states were increasingly held accountable against these standards, was in itself a considerable achievement that indicated the direction of prevailing winds in indigenous human rights protections. Litigation initiated by indigenous peoples opened a new field of discursive practice that brought to bear its own considerable structure of authority. The following discussion gives historical background to indigenous peoples' reconceptualisation of self-determination as autonomy, before examining cases before the Inter-American Court of Human Rights.

From Self-determination to Autonomy

Following the WGIP's 1983 decision permitting direct participation by indigenous delegates, the forum became more diverse and gradually transformed from one dominated by delegates from the Americas and the global North into one more representative of the diversity of the world's indigenous peoples (Muehlebach 2001: 435–6).[20] As the forum became more diverse, so indigenists adjusted their strategic orientation.

The first shifts began with the flourishing pan-Indian movement in South and Central America from the mid-1980s in tandem with nascent transitions towards less authoritarian forms of governance across the continent. Although

---

[20] Only thirty indigenous and non-indigenous participants attended the WGIP's inaugural meeting in 1982. Indigenous organisations from Asia began attending WGIP annual meetings from 1984. Among the first were representatives from the Cordillera region in the Philippines and the Chittagong Hill Tracts in Bangladesh, followed by Ainu from Japan, Naga from India, Chin from Burma and Karen from Thailand. Maori delegates began attending from 1988, followed by more delegates from the Pacific region, including from Hawaii in 1989. Also in 1989, Masai representatives from East Africa attended, followed by Twa from Rwanda, San from southern Africa, Ogoni from Nigeria and Taureg groups from West Africa. The end of the Cold War also saw representatives of 'small peoples' from the Russia Federation begin to attend. In 1992, more than six hundred delegates from five continents attended the WGIP's annual meeting; by 1999 that figure had risen to nearly a thousand. The Americas still sent the most delegations. The 1999 WGIP was attended by approximately 46 South and Central American delegations, 40 Asian, 31 North American, 23 African, 9 Australian, 6 North Asian/Siberian, 5 Pacific, 4 Inuit and 2 Saami delegations and about 6 explicitly transnational indigenous organisations (Muehlebach 2001: 420; cf. Ewen 1994).

South and Central America had been a focus area for the WGIP since its inception, indigenous delegates from Latin America often were unable to attend WGIP sessions in person, relying instead on transnational activist networks to represent their interests. Indigenous activism, along with representatives' capacities to participate in international forums like the WGIP, was restricted by a combination of military governments (Chile, Bolivia, Ecuador), Marxist revolutionary movements (Guatemala, Nicaragua, El Salvador), discredited bureaucratic infrastructures responsible for managing Indian affairs, as with Brazil's Fundação Nacional do Índio, and indigenes' economic marginalisation and social deprivation following decades of *indigenismo* policies. However, as political negotiations in several American states produced constitutional amendments and reforms and as governance structures became more open, accountable and tolerant, local indigenous communities' capacities to forge regional, transnational alliances improved.[21] These efforts were spurred at the international level by the changing legal framework and were supported by indigenous leaders' participation in international conferences, usually funded by foreign NGOs and sometimes governments (mainly European). At a national level, subsequent negotiations over constitutional reforms offered unprecedented opportunities to establish indigenous rights and legal protections in domestic law. The new pan-Indianism was also spurred by indigenous activists' desire to respond to the approaching quincentennial of Columbus's voyage and the beginning of the European conquest of the Americas. Their response included highly publicised activist interventions such as at the inaugural UN Earth Summit, hosted by Rio de Janeiro in 1992 (Little 1995). Ultimately, the UN was convinced to declare 1993 the International Year of Indigenous Peoples.[22] The International Year was succeeded by the International Decade of the World's Indigenous Peoples beginning in 1995.

This intensification of indigenous activism in Latin America also contributed to the diversification of indigenous participation at the WGIP. As a global forum for working out indigenous positions on a vast range of issues, the WGIP, particularly its annual meetings, was crucial in uniting indigenous peoples around

---

[21] Constitutional amendments were adopted in Bolivia (1994), Colombia (1991), Ecuador (1998), Mexico (1992), Nicaragua (1986), Paraguay (1992), Peru (1993) and Venezuela (1999). For discussion of specific legislative reforms, see Graham 1987, Stavenhagen 2002: 32–4, Van Cott 2006, 2002, 2000, 1994).

[22] Indigenous leaders had wanted 1992, the quincentennial year, to be the International Year of Indigenous Peoples, but accepted the UN offer of 1993 instead (following objections from Brazil, Spain and the United States) because, among other reasons, they reasoned two years to advocate their grievances was better than just one (see Ewen 1994: 21).

the world around a common experience of alienation, suffering, powerlessness and a shared project to devise legal mechanisms that would improve their respective situations. These efforts naturally fostered transnational indigenous solidarity and cohesion. Yet notwithstanding solidarity and community of purpose, there were and remain important differences between different indigenous peoples' respective struggles. In the Americas and northern Europe (and arguably parts of Australasia), indigenous struggles are quite different from those in Africa or Asia (Barnes et al. 1995, Erni 2008). For example, in Brazil and Canada, where indigenous peoples have already secured a range of rights and entitlements, indigenous struggles today are mainly focused on maintaining and protecting those achievements. In parts of Africa, by contrast, definitions of who and what constitutes indigenous are not yet settled, even provisionally. For example, Hodgson reports that San and Masai, of southern and east Africa respectively, are still engaged in a politics of identity as they struggle to form viable and durable coalitions and link themselves into the transnational indigenous rights movement (Hodgson 2002a: 1043; see also Hodgson 2002b, Mutume 2007, Sylvain 2005, 2002). Neither is the situation uniform within continental regions, as Jackson and Warren have demonstrated with reference to Central and South America (Jackson and Warren 2005, Warren and Jackson 2002a; see also Sieder 2002b, Van Cott 2002, 1994) and examples from the Russian Federation show with reference to North Asia (Xanthaki 2004, Köhler and Wessendorf 2002). More generally, states in Asia and Africa have complex histories of movement and displacement that do not fit easily with notions of a timeless past prior to a single moment of displacement by foreign settlers. Governments in Africa and Asia often draw considerable legitimacy from their claim to being indigenous too and invoke these claims to elevate post-independence nationalist unity and subordinate ethnic diversity. Indeed, this problem was highlighted at the first attendance at the WGIP of indigenous delegates from Africa, when Moringe Parkipuny, a representative of East African Masai, criticised African governments' repudiation of social diversity in favour of a chauvinist version of national unity: '... the vital need to consolidate national identity and unity ... should never be pursued to the exclusion of the protection of the legitimate rights of vulnerable minorities. To do that undermines the very objective of national unity' (Parkipuny 1987; cf. Hodgson 2002b). Some African and Asian governments have counter-argued that the problematic of indigenous peoples and state power applies only to settler societies, such as in the Americas, Australia, or New Zealand, while that in their respective polities the minority rights already established in international law, not least ICCPR Article 27, are appropriate and sufficient (on these debates, see McIntosh 2000, Niezen 2003, UNCHR 1999).

Legal scholar Karen Engle has researched these debates with reference to indigenists' shifting approaches towards securing rights. She argues that indigenist discourse distinguishes between two versions of indigenous self-determination: as a collective right to secession or statehood, and as autonomy within the state. Moreover, a preference for these versions roughly correlates with a distinction between the global North and the global South (Engle 2010: 71). Although Engle's distinction between North and South corresponds with the socio-economic distinction between developed and developing states, used, for example, in the UN's Human Development Index, she is more interested in a discursive difference: the global North, in her analysis, is marked by the political resonance of the notion of a global 'Fourth World' movement. The phrase 'Fourth World' rose to prominence in North America following the 1974 publication of *The Fourth World: An Indian Reality* by George Manuel, an indigenous leader and soon-to-become chairperson of the Union of British Columbian Indian Chiefs (Manuel and Posluns 1974). The point of comparison for Manuel was the Third World, which in the 1960s seemed to be on a path to independence in a way that had not been made available to indigenous peoples. To the extent that the Fourth World idea mobilised around post-war anti-colonialism, cited broken treaties and drew attention to 'the geopolitical situation in which indigenous peoples found themselves' (Engle 2010: 49), the global North, including Australia and New Zealand, advocated the strong form of self-determination. From its inception, 'Fourth World' has referred to all indigenous peoples around the world, not only those in the global North, and was eventually embraced globally. However, much research and activism that identifies with 'Fourth World' political struggles remains in the global North, as Engle notes (2010: 51–2). She illustrates the point with reference to the World Council of Indigenous Peoples founded by Manuel in 1975. Until its dissolution in the mid-1990s, the Council published the *Fourth World Journal* and maintained the Fourth World Documentation Project, although all but one of its nine directors were from tribes in North America (Engle 2010: 52). Today, the Council's work is continued by the Center for World Indigenous Studies. Co-founded by Manuel in 1984, the Center conducts research, offers consulting services, publishes *Fourth World Journal* and hosts the Chief George Manuel Library, for which it is credited by the Centre's Jay Taber as 'the premier indigenous think tank and archival repository serving the Fourth World' (Taber 2011).

The notion of a global Fourth World movement has not had as much resonance for indigenous peoples outside the global North. Contrasting indigenous advocacy between North and South America, Engle notes the different significance land has in these respective political contexts. Whereas land dispossession galvanised indigenous activism in North America, indigenous advocacy in South and Central America has been oriented by endangered cultures, traditions and identities, often in tandem with the exploitation of indigenous peoples' labour on lands they continued to occupy (Engle 2010: 55). As the indigenous peoples' movement has globalised via the work of the WGIP as well as expansions and consolidations of transnational indigenous networks via other forums, including NGO advocacy, this orientation towards traditions and cultures has come to distinguish the contours of indigenous advocacy in the global South, including Africa and Asia.

Having set up her analysis in these terms, Engle argues that a shift has occurred in indigenous advocacy since the late 1980s and early 1990s. Prior to this, indigenist discourse was mostly framed in terms of the anti-colonialism of a global Fourth World imaginary, including deliberations at the WGIP. However, as participation increased from the global South, a subtle shift occurred from a strong version of external self-determination towards a softer version of indigenous autonomy within states. Several factors contributed to this shift. One was the changing domestic politics of countries in South and Central America and in Africa that enabled greater participation by indigenous representatives from these states in transnational indigenous advocacy networks. This participation in turn influenced debates about desirable and acceptable forms of indigenous self-determination. Indigenous participants from parts of Asia (particularly India, Japan, Malaysia and Thailand) favoured an autonomy model. Another factor was recognition that states' unwavering resistance to indigenous challenges to their territorial contiguity, combined with lack of indigenous resources, meant the strong version of self-determination was increasingly impractical. Still another factor was the steady progress in securing legal protections in terms of individual human rights, such as ILO169, ICCPR Article 27 and ICERD. By the mid-1990s, indigenous representatives by and large had given up their claim to a strong right to external self-determination (Engle 2010: 95). Instead, indigenist discourse began to favour an array of rights and privileges guaranteeing indigenous peoples greater autonomy within the states in which they live.

Engle's analysis is somewhat over-determined in the sense that she draws the distinctions and correlations in terms that are arguably more dichotomous than has actually been the case. For example, Benedict Kingsbury (2001) traces a similar trend, but differentiates five 'conceptual structures' underpinning indigenous claims to self-determination and pays closer attention than Engle does to convergences between the competing interests of indigenes and states.

In fairness to Engle, her analysis is concerned with comparing the relative strengths and limitations of pursuing protections for indigenous peoples through collective land rights versus individual cultural rights. Moreover, the trend she characterises is widely reported and accepted (for example, Kipuri 2009, Muehlebach 2003, Wiessner 2011). The relevant point for indigenism discourse is that in recent years international human rights law has accorded greater recognition to culture and heritage in protecting indigenous peoples' rights and has thereby made available new avenues towards securing greater autonomy for indigenous peoples within the states in which they live. This shift opened new avenues for indigenist recourse and has led to new precedents in interpretations of human rights law, notably by elaborating jurisprudence around culture, religion and property rights.

Developing Engle's analysis, I want to argue that greater substate autonomy became an acceptable vehicle for self-determination claims because indigenous identity, culture and tradition had become so closely entangled with the notion of indigenous 'lands, territories and resources' that a right to heritage and culture offered a viable strategy for winning claims to land, title and tenure and therewith some degree of self-determination in relation to indigenous peoples' territories and resources. In other words, this mainstay of indigenous activism no longer necessitated a politically unwelcome, hard right to external self-determination. This viability is among the important discursive effects of a quarter-century of indigenist discourse about a unique cosmological bond linking people and place. The instrumentalisation of this special bond – first in indigenist discourse and identity politics, and then in corresponding human rights law and jurisprudence – recalls Penrose's thesis about territorialisation. It amounts to a kind of territorial praxis by which space is bounded, peoplehood is made and the collective right of peoples to determine their futures in relation to their territories is secured. Several judgments by the Inter-American Court of Human Rights (IACrtHR) bears this out, beginning with the landmark Awas Tingni case decided in 2001. They also return our attention to shamanism and therewith the problem of modernity's practical limit attitude.

Indigenism on Trial

The Awas Tingni are a community of indigenous Mayagna people living in Nicaragua and Honduras. Since the 1950s, they had been unsuccessfully petitioning the Nicaraguan government to demarcate their lands. In 1996, Nicaragua's government issued logging concessions to a Korean company in lands claimed by the Awas Tingni, prompting the community to begin legal proceedings to have the concessions withdrawn and their lands demarcated in their favour. The case eventually came before the Inter-American Court of Human Rights (hereafter IACrtHR). Although the IACrtHR has not always shown willingness to advance indigenous peoples' rights (Van Cott 1994: 7), since the 1990s the court has become a global leader in developing jurisprudence around indigenous rights (Engle 2010: 127, Wiessner 2011). The question before the court in the Awas Tingni case was whether the Nicaraguan government's decision to grant logging concessions to third parties on land claimed by the Awas Tingni community violated Article 21 (right to property) and Article 25 (right to judicial protection) of the American Convention on Human Rights, to which Nicaragua is a signatory. The court's judgment, passed by 7 to 1, affirmed the Awas Tingni community's communal ownership of their ancestral lands and instructed the Nicaraguan government to demarcate their territory as well as abstain from any actions that would affect their use and enjoyment of their ancestral lands (IACrtHR: 441).[23] From a legal perspective, the significance of the judgment was how the court interpreted the right to property protected by Article 21. Representing the Awas Tingni community, the Inter-American Commission on Human Rights (hereafter the Commission) argued for a broad interpretation of Article 21, one that recognised not only the traditional and communal nature of indigenous property rights, but also the reliance of the community on their relationship with their territory for their general well-being.

Testimony at the trial repeated familiar themes about the importance of cosmology in delimiting space and creating territory. An exchange between Judge Cançado Trindade and anthropologist Theodore MacDonald, a witness appearing for the community, is a typical example (pp. 172–3):

> PRESIDENT CANÇADO TRINDADE: I have just one question. In response to one of the questions of the Agent of the Illustrious State of Nicaragua, you referred to a relationship with the Mayagna Community, and I am referring to the expression 'in the sense of boundaries.' Could you elaborate, explain to us of what that consists, in the cosmology of the Community, this 'sense of boundaries?'

---

[23] Unless indicated otherwise, subsequent citations refer to page numbers of the trial transcript published in a special issue of the *Arizona Journal of International and Comparative Law* (IACrtHR 2002; cf. Vuotto 2004).

WITNESS THEODORE MACDONALD: Yes, I mention sense because, in the beginning, there were not many conflicts over this. They had an idea of their territory; the idea comes, as you mention, from the cosmology. If you could show me the map, that would help.

Those hills are the main ones, according to them; inside of those hills live the spirits of the mountain, chiefs of the mountain, that in Mayagna are called Asangpas Muigeni. They control the animals around that region.

In order to harvest those animals, there must be a special relationship with the spirits of the mountain. On many occasions, the *cacique*, also a kind of shaman that they called Ditelian, can maintain that relationship with the spirits; then the presence of the animals and the possibility of using the animals, through hunting, is based on the cosmology and has a lot to do with the boundaries because, according to them, those masters of the mountain are the owners of the animals, especially the mountain pigs that roam in herds, and they roam around the mountains. And to be able to take those animals, there must be a good relationship with the spirit that lives inside the mountain. To achieve that good relationship, time must pass, so there is a strong bond within the cosmology, with these sacred sites, the spirits that live inside and their brothers that are members of the Community, that have special relationships – spiritual, they can be called – with the animals of the mountain that allows them to go to the hunt. That is their sense of being with the territory.

MacDonald went on to explain that there are two kinds of sacred places in Awas Tingni cosmology. The first kind consists of cemeteries and burial sites, and the second kind consists of hills inhabited by the spirits who control the animals hunted by community members. Hunting is also an occasion to visit burial sites and visit the community's predecessors. McDonald continued: 'So ... up to a certain point, it is a spiritual act, to go hunting, and it has much to do with the territory that they enjoy.' This idea of spirits residing within the hills was introduced in the earlier testimony of Charlie McLean, a member of the Awas Tingi community, who told the court about Asangpas Muigeni, 'the spirit of the mountain; it is the same form as a human, but it is a spirit [who] always lives under the hills' (p. 156; cf. p. 146).

Sociologist Rodolfo Stavenhagen appeared as an expert witness for the community. In his testimony, he explained to the court the difference between the Awas Tingni's concept of territory and the modern concept of land. He told the court that 'the concept of the land must be extended beyond that which a certain modernity asks that we see it as land, as simply, as I said a moment ago, an instrument of production.' Expanding on this broader concept of land, he argued land must be understood

> ... as a part of the geographic space and the social space, of the symbolic space, of the religious space with which the history of indigenous peoples is connected and with which the current functioning of those same peoples is connected ... peoples whose essence is derived from their relationship with the land.

Land 'gives life to an entire culture, to an entire nation', and for this reason the concept of territory must be understood in broader terms too: 'Territory as a geographic space, as a physical space, but also as a social and symbolic space with which the culture identifies itself.' This relationship between people and territory therefore is mutually constitutive: 'land does not belong to us, but rather, that we belong to the land' (pp. 176–7).

Finding in favour of the Awas Tingni community, the court set a new precedent in the jurisprudence of indigenous peoples' human rights by judging that the right to property also protects the traditionally communal land tenure of indigenous communities. Remarking that 'among indigenous peoples there is a communitarian tradition regarding a communal form of collective ownership of the land', the judges agreed with witness testimony about the foundational significance of the relationship between people and place for indigenous culture, identity and survival:

> ... the close ties of indigenous people with the land must be recognized and understood as the fundamental basis of their cultures, their spiritual life, their integrity, and their economic survival. For indigenous communities, relations to the land are not merely a matter of possession and production but a material and spiritual element which they must fully enjoy, even to preserve their cultural legacy and transmit it to future generations. (p. 430)

This paragraph about 'the concept of property in indigenous communities' has been widely quoted by subsequent cases citing the precedent set by the Awas Tingni judgment (discussed below). The significance of the new precedent went beyond merely affirming the communal nature of indigenous property ownership. The court's judgment also affirmed in case law jurisprudence the special bond between indigenous peoples and their lands, explicitly arguing that land is a form of culture and implicitly arguing that culture is land too. Recognising the significance of their judgment and anticipating implications for human rights jurisprudence, three judges of the court, including Court President Antônio A. Cançado Trindade, authored a Joint Separate Opinion in which they commented on 'the *intertemporal dimension*' of indigenous peoples' communal form of property, a dimension they thought was one of the case's central aspects (p. 443).

The opinion begins by noting the importance of land for the community's cultural and religious development. The judges emphasised 'their [Mayagna Community's] characterisation of the territory as *sacred*, for encompassing not only the members of the Community who are alive, but also the mortal remains of their ancestors, as well as their divinities'. The judges recalled testimony about family members and material artefacts buried in particular hills, ancestral spirits residing there and obligations stemming from these fact. They cited testimony about types of 'sacred places' for the Mayagna community and their general assessment that 'the lands of the indigenous peoples constitute a space which is, at the same time, geographical and social, symbolic and religious, of crucial importance for their cultural self-identification, their mental health, their social self-perception'. They quoted from the court's judgment that 'the relationship with the land is not merely a question of possession and production but rather a material and spiritual element that they ought to enjoy fully, so as to preserve their cultural legacy and transmit it to future generations' (pp. 443–5).

It is this 'conceptual element' that the judges 'consider ... necessary to enlarge', 'with an emphasis on the *intertemporal dimension* of what seems to us to characterize the relationship of the indigenous persons of the Community with their lands'. This 'intertemporal dimension' at once gives rise to the communal form of land ownership among indigenous communities and at the same time distinguishes it from 'the civilist (private law) conception'. Noting that without the use and enjoyment of their lands the Mayagna community 'would be deprived of practicing, conserving and revitalising their cultural habits, which give a meaning to their own existence, both individual and communitarian', the judges argued that Article 21 property rights 'ought to, in our view, be appreciated from this angle' (p. 445). The difference between the perspective the judges are developing and the perspective that has normally prevailed in interpreting Article 21 protections is neatly encapsulated in the judges' repetition of Stavenhagen's testimony, that, 'just as the land they occupy belongs to them, they in turn belong to their land'. The notion that the fortunes and future of the community is identical with their lands accounts for the 'necessary prevalence' of conservation over 'simple exploitation' in indigenous concepts of land ownership and is a crucial aspect of the intertemporal dimension the judges wish to foreground:

> The concern with the element of conservation reflects a cultural manifestation of the integration of human beings with nature and the world wherein they live. This integration, we believe, is projected into both space and time, as we relate ourselves, in space, with the natural system of which we are part and that we ought to treat with care, and, in time, with other generations (past and future), in respect of which we have obligations. Cultural manifestations of the kind form, in their turn, the *substratum* of the juridical norms which ought to govern the relations of the community members *inter se* and with their goods. (p. 445)

The judges argued that the passage has been steady from cultural manifestations of integration to judicial norms and case law that recognise and protect indigenous social organisation. They cite several judgments of the IACrtHR demonstrating this. With the Awas Tingni case, however, the judges felt it was necessary to go 'into greater depth in the analysis of the matter, in an approximation to an integral interpretation of the indigenous cosmovision, as the central point of the present Judgment' (p. 446). The court's interpretation and application of Article 21

> ... represent, in our view, a positive contribution to the protection of the communal form of property prevailing among the members of that Community. This communal conception, besides the values underlying it, has a cosmovision of its own, and an important intertemporal dimension, in bringing to the fore the bonds of human solidarity that link those who are alive with their dead and with the ones who are still to come. (p. 447)

Noting that 'human rights treaties are live instruments whose interpretation must adapt to the evolution of the times and, specifically, to current living conditions', the judges were acutely aware that they were applying the law in new and innovative ways and that their ruling would have far-reaching implications for indigenous rights jurisprudence (p. 429). Jurisprudence may be construed broadly as connecting the practice of law with society. It is concerned, as Freedman explains in the eighth edition of *Lloyd's Introduction to Jurisprudence*, 'with rule-governed action, with the activities of officials such as judges and with the relationship between them and the population of a given society'. Concerned with the social nature of law and the relationship of law to justice and morality, jurisprudence has a great deal to say about the meaning of social knowledge (Freeman 2008: 3, 10–11). Legal precedent is an important aspect of jurisprudence because it references the chain of judgments that give weight and meaning to judicial authority. Defined by *Black's Law Dictionary* as 'an already decided decision which furnishes the basis for later cases involving similar facts and issues', legal precedent clearly can have a restraining effect on elaborating and developing law in new or innovative ways. As legal philosopher Ronald Dworkin explains, precedent means that jurisprudence always tends towards convergence and agreement:

> The practice of precedent, which no judge's interpretation can wholly ignore, presses toward agreement; each judge's theories of what judging really is will incorporate by reference, through whatever account and restructuring of precedent he [*sic*] settles on, aspects of other popular interpretations of the day. Judges think about law, moreover, within society, not apart from it; the general intellectual environment, as well as the common language that reflects and protects that environment, exercise practical constraints on idiosyncrasy and conceptual restraints on imagination. The inevitable conservativism of formal legal education, and of the process of selecting lawyers for judicial and administrative office, adds further centripetal pressure. (Dworkin 1986: 88)

As Dworkin emphasises, this centripetal pressure or converging tendency is inherent in jurisprudence because legal precedent is a foundational principle of rational legal argument. This is so even in precedent-setting judgments, such as the Awas Tingni case. For example, in outlining the complaint before the court, the Commission noted that Nicaragua was party to the ICCPR and recalled a 1983 judgment by the same court that cited ICCPR article 27 in affirming indigenous peoples' right to 'special legal protection' in issues relating to the integrity of their cultures (IACrtHR 2002: 56). The Commission also drew the court's attention to ILO169, CERD's General Recommendation 23, as well as the (then) draft Declaration on the Rights of Indigenous Peoples and Proposed American Declaration on the Rights of Indigenous Peoples. In this sense, the innovative aspects of practicing precedent refer to the court's granting its assent and authority to a new form of application of what was already present in the law. The court elaborates jurisprudence pertaining to indigenous peoples' issues by applying the law in new ways and granting its authority to these elaborations by way of legal judgments. These judgments in turn increase the centripetal pressure of jurisprudence as well as strengthen the architecture of indigenism.

After nearly half a century of indigenist discourse, legal precedent is a powerful means of conveying regularity into shamanism discourse. In the decade since the court's judgment, the Awas Tingni case has been cited in several subsequent judgments favourable to indigenous complainants, quoting from the judgment or using virtually identical phrasing, particularly from paragraph 149 about the indigenous concept of property. Consider the following representative cases. In a 2004 case, *Mayan indigenous communities v. Belize*, several Mayan communities complained to the IACHR about their eviction from their lands by the government of Belize. Finding in their favour, the Commission noted, 'the jurisprudence of the [inter-American human rights] system has acknowledged that the property rights of indigenous peoples ... arises from and is grounded in indigenous custom and tradition' (para. 117). Quoting from the Awas Tingni judgment, the Commission recalled that 'the close ties of indigenous people with the land must be recognised and understood as the fundamental basis of their cultures, their spiritual life, their integrity, and their economic survival' and emphasised that its approach was 'consistent with developments in the field of international human rights law more broadly'. The ruling cited the Awas Tingni case, ILO169, General Comment 23, General Recommendation 23, as well as domestic law in member states of the Organisation of American States (para. 97).

In the 2005 judgment, *Moiwana Community v. Suriname*, the court found in favour of the survivors of a 1986 massacre of indigenous Maroon villagers at Moiwana by agents of the government of Suriname. The issue at the centre of the complaint was that survivors were subsequently prevented from returning to their village and therefore were unable to resume their traditional way of life, including performing ceremonies with respect to their murdered kinspeople, whose spirits consequently were not at peace. Finding in favour of the Moiwana community, the judges recalled the Awas Tingni case: 'For [indigenous communities], their communal nexus with the ancestral territory ... consists in material and spiritual elements that must be fully integrated and enjoyed by the community, so that it may preserve its cultural legacy and pass it on to future generations' (para. 131). As in the Awas Tingni case, Judge Cançado Trindade wrote a separate concurring opinion in which he argued that 'the grave damage caused to [the survivors of the massacre] was ... a true spiritual damage, which seriously affected, in their cosmovision, not only the living, but the living with their dead altogether' (para. 78). As 'an aggravated form of moral damage' (para. 71), this spiritual damage at the centre of the Moiwana community case 'takes us even further than the emerging right to the project of life' towards 'the right to a project of after-life' (paras 66–70, 2).

Since 1990, the Xákmok Kásek in Paraguay had been trying to secure legal title to their ancestral lands. In a 2010 case, *Xákmok Kásek Indigenous Community v. Paraguay*, the court found in favour of the community. Citing the Awas Tingni judgment, the court ruled (paras 174–6):

> The culture of indigenous communities is part of a unique way of living, of being, seeing, and acting in the world, formed due their close relationship [*sic*] with their traditional lands and natural resources, not only because it is their main means of subsistence, but also because the relationship is an integral element in their cosmology, their religion, and therefore their cultural identity ... For the members of the Xákmok Kásek Community, cultural features like their own language (Sanapaná and Enxet), their shaman rituals, their male and female initiation rituals, their ancestral shamanic knowledge, their ways of commemorating the dead, and their relationship with the land are essential for developing their cosmology and unique way of existing.

The Xákmok Kásek case was the third in a decade successfully brought against the Paraguayan government by indigenous communities (The two other cases were *Indigenous Community of Yakye Axa v. Paraguay* and *Indigenous Community of Sawhoyamaxa v. Paraguay*). All three cases involving Paraguay, along with the Mayan and Moiwana cases, added to the growing body of case law applying the Awas Tingni precedent to interpreting indigenous property rights. For example, in a 2007 case, *Saramaka People v. Suriname*, the complainants quoted the Awas Tingni judgment, cited *Yakye Axa v. Paraguay*, *Sawhoyamaxa v. Paraguay* and *Moiwana v. Suriname*, as well as a familiar ensemble of international law, before reminding the court that these judgments 'have all been based upon the special relationship that members of indigenous and tribal peoples have with their territory, and on the need to protect their right to that territory in order to safeguard the physical and cultural survival of such peoples' (para. 90). As in the cases already mentioned, the court decided in favour of the indigenous complainants and ordered the offending government to adopt various remedial measures, including demarcating and titling indigenous territories.

Today, human rights jurisprudence recognises that space historically delimited in cosmological terms is sufficient grounds for recognising indigenous territorial claims and enacting protections. Recalling the rhetoric of anti-colonial independence and the hard version of self-determination underpinning indigenist discourse in the 1970s, it is perhaps surprising that indigenous religiosity has become such a consequential factor in securing legal title and control over indigenous peoples' ancestral territories. Yet recalling Penrose's characterisation of territoriality as 'a geographic strategy that connects society and space' (Penrose 2002: 279), the crucial development in human rights jurisprudence pertaining to indigenous peoples' land rights in recent decades is that it has elaborated and expanded the ways in which international law recognises that people may be connected with the spaces they inhabit. It has, in effect, broadened the ways in which law accepts that territories may be bounded and delimited. This broadened interpretation of territoriality has favoured indigenism's characterisation in cosmological terms of the special and unique bond between indigenous peoples and their ancestral lands and made indigenous cosmologies increasingly relevant among indigenists' strategic repertoire of territorial practices.

Discursive Imbrications

Dispensing with an objection is a useful way to revisit the argument outlined in this chapter. An objection may be levelled that indigenous cosmology has always been an important instrument in indigenous communities' territorial practice. Indigenous rituals and myths have always been crucial to the strategies by which people establish and affirm their bonds with a place and underwrite their self-understanding as 'of a particular place'. Although this observation is generally correct (although notions of timeless homogeneity and universality of 'indigenous cosmology' are more problematic), my point is that while these kinds of territorial practices, along with social ones such as practices affirming kinship ties, or economic ones related to occupation or utility of 'lands, territories, and resources', once were sufficient to stake territorial claims, that is no longer the case. Today, territorial practices require modern law (as opposed to customary or other forms of local law) and notions of individual rights, to property, to title, to culture. In this circumstance, indigenous cosmology has been demonstrated to be more effective at securing those rights than have social or economic forms of bonding people with place. But it is not indigenous cosmology as it is practised in ritual that matters most (although ritual matters too). Rather, what matters is how indigenous cosmology is discoursed and represented in language. It is at this juncture that shamanism is imbricated with indigenism because the centuries-long discourse about shamans offers indigenists and jurists alike a common structure of knowledge, an episteme in the Foucauldian sense, that permits mutual intelligibility.

Indigenist discursive practice has not produced a rubric signifier that subsumes indigenous religious diversity like the way 'indigenous' subsumes local cultural diversity.[24] In this circumstance, shamanic religiosity has seemed

[24] When scholars of religion consider this question, the discussion tends towards producing taxonomies of 'indigenous religion' in which 'spirit possession' and 'shamanism' often feature prominently and are increasingly supplemented by 'paganism' and the religious traditions 'indigenous' to Europe (G. Harvey 1999).

to many people, such as the witnesses and judges at the IACrtHR, to be an approximate and sufficient encompassing rubric. Discursively representing indigenous cosmology as 'shamanic' can be understood as a kind of translation that interpolates local religious diversity into a universalised category. This kind of translation continues the interpolation of particulars into universals that began in eighteenth-century Russia. Reports by European explorers indicate that local Siberian communities had many different names for their ritual specialists and these varied by community and the specialists' role within the community (Flaherty 1992: 72–5, Hutton 2001, Siikala 2004: 153). Why exactly the term 'shaman' won out among alternatives is not entirely clear; neither is it particularly relevant for present purposes. Far more relevant is that 'shaman' and its derivatives ('shamanic', shamanist', 'shamanism') entered European languages via German (*schamanismus*) and was conveyed to different regions and applications beyond North Asia via projections of European power/knowledge globally, beginning with North American anthropology in the nineteenth century. Indeed, Soviet prohibitions on shamanic religiosities following the Russian Revolution and their decline across North Asia during the period of Soviet authoritarianism coincided with the expansion of shamanism's discursive field in the Americas. As in Russia's North Asian empire, interpolations of local religiosities across the Americas into a generalised shamanic idiom relied extensively on translating local terms into the European languages in which shamanism was discoursed, notably English, French (*chamanisme*) and Spanish (*chamanismo*) (for early examples, see Eliade 1964: 297–302, 323 n. 101). From this perspective, indigenism's elevation of cosmology and ritual as a fundamental dimension of indigenous identity emerged into a space linguistically and conceptually framed by a European discourse about shamans. Thus anthropologist and witness Theodore MacDonald could tell the court in the Awas Tingni case about 'the *cacique*, also a kind of shaman that they called Ditelian' and the judges of the IACrtHR could rule on the importance of the Xákmok Kásek's 'shamanic rituals' ('*los ritos de chamanismo*') and 'ancestral shamanic knowledge' ('*los saberes ancestrales chamánicos*').[25]

The mutual intelligibility enabled by recourse to shamanism discourse also permitted the court to distinguish between what is and is not acceptable to the current values informing contemporary jurisprudential thought. Hence, we have successive Separate Opinions supplementary to the court's judgment in which several judges elaborate on the 'indigenous cosmovision' with reference

---

[25] The judgments of the IACrtHR are published in Spanish and English. The translations used here are from the court's Spanish judgments.

to 'the intertemporal dimension' they feel is insufficiently regarded in current case law but which they feel contemporary jurisprudential thought demands be addressed. The judges were self-conscious about the weight of legal precedent and the Separate Opinions were partly intended to give further elaboration and substantiation of the reasoning underlying the court's judgment. By elaborating arguments that strengthen the precedent, the judges ensured the precedent's durability, which was surely their aim. By ensuring the durability of the precedent, however, they were also strengthening a powerful structural relay for identifying certain key tropes with shamanism and proliferating and dispersing these to other jurisdictions. Emphases on rationality, precedent and citation in writing laws, delivering authoritative judgments and in developing jurisprudence have added these same qualities to the discursive regularities of shamanism discourse. Among ideas conveyed into contemporary jurisprudence pertaining to indigenous rights and identified with shamanic religiosity are the notions that plants, animals and topographical features of local environments embody spirits or are otherwise inhabited by spiritual agents, including but not limited to human ancestors. Similarly prominent in the jurisprudence of indigenous peoples' rights is the idea popularised by much neo-shamanic literature that the ordinary, material world is only the visible aspect of a larger experiential universe that includes what Michael Harner and others have termed 'non-ordinary reality' (see Chapter 5).

We glimpse here modernity's practical limit attitude and the operations of the double-hinge. Indigenous cosmology as territorial practice is practical within indigenism's political project because it connects the specificities of ontological being ('being indigenous') with the epistemological requirements of modern law. At the epistemological level, indigenous cosmology is represented in discourse in terms of shamanism and relies on universal categories developed in the course of three centuries of shamanism discourse. Yet, in rendering judgment, the court is self-consciously developing jurisprudence in a field of human rights law it feels would benefit from elaboration at the refined limits of what the court judges is just. In this sense, the court interpolates the ontological dimension of being indigenous into the epistemological requirements of law. In doing so, the Inter-American Court of Human Rights offers its unique contribution towards advancing a moral transcendence of political contingencies that is nevertheless in the form of a necessary limitation, or, as Kant might have said, within limits knowledge must renounce exceeding.

Chapter 4
Environmentalism

In Chapter 3, we saw modernity's double-hinge operating in indigenism's instrumentalisation of cosmology to secure a right to self-determination modified as greater autonomy at a substate level and the responsiveness of jurists to this solution. Shamanism was absent from much of that discussion until autonomy became an acceptable solution to the impasse indigenists found themselves at in their negotiations with states. As that solution was pursued in the Awas Tingni case and subsequent cases, the figure of the shaman emerged, apparently without much difficulty, to supply a discursive formulation with which indigenists and jurists could expand the limits of law to accommodate indigenous peoples' land rights via a right to culture. In the present chapter, I want to illustrate a different way in which modernity's double-hinge operates in shamanism discourse, by considering shamanism's imbrications with environmentalism. A qualification is necessary from the outset: environmentalism signifies a wide range of inquiries pertaining to concerns about the Earth's biosphere as human habitat, and human development within the carrying limits of natural environments. These concerns are the general background to my more focused interest in the historical specificity of what I have termed the 'indigenist-environmentalist alliance'.

The specific genesis of this alliance was an alignment of interests during the 1980s between indigenist struggles in the Amazon Basin and revisions of transnational conservation practices. This alignment reframed indigenous cultural survival as an environmental issue and linked biodiversity conservation with cultural conservation. Among the consequences of this framing was the relatively sudden visibility of indigenous peoples in transnational environmental advocacy networks and multilateral forums, a degree of visibility that in turn supplied indigenous symbolic capital to an ecocentric critique of anthropocentric mastery of nature. The basic terms of this critique may be summarised as disavowing a distinction between natural life and human life, and privileging sustainable development over economic development, biological diversity over instrumental human gain and ethical responsibilities towards future generations of life over legal obligations towards the present generation of human life (M.J. Smith 1998). The symbolic economy of indigenous authenticity stimulated by this alignment generated the idea of the 'ecological Indian' whose 'cosmovision' exemplified ecocentric values and whose lifeways embodied ecocentric ethics and sustainable practices. As an idealisation of a non-modern Other who was 'more of nature than in it' (Nadasdy 2005: 292), the ecological Indian bore much resemblance to the 'noble savage'. But whereas the noble savage was denigrated and maligned as a remnant of an outdated romanticism, the prominent contribution of indigenists to representations and portrayals of indigenous ecocentrism gave the ecological Indian considerable credibility and authority. Indigenous symbolic capital underwrote the ecocentric critique of anthropocentrism and in the same movement rehabilitated the noble savage re-identified as the ecological Indian.

These developments over a relatively short period of time inflected shamanism discourse in two important ways. First, representations of indigenous religiosity and culture emerging from the imbrication of indigenist and environmentalist fields of social practice were seen by many proponents of shamanism as validating and giving indigenous authority to an aesthetic critique of modernity in which shamans have historically featured prominently. The basic terms of this (neo-romantic) critique may be summarised as privileging unconstrained experience over subject-centred reason, intuition over scientific method, evocation over representation and perceiving amnesia and loss in place of freedom and emancipation (Tremlett 2008: 68). Within the western academy, shamanism's role in conveying an aesthetic critique of modernity is often associated with religious studies scholars interested in phenomenological approaches to studying religion, among whom Mircea Eliade is usually regarded as the apotheosis of a line that can be traced via Raffaele Pettazzoni, C.J. Bleeker, W. Breda Kristensen, Gerardus van der Leeuw, Rudolf Otto, Louis Jordan and Cornelius P. Tiele. Outside the academy, shamanism's role in conveying this critique is most frequently associated with New Age aspects of the 1960s counter-culture movements, notably Carlos Castaneda and later Michael Harner. Significantly, however, the genealogy of the critique itself goes back to the nineteenth century and the milieu of romanticism and spiritualism in Europe and its colonies,[1] as well as American transcendentalism. Indeed, several proponents of transcendentalist thought, notably Ralph Waldo Emerson and Henry David Thoreau, were key figures in the tendency towards sacralising nature and, along with wilderness preservationist John Muir, are widely regarded as among the most influential antecedents of the twentieth-century green movement. The emergence of an

---

[1]   The Siberian regionalist movement discussed in Chapter 2 is also relevant in this regard.

ecocentric critique vested with indigenous symbolic capital went a long way towards reviving and reinvigorating an aesthetic critique that had begun to appear hackneyed and stale amid the eclecticism of New Age syncretism and bricolage.

Consequently, this is the second point: as ecocentrism cached an aesthetic critique of modernity with indigenous symbolic capital, so did shamanism's styles of representation adjust to reflect these changed circumstances. Prior to the indigenist-environmentalist alliance, much shamanism discourse tended to efface the contingencies and particularities of indigenous shamanic traditions with the regularities of universal structures and patterns. Local practices still featured, but they were usually (poorly) surveyed as equivalent examples of 'traditional', 'primitive', or 'archaic' practices from a bygone era rapidly receding as the modern epoch advanced. Eliade's classic text on shamanism, as well as his frequent allusions to shamanic religiosity elsewhere in his writings, is an obvious example of this tendency, although the tendency itself is better attributed to enthusiasm for the phenomenological method, in scholarly as much as popular discourse. With the emergence of the indigenist-environmentalist alliance and increasing visibility of indigenous shamans, this kind of effacement became untenable. More than that, however, the emergence of an economy of indigenous symbolic capital ensured indigenous shamans became desirable partners in the labours of representing and promoting universal shamanism. The final discussion of this chapter develops these two interrelated inflections of shamanism discourse by considering Michael Harner's theory of 'core shamanism' and the representational strategies of his Foundation for Shamanic Studies. I have chosen this example for two reasons. First, Harner has been one of the most influential promoters of a universal, generic shaman for modern, popular audiences. As Roger Walsh and Charles Grob enthuse in their introduction to Harner's chapter in their book, 'What Yogananda did for Hinduism and D.T. Suzuki did for Zen, Michael Harner has done for shamanism, namely bring the tradition and its richness to Western awareness' (Harner 2005b: 160). Second, Harner's promotion of core shamanism straddles the indigenist-environmentalist alliance and therefore offers comparative material for testing how representations of shamans have changed over the years. The short of it is that while Harner's popular book *The Way of the Shaman*, first published in 1980, is not influenced by indigenism and mentions neither indigenous peoples nor environmental concerns, Harner's Foundation for Shamanic Studies goes to considerable lengths to align core shamanism with the new eco-politics of indigenism.

The focus of this chapter is the historical emergence of a symbolic economy for indigenous authenticity in which the essence of indigenous identity is rendered as ecocentric disposition, represented in sacred, transcendent, or numinous terms and positioned as a vantage from which to articulate a critique of anthropocentric mastery of nature. The chapter comprises three discussions. I begin with a recent example from South Africa of an indigenous community's partnership with a transnational environmentalist NGO to illustrate some of the discursive and practical effects of this symbolic economy and how these have travelled and still endure in a location at some remove from indigenist struggles in Amazonia during the 1980s. This example also introduces the problem of agency and indigenous peoples' tactical choices about self-representation to advance their interests. Whereas transnational NGOs may promote essentialist representations of indigenous peoples' inherent closeness to nature, for indigenous peoples these representations often reflect tactical choices about securing interests within structures of opportunity and constraint generated by the symbolic economy itself. These ideas are the focus of this chapter's second discussion, in which I consider the historical alignment of indigenist and environmentalist interests and trace the emergence of a symbolic economy of indigenous authenticity. Among a range of related consequences, this economy also increasingly identified shamans as exemplars of an ecocentric disposition and counterpoint to modern anthropocentric mastery of nature.[2] The chapter's third and final discussion steps back from environmentalism to consider how representations of shamans as exemplars of ecocentric disposition within an environmentalist domain have impacted shamanism discourse. I consider this question with reference to Michael Harner's theory of 'core shamanism' as an example par excellence of universal shamanism. The curious issue here is why a universal theory would need to adapt its representations to changing proclivities and contingencies. This question leads to the chapter's concluding discussion, where I revisit the analysis developed through these successive discussions from the limit perspective of modernity's double-hinged labour.

---

[2]   The gradual dissolution of the alliance since the late 1990s is not considered here because this development has not diminished or significantly altered representations of indigenous ecocentric disposition in sacred or numinous terms, as the following discussions illustrates. That said, several contemporary observers questioned the extent to which conservationists and indigenists shared common interests and some predicted a future falling out (Redford and Stearman 1993). Certainly there were always tensions. By the new millennium, cooperation between conservation organisations and indigenist associations was deeply compromised (Chapin 2004; Colchester 2003).

Ramunangi Land Claim

The vhaVenda identify themselves as an indigenous people of southern Africa whose ancestral territories are in the Soutpansberg Mountains of South Africa's northern Limpopo province. In 2005, a group of vhaVenda woman, concerned that younger generations were losing their attachments to traditional customs, initiated a project to recover, conserve and promote vhaVenda heritage. According to a timeline summary of subsequent events prepared by the Gaia Foundation in London (hereafter GAIA) and published online, 'Out of this process [the vhaVenda women] identified the degradation of sacred sites and the obligatory practices associated with them as one of the root causes for the disorder in their community' (GAIA 2010). A group of older woman, identified as Makhadzis or 'sacred site guardians', formed an organisation called Dzomo la Mupo through which they coordinated efforts between different local communities. Around 2008, the Makhadzis discovered that planning was at an advanced stage to develop a picnic site beside a waterfall near the town of Phiphidi. The Makhadzis' concern related to two sacred sites at Phiphidi Falls: a rock atop the waterfall called LanwaDzongolo and a site beneath the falls called Guvhukuvho. The Makhadzis were concerned that the development would violate customary laws, prohibitions and obligations regarding the sites. A vhaVenda clan, the Ramunangi, claimed to be traditional custodians of LanwaDzongolo and Guvhukuvhu and took up the cause of protecting Phiphidi Falls.

Clan leader Phanuel Mudau had been engaging local traditional leader Jerry Tshivhase for several years in an effort to have the Ramunangi customary claim to custody of LanwaDzongolo and Guvhukuvhu recognised by traditional authority. According to the Ramunangi's lawyer, discussions had dragged on inconclusively for at least a decade, during which time LanwaDzongolo was destroyed to quarry stones for a new road to a nearby hospital and planning advanced to develop the site at Guvhukuvhu. The Ramunangi were not consulted in either instance, while their concerns grew about the punishment their ancestors would visit upon the vhaVenda people for failing to prevent spoliation of the two sites. When bulldozers moved onto the proposed picnic site in 2010, the Makhadzi organisation Dzomo la Mupo along with several clan members obtained an interim court injunction against further construction. The injunction was extended in 2011 to the local municipality and construction company pending further litigation (Chennels 2012, 2008).

Regarded from the wider perspective of indigenous territoriality, the Ramunangi case illustrates the kind of interpolations of locality into globality and particularities into universality with which we are concerned. A document drafted in 2008 by a lawyer on behalf of Ramunangi claimants provides a striking example. Titled 'The Ramunangi Claim of Rights to the Sacred Sites of Phiphidi Waterfalls' and citing 'Ramunangi Tribal Leaders' as co-authors, the 14-page document was circulated to several government agencies to place on record the Ramunangi's claim and to establish a basis for further advocacy (Chennels 2008). Prepared with support from GAIA, it is among downloadable resources from the websites of GAIA and Earth Island Institute's Sacred Land Film Project.[3] Most of the document focuses narrowly on local details of the Ramunangi's claims at LanwaDzongolo and Guvhukuvhu. Topics include the history of the Ramunangi's presence in the region, their 'customs, traditions and beliefs', sacred sites in their territory, Phanuel Mudau's unsuccessful approaches to traditional authorities, the destruction of LanwaDzongolo and the Makhadzis' concerns that 'the gods would punish them for the lack of respect'. The document contextualises these local details in terms of 'the universality of sacred sites':

> Throughout history, sacred sites have existed in all cultures and all parts of the world. They have always been founded upon a core set of natural features, such as mountains, caves, rock outcrops, springs etc. In all cultures, sacred places are seen as crossing-over points, sited between the mundane and the spirit world: entry points into another consciousness. Not simply seen as just another place in the landscape, sacred sites carry a whole set of rules and regulations regarding people's behaviour, and imply a set of beliefs connected with the non-material world, often in relation to the spirits of the ancestors and a belief in gods or spirits.

Sacred sites, the Ramunangi's lawyer explains, are important nodes in the earth's 'immune system', 'like acupuncture points around the planet'. As 'a concentration of energy in the ecosystem', sacred sites are usually 'manifest as places of high biodiversity or areas which play a vital role in maintaining the health of ecosystems'. Thus, 'Indigenous peoples have developed an acute level of eco-literacy over generations of living in a range of eco-systems', and 'all have special custodians of these sites', who possess the right knowledge and training that enables them to 'interpret the law' governing these sites and the ecosystems that they connect: 'Indigenous peoples from around the world consider sacred sites to be places where the voice of Nature can be heard by those who are literate ... '. By protecting these sacred sites where 'cultural, spiritual

---

3   http://www.gaiafoundation.org/saving-phiphidi-falls and http://www.sacredland. org/media/Ranumangi-Claim-of-Rights_15Nov08.pdf.

and ecological significance' converge, indigenous peoples have maintained 'the health of their ecosystem, which has sustained their livelihoods over millennia'. Yet after millennia of relative health, today the Earth's immune system is weak and vulnerable. Violations of natural law are cumulatively reducing biodiversity, weakening ecosystems and placing the biosphere under the greatest strain. Tampering with sacred sites, argues the Ramunangi's lawyer, ignores the role of sacred sites in maintaining ecosystem resilience and mitigating and adapting to climate change: 'Sacred sites provide the fundamental framework that supports the energetic, biological and hydrological immune systems of the Earth. This is why indigenous peoples insist that these last vestiges of pristine nature must not be violated' (Chennels 2008: 5–7).

In this analysis, sacred sites are indicated by concentrations of life energy in ecosystems. They are places where nature speaks and spirits and ancestors reside; where mundane reality may be transcended and another kind of consciousness attained; where the false consciousness of anthropocentrism is discarded and the interdependent unity of self and natural world is revealed. But not everyone is capable of 'crossing-over'. As custodians of these 'entry points into another consciousness', indigenous peoples' high levels of eco-literacy mark them as exemplars of a relationship with natural ecosystems and Earth's biosphere that is absent among the rest of humanity. In the context of the current ecological crisis, this deficit is increasingly acute, the critique it implies is increasingly apocalyptic and the elevation of indigenous knowledge is increasingly millenarian. In this sense, indigenous peoples – the *idea* of indigenous peoples more so than particular communities of indigenes – are exemplars of an ideal that also conveys a complicated critique of industrialisation and modernity's disenchantment, as well as a lament for what has been lost in the course of becoming modern.

The analysis presented in the Ramunangi's Claim of Rights document draws extensively on a report commissioned by GAIA. Authored by Anthony Thorley and Celia Gunn (Thorley and Gunn 2007), the report argues that environmental degradation has caused permanent damage to Earth's 'life support systems', that the 'root cause' of this damage is humans' orientation toward the world, one marked by domination and exploitation in which humans are agents and the natural world is their domain of control, and that sacred sites 'as foci of spiritual belief and expression' are crucial to reorienting human beings so that catastrophe can be averted. It is notable that Thorley and Gunn specifically have in mind those who inhabit the 'secular western industrialized world' and practice 'western thinking and culture'. Their report uses variations of these and similar phrases interchangeably and repeatedly, including 'western mindset', 'secular culture', 'the industrial world' and 'industrial culture'. The qualification is important because it underpins the distinction Thorley and Gunn want to make between a modern mode of being and a non-modern one they identify with indigenous ontology. In Thorley and Gunn's analysis, this reorientation consists in a paradigm shift from a human-centred 'view of the world' to an Earth-centric 'experience of the world', in which human beings live in harmony with other members of the Earth's community, without domination or exploitation. Transforming an anthropocentric worldview into ecocentric experience is no small task, but anthropocentrists are not without help. The first principle of ecocentrism is that one is never alone, hence the importance of sacred sites where nature's voice is heard. Also, anthropocentricism did not always predominate. Although many humans, perhaps most, are no longer ecocentric, this loss is not irretrievable and neither is it universal; many humans still inhabit an ecocentric world. Hence the importance of indigenous peoples whom the authors portray as living 'harmoniously in their sacred lands' and whose 'spiritual observances' are pivotal to 'maintaining rich biodiversity and cultural coherence' (Thorley and Gunn 2007: 15–16).

On this account, environmental policies and regulatory laws will be effective only if they are premised on ecocentric experience, rather than the anthropocentrism that orients modern law. Some legal scholars and activists have embraced this profoundly challenging task as an ethical imperative stemming from ecocentrism itself. They identify their work as 'Earth jurisprudence' and their branch of law as 'wild law'. A concept pioneered by South African attorney Cormac Cullinan, who in turn was deeply influenced by Arne Næss's notion of deep ecology and the ideas of ecotheologian Thomas Berry (Cullinan 1999; cf. Burdon 2011), in a 'wild' legal system, law governs relations between not just human beings, but all life on Earth. Indeed, as GAIA director and co-founder Liz Hosken explains, law is not made by humans; 'the Earth itself is the source of law and order' and the law exists *a priori* as 'the laws of life' (Hosken 2011: 25–6). Humans are born into 'a lawful and ordered Universe' and must become aware of the laws governing it by reading them from 'the book of Nature'. This is the universal principle of Earth jurisprudence underpinning and exemplified by 'indigenous governance systems', which Hosken defines as 'maintaining a healthy relationship between the human community, the larger Earth community and the spiritual or energetic dimension of life' (ibid.: 29). Sacred sites are at the centre of indigenous governance and shamans play an essential role mediating these communal relations. As 'places of origin', sacred sites are 'the source of the law' and it is the role and responsibility of 'elders and shamans who dialogue with that source and act as interlocutors' to interpret, mediate and apply wild law of these places: 'This is what they believe is the role of the true "wild lawyer"'

(Thorley and Gunn 2007: 145). As practitioners of wild law, indigenous elders and shamans emerge from this account as ecocentric exemplars and pivotal to a critique of modern anthropocentrism. For the same reason, protecting indigenous sacred sites is an important part of GAIA's advocacy for Earth jurisprudence.

The Sacred Sites Network (hereafter SSN) is a project run by GAIA that partners with representatives of indigenous communities 'to strengthen their traditional knowledge, practices and governance systems in order to protect their sacred sites and territories' (GAIA 2012b). London-based GAIA works through partnerships with local organisations in three targeted regions. In the Altai Republic, GAIA has partnered with the Foundation for Sustainable Development of Altai and the Uch Enmek Nature Park, along with international partners Sacred Lands Film Project and Cultural Survival, to protect Karakol Valley and Mount Uch Enmek. Both are regarded as sacred places 'revered by the Altaians ... since ancient times'. In GAIA's view, Karakol Nature Park Uch Enmek, established in 2001 and managed by 'indigenous people who respect the traditional principles and ethno-ecological consciousness of their cultural heritage', is a precedent-setting model of 'ethno-park' development 'where people who choose to live respectfully towards their cultural and natural heritage are able to establish legal recognition to govern their bio-cultural landscapes according to their Earth-centred laws' (GAIA 2012c). In the Colombian Amazon, GAIA works with local partner Gaia Amazonas to protect the Yuisi Rapids on the lower Apaporis River. Reportedly regarded by local indigenes as the place where human beings were created, Colombia's Environment Minister Carlos Costa is quoted as saying, 'This area has a rich cultural tradition that includes a number of shamanistic practices and rituals that provide the humans with the knowledge necessary for living in and protecting this world' (quoted in Gaia Amazonas 2012: 10).

The last of GAIA's SSN focus areas is Phiphidi Falls. In this case, the link between local Makhadzi organisation Dzomo la Mupo and international networks of environmental NGOs, including GAIA, the African Biodiversity Network and Genetic Resources Action International, is the Mupo Foundation. Established by local vhaVenda woman Mphatheleni Makaulule, the foundation 'strengthens local communities in ecological governance by reviving indigenous seed, facilitating and encouraging intergenerational learning, and rebuilding confidence in the value of indigenous knowledge systems', according to the foundation's website at www.mupofoundation.org. GAIA's Liz Hosken serves on the foundation's board. Makaulule explains that *mupo* 'describes the origin of creation, the creation of the whole Universe. When we look at Nature we see *mupo*. When we look at the sky we see *mupo*. *Mupo* means all that is not man-made' (GAIA 2012a). On this account, *mupo* is a vhaVenda version of the ecocentric vision promoted internationally by GAIA and identified with a sacralised vision of James Lovelock's influential Gaia hypothesis, which postulates that all organisms on Earth form with their inorganic surroundings one self-regulating ecosystem.

The SSN project illustrates the transnational advocacy role that GAIA has carved out among the plethora of non-governmental organisations working at intersections between indigenism and environmentalism. It also illustrates the importance of indigenous religiosity as symbolic capital in GAIA's advocacy work and the ways in which GAIA has made symbolic capital out of partnering with indigenous communities and their representatives. For example, in November 2009, GAIA organised a week-long 'eco-cultural mapping' exercise in South Africa with members of the vhaVenda community and indigenous delegates from Colombia and Altai. A short documentary film produced and disseminated online by GAIA and its partners evidenced and validated GAIA's advocacy work by citing benefits to the indigenous communities and delegates with which GAIA works. The eco-cultural mapping exercise was also featured in a toolkit produced by the UN Environment Programme. Presented in the form of a case study, the Ramunangi example was used to illustrate how mapping indigenous culture, including sacred and spiritual aspects, onto landscapes facilitated 'a deeper understanding of how their sacred natural sites are embedded in their territory and cultural identity emerged'. This deeper communal understanding in turn fostered stronger cohesion and confidence 'to assert historical rights and responsibilities as custodians of the sacred natural sites' (UNEP 2013: 42).

The Ramunangi example illustrates how the operations of an economy of indigenous symbolic capital tends to displace the contingencies of the Ramunangi's territorial claim with abstract representations of universal indigenous religiosity. The requirement that indigenous claims such as the Ramunangi's comport with the structural logic of a symbolic economy in which indigenous religiosity is represented as laudable exemplar of ecocentrism means that the contingencies of a particular context are replaced by the economy's universalised abstractions – the purported identity between indigenous peoples and nature, indigenous knowledge and ecological knowledge, cultural diversity conservation and biodiversity conservation, indigenous development and sustainable development, along with the universality of an indigenous cosmovision and religiosity itself. At the same time, however, this replacement of contingency with universality leads to an auxiliary requirement for a re-inscription of contingency, because the specificity of indigeneity qua indigenous is its distinguishing quality and is the kernel of its value as symbolic capital. In other words, universal indigenous religiosity requires difference within what is circumscribed as universal; indigenous religiosity can only be universal if different and distinct peoples on three continents attest to this fact, not just once, but repeatedly. It is in this sense that this symbolic economy participates in the dialectic between the ontological and epistemological arms of modernity's double-hinge. Rather than an endless oscillation, however, the alternation between replacement and re-inscription is better perceived as a new instantiation on each occasion, just as the modern limit attitude labours only at the limits and does not (because it cannot) re-tread old ground. The logic of this symbolic economy is important to the analysis of modern shamanism because it accounts for its hyperreal quality and the sense in which the modern limit attitude trades in simulations of indigenous authenticity to support a posited 'core' to universal shamanic religiosity.

The Indigenist-Environmentalist Alliance

I want to draw out the logic of this symbolic economy by considering its historical emergence from transformations in conservation practices that brought about, among many consequences, an alliance between indigenous peoples and environmentalists. I will argue that the shift from a 'fines and fences' approach to preserving natural environments towards conservation practices that would sustain human development led to the emergence of an economy for reified symbols of indigenous authenticity. Within the structural logic of this symbolic economy, shamans were increasingly identified with possession and safe-keeping of valuable indigenous knowledge, about indigenous conservation practices, the healing properties of plants, indigenous stewardship of nature and ultimately what the modern world needs to do to prevent degradation of natural environments and avert the catastrophic consequences that will follow. The note of millenarian expectation in this characterisation is not hyperbolic. For example, reporting on a 2009 visit to London by well-known Yanomami shaman Davi Kopenawa, Britain's *Guardian* newspaper announced 'Shaman returns to London with warning about future of his people in the Amazon and people all over the planet'. The *Guardian* published their story under a headline announcing, 'When Davi Kopenawa Yanomami leaves home, you know the world is in trouble' (Vidal 2009). Davi Kopenawa returns to our story later. For the moment, I want to suggest that this figure is a bricolage, a variable composition of elements that together render indigeneity as ontological alterity and the measure of a difference between an ecocentric disposition towards nature as habitat and an anthropocentric inclination towards mastery of nature for purposes of prospecting resources and maximising utility.

To an extent, the ascendancy of 'sustainable development' forged a political environment more conducive to advancing indigenous peoples' interests in a way homologous to how the ascendancy of human rights utopianism created a more enabling context for indigenous peoples in the field of international law. However, the situation is more complicated than such an account would indicate. Sustainable development was also, like indigenism, a consequence of the ascendancy of human rights discourse. As it emerged into the field of environmentalism (sustainable development was not only, nor even primarily, a form of conservation practice initially), it was in the form of a critique of the omission from the 'fines and fences' approach of social and economic questions in favour of biological and ecological ones. The shift towards sustainable development as conservation practice could be interpreted as a consequence of human rights utopianism's sensitivity to the ethics of displacing or disrupting communities to establish protected conservation areas and the dilemmas of 'meeting the needs of the present without compromising the ability of future generations to meet their own needs' (WCED 1987: 24). For this reason, I consider indigenism and environmentalism as distinct but imbricated fields, each structured by differential stakes. In the field of indigenism, the stake for indigenous peoples is cultural survival, framed as a positive right to self-determination in relation to lands, territories and resources. In the field of environmentalism, the common stake for various shades of green activists is humanity's survival, framed as an imperative to devise new ways of living within Earth's ecological limits. The interests of both indigenists and environmentalists intersect around issues of control and use of lands, waters and the natural resources these contain. The range of intersections, from agreement to opposition and the variations of common- and cross-purposes between them, delimit the range of imbrication of the fields. This formulation in terms of fields and stakes is perhaps over-determined, and while it owes much to Pierre Bourdieu's theory of practice, it is also difficult to demonstrate empirically by Bourdieu's rigorous standards (for example, Bourdieu 1986, 2001). Nevertheless, this image of imbricated fields provides a useful heuristic framework: forms of capital generated and mobilised by interested practices helps to make sense of an increasingly generic image of shamanic religiosity distilled by the operations of symbolic economies of indigenous authenticity, generated in turn by the structural logic of imbricated fields of practice. This is the element I want to tease out in the following discussion.

For much of the 1970s and 1980s, as concern about the environmental impacts of modernisation policies stimulated considerable debate about what should be done, indigenous peoples and conservationists had little common ground. Conservation debates were dominated by biologists and scientists who argued that human activities were detrimental to conservation objectives, that nature ought to be protected from human interference and that coercive measures were necessary to ensure pristine nature was segregated from polluting and destructive humans. This approach to environmental conservation advocated that lands be delimited and fenced off from human activity and occupation and trespassers fined or prosecuted. It also provided a rationale for evicting indigenous peoples from their ancestral territories in the name of environmental conservation. During the 1980s, however, this 'fines and fences' approach was gradually supplanted by conservation practices oriented towards sustaining human development. The shifting emphasis recognised that simply sealing off tracts of wilderness did not address advancing environmental degradation and ignored ethical questions about the social impacts of displacing populations and restricting their activities. The new approach affirmed that human development and environmental conservation were interlinked. Conservation practices were needed that would sustain human development.

Notable moments in this shift were adoption in 1980 of the *World Conservation Strategy: Living Resource Conservation for Sustainable Development* (IUCN et al. 1980) by the International Union for Conservation of Nature, the World Wildlife Fund (renamed World Wide Fund for Nature in 1986), and the UN Environmental Programme. The *World Conservation Strategy* oriented conservation towards sustainable development and precipitated a new kind of conservation practice, the Integrated Conservation and Development Project. The *World Conservation Strategy* report was followed in 1987 by the report of the World Commission on Environment and Development. Titled *Our Common Future*, the 'Brundtland Report' as it became known (after former Norwegian Prime Minister and commission chairman Gro Harlem Brundtland) established sustainable development as the paradigm of socio-economic development in an age of resource conservation (WCED 1987). The report conveyed the consensus growing throughout the 1980s that conservation practices needed to establish collaborative partnerships with local communities. This was not yet a bottom-up approach, but it did leave more room for people than the purely scientific approaches of biologist conservationists. At the same time, sustainable development was still mainly an aspiration, a hypothesis that lacked data, a model in the early stages of testing. The shift towards conservation practices able to sustain human development therefore stimulated a search for models of sustainable use of natural resources (see Dove 2006, Fischer and Black 1995, McNeely and Pitt 1985, Stevens 1997; cf. Luke 1995).

It was in this context that indigenous peoples began to receive a warmer reception from environmentalists. Conklin and Graham (1995: 697–9) have summarised the benefits for environmentalists and indigenists of their new alliance with reference to the Amazon Basin. For environmentalists, these included opportunities to study and model indigenous practices of sustainable resource use that could feed into the demands of the new conservation and development paradigm, in turn creating an ecological rationale for defending indigenous land rights. Data about indigenous resource management also supplied evidence for an ecological critique of economic development models promoted by multilateral lending agencies. After decades of so-called underdevelopment, indigenous populations in South America and particularly the Amazon Basin were now championed for holding the keys to rational development. Partnering with local indigenous communities also strengthened environmentalists' moral position and allowed environmental organisations to claim they were defending the politically disempowered, not merely protecting flora and fauna. For indigenists, benefits included a new and potentially more compelling frame in which to promote their advocacy of indigenous self-determination. The language of biodiversity conservation and sustainable development enabled indigenists to reframe cultural survival as an environmental issue and simultaneously gained them powerful new allies. International support also offered indigenists channels to communicate their claims independently of statutory or official government channels, enabling indigenous peoples to place their grievances before the international court of public opinion. This offered valuable leverage, as the widely publicised Kayapó and Yanomami examples demonstrate (discussed below). As Conklin and Graham put it (1995: 697), 'Environmentalists discovered the value of indigenous knowledge, and environmental organizations discovered the strategic value of allying with indigenous causes.'

The alignment of indigenist and environmentalist interests was very much a tactical choice. Recalling that practice embodies a conjunction of field and habitus, of interest and disposition, one could argue that shifting from a 'fines and fences' approach towards conservation practices that would sustain human development altered the structured dispositions of indigenous peoples' habitus. Several authors have noted that the apparent convergence of indigenist and environmentalist interests was simply a pragmatic alignment that responded to shifting distributions of capital (in the Bourdeausian sense). While that is true, the shifting distributions of particularly symbolic capital were the most significant factor enabling in a remarkably short time an alliance between indigenists and environmentalists. Under the sign of a (then nascent) 'global ecological imaginary', albeit one 'based mostly on abstract notions about the convergence between native and environmental visions for the future', a vision of 'transcultural eco-solidarity' emerged that placed premium value on indigenous peoples' cultural difference and marked them as 'natural partners' (ibid.: 697). Indigenists recognised that gaining the advantages made available by the sustainable development paradigm required they carefully and tactically negotiate this difference.

As interests aligned in the new Amazonian eco-politics, a range of practical problems arose for indigenists and environmentalists alike over how they might cooperate. One of the biggest challenges was communication. Lacking a common language or familiarity with each other's cultures, misunderstandings were frequent and adumbrated a range of impediments to cooperation that became an ongoing part of managing partnerships. This problem operated in both directions, but the relationship was fundamentally asymmetrical. Environmentalists were advantaged in their partnership with indigenists by their greater familiarity and experience when dealing with transnational advocacy networks, communicating with potential supporters, lobbying decision makers, fundraising and controlling financial resources. Consequently, although environmentalists and development workers professed their willingness to listen to indigenous peoples to ensure indigenous needs were being met, indigenous communities and their representatives still carried the burden of adapting the style and form of their communication to the expectations of their new partners. As the indigenist-environmentalist alliance unfolded during the 1990s, an increasingly salient question for indigenists was: how should an Indian speak?

Framing this question with reference to Amazonian Indians, anthropologist Laura Graham researched linguistic practices employed by indigenous peoples to perform or instantiate their identity and legitimate their 'otherness'. She illustrates the issue with three emblematic examples (Graham 2002). The first is a 1991 case where a delegation of Waiãpi representatives were effectively muted when their translator was barred from participating in a meeting with representatives of Brazil's government. Graham notes that relying on an indigenous language to communicate effectively may be a serious liability when potential for political gain is solely conditional on communicating propositional content (ibid.: 192). On the other hand, this liability can be ameliorated in situations 'where the indexical, or pragmatic, properties of an indigenous language are valued'. Although this economy of value could be shut out of the closed-door meeting between the Waiãpi delegation and government representatives, the situation is different in more public forums where the cultural capital of indigenous alterity is constrained only by the structural logic of the field in which it holds currency. In such situations, indigenous cultural capital can offer political advantage. Graham's example is a public meeting in 1987 in the Brazilian city of Goiânia addressed by the Xavante leader Warodi. The first meeting between indigenous peoples, traditional rubber tappers and landless forest occupiers, the 100-strong audience included local activists, intellectuals, university students, professors and journalists. Among other outcomes, the Goiânia meeting resulted in the formation of the Forest Peoples Alliance, which subsequently became an important political force in the late 1980s and early 1990s. Warodi wore traditional Xavante attire and spoke in the Xavante's language. As he spoke, a 'palpable hush' fell over the auditorium, Graham reports: 'Although the referential content of Warodi's message was opaque, the aesthetic value of the aesthetic performance was unmistakable' (ibid.: 196). However, there is a disadvantage: resorting to translators means indigenous representatives lose control over the semantic-referential content of their message.

Translators bear a heavy responsibility for how they re-present the message they are translating. Warodi's speech was translated by Paulo, one of a handful of Xavante men sent as children to grow up in cities, learn Portuguese and acquire the cultural knowledge of Brazilian society so that they could later assist the Xavante in their negotiations with the Brazilian state (ibid.: 192–3, 196). In his translation, Paulo faithfully repeated Warodi's criticisms of government administrators and the effects of ranching, but omitted Warodi's several references to two Xavante mythological creators, The One Who Pierced His Foot and The One Who Created The Sea. As Graham explains, for Paulo these references were not germane to Warodi's principal topic and would have distracted from Warodi's point with a lengthy and disruptive explanation. Yet from a symbolic perspective, Paulo's omission denuded Warodi's discourse of symbolic weight and in the end the only noteworthy aspect of Warodi's speech was his performance. As Graham puts it, 'Part of the performance's symbolic value is literally lost in translation' (ibid.: 198).

This brings us to intercultural mediators and Graham's third example. Mastery of a dominant language means much greater control for indigenous speakers over the referential content of their message. But the trade-off for bilingual culture brokers is that demonstrating such mastery can diminish their authenticity and therewith their legitimacy as speakers for or on behalf of indigenous peoples. Challenged to underwrite the authority of their speech, speakers may insert culturally specific content, for example, by using indigenous words to refer to particular places, plants, spirits, myths, and so on. Indigenous speakers may also employ symbols of indigenous alterity to signify their authentic indigenous identity: body paint, headdresses and body ornamentation have all featured prominently in indigenist struggles in the Amazon Basin. These representational strategies have been pursued to considerable effect by several well-known indigenous representatives and have brought them national, regional and sometimes international fame (for notable examples, see Conklin and Graham 1995: 704). In this circumstance, bilingual indigenous speakers become intercultural mediators as they negotiate symbolic economies of indigenous authenticity. The three kinds of representation Graham outlines are usually combined in practice. She insists, however, that their hybrid forms cannot been regarded as 'culture loss' or lacking authenticity, concepts that reference Eurocentric nostalgia. Rather, linguistic hybridity and borrowings should be recognised for productive incorporation of new concepts ('biodiversity', 'biosphere', 'environment') and creative blending to advance indigenist interests, foremost of which are indigenous capacities to meaningfully engage the global world of which they are now a part. The downside for these cultural brokers is that fraternising with governments and NGO representatives for long periods away from the communities on whose behalf they claim authority to speak fosters alienation and frequently generates suspicions at home. Furthermore, as culture brokers' symbolic capital (authenticity, authority, legitimacy, reputation, and so on) becomes increasingly dependent on the operations of the symbolic economy of indigenous authenticity, they become increasingly vulnerable to the estimations of NGOs and funding agencies about the extent of their authenticity. Should they fail to meet expectations about how 'real' Indians speak, comport themselves and convey their concerns, they can find themselves caught by 'the essentialist boomerang' (Ramos 2003: 373–5) and swiftly stripped of their status and standing in transnational NGO support networks (Brown 1993: 317–18, Conklin and Graham 1995: 704).

Alcida Ramos has approached this problem from the opposite perspective. Whereas Graham draws attention to the communicative strategies and representational practices of Amazonian Indians, Ramos is interested in the administrative demands for rationality and efficiency in organisations seeking to support indigenous communities. Ramos begins by recounting a frequent complaint: that the professionalisation of support groups has led to the routinisation and bureaucratisation of NGOs at the expense of organisational objectives. As organisations' goals are gradually accommodated to the system of rules and regularities developed to increase administrative efficiency, the balance of resource allocation between administration and services becomes skewed and the relationship between means and ends becomes confused. This is a familiar process and relatively unremarkable of NGOs generally, at least for those of us experienced with organisational bureaucracy. For indigenous communities, however, the logic of the bureau is alien and gross misunderstandings are common. With this disjuncture in mind, Ramos poses the following questions:

> What is to be done about the Indians' otherness that is so resistant to domestication by the bureau's logic? How is it possible to control that otherness and render it compatible with the 'impersonal and functional goals' of bureaucratic organization? How can anyone overcome the disjunction between the organizational impetus of the NGOs and the need to act in the interstices of indigenes and non-indigenous polities? The Weberian vocation of the office seems especially inappropriate for dealing with the interethnic question for the simple reason that the Weberian 'rationality' it cherishes is at odds with both the ethos of most indigenous cultures and the 'irrationality' of most relationships involving Indians and non-Indians. How to rationally administer irrationality is the ultimate challenge for indigenist NGOs. (Ramos 1998: 274)

Ramos argues that NGOs working with indigenous communities solve this dilemma by creating a 'bureaucratizable Indian', a model Indian with which they can work to achieve the organisation's objectives. However, as professionalised NGOs begin working more and more with the model Indian and less and less with 'real flesh-and-blood' Indians, the organisation's objective (supporting Indians) is substituted with the means of doing so (the model Indian). Composed of signs of authentic 'Indianness', the model Indian is akin to a Baudrillardian simulacrum, a simulation of indigenous authenticity, a hyperreal Indian. Recall Baudrillard's observations on the simulacrum:

> It is no longer a question of imitation, nor duplication, nor even parody. It is a question of substituting the signs of the real for the real, that is to say of an operation of deterring every real process via its operational double, a programmatic, metastable, perfectly descriptive machine that offers all the signs of the real and short-circuits all its vicissitudes. Never again will the real have the chance to produce itself ... . (Baudrillard 1994: 2)

As 'the fabrication of the perfect Indian whose virtues, sufferings, and untiring stoicism have won him the right to be defended by the professionals of human rights' (Ramos 1998: 275–6), this hyperreal Indian is 'an ethical hologram' distinguished from 'real flesh-and-blood Indians' whose problems, demands and choices contradict and exceed the organisation's interests in defending Indians' rights. Real Indians enter into commercial arrangements with loggers and mining companies; they relinquish claim to some of their lands in exchange for title to the remainder; they request tractors, electric generators and equipment to modernise their agriculture; they splinter into competing factions and generally pursue their interests as they conceive them within the contingencies of their circumstances (ibid.: 267–70; cf. Graham 2002: 198–200). In contrast, the simulation of real Indians moulds Indians' interests to organisations' shape and needs, not least for funding. Crucially, this 'epidemic of value' (Baudrillard's phrase) is structurally unavoidable. As the model that justifies the NGO's purpose, 'the figure of the hyperreal Indian is bound to spread ... in a mounting process of conformity and uniformity until indigenous grievances and NGO responses become virtually undifferentiated' (Ramos 1998: 278–9; cf. 2003).

Between NGOs' simulations and 'flesh-and-blood' Indians' self-representations is a complex circulation of images mediating between what NGOs want to support and what Indians want to obtain. Admittedly, Ramos's somewhat abstract analysis fails to acknowledge the considerable diversity within 'the third sector', the relative newness of this phrase perhaps testimony to the rapid expansion of this segment that is neither of the market nor the state (cf. Fisher 1997). None the less, I think Ramos's analysis usefully conveys in general terms the operations and implications of a symbolic economy of indigenous authenticity that arose amid an alignment of interests between indigenists and environmentalists. Moreover, her analysis has much in common with related discussions of the operations and implications of this economy in the Latin American context (Becket 1996, Brown 1998, Jackson and Warren 1995, Varese 1996) and several ethnographic studies exploring indigenous peoples' practices in relation to economies of 'Indianness' in Latin America (Canessa 2007, Fisher 1994, Gow and Rappaport 2002, Lucero 2006, Santos-Granero 2009, Veber 1996, 1992). As transnational indigenism has become more prominent in parts of Asia, a similar critique of political instrumentalisations of indigenous authenticity by NGOs and indigenous peoples alike has emerged there too, for example, with reference to China, Indonesia and Thailand (see Hathaway 2010, Li 2000, Santasombat 2004, Walker 2001).[4] As a spokesperson for the Rainforest Foundation explained to political scientist Alison Brysk: 'The rainforest card is stronger than the indigenous card. They [indigenous people] know that, and we [NGOs] know that – and without that, indigenous peoples wouldn't have a chance in hell.' Less blunt is the assessment of a representative

---

[4] See contributions to the special issue of *Identities* (1999) on 'Environmentalism, Indigenous Rights, and Transnational Cultural Critique'.

of Cultural Survival, a prominent indigenous rights advocacy NGO, who told Brysk, 'We see ourselves as a human rights organization in the broadest sense, and that was certainly our first track of contact with indigenous rights. But we've moved into ecology ... clearly, it works better' (Brysk 1994: 36).[5]

At stake in Graham's and Ramos's respective analyses is the structural logic of a symbolic economy for indigenous authenticity. If indigenous peoples want to be heard by audiences they recognise have some influence in addressing their needs, they are required to present their problems and concerns in ways that conform to their audiences' expectations of how authentic indigenous peoples ought to speak, dress and behave. Precisely what these expectations are depends on the audience, but within the general economy of the indigenist-environmentalist alliance, elements include a 'natural' or 'innate' disposition towards living in balanced harmony with natural environments, consuming only as much as they need, and not exceeding nature's capacity to replenish. As we saw earlier with the Ramunangi example, this disposition is typically identified with an indigenous world-view or cosmovision in which ecological conservation and sustainable living are regarded as spiritual principles, conveyed in myth and vested with sacred value, with attendant rites and obligations. The difficulty with this structure of expectation and requirement is that it establishes its own principle of authority and legitimacy and becomes inescapable. Thus, every instance of indigenous self-representation becomes, for non-indigenous audiences at least and arguably for indigenous ones too, the measure of authenticity for subsequent representations. Far from a neat, sequential, or linear process implied by the simplest version of this formulation, it is more accurate to conceive this process as a cascade of imitations and modified improvisations. Lacking an original referent of authentic indigeneity but still deeply reliant on a notion of indigenous authenticity, one is left with a Baudrillardian simulacrum, a hyperreal simulation, no less real, affective, or consequential, but impossible for any one indigene to embody without qualification or mitigation of their shortcoming, even if that shortcoming is framed as cultural loss attributable to territorial conquest, environmental degradation and encroachments of modernity. Thus the indigenist-environmentalist alliance gives rise to a symbolic politics of indigenous authenticity in which indigenous peoples' ecological and

---

   5   Brysk's distinction between three different kinds of 'networks' within 'the northern green community' graded by the extent to which they affirm or reject indigenous priorities in advocating green policies adds a measure of differentiation to Ramos's homogenous NGO managerialism. Brysk differentiates between indigenist environmentalist, conditional indigenist, and conservationist NGOs.

spiritual proximity to nature is both a kind of identity and a site of difference, a laudable fact and an aspirational desire and a means to an end.

Writing in the mid-1990s, Conklin and Graham researched the (then) new eco-politics shaping local struggles in the Amazon Basin. Drawing on Bourdieu, they argued these were primarily 'symbolic politics' in which ideas and images more than common identity or economic interests mobilised political actions that drew together actors across wide gulfs of distance, language and culture. As Amazonian conflicts were linked into growing anxieties in the global North about unsustainable futures, indigenous peoples became key symbols in a wider effort to rethink modern societies' relationships with natural environments and devise appropriate legislative and policy reforms to put the planet on a sustainable path. Conklin and Graham noted that positive ideas about Indians and their relations to nature became a potent symbolic resource in transnational politics (Conklin and Graham 1995: 696).

In fact, from the earliest days of indigenism, indigenists sought to instrumentalise positive ideas about indigenous peoples' relations with nature to underwrite their claims to self-determination. Framed in terms of indigenous guardianship or stewardship of nature, these ideas and images were usually conveyed in the form of a critique of 'Western civilisation'. An early example is a presentation by representatives of the Hau De No Sau Nee to the UN NGO conference in Geneva in 1977, who informed the conference that 'The technologies and social systems which have destroyed plant and animal life are also destroying the Native People. And that process is Western Civilisation' (anonymous, in *Akwesasne Notes* 1991: 77). In similar vein, in 1979, the WCIP's George Manuel told an international conference in Mexico, 'Not until the emergence of the nation or the political state was the harmony between human beings and the environment upset':

> This world exists as a balance between natural and supernatural forces. Both forces make up the real environment that one must accept ... The balance between the natural and the supernatural was and continues to be violently disrupted by those who would seek short-term benefits by extracting natural resources at rates, and in amounts, greater than can be naturally replaced. (WCIP 1979)

Whereas nation states are motivated by 'growth, consumption and the idea of progress', Manuel insisted that indigenous peoples believe human beings are 'thinking, acting and growing individuals with souls and spirits' and extend 'this belief ... to animals and plants that fill our environment':

> Because indigenous peoples live in close proximity to the natural world and the
> supernatural world, a relative balance is maintained through limited growth and
> moderate consumption ... Indigenous peoples have, by virtue of their way of life,
> protected and preserved lands, water, plants and animals that represent the last
> major undeveloped resources in the world. (Ibid.)

These ideas were developed by the National Aboriginal Conference in a position
paper drafted ahead of the WCIP's General Assembly meeting in Canberra,
Australia, in 1981 and underpinned the Conference's presentation to the
International NGO Conference on Indigenous Peoples and the Land held that
year in Geneva, Switzerland (C. Jacobs 1981; WCIP 1981).

Claims about indigenous peoples' closeness to nature operate on two
levels. First, they distinguished 'indigenous peoples' at an ontological level
by emphasising indigenous peoples' otherness from modern subjectivities
in terms of their rejection of a distinction between natural and supernatural
worlds. Conveyed in the mode of a critique, indigenists have portrayed this
modern distinction as posing a growing threat to the long-term future of
humankind. Second, indigenous peoples' closeness to nature have underwritten
indigenous peoples' claim to special legal protections and privileges. So, at the
Mexico conference, which was about fisheries resources, Manuel concluded
his presentation by emphasising that 'Where tribal people or other indigenous
peoples can be defined as the principle guardians over a resource like fish, they
must be recognized as the permanent authorities over the use and management
of the resource'. As we saw in Chapter 3, ontological alterity is put forward as
the basis for legal right. During the 1970s, indigenous ontological alterity held
limited symbolic currency beyond certain networks of New Age enthusiasts
(of whom indigenists were highly critical: Churchill 2003, V. Deloria 1973)
and counted for little where it mattered most, in the field of international
human rights law. However, the shift towards sustainability in transnational
environmentalism and development – for which resource-rich rural regions
of underdeveloped countries were a key focus – foreshadowed a considerable
increase in the symbolic capital of indigenous ontological alterity.

If indigenous symbolic capital was a traded stock, it spiked sharply in 1989. In
that year, the Kayapó people in Brazil's Pará province persuaded the World Bank
to withdraw funding from the Brazilian government's Belo Monte hydroelectric
dam project. The Kayapó delivered this blow to encroachment on their
territories not by lobbying the World Bank directly (although see Ramos 1998:
216), but by producing a protest spectacle at a meeting with representatives of
Eletronorte, the company behind the project. The confrontation at the town of

Altamira produced headlines around the world. The Kayapó had secured their international audience the previous year when two of their leaders undertook a speaking tour of Europe and North America to draw attention to both the development and the meeting at Altamira. Partly arranged by Friends of the Earth and Survival International (environmentalist and indigenist NGOs respectively), the appearance of these exotic Amazonian Indians at news conferences in the UK, Holland, Italy, Germany, Belgium, Canada and the United States drew considerable attention and attracted celebrity support, notably from British rock star Sting and Anita Roddick, founder of cosmetics company The Body Shop. Sting invited Kayapó chief Ropni to join him on his concert tour, while Roddick subsequently used images of Kayapó in traditional dress in her company's Trade Not Aid advertising campaign. The contingent of foreign media who trekked to Altamira witnessed a mixture of popular protest and political rally, while dramatic images of hundreds of Kayapó men and woman adorned with traditional headdresses, face paint, body ornaments and brandishing machetes and clubs at Eletronorte representatives made headlines around the world (Moore 1994; Ramos 2003, 1998; T. Turner 1995, 1991).

The Kayapó halted the hydroelectric project with a combination of 'their keen instrumentalization of cultural primordialities, their shrewd political sagacity, and their tremendous organizing drive' (Ramos 2003: 363).[6] Yet media coverage missed much of the point, which was the Kayapó's demand for an end to decisions about Amazonia's development without their participation in decision making (Ramos 1998: 217). Rather than greater agency in decision-making processes that affected Kayapó society, arguably the most significant outcome of the protest rally at Altamira was that it firmly established the link between threats facing indigenous cultures and threats facing natural environments. Indeed, later that same year the Coordinating Body of Indigenous Organisations of the Amazon Basin called on 'the community of concerned environmentalists' and 'international funders of Amazonian development' to 'consider allying yourselves with us, the Indigenous Peoples of the Amazon, in defense of our Amazonian homeland' (COICA 1989). In May 1990, representatives of 14 indigenous organisations and 24 international environmental organisations signed the Declaration of Iquitos, a formal 'Indigenous and Environmentalist Alliance for an Amazon for Humanity' (COICA 1990a, 1990b; cf. Mato 1997). COICA subsequently formed the Alliance for the Environment, a

---

[6] This proved only temporary. Two decades later, Brazil is less dependent on foreign financing and less susceptible to international pressure. In June 2011, Brazil's environmental regulatory agency approved the project, prompting a new campaign against the development.

network of sister-city partnerships linking over 400 European municipalities with the new eco-politics of local struggles in Amazonia (Brysk 2000: 98). The Altamira meeting did not inaugurate the framing of cultural survival in terms of environmental conservation, but the vivid depiction of this frame dramatically increased the symbolic capital of indigeneity.

Another example of local politics mediating transnational anxieties about ecological destruction in Amazonia is the case of the Yanomami people of Brazil's northern border region with Venezuela. The plight of the Yanomami first came to the attention of concerned publics beyond Brazil in 1989 when a Yanomami shaman and community leader, Davi Kopenawa, travelled to Sweden to receive the Right Livelihood Award on behalf of Survival International.[7] In the mid-1980s, Yanomami lands were overrun by an army of *garimpeiros* (small-scale gold prospectors), who brought with them epidemics of measles and other diseases, slashed and burned the forests and murdered local Yanomamis. Survival International estimated that by the late 1980s 40,000 *garimpeiros* had overrun Yanomami territory and 20 per cent of the Yanomami had died of respiratory infections, malnutrition and malaria introduced by the miners (Survival International 2012). As with the Kayapó, the Yanomami case generated international headlines and Davi Kopenawa, much like Kayapó leaders Payakan and Chief Ropni, became both a cultural broker mediating the plight of his people for far-away audiences and an emblem of the link between cultural survival and ecological conservation. International attention to the Yanomami's plight prompted much debate within Brazilian society about what should be done. One outcome was that Brazil's government proclaimed a series of protected areas reserved for Yanomami use and habitation. However, a different range of outcomes deeply inflected how the challenges facing Amazonian indigenous populations were represented in public debate, both at the level of Brazilian national politics and at the level of transnational environmentalism (Conklin 2002). Amazonian Indians became, for northern audiences particularly, emblems of an emerging 'global ecological imaginary'. Dislocated from the contingencies of cultural production and consumption, however, this imaginary trades in increasingly reified and abstract images and tropes of indigenism, while the range of application of ideas signified and re-signified by these representations is increasingly universalised and absolute. As Ramos has put it with reference to Brazil, 'Brightly colored feathers and esoteric shamanic séances are some of the most fitting items for this purpose both for

---

7   Known as the alternative Nobel Prize, the annual Right Livelihood Award is awarded in Stockholm in the days before the Nobel Prize winners are announced.

their visual appeal and for the reassuring confidence that, thanks to protective ethnographic ignorance, social distance is comfortably preserved' (Ramos 2003: 378; cf. Conklin 1997).

One of the key tropes of this ecological imaginary was that indigenous peoples possess arcane knowledge that would unlock the solution to sustainable development. In the early 1990s, the notion that indigenous peoples live in close harmony with nature fitted neatly with the new demand for examples of sustainable development that could be modeled and replicated. From this vantage, 'tradition' was seen in a new light. Data about how indigenous communities mitigated against drought, fires and floods; cultivated crops and stored surpluses; mediated and resolved conflicts; protected against or healed affliction and a host of similar inquiries related to the reproduction of indigenous life, became a focus of interest for ecologists and development practitioners, along with NGOs, funding agencies and other institutional actors. The operations and dilemmas of this economy of essentialised representations of indigeneity – by which I mean framing strategies, juxtapositions, associations, occlusions and handling of contradictions – have been important in validating and giving authority to 'indigenous knowledge' framed in terms of biodiversity conservation and sustainable development. For example, Conklin has demonstrated how reframing indigenous peoples' public image from combative 'warriors' to 'stewards of the forest' shifted the locus of indigenous identity from historical occupation and subsequent dispossession of lands and territories to possession of local knowledge about environmental resources, plant and animal species and biodiversity. This reformulation generated increasingly generic representations of shamans as keepers of valuable local knowledge and placed medicinal and ritual plant use at the centre of shamanic practice and expertise (Conklin 2002: 1056–7; cf. Langdon 2006). The campaign to protect the Yanomami and particularly the role of Yanomami shaman Davi Kopenawa was an important factor in cementing the association between the need to conserve arcane 'indigenous knowledge' and the specialist role of shamans in indigenous societies. Indigenous knowledge and particularly shamans' knowledge became synonymous with an ecological critique of disenchanted modernity, in much the same terms as had been articulated since the 1970s by indigenists like Vine Deloria and George Manuel. Indeed, indigenists adapted notions of indigenous guardianship or stewardship of nature to the discursive regularities of 'indigenous knowledge' in the service of biodiversity conservation and sustainable development (Dove 2006, Escobar 1998, Muehlebach 2001). Largely detached from local contingencies and complexities, reified notions of indigenous knowledge and cosmology mobilised symbolic capital cached in essentialised images and tropes of indigenous peoples' proximity to nature. So, for example, when Davi Kopenawa addressed the UN General Assembly at the launch of the International Year of Indigenous Peoples on Human Rights Day in 1992, the affect of his speech relied less on the referential content of Yanomami cosmology and more on the symbolic capital of indigenous ontological alterity, by aligning notions of nature and knowledge with shamans to convey a critique of industrial development couched in apocalyptic anxiety. Davi Kopenawa told the General Assembly he brought to the UN a message from *Omam*

> ... the creator of the Yanomami and the creator of the *shaboris*, who are our shamans. The *shaboris* have all the knowledge, and they have sent us to deliver their message to the United Nations: stop the destruction, stop taking minerals from under the ground, and stop building roads through forests. Our word is to protect nature, the wind, the mountains, the forest, the animals, and this is what we want to teach you. The leaders of the rich, industrialized world think that they are the owners of the world. But the *shaboris* are the ones that have true knowledge. They are the real First World. And if their knowledge is destroyed, then the white people too will die. It will be the end of the world. This is what we want to avoid. (Davi Kopenawa Yanomami, in Ewen 1994: 110–11)

The notion that indigenous peoples possess arcane knowledge that holds the key to ecological conservation and sustainable development has hardly been without controversy or criticism. Several scholars have argued that the notion of 'indigenous knowledge' as distinct from and independent of western science or modern epistemology does not stand up to scrutiny (for example, Nygren 1999; see also Dove 2006, Escobar 1998). Furthermore, the notion of a profound distinction between local science and global science is hardly neutral and 'may privilege political, bureaucratic authorities with a vested interest in the distinction (whether its maintenance or collapse)' (Dove 2006: 196; although see De la Cadena 2010, Povinelli 2001). Moreover, recalling the saliency of notions of the 'noble savage' in North American history (Harkin and Lewis 2007, R. Jacobs 1980, Krech 1999, Vecsey 1980), several observers have argued that celebrations of indigenous peoples and indigenous knowledge as a solution to the environmental challenges facing the world updates the romantic trope of the noble savage with that of the ecological Indian. Distinguished from modern man by a laudably primitive but harmonious relation with the environment – 'more of nature than in it' (Nadasdy 2005: 292) – the ecological Indian has been hugely controversial, not least for indigenous peoples who have taken aim at many environmentalists' romantic idealisations (Hames 2007, Redford

1991). However, the controversy is complicated by indigenists' advocacy of environmental stewardship which relies on similarly essentialist notions that indigenous peoples are best suited to managing environmental resources because, being indigenous, they have a close bond with the natural environment (for example, see *Akwesasne Notes* 1991, Eaglewoman 2009, Martinez 1998), despite indications that essentialising strategies risk undermining indigenous claims for a greater share of natural resources and development assistance (Walker 2001). In fact, the symbolic politics of the indigenist-environmentalist alliance have imputed a range of ecocentric ideas to indigenous religiosity, indigenous cosmovisions and indigenous ritual specialists and instrumentalised these to distinguish indigenous peoples as exemplars of an ecocentric orientation towards the world we all inhabit. In this way, the noble savage was modified and revived as the ecological Indian, weighted with the moral authority and political capital of indigenism and amplified by alarm at ecological destruction on a planetary scale. Now rendered as the ecological Indian, representations of indigeneity in an ecological imaginary arguably instrumentalise primitivism in an ecological register to lament what has been lost in the course of becoming modern. The Gaia Foundation's report on Sacred Sites discussed earlier is a good example. Chris Tennent (1994: 7) has noted the double role of this figure, 'representing not only what has been left behind in the progress of modernity, but also providing a site for millenarian aspirations for a transformation and redemption of modernity, through a "return to the primitive"'.

As such, the indigenist-environmentalist alliance forms part of a much longer tradition of critiquing anthropocentrism with representations of indigenous cultures and cosmologies. Traces of this critique can be discerned in the European romantic tradition, notably in the work of Edmund Burke and Jean Jacques Rousseau, along with nineteenth-century American transcendentalists such as Ralph Waldo Emerson and Henry David Thoreau. The latter, along with John Burroughs, an exemplar of 'the Arcadian impulse in American culture' (B. Taylor 2009: 59) and American wilderness preservationist John Muir, are often regarded as among the most influential antecedents of the twentieth-century green movement (Albanese 2007, 1990; B. Taylor 2009; although also see Grove 1995, Guha 2000). Within the green movement, the critique of anthropocentrism has been most closely associated with Norwegian ecologist Arne Næss's advocacy of 'deep ecology', a term Næss first proposed in 1973 (Næss 1973) and scientist James Lovelock's Gaia Hypothesis, an idea Lovelock first conceived in the early 1960s while researching methods of detecting life on Mars and later popularised in an accessible non-specialist book *Gaia, a New Look at Life on Earth* (Lovelock 1979). From early on, the critique of anthropocentrism operated spiritual, mystical and transcendent tropes, and although not all contemporary deep ecologists conceive of nature in transcendent terms, a significant proportion do conceive of nature as numinous in one way or another (B. Taylor 2009; also see Chapter 6).

The problematic I want to draw out is how a symbolic economy for indigenous authenticity and politics of representation generated by the indigenist-environmentalist alliance linked a range of ideas about indigenous identity and religiosity with nature and ecology. As Indians and environmentalists learned 'how to speak' and 'play the game' of the new transnational environmental advocacy, tactical choices about contextual specificity were combined with reified notions of 'indigenous knowledge', 'biodiversity conservation' and 'sustainable development' in a generic discourse about indigenous peoples' closeness to nature. These kinds of representations and references were mobilised by indigenists and environmentalists alike to signify a subject position that, in relation to the current ecological challenges facing the modern world, indicated a site from which economic development could be critiqued, modernity lamented, and indigeneity lauded in a millenarian anticipation about indigenous peoples' important role in saving the world from itself.[8] At the same time that these reified and abstract elements construed a useful distinction between modern and indigenous ontology represented as difference between anthropocentric and ecocentric epistemologies, the free-flowing recombinations of these elements and their intense mediation among transnational audiences eroded contextual contingency within the realm of indigeneity and opened the way to hyperreality.[9] Differentiation between specific communities of indigenes, their distinct histories, cultures and traditions gave way to simulations of indigenous identity in which shamans, their cosmologies, ritual practices and indigenous ('shamanic') knowledge featured prominently. The way in which the Ramunangi's concerns about spoliation of LanwaDzongolo and Guvhukuvhu became transnational emblems of 'wild law', Earth jurisprudence, ecocentric disposition and ontological alterity also illustrate this point. Among the consequences of the indigenist-environmentalist alliance was that it distilled an increasingly generic image of shamans as keepers of valuable local knowledge and placed indigenous healing techniques at the centre of shamanic practice and expertise. Significantly, however, this image also de-emphasised older

---

8   Typical of this genre is David Maybury-Lewis's *Millennium: Tribal Wisdom and the Modern World*, based on a 1992 television series of the same name.

9   Documentary film and television, print and broadcast media, public awareness and fundraising campaigns, lobbying efforts and the like have all been prominent strategies of the indigenist-environmentalist alliance since the late 1990s.

representations of shamans as implicated with conflict, killing and death and was supplemented by the notion that shamans, among all indigenous peoples, are the most knowledgeable about how human beings can live sustainably as part of, rather than masters over, the natural world. Rendered in these generic terms, the term 'shaman' became even more easily translatable and local names for traditional healers around the world became (and continue to be) translated as so many local equivalents of a transnational generic 'shaman' category. The discussion in Chapter 2 on shamanism's 'emigration' to North America illustrated early examples of this kind of assimilation by translation. A similar discussion in Chapter 5 illustrates how this process is also assimilating local southern African indigenous religiosities to a generic shamanic idiom.

Rendering shamans as exemplars of indigenous ontology framed in terms of an ecocentric disposition retains the notion of shamans as mediator between worlds. However, the distinction between worlds is now represented as between an ordinary world oriented by anthropocentric mastery of nature and an ordinarily hidden world in which humans are only one part of an ecological system that ultimately comprises all natural things. This distinction, in which the latter enables a critical perspective of the former, is mirrored in a distinction between 'Western' 'scientific' knowledge and 'indigenous knowledge'. The shaman is valued for their possession of indigenous knowledge that they draw on in their role as healer, which is now represented as their primary social function. Practising shamanic techniques accesses this nonordinary world and if performed correctly the hidden world reveals itself to the shaman possessed of the right knowledge and technique. Through a combination of bodily and spiritual techniques, the shaman intervenes in this ordinarily hidden world to affect the desired healing outcome. Noteworthy is the occlusion of negative images of shamans. By singling out benevolent indigenous knowledge and healing as the core of shamanic practice and expertise, the indigenist-environmentalist contributed towards distilling a generic image of shamanic religiosity that downplayed older images of shamans as implicated in conflict and violence. This generic image has increasingly become the global template of the traditional-healer-as-shaman tapped by spiritual entrepreneurs and increasingly subject to state regulation, both topics I address in Chapter 5.

In the last discussion of this chapter, I want to look at this shaman more closely. On the one hand, this shaman appears to have shrugged off resemblances to specificity and contingency to the extent that all that remains are simulations of shamans as the image of ontological alterity, a last resemblance on the threshold of hyperreality. On the other hand, however, the simulacrum of universal shamanic religiosity relies on symbolic capital cached in the specificities of indigenous identities to vouchsafe its universal claims. To demonstrate this point, I want to consider how Michael Harner's theory of 'core shamanism' has adapted its representation of shamans in the wake of the indigenist-environmentalist alliance.

Core Shamanism

Michael Harner is a former professor and chairman of the Graduate Faculty Department of Anthropology at the New School of Social Research and has taught at the University of California at Berkeley, Columbia University and Yale. In the course of his academic career, he published two anthropological books (Harner 1972, 1973) and several journal articles based on his fieldwork among indigenous communities in Amazonia during the 1950s and 1960s (Grimaldi 1997). This fieldwork stimulated Harner's interest in what he would later term the 'shamanic state of consciousness' and is a frequent reference in his theory of core shamanism.

Harner defines core shamanism as 'the universal, near-universal, or common principles and practices of shamanism not bound to any specific cultural group or perspective ...' (FSS 2012d), as outlined in his book *The Way of the Shaman*.[10] For Harner, a shaman is 'a man or woman who enters an altered state of consciousness – at will – to contact and utilise an ordinarily hidden reality in order to acquire knowledge, power and to help other persons. The shaman has at least one, and usually more, "spirits" in his personal service' (pp. 25–6). 'Shamans are especially healers' and move between ordinary and 'ordinarily hidden' realities to perform their healing work (p. 55). In Harner's view, ordinary and ordinarily hidden realities are both equally real. Harner rejects as unproven, 'even in the sciences of ordinary reality', the contention that there is only one state of consciousness that is valid for first-hand observations on which basis is determined the empirical definition of reality (p. xvii). Therefore, Harner proposes another duality, the shamanic state of consciousness (SSC) in contrast to the ordinary state of consciousness: 'The SSC is the cognitive condition in which one perceives the "nonordinary reality" of Carlos Castaneda and the "extraordinary manifestations of reality" of Robert Lowie' (p. 26). As an intermediary between ordinary and nonordinary realities, the shaman is 'a magical athlete of states of consciousness'

---

[10]   Although Harner did not coin the term 'core shamanism' until later, *The Way of the Shaman* is Harner's key text and is promoted as a kind of textbook of core shamanism by his Foundation for Shamanic Studies. Unless otherwise indicated, subsequent page citations reference Harner (1980).

(p. 56). However, the shamanic state of consciousness is not a place of play: 'The shaman is a person with work to do in the SSC and he must know the basic methods for accomplishing that work' (p. 27). These methods entail knowledge, of the 'cosmic geography of nonordinary reality', of speaking with non-human beings, including animals, trees and spirits and of working with guardians and spirit helpers (pp. 26, 74–5, 81–3). This knowledge can be acquired in many ways, including apprenticeships and textual sources such as his book.[11] However, mainly shamanic knowledge is acquired through experience: 'The shaman is an empiricist ... And indeed the shaman depends primarily on firsthand experience of the senses, to acquire knowledge' (p. 58). According to Harner (pp. 52–3), 'the remarkable worldwide consistency in basic shamanic knowledge' is a hallmark of shamanic practice and is widely reported by scholars (his examples are Eliade and anthropologist and folklorist Johannes Wilbert). Indeed, Harner suggests this consistency is because 'the ancient methods of shamanism are already time-tested' (p. xiv). 'Shamanic methods' are very ancient, according to Harner, 'at least twenty or thirty thousand years old' and possibly 'two or three million years' when 'primates that could be called human' populated the planet (Harner 1980: 51). Like knowledge produced by scientific experimentation, knowledge produced by shamanic methods has distilled and separated what works from what does not. Shamanic knowledge is therefore not only consistent, but reliable too.

Shaman*ism* for Harner is the method of applying shamanic knowledge; it is 'the most widespread and ancient methodological system of mind-body healing known to humanity' (p. 51). Although 'the achievements of Western scientific and technological medicine' are 'miraculous in their own right' (p. 176), shamanism is not taken seriously in the modern world because 'our Western culture' is 'cognicentric', by which Harner means 'prejudiced against a concept of nonordinary reality'; cognicentrism is 'the analogue in consciousness of ethnocentrism' (p. xvii). In contrast to western cognicentrism, 'primitive peoples' already understand 'the two-tiered nature of their experiences' and don't distinguish between ordinary and nonordinary reality. Yet, '[b]ecause our Western culture is not shamanic' and 'is simply unsophisticated from a shamanic point of view', it is necessary when teaching shamanism to make these distinctions clear. If you become a shaman, however, 'you will find it no more necessary than a Jívaro or an Australian aborigine to specify

---

11   On whether shamanic knowledge can be learned from a book, Harner states, 'You must learn the methods in order to utilize them ... In Western culture, most people will never know a shaman, let alone train with one. Yet, since ours is a literate culture, you do not have to be in an apprenticeship situation to learn; a written guide can provide the essential methodological information' (Harner 1980: xv).

the state of consciousness you were in when you had a particular experience. Your audience, if composed of persons of knowledge, will know' (pp. 60–62). Western cognicentrism notwithstanding, Harner claims students attending his training workshops 'have demonstrated again and again that most Westerners can easily become initiated into the fundamentals of shamanic practice'. Indeed, '[t]he ancient way is so powerful, and taps so deeply into the human mind, that one's usual cultural belief systems and assumptions about reality are essentially irrelevant' (pp. xiv–xv). Harner terms these 'fundamentals of shamanic practice', along with the body of knowledge on which the practice relies, 'core shamanism'. At the centre of core shamanism is the shaman's experience, beginning with his or her transition into shamanic state of consciousness and followed by journeys in nonordinary reality. Harner describes the shaman's experience as follows:

> In the SSC, the shaman typically experiences an ineffable joy in what he sees, an awe of the beautiful and mysterious worlds that open before him. His experiences are like dreams, but waking ones that feel real and in which he can control his actions and direct his adventures. While in the SSC, he is often amazed by the reality of that which is presented. He gains access to a whole new, and yet familiarly ancient universe that provides him with profound information about the meaning of his own life and death and his place within the totality of all existence. During his great adventures in the SSC, he maintains conscious control over the direction of his travels, but does not know what he will discover. He is a self-reliant explorer of the endless mansions of a magnificent hidden universe. Finally, he brings back his discoveries to build his knowledge and to help others. (p. 27)

The purpose of Harner's core-shamanism training is to recommend specific techniques by which one may journey into the shamanic state of consciousness and nonordinary reality and there partake of one's own ineffable experience (pp. 38–40). First, the journeyer must be calm and relaxed. They should avoid psychedelic or alcoholic stimulants for at least 24 hours 'so that your centeredness and power of concentration will be good, and your mind clear of confusing imagery'. Similarly, Harner recommends fasting or eating only lightly. When they are ready, they should lie comfortably on the floor in a dark and quiet room wearing light clothing without shoes or pillow. They should take a few minutes to relax arms and legs and take a few deep breathes while contemplating the journey they are about to begin. Finally, they should close their eyes and cover them with a hand or forearm to keep out any light. They are now ready to begin. First, they should 'visualize an opening into the earth that you remember from some time in your life'. Any kind of opening will do – a burrow, cave, tree hollow, spring, or 'man-made opening'. After visualising the opening for a few minutes, they should instruct a companion to begin beating a drum 'in a strong, monotonous, unvarying, and rapid beat' of between 205 and 220 beats per minute. The journey through the tunnel takes several minutes, during which time 'The steady, monotonous beat of the drum acts like a carrier wave, first to help the shaman enter the SSC, and then to sustain him on his journey' (p. 65):

> When the drumming begins, visualize your familiar opening into the earth, enter it, and begin the journey. Go down through the opening and enter the Tunnel. At first the Tunnel may be dark and dim. It usually goes underground at a slight angle, but occasionally it descends steeply. The Tunnel sometimes appears ribbed, and often it bends. Occasionally one passes through the Tunnel so fast it is not even seen. In following the Tunnel you may run up against a natural wall of stone or some other obstacle. When this happens, just go around it or through a crack in it. If this fails, simply come back to try again. In any case, do not exert yourself too hard in making the journey. If you do this work correctly, it will be relatively effortless. Success in journeying and seeing depends on an attitude that lies between trying too hard and not trying hard enough. (p. 40)

If the journey is successful, the shaman emerges onto a landscape. Harner recommends the journeyer 'examine the landscape in detail, travel through it, and remember its features'. When signalled to return by the drumming companion, the shaman should return to the ordinary state of consciousness by way of the same tunnel. Finally, Harner recommends the shaman describes their experience to their companion to assist them retain the knowledge learnt. Harner also recommends writing down these recollections or dictating them into a voice recorder: 'The act of remembering these experiential details is the beginning of your accumulation of SSC knowledge' (ibid.)

This account of the shaman's journey into shamanic state of consciousness and nonordinary reality is the basic pattern of core shamanism. It is the template from which other kinds of shamanic journeys take their variation, including journeys to recover a power animal, spirit canoe journeys and journeys to remove intrusions or to restore a soul. It is the origin of shamanic knowledge and healing practice. On this point, Harner insists that 'truly significant shamanic knowledge is experienced, and cannot be obtained from me or any other shaman. Shamanism is, after all, basically a strategy for personal learning and acting on that learning' (p. xxii).

Shamanism may be a strategy for personal learning, but it is also an object of study in its own right. In 1979, Harner established the Centre for Shamanic

Studies, based in Norwalk, Connecticut. In 1987 Harner retired from universities to dedicate himself fulltime to shamanism studies, and renaming his organisation The Foundation for Shamanic Studies. A non-profit, public charitable organisation currently based in Mill Valley north of San Francisco, the Foundation for Shamanic Studies (hereafter FSS or Foundation) gives its purpose as 'the preservation, study and teaching of shamanic knowledge for the welfare of the Planet and its inhabitants' (FSS 2012a, Harner 2005a). This purpose is envisaged as 'a three-part mission'. Historically, teaching shamanism has been the most important part of the Foundation's work and has been organised around a menu of courses offered through the Foundation and taught by Harner and an ever-growing college of FSS faculty members, all of whom are themselves graduates of the Foundation's advanced-level courses.

The introductory-level Basic Workshop in Core Shamanism is modelled on *The Way of the Shaman* and is a prerequisite for proceeding to more advanced-level courses. Since the basic course was developed in the 1980s, a wide range of advanced-level offerings have been developed by Harner and the Foundation's alums. These range from weekend workshops, to two-week intensive courses, such as the Shamanic Healing Intensive and a Three Year Program of Advanced Initiations in Shamanism and Shamanic Healing. The typical offering of advanced-level weekend workshops include Shamanic Extraction Healing Training; Shamanism, Dying, and Beyond; Shamanic Divination Training; Shamanism and the Spirits of Nature; Shamanic Dreamwork; Shamanic Training in Creativity, and Shamanism Practicum (FSS 2012k). Most courses are taught in North America and as more graduates have moved on to advanced levels and become faculty members, so the number, diversity and availability of courses has increased. Scheduled offerings published in the Foundation's monthly newsletter indicate that since 2010 the Foundation has offered between 30 and 35 basic courses and 40–45 advanced-level courses across North America.

The Foundation's success over a sustained period has also led to a network of international faculty who teach the Foundation's courses beyond North America through local affiliates. The largest of these is FSS Europa based in Vienna. Among the most active European affiliates are Centro Studi Sciamanici (Italy), Chamanisme (Switzerland), Chamanisme-FSS (France), FSS Europe Portugal (Portugal), Formación en Chamanismo Transcultural (Spain) and the Sacred Trust (United Kingdom).[12] Each offer a regular schedule of basic and

---

[12] The websites of these organisations are respectively, http://www.studisciamanici.it, http://www.chamanisme.ch, http://www.chamanisme-fss.org, http://www.xamanismo.net, http://www.estudioschamanicos.com and http://www.sacredtrust.org (accessed 29 March 2012).

advanced courses. Although less frequent, FSS courses are also taught by FSS faculty in Argentina, Australia, Japan and Taiwan.

The various courses offered around the world by FSS faculty members, along with prerequisite conditions for enrolment, graduation through higher levels of advancement and certification upon completion suggest some of the ways FSS produces disciplinary knowledge about shamanism ('shamanic knowledge'), along with mechanisms for authorising and regulating standards. White, Bronze and Silver certifications are issued with respect to completing combinations of advanced-level courses of two weeks or longer, while Gold certification is issued upon completion of 'all standard advanced Foundation trainings in Core Shamanism' (FSS 2012b). The certification 'Harner Method Shamanic Counselor', the most esteemed of FSS's certifications, is instructive (FSS 2012j). Among other requirements, candidates must complete FSS Basic Workshop; complete the five-day shamanic counselling training course; submit a 5,000-word essay on the topic 'What should the standards be for the shamanic counselor, and how do I meet these standards?'; attend at least twenty meetings of a 'core shamanic drumming circle'; complete 125 hours of 'core shamanic training' in advanced-level FSS courses; submit audio recordings and written reports of shamanic counselling sessions, and complete a 5-day 'Teaching Examination in Shamanic Counseling' and oral examination. Although FSS stopped issuing Harner Certified Shamanic Counseling certifications in 2008, the certification remains valid for those who had already received it, including nearly a hundred Harner Method Certified Shamanic Counselors listed on the Foundation's website (FSS 2012c).

Besides teaching, in recent years FSS has begun placing more emphasis on research. In 2006, the Foundation established the Shamanic Knowledge Conservatory. According to FSS, the conservatory holds 'over 65,000 indexed pages related to shamanism and shamanic practices ... culled from 396 cultures', as well as books, manuscripts, artifacts, drums and audio-visual media. Mostly preserved digitally and stored in multiple locations to ensure survival in case of 'a future calamity', the material is organised into five categories: shamanic healing, about shamans, cosmology, eschatology and divination (FSS 2012g). A second FSS research project, concerned with 'mapping nonordinary reality', claims to have amassed over 70,000 pages of researched data on cross-cultural shamanism and shamanic healing, along with a further 6,000 books and journals, as well as 35,000 pages of first-hand descriptions of shamanic journeys 'and other visionary experiences of contemporary Westerners', including, according to FSS, 'the very first shamanic journeys contemporary Westerners have experienced' (FSS 2012g). Finally, FSS also runs a Shamanism and Health programme that researches the efficacy of shamanic healing methods. Envisaged as 'a progressing effort to find how shamanic practices complement mainstream medicine', the Foundation invites 'shamanic healing practitioners' to complete a questionnaire, although no time frame is given for when findings will be published (FSS 2012h). Between these transcultural research and transnational teaching labours, FSS strongly resembles a conventional academic institution, as indeed is the Foundation's intention. As Harner has said, 'Our Foundation for Shamanic Studies is a kind of university of shamanism' (Harner 2005b: 170).

The third part of the Foundation's mission is given as 'preservation and revival of indigenous shamanism'. The Foundation has two programmes for accomplishing these goals. The Living Treasure of Shamanism award was inaugurated in 1992 to assist 'exceptionally distinguished indigenous shamans' pass on their knowledge to a new generation in less-developed countries where 'their age-old knowledge of shamanism and shamanic healing is in danger of extinction'. Support is in the form of a lifetime stipend. Anyone can nominate an awardee and nominations are considered annually by the FSS Board. Among award recipients listed on the Foundation's website are a Daur shaman in Inner Mongolia, Tibetan shamans in Tibet and Nepal, several shamans of three different 'small peoples' of Siberia and Central Asia and several shamans in Amazonia (FSS 2012f). The second programme, titled 'Preservation, Revival, and Urgent Indigenous Assistance', is more interventionist: 'When invited by indigenous peoples who have largely lost their shamanic knowledge, the Foundation may send a team to help them establish firsthand shamanic contact with their own spirits and learn from them' (FSS 2012a). As of March 2012, the Foundation had sent 'basic training teams' to Australia, Canada, China, Samiland (Scandinavia), Siberia, Tuva and the United States. The Foundation states it is also 'actively engaged in preservation work in Nepal, Siberia, China, Central Asia, the Amazon, and elsewhere' (FSS 2012f). Certainly, this kind of direct intervention could be viewed askance as a form of proselytising, which is probably why FSS stresses this 'assistance' is by invitation only and is provided by FSS 'Field Associates', of which the Foundation lists thirty spread around the world. The Foundation's 1993 'expedition' to 'Tuva, Land of Eagles', mentioned in Chapter 1, pioneered this form of 'indigenous assistance'.

A more recent example is a project to support 'shamanic revival' among the Baniwa people of north-west Amazonia (FSS 2012i). The focal point of the Foundation's effort is Mandu da Silva, a local Baniwa chief (*mandu*) and reportedly the last snuff-jaguar shaman. Anthropologist Robin Wright has undertaken field research among Baniwa communities and other Awaraklanguage groups on the Brazilian side of the border with Colombia since the 1970s and da Silva has been one of his key informants. Wright, who has also been a close observer of the alignment of indigenism with sustainable development in Amazonia (Wright 2009, 2007), illustrated the cover of his monograph *Cosmos, Self, and History in Baniwa Religion* with a 1977 photograph of da Silva in shamanic trance (Wright 1998; cf. Wright 2011). Some time around 2009, Wright persuaded FSS to support a project to promote 'shamanic revitalization' among the Baniwa. Wright became an FSS Field Associate and Mandu da Silva became a Living Treasures of Shamanism award recipient. Whether the Foundation was aware of, or indeed interested in, how their support might fit within the larger political context of Amazonian cultural politics or transnational indigenism is not clear, although there is no acknowledgement of this history in the Foundation's account of 'the shamanic revitalisation of the Baniwa people'. The project's first major objective was to establish a 'cultural centre' in a purpose-built 'traditional longhouse' to house a library of books, tapes and audio-visual material to be made available to schools in the Aiary River region. More than an archive of Baniwa culture, the centre was to be a focus of Baniwa shamanic revival. With FSS funding, the longhouse was built in 2009. Titled the 'Shaman's School of Knowledge', FSS was pleased to report that 15 young Baniwa men had subsequently apprenticed to da Silva. FSS was particularly pleased that all 15 were schoolteachers because this fact was regarded as advancing one of the project's goals, to ensure that 'the knowledge of the shamans' be included in the educational curriculum. Towards this end, FSS explained that the next phase of the project would produce a series of illustrated booklets about shamans' work to be used in classrooms. At the same time, cultural conservation would continue by recording shamanic knowledge on film and with audio and photographic equipment to be lodged in the Cultural Centre. In this way, the Shaman's School of Knowledge would become a living library of Baniwa culture. This support for Mandu da Silva and his community is one of several projects providing 'indigenous assistance' which are prominently advertised on the Foundation's website and in its newsletters. Subscribers and website visitors are reminded that 'ongoing assistance is needed to continue the revitalization' and are encouraged to donate to the Foundation's Fund to Save Shamanic Knowledge (FSS 2010b). The fund is one of three to which donors can make earmarked contributions (the others are the Fund to Study Shamanic Knowledge and the Fund to Teach Shamanic Knowledge). Donors have the further option to contribute a one-off donation, join the Guardians Circle by donating monthly, or the Partners Circle by donating $5,000 or more annually for three years (FSS 2012e).

It is hardly surprising that Harner and the numerous shamans and shamanic enthusiasts associated with the FSS would want to disseminate the principles of core shamanism. Neither is it surprising that they would want to support indigenous shamans and local indigenous communities. Yet there is a sense that there is something more than enthusiasm or altruism implicated in these efforts. Two important clues bear some consideration. The first is the tension between representations of shamanic experience promoted by core-shamanism training on the one hand, and the various examples of indigenous shamanic practice conveyed in the FSS's various research, conservation and revival programmes on the other. The second is the sense in which FSS's labours are indispensible to the internal structure of the theory itself. Both clues are related, but whereas the former draws attention to the operations of the symbolic economy for indigenous authenticity operating in the FSS's programmes, the latter brings into focus the always incomplete task implicated in the modern limit attitude.

Consider how Harner's representations of indigenous peoples and indigenous shamanic religiosities have changed since he first published *The Way of the Shaman*. Central to core shamanism is a critique of Euro-American modernity. The theme of the loss of shamanic knowledge in modern culture is an organising trope of core shamanism, along with the auxiliary claim that among indigenous peoples 'shamanism and shamanic knowledge is in danger of extinction' (FSS 2012f).[13] In *The Way of the Shaman*, however, Harner does not mention 'indigenous' peoples, although he frequently refers to 'primitive' communities and 'tribal' cultures. For example, he claims that 'Today shamanic knowledge survives primarily among people who, until recently, had primitive cultures' and argues that 'shamanic knowledge [is] basically consistent in different parts of the primitive world' (Harner 1980: 51, 53). Harner affirms the identical idea in a 1997 article in *Natural History Magazine*, but substitutes 'primitive' and 'tribal' with 'indigenous': 'the fundamental principles of shamanic practice' are 'basically the same among indigenous peoples' (Harner 1997: 51). This is more than a gesture towards political correctness. Although all three terms – 'primitive', 'tribal' and 'indigenous peoples' – are used to reference non-modern ontological alterity and carry the same indexical value in core shamanism's discourse, this lexical shift foreshadows the FSS's better positioning itself to appropriate and instrumentalise indigenous symbolic capital in ways that had long ceased to be advantageous with reference to the older terms. Another

---

[13] We see in this formulation – western peoples 'lose' shamanic traditions; among indigenous peoples it becomes 'extinct' – traces of the noble savage/ecological Indian who is more of nature than in it and for whom the natural history category of 'extinction' is a problem.

example: in April 2010, the FSS announced Harner would be running a new weekend course titled 'Shamanic Dreamwork' beginning in September that year (FSS 2010a). In a subsequent article titled 'A Core Shamanic Theory of Dreams' and published in the FSS's journal, Harner repeatedly emphasises that his theory derives from his 'years of cross-cultural study of indigenous shamanism' and reflects 'indigenous shamanic concepts and practices'. He expresses the hope that 'indigenous shamans' will regard his exposition as 'an example of a long overdue Western recognition of the validity of what they and their ancestors have known since ancient times'. Similarly, he concludes his article with the hope that 'this brief article may encourage more research on the wealth of indigenous knowledge, published and unpublished, that is awaiting respectful study' and in a footnote recommends the Shamanic Knowledge Conservatory for this purpose (Harner 2010: 2, 4).

The extent to which Harner became sensitive to the new language of indigenism during the 1980s is evident in his Preface to the tenth-anniversary edition of *The Way of the Shaman* (Harner 1990). Harner notes that before the first edition was published in 1980, missionaries, colonists, governments and commercial interests were overwhelming 'tribal peoples and their ancient cultures' and 'shamanism was rapidly disappearing from the Planet'. Since then, however, there has been a remarkable 'shamanic renaissance', which he attributes to three developments. First, 'thinking people' have lost trust in 'ecclesiastical dogma and authority'. They have 'left the Age of Faith behind them' in favour of the 'higher standards of evidence' provided by direct, unmediated experiences of 'realms of the spirit'. Second, 'holistic health approaches' discovered 'techniques long used in shamanism' and incorporated these into contemporary holistic healing practices. Third, 'In this time of worldwide environmental crisis, shamanism provides something largely lacking in the anthropocentric "great" religions: reverence for, and spiritual communion with, the other beings of the Earth and with the Planet itself'. More than merely nature worship, shamanism connects us with 'the awesome spiritual power and beauty of our garden Earth'. Shamanism 'is spiritual ecology'; from the shaman's viewpoint, 'our surroundings are not "environment," but family' with whom 'we need to communicate intimately and lovingly ... not just with the human peoples, but also with the animal people, the plant people, and all the elements of the environment, including the soil, the rocks, and the water' (Harner 1990: xi–xiii). As ecocentric disposition became the standard measure of indigenous ontological alterity and increased the symbolic value of specifically 'indigenous' identity, Harner and his Foundation adjusted representations of ontological alterity in core shamanism. The Foundation represents its programme of 'indigenous assistance' as helping indigenous communities such as the Baniwa recover their shamanic knowledge, revive their ecocentric disposition and promote both cultural and environmental conservation.

Recalling Bourdieu, we could say that the FSS mobilises stores of capital, converting between economic, cultural and social forms, and reinvesting prudently to cache the theory of core shamanism with indigenous symbolic capital. These kinds of intrumentalisations operate in ways basically similar to the symbolic politics of the indigenist-environmentalist alliance: partnerships with local indigenous communities are cited as evidence of the organisation's good work, testimony to the legitimacy of this work and surety of the organisation's authority as world leader in a field reconfigured by new indigenous participants for whom shamanism is an important representational strategy in a new transnational eco-politics. At the same time, it is precisely this grounding of core shamanism in a transnational politics of representation, a symbolic economy in the Bourdieusian sense, that prevents it from crossing a threshold into hyperreal simulation. For what would core shamanism be without progressive advancement through more advanced levels of study; without the roughly 150,000 'indexed pages' of data 'culled' from 396 cultures, academic sources and first-hand descriptions; without 'living treasures' and 'basic training teams' dispatched around the world to teach core shamanism to indigenous communities whose own shamanic traditions have dissipated and transformed amid modern encroachments on their lands, territories and resources? It seems to me that if core shamanism's representation of shamanic practice is a hyperreal simulation of shamanic authenticity, a thin, fragile representation so thoroughly stripped of its resemblance that it verges on hyperrealism, it is none the less sustained by forms of indigenous symbolic capital in which the locus of value is its capacity to connect the putative 'core shaman' and the eponymous hero of *The Way of the Shaman* with specific, geographically dispersed indigenous cultures and territories, even if mediated by representational politics and indigenes' tactical choices about positioning and speech. By providing universality with a locus of specificity, the figure of the 'core shaman' remains wedded to a referent, even several substitutable referents, and is thereby restrained from an uncoupling that would otherwise propel it across a threshold into hyperreality, even as the distillation of 'core' shamanic elements from an ever-growing sample of exemplars draws the connection ever more taut and perpetually threatens to sever the link. The 'core shaman' is an intensely liminal figure, constantly pushing a threshold but never quite escaping the centripetal pull of a symbolic economy that stores premium value in the specificity of place.

The second clue regarding the internal structure of the theory of core shamanism begins to come into focus at this point. Noteworthy in Harner's account of core shamanism is the contrast between his relatively detailed description of a journey into shamanic state of consciousness – an opening in the ground, a tunnel, features of the tunnel, possible obstacles and circumventing them, rate and inclination of descent – and his abstention from describing a nonordinary landscape seen upon exiting this tunnel. Harner's stated reason is that he is reluctant to provide (or impose on) his readers details of an experience that is valued for its uniqueness (Harner 1980: xx–xxi). Recall that Harner's recommendations (really, instructions) – abstinences that help clear the mind of confusing imagery; preparation of a comfortable, dark room; drumming at a specified range of beats per minute; recommended visualisations; and the guided journey itself – these recommendations are promoted as techniques for accessing an other-than-ordinary state of consciousness that also suspends a cognicentric prejudice against the reality of the experiences had within that other-than-ordinary state of consciousness. Harner identifies these experiences as essentially shamanic (core shamanism) and this other-than-ordinary state of consciousness as the shamanic state of consciousness.

Harner is reluctant to describe nonordinary reality beyond the tunnel into the shamanic state of consciousness because eidetic reduction is pivotal to core shamanic practice. One might say that the core of shamanism is the practice of eidetic reduction. Indeed, Harner describes *The Way of the Shaman* as a phenomenological presentation (Harner 1980: xx). He insists every shaman's experience is different and unique, but is none the less a variant of a single phenomenon, the essence of which is shamanic knowledge. To know this essence requires comparison of variations of the perceptual object, hence Harner's emphasis on lifelong learning: 'In its essence, shamanic initiation is experiential and often gradual ... shamanic initiation is a never-ending process of struggle and joy ...' (Harner 1980: 56–7). At the same time, this emphasis on the ontology of a unique experience is supported and sustained by providing similar data with which a core shamanic practitioner may compare their unique experiences. In *The Way of the Shaman*, Harner offers his readers personal accounts of his shamanic experiences, particularly during time spent with Jívaro (Shuar) and Conibo shamans in Ecuador and Peru, as well as lengthy first-hand accounts of shamanic experiences provided by his students. Harner invites his readers to compare these experiences with their own and so engage an eidetic reduction of essential shamanism. Significantly, this reduction is endless because it is always incomplete. Harner likens shamans' personal revelatory experiences to pieces of a great cosmic jigsaw puzzle and cautions his readers that a high degree of knowledge of this puzzle requires many years of shamanic experience. Harner advises that 'The master shaman will try to integrate even the most unusual experiences into his total cosmology, a cosmology based primarily on his own journeys', but even so they do not expect to complete the puzzle in a 'mortal lifetime' (ibid.: 57). Harner's invitation recalls Husserl's celebration of 'this wonderful correlation between the phenomenon of knowledge and the object of knowledge'. Like a master shaman, Husserl too saw eidetic reduction as a responsibility that cannot be shirked: 'The task is this: to track down, within the framework of pure evidence or self-givenness, *all correlations and forms of givenness*, and to elucidate them through analysis' (Husserl 1999: 68). However, this task has become considerably more challenging since Harner and the FSS began instrumentalising indigenous symbolic capital to vouchsafe shamans' ontological alterity. Put simply, accumulations of indigenous symbolic capital also supply multitudes of comparative data and related 'forms of giveneness' that surely overwhelm core-shamanic practitioners. Consider the Shamanic Knowledge Conservatory's 65,000 indexed pages related to shamans, shamanic healing, cosmology, eschatology and divination; 70,000 pages of cross-cultural analysis; 35,000 pages of first-hand descriptions of shamanic journeys, and so on. These comprehensive accumulations of forms of universal shamanism are living resources and the shamans' epistemological labours of integrating them are a living practice. However, tasked with integrating even the most unusual accounts into their total cosmology, the master shaman clearly has their epistemological labour cut out for them. At the same time, this task is the responsibility of the master shaman and may not be refused.

Core shamanism is an excellent example of the modern limit attitude in operation, demonstrating at once its epistemological and ontological dimensions, its form as a task that may not be refused as well as its tendency to generate new practical limits, cascade new surfaces of appearance of a knowing self and amplify practical social effects. Some of these will be revisited in Chapter 5. So where does environmentalism figure in this analysis? I have deliberately stayed close to the historical specificity of the indigenist-environmentalist alliance rather than the wider range of inquiries pertaining to environmentalism as historical concern about the Earth's biosphere and human habitat. The indigenist-environmentalist alliance adumbrated one domain in which emerged these wider concerns about human development within carrying capacities of natural environments. This domain's economy of practice revised indigenous identity, so that proximity to nature became an essential element of indigenous ontology and indigenous knowledge pertaining to biodiversity conservation and sustainable development became an essential element of indigenous epistemology. Indigenists and environmentalists alike embraced indigenous cosmovisions and world-views to represent these ontological and epistemological dimensions of essential indigenous identity, with a concomitant elevation of the figure of the shaman as exemplar of indigenous ecocentric disposition. Recalling the importance in shamanism discourse of the shaman's ontological alterity, this elevation held significant implications for shamanism. As ecocentric disposition became the contemporary mode of representing ontological alterity, so did representations of shamans adjust to comport with the new symbolic economy of indigenous authenticity. While this adjustment enabled contemporary shamanists like Harner and the FSS to remain relevant and competitive in the shamanism field, it also offered a timely opportunity to invigorate a discourse that had lost some of its lustre since its counter-culture heyday. With this in mind, revivals of indigenous shamanism might be better regarded as reviving a putative universal shamanism, by stimulating universalism with new particularities and contingencies and indicating new limit horizons towards which shamanists can direct their labours.

Chapter 5

Neoliberalism

The analysis presented in Chapter 4 showed how the emergence in history of an alliance between indigenists and environmentalists generated a symbolic economy of indigenous authenticity that represented indigenous ontological alterity as ecocentric disposition. This economy endures today, and ecocentric disposition as the measure of indigenous ontological alterity remains a compelling image as the Ramunangi and FSS examples illustrate. Typically, this disposition is identified with an indigenous world-view or cosmovision in which indigenous peoples' ecological and spiritual proximity to nature is both a kind of identity and a site of difference: a laudable fact and an aspirational desire, and a means to an end. However, if ecocentric disposition signifies a kind of difference with reference to anthropocentrism, fundamentally this difference pertains to a relation between a human body and nature, where the difference pertains specifically to a relaxing of distinctions and enhancing of mediations between an embodied self and the natural world so that they may form an identity. As we saw with the Awas Tingni case discussed in Chapter 3, shamanism's discursive language is amenable to representing these mediations by emphasising shamans' relations with spirits, including spirits associated with specific plants, animals, topographical features of landscapes and ancestors residing there. In the present chapter, I want to consider the reverse perspective by paying attention to shamans' relations with their body. If, in the wake of the indigenist-environmentalist alliance, shamanism signifies a difference between worlds oriented by anthropocentrism and ecocentrism, then the shamans' body has become a figure of this mediation. However, read in tandem with the neoliberal critique of labour, shamans' ability to engage with spirits can be recast as a form of embodied capital that can be invested to generate an income stream over time. Indeed, the various discussions presented in this chapter argue that this is precisely what is happening.

Neoliberalism is shorthand for far-reaching structural transformations in the global economy in recent decades. Usually associated with the policy and legislative agendas of Thatcherism and Reaganism during the last decade of the Cold War, neoliberalism is conventionally summarised as an approach to economic policy that promotes deregulation of state-centric control of markets, liberalisation of financial products and services, and the almost wholesale transfer of custodianship of the economy from public to private sectors (Birch and Mykhnenko 2010, D. Harvey 2005, Larner 2000). The term 'neoliberalism' is much older, however, dating to the 1930s, when some economists and intellectuals became concerned about the central planning of national economies in politically liberal states – the British Keynesian state and the New Deal in the US being obvious examples – to which we could add ordoliberalism in West Germany following the Second World War. Advocating that economic theory should be reoriented away from concern with the structure of the economy and towards the individual as economic agent, they coined the term 'neoliberalism' to distinguish their theories from the prevailing economic orthodoxy of their time. The reorientation advocated by scholars such as Milton Friedman, Friedrich Hayek, George Stigler and Ludwig von Mises (and later Theodore Schultz and Gary Becker) sought to recover some elements of classical liberal theory, notably the primacy of individual choice. However, it also radically revised classical economics, most notably the classical theory of labour. This is Foucault's analysis, and in typical Foucauldian fashion, the emergence of a specifically neoliberal *homo economicus* is only half the story, and correlation of a much larger transformation, from the exercise of power by a sovereign in relation to that which they owned, to a form of power that exercised multiform tactics, targeted the population, and had as its objective optimising the distribution of things towards desired ends. Henceforth the art of government would entail an economising rationality to coordinate an optimal allocation of scarce means to desired ends, a new kind of practice that instilled the principle of economy as a form of reason intrinsic to the state. Foucault's insight was to recognise that neoliberal *homo economicus* embodied this economic principle and practiced the art of government in relation to their own self.

This chapter considers shamanism in relation to Foucault's analysis of *homo economicus* and governmentality. It draws out a troubling dilemma for practices of sovereign power, a problem that is particularly well illustrated by shamans: sovereign power desires neoliberal subjectivities who are eminently governable because they embody the state's economising principle; however, shaping citizens in the mould of neoliberal *homo economicus* also increasingly places them beyond sovereign reach. The crux of this problem – that the neoliberal art of government is a practice undertaken by sovereign governments as much as by sovereign individuals – is the focus of this chapter's two main discussions, which are preceded and framed by a summary discussion of Foucault's critique of governmentality and neoliberalism.

The first discussion considers how the neoliberal critique of labour enabled the notion of engaging with spirits to be recast as a form of human capital that could be developed, trained and invested to generate an income stream over time. The argument is illustrated by professional shamans, the strategies they use to develop their profession, and the techniques they employ to invest in and capitalise their embodied human capital. As another vehicle conveying shamanism discourse at a transnational level, however, neoliberalism has also contributed to the kinds of proliferations and intensifications previously considered in relation to indigenism and environmentalism. These movements are illustrated with reference to transatlantic circuits of bodies and ideas linking southern African *sangomas* with North American shamans. Examples from these regions have been selected for several reasons. With regards to North America, Harnerian core shamanism has been a key factor propelling neoliberal shamanic practice, and emerging professional networks of shamans suggests the extent to which markets for shamanic goods and services have grown in North America since the 1990s. Transatlantic circuits involving southern African *sangomas* also demonstrate shamanism's discursive power and the ways it assimilates heterogeneity to its regularities and order. A different range of reasons becomes clearer in the second half of this chapter where the discussion turns to neoliberal governmentality. Since the late 1990s, successive South African governments have engaged in an ambitious project to restructure the state, initially to dismantle apartheid, but increasingly to orient South Africa towards what the government considers will be the opportunities and challenges of the twenty-first century. South Africa has hardly been alone in these efforts during this period. However, South Africa is a compelling example of economy as the principle of state reason in relation to indigenous ritual specialists and traditional healing practices. A raft of policies, supported by new legislation and an array of regulatory authorities, amount to an ensemble of tactics designed to bring *sangomas* and other categories of 'African traditional healers' into the ambit of things coordinated by government as it seeks to optimise an arrangement disposed towards desired ends. This coordinated exercise of biopower raises dilemmas, however, because by inculcating the principle of economy in citizens, the art of government also promotes formation of a specifically neoliberal subjectivity in relation to a domain increasingly beyond sovereign reach. This problem is taken up in this chapter's concluding discussion where the dialectic between *homo legalis* and *homo economicus* provides another illustration of the modern limit attitude operating in shamanism discourse.

Foucault's Critique of Neoliberal Economy

Foucault's account of neoliberalism fits into his larger analysis of the emergence of governmentality and biopolitics, the subjects of his 1978 and 1979 lectures at the *Collège de France*. One could argue that the 1978 course, which took the historical emergence of governmentality as its primary subject, set up the argument Foucault developed in his 1979 lectures on biopolitics, in which he showed that the neoliberal critique of classical economics was another mode of articulating the historical emergence of governmentality's rationality and inculcating that rationality in the biological person as a proclivity towards economic conduct. Read together, the lectures give a history of governmentality in the twin registers of sovereign state and individual autonomy. Indeed, one of Foucault's most important insights was showing how these two domains co-determine each other's emergence (Lemke 2001: 191).

The key issue for Foucault's account of governmentality is the ways in which the conduct of individuals, both in the sense in which they conduct themselves and in which they are influenced or impressed upon to conduct themselves, emerged, and how this question of individual conduct became an increasingly important part of the exercise of sovereign power. Foucault argues that during the seventeenth century a discourse on the art of government emerged as part of a critique of sovereign power as that which is exercised by the sovereign to reinforce, strengthen and protect what he owns (that is, his territory and subjects), for which Machiavelli's Prince and Hobbes's Leviathan remained the basic model (Foucault 2009: 91–2). This new kind of practice modified sovereign power in several ways. Notably, it was immanent to the state (as opposed to above or external to it), it existed in a plurality of forms,[1] and perhaps most significantly, it was essentially continuous in all its forms. This principle of continuity was its 'economy', and the task of establishing this continuity and ensuring its endurance was the proper art of government. Henceforth, government will be essentially concerned with the introduction of economy into political practice, which is to say (quoting Guillaume La Perriére), achieving 'the right disposition

---

[1]   Foucault's examples are monarch, emperor, king, prince, lord, magistrate, prelate, judge, and so on; to which he adds 'governing' a household, souls, children, a province, a convent, a religious order and a family (Foucault 2009: 131).

of things arranged so as to lead to a suitable end' (ibid.: 96). Elaborating on the political economy of optimising an arrangement of things, Foucault noted that the art of government takes as its object, not territory and its inhabitants, but rather 'men in their relationships', with their means of livelihood, the resources at their disposal, their social and cultural context, and especially the variability and changing character of these relations over time (ibid.: 96).

Emerging here is an important transformation, not simply of sovereign power, but of a particular kind of reason intrinsic to the state and separate from, and not reliant on (or at least decreasingly reliant on), natural or divine laws or traditional virtues of wisdom and prudence. Up to the early eighteenth century, this kind of reason formulated as the art of government was still constrained by prevailing theories of sovereign power. The art of government could not fully articulate the specifically economic principles of its rationality so long as sovereign power meant exercising power in relation to territory and its inhabitants through political institutions armed with laws and decrees. The breakthrough event, if one can call it that, that enabled the art of government to assert economy as the principle of state reason (*raison d'état*) was the emergence of the problem of population out of a series of mutually reinforcing transformations related with population growth, increasing availability of money, and expansions of agricultural production. The perception of specific problems to do with population enabled 'the isolation of a level of reality that we call economy' and therewith it became possible 'to think, reflect, and calculate the problem of government' outside of the juridical framework of sovereign power (ibid.: 104). Thus, statistics gradually revealed that the population possesses its own regularities in rates, incidences, distributions and aggregates, and is therefore amenable to quantitative analyses. Population appeared, for government, as both its end and its instrument; as subject of needs and aspirations, and as object of government manipulation; aware of its wants and unaware of what was being done to it (ibid.: 105). These kinds of practices of power instantiated in tactics targeting the population Foucault called 'biopower', and the specific kind of economising rationality coordinating the art of governance Foucault called 'governmentality'. However, an analysis of biopower that attributes its effects to the emergence of an economising rationality applied to the population is incomplete without a complementary analysis that accounts for inculcations and incorporations of the principle of economy into the individual self, who will then carry it, by practicing it, to domains that are not immediately and directly economic. In other words, Foucault's analysis of governmentality implies an analysis of subjectivity that correlates with the principle of economy underpinning the new art of government.

Foucault's earlier studies of subject formation in relation to madness, the clinic and prisons tended to overemphasise techniques of domination; his lectures at Dartmouth in November 1980 acknowledged as much (Foucault 1993: 204). Foucault's subsequent development of a genealogical method during the 1970s led him to recommend that an analysis of the genealogy of the subject in western civilisation must take into account both techniques of domination and techniques of the self, or better still, take into account their co-determination. This is precisely where governmentality enters Foucault's analysis. Government is the 'contact point', and governmentality is the interactive zone where these two types of techniques constantly adjust to one another in a struggle for equilibrium between techniques that assure coercion and processes through which a self constructs and modifies their self (ibid.: 203). Foucault takes up the question of subjectivity in relation with governmentality in his 1979 lectures on the birth of biopolitics. A key issue in the lectures is the transformation of *homo economicus*, a person who in the eighteenth century is the subject of *laissez-faire* liberalism and who government ought to leave alone, but who by the twentieth century accepts their environment as given reality and responds systematically to its modification by sovereign power. As Foucault observes, *homo economicus* is someone who is eminently governable: 'From being the intangible partner of *laissez-faire, homo economicus* now becomes the correlate of a governmentality which will act on the environment and systematically modify its variables' (Foucault 2008: 270–71).

The 1979 lectures on the birth of biopolitics were concerned with demonstrating the emergence of economy as the principle of governmentality in relation to the exercise of biopower.[2] Foucault did not precisely distinguish biopower and biopolitics. However, we could say that biopower references practices that intervene in the biological dimensions of human existence, while biopolitics references the range of practices related to determining the intervention, its instruments, the goals and objectives it will pursue, the coordination of its efforts, and the production of consent that confers legitimacy on state-sanctioned exercises of biopower (Rabinow and Rose 2006: 196–7). Recalling Foucault's previous rendering of governmentality as 'conducting conduct',[3] we could say that biopolitics is the conduct of biopower. The lynchpin of Foucault's analysis is the transformation of the field

---

[2]   Foucault's concepts of biopower and biopolitics have been both criticised and elaborated, notably by Giorgio Agamben and Antonio Negri. For discussions and critiques, see Coleman and Grove (2009), Esposito (2008), Genel (2006) and Rabinow and Rose (2006).

[3]   See particularly the lecture of 8 March 1978.

of economic analysis, the constitution of its objects, and the domain of its reference. Foucault suggests this transformation did not really come into its own until the twentieth century and the articulation of a critique of liberalism by a generation of economists who wished to defend liberal economic principles against various forms of central planning that had gradually come to dominate economic thought during the 1930s (cf. R. Turner 2007). These critics identified their concern as neoliberalism to distinguish it from classical economics. Whereas classical economists since Adam Smith broadly understood their object of analysis to be the mechanisms of exchange of utility between producers and consumers of goods and services, for which Smith's image of the market's 'invisible hand' is an enduring metaphor, neoliberal economists conceived their object as the calculus of substitutable choices that allocates scarce means towards achieving competing ends. Neoliberals thought the starting-point of economic analysis should not be the structure of economy, but the individual as economic agent. Economic analysis should be concerned with the ways in which individuals allocate their scarce means to alternative ends (Foucault 2008: 222).

This concern with personal choice and the (economic) calculation that connects allocation with desirable ends necessitated a fundamental reconceptualisation of the classical theory of labour. Foucault contends that classical political economy never really analysed labour itself, as distinct from land and capital (together, the three primary factors of production). Instead, classical economics reduced labour to a quantitative variable. From David Ricardo through to John Maynard Keynes, labour was analysed simply in terms of expenditures of time, so that increasing productivity meant simply adding more labour hours. Likewise in Marx's theory of capitalism, labour is abstracted from the real conditions of workers' lives. But whereas Marx attributed this abstraction to the alienating effects of capitalist production, neoliberal theorists attributed it to the omission from classical economic theory of a serious analysis of labour 'in its concrete specificity and qualitative modulations'. In other words, whether purchased on the market or calculated as a production input, labour was not regarded by classical economists as a subjective choice among other activities (Dilts 2011: 135, Foucault 2008: 220–21). Neoliberal economists conceived labour as essentially 'economic conduct practiced, implemented, rationalised, and calculated by the person who works' (Foucault 2008: 223). Work was no longer regarded in the quantitative sense of time expenditure but in the qualitative sense of investment, with attendant consideration to strategic discrimination between alternative kinds and means of investment, as well as risks and dividends. In this process, the worker is transformed from an object in an economic analysis into an active economic subject. Neoliberal economists began by breaking down labour into capital and income, where the latter is the wage earned from work and, as an income, is the product of a capital, which is the worker's abilities and skills. In other words, in this neoliberal analysis the worker is her or his capital and this capital – their capital – is inseparable from their person. Developing the classical idea that capital investment increases income, neoliberal economists suggested a worker can increase their income by investing in their corporeal being, by improving their skills, capabilities, capacities, and so on.

In this way, neoliberal theory revised the classical idea of *homo economicus*. Classical *homo economicus* engaged in economic activity on the basis of an analysis of wants and needs that allowed them to describe or define a utility and thereby enter into exchange transactions. Neoliberal *homo economicus* is not a partner in exchange in any sense; s/he is an entrepreneur of her/himself, 'being for himself the source of (his) earnings' (ibid.: 225–6). Rather than obtaining a wage in exchange for one's labour, now it is one's embodied capital that generates income. Since income is increased by investing in capital, one can increase one's income by investing in oneself, say by enrolling in further education and training, obtaining more experience, building networks, and so on, prompting a range of choices about allocating scarce means to alternative ends. If one's self-investments are prudent and wise, then one's income will increase commensurately. Thus neoliberalism posits a theory of *homo economicus* as an entrepreneur of the self. No longer a producer and consumer via a mechanism of market exchange, neoliberal *homo economicus* is a self-entrepreneur of their embodied capital and a producer of their own satisfaction in which consumption is an enterprise activity.

Neoliberal economists called this store of embodied capital 'human capital', and in the decades since Gary Becker, Theodore Schultz and their contemporaries theorised the advantages to organisations, the notion of human capital has become a mainstay of contemporary corporate managerialism, particularly talent management strategies aimed at attracting, retaining and developing the best available skills and expertise (Becker 1964; Schultz 1970, 1961; cf. M. Johnson 2000). Much human capital is acquired though strategies and techniques devised for 'self-development' and 'self-improvement', and an important implication of the neoliberal analysis is that acquisition of forms of human capital (or failure to acquire and develop human capital) is the responsibility of the individual as self-entrepreneur. Equally important are the innate elements of human capital, hereditary elements acquired from one's parents and incorporated into the body during foetal development.

These comprise the entire range of one's physiological distinction from other humans, and draws attention to political dimensions of neoliberal economics. For example, genetic information about the offspring of a union raises ethical questions, about whether, how, or how much a genetic profile can be manipulated to improve the resulting child's human capital, or indeed, whether to continue or abort a pregnancy. Since these kinds of decisions involve costs and perceived benefits, they become economic calculations about optimising correlations of scarce means to alternative ends. But they also prompt political interventions to regulate the permitted range of choices under stipulated conditions and channel conduct towards desirable ends (for example, education campaigns, resource allocations, tax regimes, state benefits entitlements, and so on).

For an economic programme that advocates less government involvement in the formal economy and simultaneously advocates expanding the economic enterprise form into all parts of the social realm, the notion of neoliberal governmentality may seem like an oxymoron. The distinction between government and governance is important here; neoliberalism advocates less of the former, but requires more of the latter (Larner 2000). Specifically, it requires strategies of rule that will constrain, condition and channel conduct of individuals, institutions and corporations, and the population as a whole towards producing and guaranteeing conditions conducive to constituting and consolidating a specifically neoliberal subjectivity, which is to say, neoliberal *homo economicus* (see also Lemke 2001: 201–3, Hamann 2009: 42). Neoliberal subjects are eminently governable because they embody the principle of economy in their conduct and therefore more readily conduct themselves towards optimal arrangements disposed towards desired ends. Yet this fostering of an eminently governable neoliberal subject also creates a dilemma for sovereign power: the delimited and circumscribed space of sovereign power, its jurisdiction so to speak, becomes increasingly inhabited by economic subjects who, by their very ontology, increasingly resist circumscription.

Professionalising Shamanism

The Society for Shamanic Practitioners (hereafter the SSP or Society) describes itself as a public benefit corporation 'whose goal is to support the re-emergence of shamanism into modern, western culture'. While other shamanic organisations tend to 'document and learn from what has been done in the past', the SSP's focus is documenting in the present 'how shamanism is ... being used as it interfaces with the twenty-first century world'. Most of the Society's founding members have been shamanic practitioners since the 1980s, have completed the FSS's advanced-level courses, and are established professionals working at the intersection of psychotherapy, counselling, holistic health and integrative medicine. Some are long-time FSS associates and core-shamanism practitioners who have developed their own shamanic specialisations, for example, in soul retrieval or Celtic shamanism. According to the Society's website, the SSP was established as a nonprofit corporation in California in 2004. In that year, a board of directors was appointed and membership recruitment began. In 2005, $10,000 was raised towards establishing a professional journal, the inaugural annual meeting drew a hundred delegates to Monterey, California, and membership reached five hundred quickly thereafter. In the years that followed, the SSP began publishing *The Journal of Shamanic Practice* at a rate of two issues per year, as well as publishing two edited volumes, *Spirited Medicine: Shamanism in Contemporary Healthcare* and *Shamanism without Borders: A Guide to Shamanic Tending for Trauma and Disasters*, the latter modelled on the international medical humanitarian organisation Médecins Sans Frontières. By late 2009, membership reached around 860 members in 16 countries. Frequent regional meetings in California, Michigan, New Mexico, New York and Ontario in Canada have helped establish networks of professional shamanic practitioners across North America. The Society has also branched into the United Kingdom, where annual meetings held in Dorset since 2007 have consistently drawn around a hundred delegates. The bulk of the Society's website is designed to develop these regional, national and transnational networks by listing advertisements in a variety of thematic areas, including shamanic consultants and services, radio programmes, retreat centres, training, and equipment including books, tapes, drums, rattles and jewellery. By 2014, shamanic services were advertised in 35 US states, as well as Canada, Germany, Ireland, Mongolia, Mexico, Peru, Sweden, Switzerland, and the United Kingdom. SSP board member Tom Cowan explains the importance of developing networks of shaman practitioners in a short online video introducing the SSP. Cowan notes that many shaman practitioners feel alienated and 'outside the mainstream of our culture' because 'the community we live in isn't shamanic'. Whereas 'shamans always have worked in a community, in a tribe, village, clan', many modern shamanic practitioners 'discovered shamanism without a community'. According to Cowan, whose own shamanic specialisation is Celtic visionary and healing techniques, the SSP brings together practitioners 'to have that sense of community and to work together and to learn from each other'. Cowan's assessment, is echoed by fellow board members Martha Lucier and Sandra Ingerman. Ingerman thinks it is important 'to connect shamanic practitioners, who are doctors, who are lawyers, who are school teachers, who work in their communities ... to make [shamanism] more accessible to a modern day culture'. Lucier, who also founded the Canadian Centre for Shamanic Studies, explains that at this historical moment 'we're being asked to come into unity, to come into unity with all our relations and with our peers' (Rachelatssp 2011, SSP 2014).

The SSP is a good example of how in recent years shamanism discourse has adopted the language of professionalism and entrepreneurialism. Increasingly, shamans are professional practitioners. They offer services, have peers, and form professional societies and associations. They contribute to industry publications rather than scholarly journals, and the most successful shamanic practitioners have significant online presence, frequently via their own websites as well as across several social media platforms. While Facebook and Twitter have been an important part of growing markets for shamanic goods and services, professional networking websites like Linked-In have been equally important in establishing shamanic practice as a profession. Linked-In's Shamanism group, established in December 2008, had 31 members on 5 July 2010. One year later, membership had grown to 167, by July 2012 had reached 687, and by early 2014 was nearing 2,000 (Linked-In 2014).

The temptation should be resisted to regard these developments as relevant only to shamanic practitioners in the global North who tend towards New Age spiritualities, alternative medicine, or holistic health approaches. The distinctions on which these categories rely obscure the extent of similarity, overlap and convergence between so-called neo- and traditional shamanic religiosities. It is more accurate to recognise that emerging in contemporary shamanism discourse is a neoliberal entrepreneur of the self, and this emergence is as evident in the global North as it is in the global South. If there is a division that broadly correlates with a North-South distinction, it is that the important implications of this emergence with respect to sovereign power are more readily apparent in the South, or rather, in postcolonial contexts, because it is here where the dialectic is most clearly evident between a neoliberal *homo economicus* who inhabits an economic domain beyond the reach of a sovereign power and a *homo legalis* who inhabits a realm circumscribed by that same power. The second half of this chapter considers this dilemma with reference to South Africa and the chapter's concluding discussion relates it to the modern limit attitude and the double-hinge animating modernity. In the following discussion, I want to stay with the question of neoliberal *homo economicus* in relation to shamanic practitioners.

In several southern African cultural traditions, a *sangoma* is a spirit medium who becomes temporarily 'possessed' or 'inhabited' by ancestors in the course of ritual divination of affliction and prescription of cures. Originally a Zulu term, *sangomas* are differently named in other local languages (Thornton 2009; cf. Wim van Binsbergen 2005: 321), although arguably these are being displaced in a process similar to the emigration of 'shaman' to North America described in Chapter 2. Indeed, '*sangoma*' is emigrating to North America too. Consider, for example, shamanic practitioner Gretchen Crilly McKay. A former teacher with 26 years' experience in elementary schools in California, in the mid-1990s McKay began enrolling in FSS workshops and over several years completed courses with Michael Harner, Tom Cowan, and eventually Sandra Ingerman's two-year shamanic teacher-training course. In June 1999, McKay met Petros Hezekial Mtshali, a *sangoma* from Swaziland who was visiting the United States as a guest of Susan Schuster Campbell. In her book *Called to Heal: African Shamanic Healers* (S. Campbell 2000), Campbell had written about Mtshali and invited Mtshali to attend the annual Comprehensive Cancer Care Conference in Washington (DC). McKay later wrote that meeting 'the Zulu *sangoma* (shaman) changed my life.' According to McKay, Mtshali advised her that she was a traditional healer, that her ancestors called her to this role, and that if she accepted the call, the ancestors would guide her 'on an accelerated path'. In July 2000, McKay travelled to Swaziland where she spent two weeks training with Mtshali at his Luvengwa Traditional Clinic at Siteki, near the border with Mozambique. Following a further 'two rigorous months of sacred work' in Swaziland, McKay completed her training in 2001 (for an account of McKay's graduation ceremony, see Mtshali 2004: 60–64). Back in her Los Angeles home, McKay left teaching and focused full-time on growing her shamanic practice around her specialisation in *sangoma* divination techniques and communing with ancestors (McKay 2009, Mtshali 2004: 60, Stolfo 2009).

McKay's Linked-In profile identifies her as 'a shamanic practitioner and teacher for more than 15 years, studying with master shamans in the U.S. and Africa' (McKay 2012b). She states that she 'graduated in a traditional ceremony as a *sangoma* under the mentorship of Zulu shaman P.H. Mtshali in Swaziland, Africa', and diagnoses 'physical, emotional, and spiritual issues' by using 'the African divination system called "throwing the bones"'. In McKay's repertoire of shamanic healing, African divination complements 'spiritual extraction, soul retrieval and healing with spiritual light', and the blend represents McKay's synthesis of African shamanic practice. In her essay *Journey of an American*

Sangoma, McKay is clear that there is little difference between *sangomas* and shamans. Noting that 'The training I received in Africa has merged with my shamanic training in the United States', McKay claims that *sangomas*, 'like shamans throughout the world, believe that they are here for only one purpose, to heal through love and compassion, and take an oath to cause no harm' (McKay 2009: 8, 2). This view is the premise of McKay's 'shamanic services' detailed on her website Ancestral Wisdom. These include 'African Bone Readings and Connecting with the Ancestors, Soul Retrieval and Soul Remembering, Spiritual Extraction, Psychopomp, Blessings/Clearings and Sacred Ceremonies, Herbalist and Aromatherapist, Shamanic Teacher and Spiritual Life Coach', for which she charges on a sliding scale from $90 per hour to $640 per day (McKay 2012a, 2012d).

McKay is little different from countless other shamanic practitioners operating private practices in the burgeoning self-improvement industry. Reliable data is difficult to come by, but an ongoing study of the US market by Florida-based market research company Marketdata Enterprises, Inc. concludes that the US market is worth around $11 billion and still has plenty of growth opportunities. Marketdata Enterprises' forecast until 2014 predicts the biggest growth segments after motivational speakers (forecast 6.8 per cent) will be personal coaching and holistic institutes, each forecast to grow at 6.2 per cent annually. For speakers and coaches, an important vehicle for their self-entrepreneurialism is authoring books. According to Marketdata Enterprises, self-improvement book sales, worth $406 million in 2009, will double to $854 million in 2014. Audiobooks are also predicted to grow faster than conventional books. From $406 million in 2009 or 17 per cent of the total US audiobooks market, audiobook sales until 2014 are forecast to grow by 6 per cent annually, compared with 3.4 per cent annual growth in the conventional books market. In 2011, more than 24 million Americans were listening to audiobooks (Marketdata Enterprises 2013, 2012a, 2010). This all bodes well for self-employed shamanic entrepreneurs like McKay, Cowan, Ingerman and their professional peers registered with the SSP. By professionalising their shamanic practice, they and countless other shamanic practitioners are creating new opportunities in an expanding marketplace for shamanic goods and services. Advertisements of their services and websites are listed in countless industry magazines and online forums, from publications like the *Journal for Shamanic Practice* and *Sacred Hoop* magazine, to the websites of the FSS, the SSP, the Shamanic Teachers and Shamanic Practitioners websites (published in German, Spanish, French, Italian, Dutch, Portuguese and Romanian), and Indie Shaman, a UK-based organisation 'for independent spirits' that offers 'support, training and information on Shamanism and on living a Shamanic lifestyle' (Indie Shaman 2012). The proliferation of interest groups, networks and subscription services on social media platforms like Facebook, Twitter, Ning and Linked-In has also increased interest in shamanic practice and grown the market for shamanic goods and services. As with any entrepreneurial venture, success requires differentiating one's product from competitors. Marketdata Enterprises announced its 2012 survey results by proclaiming 'self- improvement market has unfilled niches for entrepreneurs' (Marketdata Enterprises 2012b). For several shamanic practitioners, one of these unfilled niches is southern African spirit mediumship.

McKay's journey from North America to southern Africa to train as a *sangoma* is a well-trodden path. Before McKay, Chicagoan James Hall was also initiated as a *sangoma* and published his account in *Sangoma: My Odyssey into the Spirit World of Africa* (Hall 1994). Nicky Arden has similarly written of her 'mystical journey into the African spirit world' (Arden 1999, 1996). In 2005, shamanic counsellor and healer Shilo Satran spent a month with McKay's mentor Mtshali who taught her 'the age old arts of throwing the bones ... and working with herbs' (Satran 2012). Probably the most well-known *sangoma* practicing in the US and also a student of Mtshali is surgeon and urologist David Cumes. A South African expatriate who settled in the US in 1975, Cumes opened his private practice in Santa Barbara, California in 1981. In the early 1990s, he visited South Africa and spent a month in the Kalahari 'with the San (Bushmen), the last hunter-gatherers of Africa' (Cumes 2004: vii).[4] During subsequent visits, Cumes met independently with several *sangomas* who 'threw bones' for him. A traditional divination practice well-known in southern Africa, 'throwing the bones' consists in casting specially selected bones (and sometimes dominos and dice) and then interpreting the fall of the bones as conveying messages from ancestors. On each occasion, their message was unequivocal: Cumes was ignoring his destiny; he should train to become a *sangoma* (ibid.: vii). In 1999, Cumes began training with Mtshali.

Cumes's 'odyssey into the spirit world of African healing', as he subtitled his subsequent book, continued a journey he began in 1990. While performing a shamanic ritual in Peru, Cumes had a vision of the South African bushveld

---

4 Commenting on the appropriateness of the designations 'San' and 'Bushmen', South African archaeologist and rock art specialist David Lewis-Williams has noted that the term 'bushman' is often seen as a pejorative term for the indigenous inhabitants of the Kalahari region and that the term 'San' is generally preferred. However, he notes too that 'San', a Nama word, means something similar to vagabond or vagrant and is also pejorative. Unfortunately, there is no suitable name for these indigenes, although many of them chose either or both these terms to identify themselves (see Lewis-Williams 1995: 82, n. 1).

and a dilapidated house without a roof. The dream was the first of three over several years that would eventually lead Cumes to Tshisimane, a farm in South Africa's Soutpansberg mountains, that he purchased around 2002 to establish the Tshisimane Healing Centre. The healing centre in the mountains is premised on the idea that, as Cumes puts it, 'Nature is a magnificent microcosmic representation of the Divine. The wilderness is God's showpiece. She is the ultimate healer and can provide the strongest medicine. Indigenous healers know this truth, and their "natural" medicine will never be outdated' (ibid.: 112). Cumes first tested this idea in 1995 when he founded Inward Bound, 'an organisation dedicated to the idea that nature provides the best healing available'. Inward Bound promoted 'restoration and self-transformation' by offering experiential tours into remote wilderness areas so that participants could benefit from an 'inner journey into the wild outdoors': 'the purer one's exposure to remote wilderness, the more powerful is the effect of what I call wilderness rapture' (ibid.: vii, 63). Cumes's first book, *Inner Passages, Outer Journeys*, took Inward Bound and wilderness rapture as its principle subject.

Cumes's second book, *The Spirit of Healing*, takes readers on a journey with Cumes 'to distant lands where healing is practiced in a different way'. Via visits to the 'primitive cultures' inhabiting the Kalahari Desert, Tibet's mountains and Amazonia's jungles, Cumes leads his readers 'towards the ultimate discovery – that we cannot separate modern medical practice from inner healing without a negative impact on our health'. For a surgeon like Cumes, this discovery fundamentally challenges professional allopathic practices of patient treatment and care. Cumes's training with the Swazi *sangoma* Mtshali was as much a response to the calling of his ancestors as it was his attempt to engage the challenge posed to his allopathic training:

> The healing that the sangoma does, like the San healing, is the first medicine; it has not changed and will not change. This therapy arises from nature, and like us it will return to nature. The principles are always true and always pure since they come from the Divine and thence from the ancestors. It is in those areas closest to wilderness, where the bush is most pristine, that the best *muti* [medicine] is available and where the healing is the most uncontaminated. (Ibid.: 64)

Beginning in 1999, Cumes's training lasted two years. During this time, he took periodic breaks from his Santa Barbara practice to train with Mtshali in Swaziland. Back in Santa Barbara, he built his own *ndumba* or special home for the ancestors, although Cumes modelled his on the Asian yurt and made it of canvas rather than the round mud and thatch hut found in southern Africa. In his third book, *Africa in My Bones*, wherein he recounts his experience training to become a *sangoma*, Cumes admits he worried that his 'patient base' would dwindle. 'Paradoxically', he reports. 'my Western practice has increased since I began throwing bones and dispensing *muti* out of my *ndumba*.' Although his surgical practice is standard and conventional, 'figuratively' he carries his *sangoma* medicine bag wherever he goes; 'this practice has added to my Western skills' (ibid.: 114–15).

The elaboration of Cumes's skills is indicated by the different photographs of Cumes displayed on the covers of *The Spirit of Healing* and *Africa in my Bones*. *Spirit* displays Cumes in the pose of a male medical professional. Photographed from the waist up with arms folded across his chest, he wears blue surgical scrubs and has a stethoscope draped around his neck. His image is cut out of its original setting and displayed against a plain white background, as if to underline that professional medical practice is not context-bound and easily transposable. Slightly greying, clean-shaven and smiling broadly, Cumes is somewhat reminiscent of a cardboard cut-out of George Clooney's character in the television series *ER*. The cover of *Bones* displays Cumes very differently. Rather than standing arms folded facing the viewer, Cumes is seated cross-legged with unfolded arms resting on his thighs. Rather than a cut-out against a white background, he is seated on a reed mat inside his *ndumba* surrounded by woven and beaded baskets, with his bones set scattered before him. In place of his stethoscope, in his hand he holds a pointing stick and criss-crossing his chest are two beaded strings, signifying his *sangoma* status. Cumes's 'odyssey into the spirit world of African healing' conveyed by the accoutrements of the *sangoma*'s practice is emphasised by the compositional perspective; rather than confronted by Cumes's assertive authority as he stands arms folded before the viewer, now our perspective is slightly declined as we view Cumes seated humbly and patiently before us on the ground. Finally, that it is a surgeon who has undertaken this odyssey is indicated by the only similarity with *Spirit*'s photograph of Cumes: he still wears surgical scrubs and the same engaging smile accompanies his gaze directly at the camera.

A few months before publication of *Bones*, in late 2003 Cumes launched his website at www.davidcumes.com under the banner 'holistic urology & surgery psycho-spiritual healing'. The website explained the principles of 'African healing rituals and divination', advised how visitors may engage Cumes as a keynote speaker or workshop facilitator (suggested topics included 'South African shamanism' and wilderness- and nature-related themes), listed two dozen 'sponsoring organisations' (including the American College of Surgeons, the Institute of Noetic Sciences, and the American Holistic Nurses Association), as well as advertised his books, Inward Bound, the healing centre at Thisimane, and somewhat incongruously, the Cumevac, 'the original single fill bladder evacuator'. Cumes has periodically updated his website, adding video from his travels in South Africa, a documentary film about his ancestors' calling, a podcast link, and a link to his webpage at the independent online music store CDBaby.com where visitors can purchase any of the twelve albums Cumes has released since 2007. With titles such as 'Sacredness', 'Indigenous Voices', 'The Ancestors' and 'Spirit Healing Songs', they can be found in CDBaby's 'shamanic', 'new age' and 'world traditions' genres.

Like McKay, Cowan, Ingerman, Shilo Satran and most professional shamanic practitioners for whom practising without a presence in cyberspace would be a formidable handicap, Cumes's personal website is a homology of his professional presence in the world. The implication that Cumes's medical rooms in Santa Barbara have been displaced recalls an important element of Foucault's critique of neoliberalism. There is a resemblance between Cumes's journey from physician to surgeon to *sangoma* to shamanic practitioner and entrepreneur, and the transformation from classical into neoliberal *homo economicus*. Recall Foucault's argument that in place of entering into exchange transactions on the basis of wants, needs and a utility that may be defined and satisfied, neoliberal *homo economicus* is an entrepreneur of their self, increases income by investing in their own embodied human capital, and produces satisfaction by reconceiving consumption as an enterprise activity. In a neoliberal context, there is no distinction between personal and professional identity because neoliberal *homo economicus* is identified less by profession than by entrepreneurial pursuits that have their locus and unity in the ontology of *homo economicus*. Cumes carries his *sangoma* bag with him everywhere he goes, and while he describes this as 'figurative' luggage, to the extent that it symbolises his human capital, it is less figurative than embodied. Indeed, if 'David Cumes' *is* the product of his own satisfaction, then the eponymously named Cumevac, patented in 1989, may be regarded as an early experiment in Cumes's neoliberal entrepreneurialism, for which Cumes's website is the maturation. As Cumes's undifferentiated personal-professional presence in cyberspace, davidcumes.com is homologous to Cumes's embodied neoliberal entrepreneurial self.

Like American *sangomas*, African *sangomas* have also been investing their human capital. However, whereas identifying their human capital with *sangoma* traditions is valuable for North American practitioners, African *sangomas* have found value in identifying their human capital with shamanism. Although *sangomas* and other kinds of traditional healers and ritual specialists across Africa have been represented as 'shamans' for at least a century,[5] assimilations of African indigenous religiosities to a transnational popular shamanic idiom accelerated sharply during the 1990s. There are likely several contributing factors explaining these developments, including the global revolution in digital technologies and relative political stability that followed the end of apartheid in South Africa. However, I think an important but neglected facilitating factor has been neoliberal spiritual entrepreneurialism, in the Atlantic world generally, and in southern Africa particularly. While Americans have been journeying to southern Africa to be initiated in the ways of indigenous African healing, African shamans have been heading to North America, apparently doing as Mtshali charged Cumes: 'to tell the white people that they have lost the way' and need to 'get back to what we in Africa know' (Mtshali, quoted in ibid.: ix).

Consider Mandaza Augustine Kandemwa, a *Svikiro* or 'carrier of many earth and water spirits' and a *Mhondoro* or 'one who is in constant prayer on behalf of others'. According to his website at www.mandaza.org, Kandemwa is 'a vessel of spirits' who 'receives visions and dreams, makes offerings, performs healing rituals, and serves as a messenger for the Ancient Ones'. Kandemwa's priority is 'to pass on to ... all citizens of Planet Earth, business people, politicians, presidents, prime ministers, kings and queens – the powerful messages I receive in my dreams and visions' and to 'share the deeper meanings of Love, Truth, Justice and Peace as given to us by Our Creator, Ancestors, and Spirits' (Kandemwa 2012g). Since the early 2000s, Kandemwa has steadily increased his penetration of a growing network of enthusiasts in North America for southern African indigenous religiosities. Kandemwa's first contact into this network was Michael Ortiz Hill and Deena Metzger. Hill's background is nursing and his interest in healing and compassionate care is the subject of several books and essays; Metzger is a feminist writer and storyteller who has published widely in both academic and non-academic forums (for examples, see Hill 2012; Metzger 2012). Together, Hill and Metzger are credited with introducing the Shona practice of *daré* or community council to North America. They can also be credited with introducing North American enthusiasts for African religiosities to Mandaza Kandemwa.

Following the 1992 Los Angeles riots, Hill became interested in African-Americans' dreams about white people. 'To do justice to the dream life of African

---

[5]   As early as 1868, an anonymous review of T.P. Lesley's *Man's Origin and Destiny* suggested that 'African fetichism is, in reality, the same superstition as the Shamanism, or so-called devil worship of Asia' (Anon. 1868: 365; also see Lang 1891; I. Lewis 1981, 1971; Nadel 1946; Ngubane 1977).

Americans', Hill proposed studying 'the African (predominantly Bantu) world that gave birth to black American culture'. He headed for Africa where he met 'the Bantu healer Mandaza Kandemwa' in Zimbabwe in 1996. Kandemwa initiated Hill 'into the ritual tradition anthropologists recognize as the headwaters of what was to become African American culture'. It also led to a series of books co-authored with Kandemwa. *The Village of the Water Spirits*, published in 2006, is the result of Hill's racial dreaming project. According to Hill's website, Kandemwa's interpretations of 'the racial dreams of black Americans' outline 'a compelling picture of the African shape of the African American soul'. The other two books revolve around Hill and Kandemwa's relationship, introduced in *Gathering in the Names: A Journey into the Land of African Gods* in terms of their kinship bond as healing practitioners, and culminating in *Twin from Another Tribe: The Story of Two Shamanic Healers from Africa and North America*.

Kandemwa built his North American network through collaborations with Hill and Metzger. Metzger was particularly taken with the Shona *daré* (Beath 2005: 138–40). In Shona, *daré* generally refers to a community court or council with executive authority. However, as the concept has been developed by Metzger and a growing community of *daré* enthusiasts in North America, it refers to 'a sacred community gathering' constituted for the purpose of dialogue, with participants as much as with spirits and ancestors. Rituals are important. Among the most active *daré* communities in North America are Cape Cod Daré in Massachusetts, Bay Area Daré in California, and Topanga Blue Flag Daré at Hill's and Metzger's home north-west of Los Angeles. According to the Bay Area Daré website (www.bayareadare.com), meetings open with invocations of spirits, and drumming and dancing are regarded as essential as the community 'aligns itself with timeless ways of knowing, placing healing, peace building and the restoration of our world at the center of our community, consciousness and actions'. Kandemwa describes *daré* as 'a gathering together of community to give and receive healing to one another and the community at large – to share ideas, stories, dreams and gifts; to create and to celebrate; to honor Spirit – and between us, to find the wisdom to proceed on a path of peacemaking' (Kandemwa 2012a).

These and other locations are important destinations on Kandemwa's annual visits to North America. From 2004 to 2008, Kandemwa visited annually with the *daré* community at Cape Cod where his presence was a celebrated focus. In 2009 he attended the SSP's annual conference in New York's Catskill Mountains where he gave two keynote addresses, on 'Becoming a Temple of Spirit' and 'Holding Dreams in Reverence', and performed a 'sacred dream ceremony'. Kandemwa's keynote was probably facilitated by Metzger, who serves on the SSP's

Advisory Board. From 2009 until 2012 Kandemwa was also a featured speaker at the Society for the Study of Shamanism, Healing and Transformation's annual conference in San Rafael, California. Coincidently, the 2010 conference, themed 'Wisdom of Our Ancestors – Bridge to the Future', also featured American *sangoma* David Cumes. No doubt Kandemwa was fêted at similar conferences and sacred communities around the US and Canada, although the inherent transience of webpages, most of the time the only readily available sources for this kind of discovery, makes tracing Kandemwa's movements and activities challenging. However, Kandemwa's 2010 calendar suggests something of the scale and scope of his itineraries in previous years. Somewhat reminiscent of a touring rock band, Kandemwa's 2010 'international tour dates' comprised 14 cities in 15 weeks, beginning in Germany, then Canada, followed by events from Boston and Cape Cod to Los Angeles and the San Francisco Bay area, before ending in Hawaii in late September (Kandemwa 2010). The following year was still more ambitious. Kandemwa was on the road for more than five months, travelling to 29 different locations, including 12 in Canada (Kandemwa 2012f).

It is worth recalling that for more than a decade, the economy of Kandemwa's native Zimbabwe has all but collapsed. Kandemwa can probably do more to support himself and his family by his entrepreneurial endeavours in North American than he can with the limited opportunities in southern Africa. At any rate, giving economic assistance to Kandemwa's family in Zimbabwe is advertised as a rationale for seeking out Kandemwa's 'Teachings, individual sessions and water and fire ceremonies' during this 'critical time period as Mother Earth heals and re-balances' (SME 2009). Certainly the collapse of the Zimbabwean dollar has caused great suffering for many Zimbabweans and provides a compelling rationale for engaging Kandemwa's spiritual services by way of offering support to at least one affected family. Significantly however, support for Kandemwa and his family entails more than simply purchasing divination readings or attending spiritual retreats and speaking engagements. Kandemwa's North American supporters have gone to some length to facilitate an entrepreneurial project built around 'Mandaza Kandemwa, African shaman, healer and peacemaker', including establishing and managing his presence online, as well as fundraising and sponsorships. The American sangoma Gretchen McKay designed Kandemwa's website and links to it from her own, while instructions for contacting Kandemwa direct inquirers to a member of Cape Cod Daré (Kandemwa 2012c; McKay 2012c). Indeed, the sense that Kandemwa is not the exclusive author of his online presence is highlighted by the observation that his website and webpages on the social networking platforms Facebook, Ning, and Peace Villages are written in the third person (Kandemwa 2012d, 2012b, 2012e).

Yet as a mode of support, neoliberal entrepreneurialism involves some risks. Kandemwa's friends founded Tatenda, a nonprofit organisation, with a threefold purpose:

> Tatenda ... has been set up to support and sustain traditional healers and their communities in Africa as well as helping to preserve these living cultures so critically endangered by poverty, inter-racial and ethnic conflicts and the demands and circumstances of modern life. In addition, Tatenda seeks to create dialogue and collaboration between practitioners of western medicine and the healing arts internationally for their mutual benefit and enlightenment. (Cape Cod Daré 2012)

Like many small nonprofit projects in the US, Tatenda used a 'fiscal sponsor', which is to say, an organisation already registered with the US tax authorities as a tax-exempt, nonprofit organisation. For a fee, fiscal sponsors manage project accounts, make payments and ensure compliance with relevant laws. Tatenda's fiscal sponsor was International Humanities Center, a California-based organisation founded in 2003 that at its peak managed over 300 nonprofit projects. In late 2011, International Humanities Center collapsed amid allegations of misappropriation and fraud; losses are estimated at over $1 million, including $60,000 for Tatenda (Cohen 2012).

Mandaza Kandemwa is a relative newcomer to the field of African shamanic entrepreneurialism. The pioneer of this field is surely Malidoma Patrice Somé, a self-professed African shaman and envoy to the West of the Dagara people of West Africa. Somé explains in his autobiography *Of Water and the Spirit: Ritual, Magic, and Initiation in the Life of an African Shaman* (Somé 1995) that as a child he was kidnapped from his rural village in Burkina Faso by Jesuit missionaries who forcibly converted him to Christianity. At age 20 he escaped, but discovered rejoining his community was near to impossible; he had lost his indigenous language and culture. The village decided Somé needed to be initiated back into the tribe, and a month-long ritual followed. At the end of it, Somé was restored to the community. But because he retained his 'Western education', he felt like 'a man of two worlds – trying to be at home in both of them' (ibid.: 3). As a man of two worlds, Somé is in a better position than most to recognise, as he explains in his book:

> ... at this time in history, Western civilization is suffering from a great sickness of the soul. The West's progressive turning away from functioning spiritual values; its total disregard for the environment and the protection of natural resources; the violence of inner cities with their problems of poverty, drugs, and crime; spiraling unemployment and economic disarray; and growing intolerance toward

people of color and the values of other cultures – all of these trends, if unchecked, will eventually bring about a terrible self-destruction. In the face of all this global chaos, the only possible hope is self-transformation. (Ibid.: 1).

At his elders' behest, Somé returned to 'the white man's world ... to share what I had learned about my own spiritual tradition through my initiation' (ibid.: 3): 'My elders are convinced that the West is as endangered as the indigenous cultures it has decimated in the name of colonialism.' In terms somewhat reminiscent of the FSS's expeditions to Siberia to assist indigenous communities recover the traditions they have lost, Somé's task was to be a Dagara envoy to the West, to teach the West about the spiritual values it has lost, to restore regard for environment and nature, and to replace violence with tolerance and understanding. Somé's first assignment was to obtain a university education, and in his first book he claims to hold three master's degrees and two doctorates, one each from the Sorbonne and Brandeis University.

Following a brief stint teaching at the University of Michigan, Somé left academia in the early 1990s to become a full-time public speaker. He gained some prominence in the men's movement by offering an African indigenous perspective on such issues as home and community, sexual intimacy and initiation, the latter in collaboration with mythologist and poet Michael Mead and James Hillman, director of studies at the Jungian Institute following Jung's death and an important figure in the Jungian orientation of the men's movement during the 1980s and 1990s (Somé 1993, Somé and Somé 1994, Hillman, Meade and Somé 1992; cf. Kimmel 1995). Somé was the subject of the documentary film *Thinking Aloud: African Ritual and Initiation*, was interviewed for *Mother Jones* and over the next few years published the three books that extended his influence beyond the men's movement and established him as a fixture of the alternative spiritualities circuit. The first was *Of Water and the Spirit*, his autobiographical account of 'life as an African shaman', followed by *Ritual: Power, Healing and Community*, and finally *The Healing Wisdom of Africa*. The first and last are still in print, have been recorded as audiobooks, and translated into German. Somé also founded a charitable organisation, but whereas Kandemwa opted for the fiscal sponsor option, Somé registered his as a nonprofit organisation and assumed responsibility for managing its finances. In *Of Water and the Spirit*, Somé wrote of his role 'as both a bridge and a conduit' between two worlds. Echoes of the Ancestors, Inc. was conceived as the vehicle with which to traverse the distance. Through Echoes of the Ancestors, and particularly his website at www.malidoma.org, Somé offered over twenty courses and workshops on divination, healing with ancestors, and African shamanism, including courses on 'African Shamanism in the Business World' and a 'three year intensive' titled 'into the Heart of African Shamanism' (Somé 2012). While African shamanism travelled west, Somé advertised development projects in Burkina Faso he hoped would draw funding eastward. Details, applications, payment and donations were all handled through Somé's website.

By 2010, Somé had transferred his website to a .com domain (www. malidoma.com) and revamped its design. He scaled back his services to telephone consultations and personal divinations and reduced his intensive African shamanism course to two years. Retitled 'Indigenous African Spirit Technologies: An Introduction Into a Dagara-Inspired Way Of Walking on the Earth', the course is designed 'to lay the groundwork, deeply and personally, for a leap into the magical and spiritual technological legacies of our ancestors'. It includes 'radical exploration of the elements of cosmology, Fire, Water, Earth, Nature, and Mineral', 'ancestralisation' rituals, 'cowry shell divination', and 'the art and science of talisman making' (Somé 2012). Somé also replaced Echoes of the Ancestors with a new nonprofit organisation called Aviela, Inc. Aviela's two purposes are, first to acknowledge and thank 'the elders and diviners, the healers and shamans of West Africa' for giving of 'their time, knowledge, and dedication to the ancestors ... often without compensation or acknowledgement'; second, Aviela 'provides a vehicle' to realise Malidoma's vision of 'a training/healing/ retreat center, a home for the ancestors, here in the west':

> This place would be dedicated to the ongoing offering of ritual training, teaching and intense experiential healing that comes from the work Malidoma facilitates. It will be a space, in the west, that holds the collective energies of all those who come to deepen their relationship with the other worlds, via the teachings of indigenous Africa. (Ibid.)

'AVIELA provides a container for saying "thank you", in a monetary way', and anyone may donate with Paypal via Somé's website.

One may wonder what exactly is so neoliberal about spiritual entrepreneurs like African shamans Kandemwa and Somé, American *sangomas* McKay and Cumes, and innumerable examples like theirs. Recalling Foucault, the key issue is how neoliberal theory reconceives labour. The classical theory of labour as sold at the market price for a given skill or competency level is challenged by the observation that a worker's skill is embodied, inseparable from their corporeal being, and therefore cannot be sold from time to time on the market. Instead, labour can be separated into components of capital and income, where the latter is the wage earned from work and, as an income, is the product of a (human) capital, which is the worker's abilities and skills. As against the Marxist account of the worker as an alienated machine, Foucault understands this machine in the positive sense as one constituted by a worker and their ability bound together and remunerated over time by a series of wages that will produce an income stream. Foucault's account of a 'machine-stream ensemble' is very different from the conception of labour power sold at the prevailing market price; the ensemble presents 'a conception of capital-ability ... so that the worker himself appears as a sort of enterprise of himself' (Foucault 2008: 224–5).

This kind of enterprise of the self distinguishes neoliberal from classical *homo economicus*. It is also particularly well suited to shamanic practitioners, whose ability to enter a shamanic state of consciousness and commune with ancestral and other spirits is both paradigmatic of their practice and quintessentially inalienable from their corporeal being. If this analysis is correct, however, then what do neoliberal spiritual entrepreneurs impart that in imparting is none the less not alienated from them? I suggest it is an experience in the person with whom they are transacting, catalysed by the entrepreneur's representation (via autobiography) of their experience (engaging with spirits) which also testifies to their skills and abilities (as shamanic practitioners): Cumes's 'pure experience' of 'wilderness rapture', the centrality of 'ancestral wisdom' in McKay's and Somé's respective projects, Kandemwa's *darés* that 'honor spirit', indeed Harner's account of core shamanism as cultivating shamanic knowledge via shamanic experiences, or as one participant enthused on Mandaza's Facebook webpage in August 2011 about a joint workshop with Somé and Kandema, 'such an incredible experience witnessing Mandaza and Malidoma meeting in person'. Experience has been one of shamanism's discursive regularities since at least the nineteenth century. In the neoliberal era, however, the entrepreneur's representation of their experience increasingly emphasises technique. Unlike entrepreneurs of Harner's and Castaneda's generation for whom technique meant a means of accessing shamanic consciousness and non-ordinary reality, for today's spiritual entrepreneurs technique increasingly means recovering an alternative epistemology as a move towards founding a new ontology that will reverse the deleterious effects of anthropocentric mastery. Consider, for example, Somé's two-year course on 'Indigenous African Spirit Technologies':

> The time for a vigorous act of devotion to, and embracing of the wisdom of indigenous Africa has come ... the continent is ... the repository of profound unseen powers and technologies on standby to contribute to a radical healing change much needed in the world today. This calls for ... those in whose heart ancient Africa speaks, to check in for this exciting and compelling journey home

where they can expect to find how much of the old in them has been waiting to burst in service of the world's need to heal and to transform. This training is offered in response to that call. (Somé 2012)

Certainly this training is also an object of commercial transaction and resembles a product of labour exchanged for a monetary value at the market price, in accord with classical economics. Yet, this understanding misrecognises the nature of the object and the larger process of which it is a part. Rather than a product of labour, the training (and its experiential content) is a product of human capital, which is Somé's embodied and inalienable abilities and skills as a shamanic practitioner. With his capital, he generates an income, which is his wage for his labour. Secondly, by emphasising the transaction, the classical understanding fails to convey the sense in which it is one transaction in a complicated web linking it with other transacted products (books, talks, workshops, retreats, and so on) and in its temporal dimension is akin to an income-stream that returns to Somé the dividends of his investments in his embodied human capital.

Shamanism's neoliberal moment emerged because the new premium neoliberal theory placed on embodiment meant that engaging with spirits could be recast as a form of human capital. Shamanic practice, like other professional practices, could be trained and improved, and as an investment in human capital, would generate an income stream over time. Today shamanic practice is regarded by aspiring shamanic practitioners as a viable career option. Consider the professional biography of shamanic practitioner Lenore Norrgard (2012a, 2012b). Drawn to shamanism in the late 1980s, Norrgard enrolled in FSS courses and graduated in 1993 as a Harner Method Shamanic Counsellor. From the mid-1990s, she began designing and offering professional shamanic counseling services and courses from offices in downtown Seattle, including a Shamanic Healing Apprenticeship Programme (Norrgard 2012c). By the end of the decade, she was consulting with US health insurance giant Kaiser Permanente in preparing a grant application to the National Institutes of Health to research the efficacy and cost-effectiveness of shamanic healing. Norrgard participated in the subsequent study (see Vuckovic et al. 2007, Norrgard 2012a, 2012b). Another shamanic practitioner is Christina Pratt, a former student of both Harner and Somé and author of *An Encyclopedia of Shamanism* in two volumes. Since January 2009, Pratt has hosted a weekly podcast titled 'Why Shamanism Now'. The podcast is available online and via Apple's iTunes service, and over the years has featured interviews with Cowan, Ingerman, Lucier, McKay and Norrgard, among many others (Pratt 2012). In the new millennium, Pratt, like Norrgard and a growing number of practitioners registered with the Society for

Shamanic Practitioners and similar associations, are among a new generation of shamans working hard to develop shamanic practice as a profession.

This kind of professionalisation is not without controversy, not least because capital, whether embodied or otherwise, is always acquired one way or another. Since much professional shamanic practice in North America is based on Harner's core shamanism and stripped of reference to specific contexts and cultures, it is less vulnerable to charges of unethical appropriation of indigenous cultures and traditions. However, modes of acquisition become highly contested in cases of indigenous culture and knowledge that are identifiable with specific local cultures and contexts. Accusations of appropriation, commodification and exploitation of indigenous traditions and native authenticity have long been topical issues in this regard,[6] and controversies over intellectual property rights are among the most salient examples of intersections between indigenism, environmentalism and neoliberalism. These controversies intensified during the 1990s, partly because transnational indigenism increased sensitivity to exploitation of indigenous cultures, but particularly because surging interest from pharmaceutical companies in indigenous peoples' knowledge of healing properties of plants prompted accusations of neocolonialism and 'green colonialism', from Yanomami shaman Davi Kopenawa among many others (Jowitt 2007).

The Swazi *sangoma* P.H. Mtshali recounts that in 1985 his senior ancestor King Luvenga told his family a new independence struggle was needed in Africa: '... nations of Africa have struggled and fought for independence from the bondage of colonialism and imperialism. Now that political freedom has been gained it is time for the next step – to gain professional independence for traditional healers.' Mtshali reported that all the ancestors agreed with King Luvenga and charged the president of Swaziland's Traditional Healers Organisation 'to be their mouthpiece'. In this new independence struggle, *sangomas* need help, and not only from their ancestors. Mtshali continued:

---

[6]   These issues became topical in New Age contexts in the 1980s (Churchill 2003, P. Deloria 1994, Raibmon 2005, Kehoe 1990, P. Jenkins 2004, Wernitznig 2003). An analogous controversy has emerged in southern Africa where *sangoma* traditionalists have argued that white people shouldn't be initiated as *sangomas* because, as descendants of Europeans, they don't have African ancestors (Gophe 2000). John Lockley, a white *sangoma* and self-proclaimed African shaman who was featured on Pratt's radio show (Pratt 2010), counters that since Africa is the birthplace of humanity, 'we all have ancient African ancestors' (Lockley 2010; cf. IOL 2007). Academic researcher and white *sangoma* Jo Wreford has written on these issues (Wreford 2008, 2007, 2006).

I believe that each country should collect and preserve traditional healing skills which are rapidly disappearing. The traditional medical knowledge of herbs ... should be for the benefit of all people, not just make a few drug companies rich. These companies steal our knowledge and then make the drugs so expensive that the people who collected the knowledge in the first place cannot afford to use and benefit from them. Is this fair? I say no, and the way around the problem is to have governments collect the knowledge worldwide for the benefit of everyone. (Mtshali 2004: 117)

The second part of this chapter shifts perspective from neoliberal *homo economicus* who is an entrepreneur of her or his self towards neoliberal governmentality and the art of maintaining things in their right disposition so that the principle of economy extends, capillary-like, to the farthest ends of the social order. There are many examples of intersections between neoliberal governmentality, entrepreneurialism, and indigenous identity and culture that illustrate the issues discussed below. Chapter 1 touched on examples from Central and North Asia, where shamanic revivals in autonomous federal republics of Altai, Sakha (Yakutia), Tuva, and Buryatia (and among ethnic Buryats in Mongolia) have vitalised post-Soviet ethnic nationalisms. Integrations of ethnic nationalisms into global circuits of shamanism discourse have brought Siberia to the wider world, but have also brought the shifting discursive regularities of transnational shamanism to Siberia. Vitebsky's comparison of the Sora and Sakha illustrated how coupling environmental concern with privileged indigenous knowledge that began in Brazil has been instrumentalised in Sakha Republic. In the idiom of environmentalism, indigenous claims cached with histories of dispossession and subjugation become future-oriented and hence all the more powerful in legitimating ethnic claims in the political vacuum that followed the disintegration of the Soviet Union. A different series of examples can be found in the United States where Alaska's Native Claims Settlement Act provided a uniquely neoliberal solution to indigenous claims to sovereignty over lands, territories and resources. The Act transformed all twelve of Alaska's regional native associations into over two hundred 'Native Village Corporations', such as the Chenega Corporation of Prince William Sound and the Afognak Native Corporation of Kodiak Island. With offices across the US, including Anchorage, Honolulu, Dallas, Denver, San Diego and Washington, the Afognak pursue their goal 'to optimize financial benefits, land use and preserve our culture for the well-being of our shareholders', according to the corporation's website at www.afognak.com. To these examples we could add South Africa, where an ensemble of tactics targeting *sangomas* provides another exemplary illustration of neoliberal governmentality implicating shamanism.

Neoliberal Governmentality

In 1997, the South African government's Department of Health adopted a National Drug Policy (DOH 1996). Comprising health, economic and 'national development' objectives, the policy committed the government to investigating the effective and safe use of 'African traditional medicines' in primary healthcare. The policy aimed to encourage 'traditional healers' to work more closely with 'the formal health care sector', and committed the government to investigating the efficacy, safety and quality of traditional medicines. The following year, the Medical Research Council of South Africa established a Traditional Medicines Research Unit and a National Reference Centre for African Traditional Medicine. An expert committee on African traditional medicines was also established to advise the Medicines Control Council on regulating, registering and controlling indigenous traditional medicines. From a healthcare perspective, these efforts were important, particularly given that 70–80 per cent of South Africa's population relied on traditional medicine for their primary healthcare needs and South Africa's disease burden included epidemics of HIV and tuberculosis. Beyond healthcare, however, these efforts to regulate and control African traditional medicine also signalled an extension of neoliberal governmentality into social domains in which economy as the principle of *raison d'état* had not previously been present, or at least less intensely. Indeed, since the late 1990s, successive governments' strategies to modernise and develop the post-apartheid state have extended and consolidated the principle of economy across all sectors of South African society, in accord with former president Thabo Mbeki's version of a developmental state. It was a cornerstone of Mbeki's vision of an African Renaissance and the motivating factor in prioritising 'Indigenous Knowledge Systems' (hereafter IKS) in the government's economic development strategy (Odora Hoppers 2002).

The government's Indigenous Knowledge Systems Policy, designed by the national Department of Science and Technology (hereafter DST) and adopted by the Cabinet in 2004, is structured by four 'IKS Policy drivers': 'affirmation of African cultural values in the face of globalisation', 'development of services provided by traditional healers', contribution of indigenous knowledge to employment and wealth creation, and interfaces with other knowledge systems (DST 2004: 9, 12–15). The policy established a National Indigenous Knowledge Systems Office within the DST and charged it with responsibility for coordinating IKS-related matters between twelve relevant ministries, in multilateral and bilateral relations with other states, and with the private sector. The policy also made clear that the state too intends prospecting indigenous knowledge. Indeed, the government's *Ten-Year Innovation Plan for South Africa* published in 2008 intends transforming South Africa into a 'knowledge-based economy' by 2018 (DST 2008; cf. Green 2008a). The four pillars of this vision are given as innovation, education, information infrastructure, and 'the economic and institutional regime'. '[H]uman capital development' is prioritised, and the Plan explains that 'the government needs to set the focus, establish the scale, and give appropriate signals to ensure that enabling conditions are in place' (DST 2008: 31). The ten-year plan is premised on an analysis that the world is entering a new phase of technological innovation it calls 'bio-economy' and compares this economy's stage of development in 2007 with the steam age around the 1840s and the information age around the 1970s (ibid.: 3). Faced with this bio-economic future, the plan identifies several 'grand challenge areas', including the '"Farmer to Pharma" value chain to strengthen the bio-economy'. The Plan insists that by 2018 'South Africa must become a world leader in biotechnology and the pharmaceuticals [*sic*], based on the nation's indigenous resources and expanding knowledge base' (ibid.: viii). Far from guarding healing practices from commercial exploitation, the healing practices of *sangomas* like Mtshali are a key part of the government's strategic goal: 'an economy in which new knowledge-based industries, and knowledge workers and systems, fuel stronger economic growth' (ibid.: 31). The DST's commitment to developing South Africa's knowledge economy is endorsed by the National Planning Commission (hereafter NPC). Established in 2009 and situated within the president's office, the NPC's role is to coordinate strategy, policy and actions across ministries and state agencies. The NPC's *National Development Plan 2030* sets out key drivers and challenges for social and economic development for the next two decades, including the importance of knowledge innovation (NPC 2011, 2012): 'The only form of investment that allows for increasing returns is in building the stocks and flows of knowledge that a country (or company) needs, and in encouraging new insights and techniques.' Knowledge production and innovation is important because it 'allows a citizen, a worker, a manager, or a finance minister to act purposefully and intelligently in a complex and demanding world' (NPC 2012: 94). The NPC's plan emphasises the need for a policy framework governing how traditional medicine fits into the overall health sector and insists that regulatory institutions and professional bodies within the health sector should be strengthened to support reforms, while state agencies like the Competition Commission and National Consumer Council should take cognisance of national health goals in pursuing their mandates (ibid.: 349–50).

One can appreciate why South Africa's government thinks the future of technological innovation is bio-economy and biotechnology. The World Health Organization estimates that 80 per cent of the world's population use herbal medicine for some aspect of primary healthcare (WHO 2008). Although proportions of population who use herbal medicines are highest in developing countries, in economic terms, the most valuable markets for phytomedicines are in western Europe, North America, and China. In 1993, the phytomedicines market in Europe, Asia and North America combined was worth $8.4 billion. Only four years later, in western Europe alone it was valued at $7 billion (Laird and Wynberg 1996, Okigbo and Mmeka 2006: 88). In 1993, American consumers spent almost $1.5 billion on 'herbal remedies'; by 1999, the US market had grown to $5 billion (Neddermeyer 2009, Okigbo and Mmeka 2006: 88). Market size in developing countries is more difficult to measure, although Grunwald (cited in Okigbo and Mmeka 2006: 88) reported that in 1993, over $2.4 billion worth of traditional Chinese medicines was sold in China and another $400 million worth was exported. The World Health Organization estimates that sales of herbal products in China totalled $14 billion in 2005 and in Brazil were worth $160 million in 2007 (WHO 2008). Figures published in 2006 showed that South Africa's market for African traditional medicine contributed an estimated R2.9 billion annually ($260 million) to South Africa's economy and employed at least 133,000 people (mostly rural women) (Rautenbach 2011: 39). In 2006, the annual global market value for phytomedicines was roughly $43 billion (Okigbo and Mmeka 2006: 88). Although the notion of using natural materials, whether plant, animal, or mineral, to treat ailments is probably as old as humanity, the expansion of market economics into this domain on the scale seen over the past quarter-century is unprecedented in human history. Some countries, notably those with high measures of biodiversity, think they have a competitive advantage. South Africa's 24,000 indigenous plants represent approximately 10 per cent of all vascular plants on Earth, according to government literature (DOH et al. n.d.: 5), and entirely includes one of the Earth's six floristic kingdoms.[7] Many of these plants can be purchased in local markets in towns and cities across South Africa and online through companies like African Shaman (www.africanshaman.com), although consumption rates of 200,000 tonnes of plant material per year alarm conservationists and *sangomas* alike (Mhlabane 2002, Rautenbach 2011: 39).

---

[7]   In botanical taxonomy, Earth's flora consists of six kingdoms, 35 floristic regions, and 152 floristic provinces. The South African floristic kingdom is the smallest and is entirely contained within South Africa's south-west region.

If growing global demand for phytomedicines indicates that the future bio-economy is already upon us, one can appreciate the South African government's sense of urgency, especially given South Africa's unique supply of plant resources. Indeed, like many governments around the world, South Africa is trying to catch up with transnational corporations that have been prospecting indigenous knowledge for the therapeutic properties of plants since the early 1990s. That decade saw an explosion of private-sector interest in plant materials, spurred on by advances in genetic science that allowed researchers to screen biological material for health properties far faster than trial-and-error methods. However, given that the Earth has hundreds of thousands of plant species, researchers reasoned that traditional healers are a good source of research leads and would add another level of screening. One South African researcher estimated screening efficiency increased by more than 400 per cent when researchers took their leads from *sangomas* and traditional healers (Koch 1995). At least one company, California-based Shaman Pharmaceuticals, made data collection from indigenous communities and traditional healers a cornerstone of their research strategy. During a 1995 visit to South Africa, Shaman Pharmaceuticals' chief medical anthropologist reportedly held extensive discussions with a local healers' organisation and talked about funding the organisation through South Africa's statutory Council for Scientific and Industrial Research (ibid.). Although Shaman Pharmaceuticals ultimately failed as a company and declared bankruptcy in 2001, their failure has not deterred other companies who have drawn lessons and are staking their claims in the new world of bioprospecting (Clapp and Crook 2002).

Foremost among the ethical issues raised by bioprospecting is fair compensation agreements and benefit-sharing with communities whose knowledge corporations convert into intellectual property and patents. When benefits are not shared equitably with communities, bioprospecting becomes biopiracy. The Rural Advancement Foundation International or RAFI, renamed in 2001 to Action Group on Erosion, Technology and Concentration or ETC Group, coined the term 'biopiracy' in the early 1990s to refer to 'the appropriation of the knowledge and genetic resources of farming and indigenous communities by individuals or institutions seeking exclusive monopoly control (usually patents or plant breeders' rights) over these resources and knowledge' (Robinson 2010: 14, 18). Although a formal definition of biopiracy has not been adopted by transnational regulators like the World International Property Organization, and ethical issues, legal complexities, and controversies abound (Dutfield 2003, Farhat 2008, McGown 2006, Robinson 2010), RAFI's definition remains an influential benchmark and was used, for example, by the report of the UK government's Commission on Intellectual Property Rights (CIPR 2002). If bioprospecting frames the future bio-economy in terms of opportunities, biopiracy frames it in terms of dangers. In recent years, these dangers have been brought into sharp focus by several controversial patenting decisions. For example, India's government became embroiled in complicated legal wrangling to reverse decisions by US and European patent authorities to grant patents on turmeric, neem tree extracts and basmati rice, while Bikram Choudhury's franchising of 26 yoga postures precipitated 'yoga wars' in the multi-billion-dollar yoga industry, in the US alone valued at $6 billion and up to $30 billion when accessories, equipment, instructional books and DVDs are included (Marden 1999, Wax 2010). Governments have recognised that a proactive approach requires measures along the lines advocated by Zulu *sangoma* Mtshali. India's government responded to the Bikram Yoga franchise by dedicating a 200-strong team of yogis and scholars to documenting and archiving 900 postures scanned from the *Mahabharata* and the Yoga Sutras, among other sources. This labour was part of a larger project to 'safeguard the sovereignty of [India's] traditional knowledge' under the auspices of the Traditional Knowledge Digital Library, a government-sponsored project to archive traditional knowledge found within India's sovereign territory in a searchable digital archive catalogued according to the specifications of international patent classification systems. Agreements with patents offices of Japan, the European Union, United Kingdom, United States, and the World Intellectual Property Organization grant confidential access so that patent applications in these jurisdictions can be checked against India's catalogue. The project includes an ongoing effort to translate the archive into English, French, German, Japanese and Spanish (TKDL 2012).

The Indian example illustrates three important issues for the problematic of neoliberal governmentality and indigenous knowledge. First, safeguarding indigenous knowledge from biopiracy requires assimilating it to neoliberalism's economic principle by converting indigenous knowledge into intellectual property. That conversion is achieved by describing the unique properties of an object in such a way that the description conforms to the systematicities and regularities of transnational intellectual property management regimes. Second, when Mtshali recommends that governments should collect traditional healing practices to safeguard them against appropriation by transnational pharmaceutical companies, the implication is that governments should collect this knowledge from people who already possess it, that is, yogis in the Indian example just mentioned and *sangomas* in the South African example cited earlier. A similar logic played out in Brazil. Among the changes wrought by the new Amazonian ecopolitics discussed in Chapter 4, Brazilian nationalists reversed the earlier exclusion of indigenous tribes from Brazilian national imaginaries and began portraying shamans as a bulwark against biopiracy by foreign corporate interests. The xenophobic element is important. Whereas previously Brazil's nationalists viewed Amazonia's indigenous populations as suspicious outsiders, in the new conjuncture they were increasingly included in the Brazilian 'nation' and identified as strategic partners in efforts to regulate bioprospecting in the national interest (Conklin 1997). From this perspective – and this is the third point – 'bioprospecting' and 'biopiracy' appear in a new light in which the prefix 'bio-' refers less to the properties of naturally occurring materials and more to the biological being of people in whom this knowledge is embodied. Bioprospecting and biopiracy in this sense have less to do with genetic plant materials and more to do with biopower: bodies are targeted by government interventions in the name of defending the state, as well as developing it via better regulation and prospecting of indigenous knowledge resources.

This perspective casts South Africa's ten-year innovation plan in a different light. 'Bio-economy' now appears less as an epoch of technological innovation akin to last century's information age or the steam age the century before that. Instead, bio-economy is the principle informing the *raison d'état* of the South African republic. The plan's emphasis – that 'the government needs to set the focus, establish the scale, and give appropriate signals to ensure that enabling conditions are in place' (DST 2008: 31) – recalls Foucault's definition of the art of government as the conduct of people in their multiform relationships toward an arrangement suitable to desired ends (Foucault 2009: 96, 1993: 203). This entails extending the principle of economy into new domains as well as deepening its penetration in those domains in which its organising rationality is already felt. Ultimately, however, the condition most enabling of neoliberal governmentality is neoliberal subjectivity. Neoliberal subjects are eminently governable because their self-conduct is informed by the same principle of economy that informs the conduct of people towards an optimal arrangement. The continuity of sovereign power across the plurality of its forms is sustained and enhanced when individuals' self-conduct is a correlate of *raison d'état*. Seen from this perspective, the ensemble tactics targeting the population are geared towards producing and guaranteeing conditions conducive to forming neoliberal subjectivity as much as towards the specificities of policy objectives. This ensemble, which includes policy, legislation and institutional authorities, operates a microphysics of power at the extremities of embodied subjectivities, 'where power reaches into the very grain of individuals' (Foucault 1980a: 39).[8] This kind of shaping and moulding of a desirable subjectivity can be likened to supplying sensation to a nerve, in which case South Africa's ten-year innovation plan is perhaps more aptly characterised as an innervation plan.

An important issue stemming from Foucault's analysis of governmentality is what becomes of law when sovereign power is no longer constituted by obedience to the sovereign's laws but instead becomes the art of government. In Foucault's analysis, the notion of the sovereign's divine right to command obedience recedes. In its place, legislation becomes one aspect of an ensemble of tactics combining policy objectives, institutional requirements, regulatory oversight, and inducements in the form of advantages and benefits obtained through compliance with legislation. Examples from South Africa have already been mentioned. The drugs policy and later the IKS policy established a National Reference Centre for African Traditional Medicine, an expert committee to advise the Medicines Control Council, a National Indigenous Knowledge Systems Office to coordinate IKS-related matters between relevant ministries, in foreign relations, and with the private sector, and articulated a rationale for prospecting indigenous knowledge in terms of the government's strategic vision of a knowledge-based economy. However, within this ensemble, legislation retains an important role. Legislation makes a practical task of citizenship by compelling compliance with the calculus of an economising rationality, and elaborates continuity between neoliberal subjectivity and *raison d'état*. Legislation coordinates the tactical operations of the micro-physics of sovereign power and, by ensuring the principle of economy pervades all forms of sovereign power, gives governmentality its art.

The South African government's efforts to incorporate *sangomas* into the ambit of governmentality and place individual *sangomas* within reach of sovereign power provides an exemplary illustration of this coordinating role of legislation. The *Traditional Health Practitioners Act* (hereafter THPA or the Act) was signed into law in 2007. Introduced to Parliament in 2001 as the Traditional Healers Bill, the stated purpose of the THPA is to provide 'a regulatory framework to ensure the efficacy, safety and quality of traditional health care services', and 'to provide for the management and control over the registration, training and conduct of practitioners, students and specified categories in the traditional health practitioners profession'. From the perspective of neoliberal governmentality and shamanism discourse, two

---

[8]   On capillary power, see Foucault 1977a: 26–7, 1980b: 96; cf. Foucault 1980a.

aspects of the THPA are particularly noteworthy. The first is the effort in the name of the state to fix in law coherent, stable and universally applicable definitions of several key terms of local discourses about *sangomas* and African traditional healing practices more generally. The second is the effort in the name of the state to found institutions and regulatory mechanisms that will govern traditional healers in their profession as traditional health practitioners.

Regarding definitions, Article 1 defines 'traditional health practice' as 'the performance of a function, activity, process or service based on a traditional philosophy that includes the utilisation of traditional medicine or traditional practice'. 'Traditional philosophy' is defined as

> ... indigenous African techniques, principles, theories, ideologies, beliefs, opinions and customs and uses of traditional medicines communicated from ancestors to descendants or from generations to generations, with or without written documentation, whether supported by science or not, and which are generally used in traditional health practice.

This broad and inclusive definition of 'traditional health practice' with reference to 'indigenous African techniques' is supplemented by differentiation from and specific exclusions of 'professional activities of a person practising any of the professions contemplated in the Pharmacy Act ... the Health Professions Act ... the Nursing Act ... the Allied Health Professions Act ... or the Dental Technicians Act ... and any other activity not based on traditional philosophy'. Having staked out a domain of application in these terms, the centrepiece of the Act is the Traditional Health Practitioners Council of South Africa. The 20-member council was established in early 2013 and is responsible for, *inter alia*, facilitating contact between different 'fields of training ... within the Republic and to set standards for such training', maintaining ethical and professional standards, and ensuring traditional health practice 'complies with universally accepted health care norms and values'. Article 6 requires the Council to maintain registers of traditional health practitioners, to 'control and exercise authority in respect of all matters concerning the training of persons in traditional health practice and the conduct of its members', and, in consultation with the Minister of Health, to 'determine policy, and ... make decisions regarding ... educational framework, fees, funding, registration procedure, code for professional conduct and ethics, disciplinary procedure and scope of traditional health practice'. The Act, which gives the Council statutory equivalence to the professional councils that respectively regulate pharmaceutical, allopathic, nursing, complementary and dental health practitioners, requires traditional healers to register with the

Council in at least one of four practitioner categories identified as 'diviner', 'herbalist', 'traditional birth attendant' and 'traditional surgeon'. Definition of these categories is deferred to the Council. The Act prohibits anyone from practicing as a traditional healer who is not registered with the Council, establishes the office of a Registrar responsible for maintaining a register of traditional health practitioners, as well as providing for disciplinary procedures to secure the integrity of the profession. Stipulations about accreditation, examination, qualification and certification are also specified, although the details are again deferred to the Council to determine. Altogether the Act intends professionalising traditional healthcare by extending government regulation of public healthcare providers to traditional healers.

Certainly there are good reasons for this intervention. An estimated 27 million South Africans rely on traditional medicine that they obtain through the services of an estimated 200,000 traditional healers (Gqaleni et al. 2007: 178, Moagi 2009: 119). With more than 50 per cent of the population – and up to 70 per cent or even 80 per cent by some estimates (Moagi 2009, WHO 2008, although see Jones 2006: 179–80) – receiving healthcare from providers whose qualifications, prescriptions and therapeutic techniques are neither regulated nor standardised, in a population with amongst the highest tuberculosis and HIV infection rates in the world, one might expect state intervention. Indeed the NPC estimates South Africa's burden of disease creates additional costs for the national health budget of around 0.7 per cent of GDP (NPC 2012: 339). Yet although the interventions provided for in the THPA models the same basic regulatory infrastructure governing other healthcare providers, traditional healers are also unique among health practitioners because their practice extensively involves working with spirits.

This is where the THPA extends the economic principle of *raison d'état* into domains previously relatively insulated from it, notwithstanding criticism such as Moagi's (2009:116) that 'the Act sets out a number of objectives for government, [but] talks little about the practical regulation of spiritual healing'. Indeed, the THPA does not mention religion, initiation, spirits, mediumship, or trance states, all of which are important and well-known aspects of traditional healing in South Africa (Thornton 2009: 21). Arguably, the Act downplays aspects of African traditional medicine because they might be viewed askance by other kinds of health professionals, although that seems unlikely because the facts of African traditional healing are so well known it is hardly credible that they can be suppressed. It is more plausible that the 'spiritual' or 'religious' aspects of traditional healing are not specifically mentioned simply because it is not necessary. The all-encompassing definition of 'traditional philosophy' and the legislated practitioner categories, particularly 'diviner', are sufficient for the Act's purpose. Far more significant than the Act's perceived omissions or obfuscations is the fact that the government seeks to intervene in spiritual healing in the first instance. Accession of the THPA was after all perhaps the first time in modern history that a liberal democratic state recognised the occult category of 'ancestors' as a source rather than an object of knowledge (ibid.: 22–3). Indeed, viewed from the perspective of governmentality, the THPA's perceived shortcomings are less omissions than deferrals to other apparatuses and technologies that as an ensemble exercise a form of power that targets the population. These include institutional bodies and regulatory authorities established by the THPA and tasked with translating varieties of local folk traditions into a profession, with its range of regularities, consistencies, standards of behaviour, ethical conduct, and common language and terminology conventions; related legislation, for example, the *Intellectual Property Laws Amendment Act* that incorporates 'indigenous cultural expressions or knowledge' into the existing regime of regulations governing copyright, patents, trademarks, and designs; state agencies and institutions such as the Medicines Control Council and National Reference Centre for African Traditional Medicine, but also fiscal authorities like the South African Revenue Service; public-sector service providers including hospitals and clinics, but also schools and state employers who must decide whether diagnoses from traditional health practitioners are acceptable for school absences and processing employees' annual sick leave; private-sector partners such as pharmaceutical companies, whom we have seen were ahead of the government in targeting traditional healers, but also mining companies who were among the first private-sector institutions in South Africa to recognise and incorporate traditional healers into their workers' medical insurance schemes; regional and national healers' associations, many of whom have enthusiastically supported the state's intervention from the Act's first draft and have vocally advocated implementation of its provisions,[9] and the overall coordination of this effort across these domains by the calculations and objectives of the government's policy framework.

---

[9] The most vocal association is the Traditional Healers Organisation which claims 29,000 members, offers accredited training certifications and lobbies the government on policy and legislation reforms (THO 2012). Other traditional healers' organisations in South Africa are the Tshwane Healers Forum, Dingaka Healers Association, Nyangazezizwe Traditional Healers Organisation and the African Traditional Health Practitioners' Union.

The Culture of Neoliberalism

A frequent criticism of the THPA is that it represents traditional health practice and traditional philosophy as an unchanging system of knowledge passed down from ancestors or through generations from a precolonial past (Thornton 2009, Rautenbach 2011). This representation is a pronounced problem in the South African government's 'indigenous knowledge systems' policy and is evident too in other applications of neoliberal governmentality to forms of indigeneity in South Africa, most obviously incorporations of 'indigenous cultural expressions or knowledge' into intellectual property rights regulations. For example, the *Intellectual Property Laws Amendment Act* amends several laws governing patents, copyright, trademarks and designs (hereafter PCTD) to recognise and protect 'certain manifestations of indigenous knowledge as a species of intellectual property'. To this end, the Act establishes a National Database of forms of indigenous knowledge that is integrated with national registers of PCTD, a National Trust for Indigenous Knowledge to administer and redistribute royalties, and a National Council for Indigenous Knowledge to advise the Minister of Trade and Industry and respective PCTD registrars. However, some observers emphasise that knowledge is situated and practical and therefore difficult to moderate with legislation. For example, Green (2008b: 149–50) proposes 'knowledge practices', 'knowledge traditions', or 'knowledge diversity' to designate what governments from South Africa to India to Brazil call 'indigenous knowledge'. Making the same point, Thornton criticises approaches to 'traditional healing' that fail to recognise that tradition is 'a category of critical and dynamic knowledge that is as much part of modernity as any other field of knowledge':

> The *sangoma* tradition has multiple roots that extend across time, cultures and languages, and derives partly from pre-colonial African systems of belief. While its appeal is broadening, it is also changing as *sangomas* are exposed to a wide range of other healing traditions and religious views. Today many of their practices scarcely resemble the older traditions reported in the early ethnographies, though some, like divination, remain … *Sangomas* offer a wide range of counselling, divination/ diagnostic, medical and other services. The *sangoma's* art is rarely directed simply at organic causes of physical disease. They prepare *muti* ('medicine') to protect clients from motor accidents, theft, witchcraft, infection, unemployment and loss of love, lovers or spouses. They relieve anxiety and depression, assist clients to make decisions and help to find lost or stolen objects. The *sangoma* is not a poor

man's doctor; they generally charge as much as a registered medical practitioner would. (Thornton 2009: 17)

On this account, *sangomas* do not need interventions like the THPA to establish their status as professionals; they already consider themselves members of a profession with a distinct intellectual tradition that is constantly made and remade in dynamic processes of circulation, critical reflection and change (see also Van Binsbergen 2005). Not only does this account of the epistemological labours of *sangomas*' practices contradict the concept of indigenous knowledge operated by the multiform tactics of *raison d'état*, it also suggests that the principle of economy is well established in the domain of African traditional medicine prior to the state's exercise of biopower targeting traditional healers. Does this contradict the foregoing analysis that the ensemble of apparatuses and technologies of biopower, including the THPA and its regulatory mechanisms, extend economy as the principle of state reason into domains where previously this principle was less established? I do not think so. What is changing here is that it is the state, actually a ruling government exercising a sovereign power that is constitutive of the state, which monopolises these apparatuses and applies these technologies to the population.

But this critique of the THPA and more generally of the ensemble of tactics of which it is a part draws attention to an important implication of the principle of economy for *raison d'état*: the art of government cannot bound or define the limits of the economic domain or circumscribe portions of it, whether as 'African traditional medicine', 'indigenous knowledge systems', or any other delimiter. The reason is simply that there is no bird's-eye view, no Archimedean vantage, from which sovereign power can grasp the totality of the economic domain and rearrange its elements to optimise the disposition of things towards desired ends. The invisible hand of the market is invisible to the sovereign too. The problem is that the juridical form of sovereign power cannot master economic processes, even as these are becoming the essential element of society's life. Thus the dilemma of sovereign power's desire for eminently governable neoliberal subjectivity: what is gained with respect to governance is lost with respect to control.

Since the 1990s, the prominence of ethnic bodies, occult economies (defined as the 'deployment of magical means for material ends' (J. Comaroff and Comaroff 1999: 297 n. 31), and 'the kingdom of culture' in South African political economy has stimulated a range of researches (for example, Ashforth 2005; Chidester 2012, 2006; J. Comaroff and Comaroff 2005, 2004, 2000, 1999; J.L. Comaroff and Comaroff 2009; Kohnert 2003; Leatt 2009; Mitchell and Mullen 2002; Ndlovu-Gatsheni 2007; Robins 2005, 2003, 2001; Settler 2015,

2010; and more generally Chabal and Daloz 1999; J. Comaroff and Comaroff 2006, 2001; Engelbert 2002; Mbembe 2002, 2001). The work of Jean and John Comaroff in particular is distinguished by their sensitivity to how neoliberalism challenges not only conceptions of sovereign power in South Africa, but also commodification and the commodity form. Not long ago, commodification was considered the worst kind of appropriation. Lacking even the merit of good intention, commodification was the vanguard of modernity's 'incursions' into indigenous societies (Olupona 2004: 13–14). Whereas appropriation signified a loss of auratic authenticity, commodification was regarded as outright corruption that defiled the imputed purity of social relations unsoiled by the predations of commercial interest and financial transaction. Ertman and Williams (2005: 4) observe that the term 'commodification' is reserved for certain kinds of sales: it is seldom used with regard to milk delivery or garbage collection, for example. They suggest commodification is invoked when boundaries between market and non-market are contested and poses questions about whether something should be in or out of the marketplace and which social relations should be managed by market forces.

The Comaroffs give a different account of commodification. They see in South Africa profusions and intensifications of 'ethno-preneurialism' dialectically positioned between a tendency towards social disorder and violence on the one hand, and towards recourse to law as first recourse on the other.[10] They argue this dialectic between law and disorder increasingly characterises contemporary societies in general but is most pronounced in postcolonies, for which South Africa is their primary example. Both tendencies they attribute to intensifications of neoliberalism, evident in the art of government as well as the economic conduct of individuals, which they suggest is displacing older mechanisms of state authority and monopolies on violence (J. Comaroff and Comaroff 2006, J.L. Comaroff and Comaroff 2009). Significantly, as against an older, negative account of commodification, they suggest that the reduction of culture to commodity, commerce and cash does not necessarily denude culture of all auratic, affective, or social worth. Commerce has become a mode of cultivating deep and powerful attachments to chosen lifestyles and the values underpinning and framing them. What's more, commerce is a means of

---

[10]   Their analysis combines Benjamin's observations that transgressing law founds another law and gives violence law-making power, with Derrida's observations that this terrifying moment is also the whole history of law, 'in which the foundation of law remains suspended ... by a pure performative act that would not have to answer to or before anyone'. '*This moment always takes place and never takes place in a presence.*' (Derrida 2002b: 169–70; cf. Benjamin 1986a: 283, 295).

accomplishing them, of exercising agency and making selfhood. The point is that commodification is not a one-way street and as culture is commodified, so is the commodity rendered explicitly cultural, and thus is increasingly apprehended as 'the generic source of sociality' (J.L. Comaroff and Comaroff 2009: 28; cf. Muir 2007). The culture of neoliberalism is, in this sense, the world seen from the perspective of commodity as generic source of sociality, in which culture is commodity, knowledge is property, tradition is patent, identity is asset, and indigenous religiosity is human capital.

From the perspective of sovereign power, however, this circumstance is deeply problematic. Not only is the sovereign's political-juridical world which he grasps in its totality incompatible with the economic world which he does not, so are *homo legalis* and *homo economicus* absolutely heterogenous and not superposable. Foucault sums up the problem as follows: 'the art of government must be exercised in a space of sovereignty – and it is the law of the state which says this – but the trouble, misfortune, or problem is that this space turns out to be inhabited by economic subjects.' The absorption of sociality into the economic domain, or rather, incorporation and expansion of the principle of economy into cultural and social relations binding society, transforms everyday life into economic process and thereby steals away ever more of 'the essential element of a society's life' from the sovereign's realm, so to speak (Foucault 2008: 282, 294).

From a Foucauldian perspective, we could interpret the dialectic between law and disorder analysed by the Comaroffs in terms of the government's efforts to found sovereignty (not assert, but endlessly re-establish sovereignty) by exercising its monopoly on violence through lawmaking, by mobilising the violence inherent in the law to found the state. On the one hand, law circumscribes, delimits and bounds a realm of application of the sovereign's power; on the other hand, these boundaries are also the limitations of its effort and mark the beginning of a domain of disorder, which is to say, a domain that cannot be totalised and is not ordered by sovereign power. Both the sovereign's realm and the economic domain are structured by the principle of economy, but whereas practices of neoliberal governance by a sovereign government seek to harness this principle to optimise exercises of sovereign power, the disordered economic domain is populated by autonomous individuals who, as neoliberal *homo economicus*, each embody the principle of economy, and as economic actors each invest in their human capital as they make entrepreneurial enterprise with their ontological being. The art of government – 'the right disposition of things arranged so as to lead to a suitable end' – is a practice undertaken by sovereign governments as much as sovereign individuals. Sovereign governments desire neoliberal subjects whose self-conduct is a correlate of *raison d'état* and are therefore eminently governable. The problem for sovereign governments is that this art of optimising preferred arrangements (including conditions conducive to forming and sustaining neoliberal subjectivity) also transforms subjects of right into autonomous economic actors in relation to a domain increasingly beyond the reach of sovereign power. Sometimes an arrangement of things within an economic domain will approximate sovereign governments' preferred arrangements, for example, when autonomous individuals freely form themselves into professional associations of traditional healers or shamanic practitioners. This ought not surprise us since it is the invisible hand of the economic principle embodied in neoliberal *homo economicus* that gives rise to these initiatives. The important point, however, is that these and similar initiatives are not at the sovereign's behest. The sovereign is always in the position of catching up, of trying to gain mastery over a field that it does not control ('African traditional medicine', 'indigenous knowledge systems'), often with only a rudimentary map compiled from accounts of travellers who have gone before. This is also why sovereign power places a premium value on knowledge of the population, because it enables government to optimise its targeting of biopower, but also fills out the map with a bird's-eye view of obstacles, opportunities and above all, scale and boundaries. But the security obtained by representing the population in this way – by totalising the sum of individuals in the detail of their healing modalities, techniques and specialisations, prescriptions, their training, its content, location, duration and supervision, and any number of regularities and generalities generated by analyses of these details – this security is as fleeting as the correspondence between an object and its representation. The map, after all, only ever sustains an incomplete correspondence with territory.

Regarded from this perspective, neoliberal shamanism appears as another instance of modernity's double-hinged dialectic. On one side, the sovereign's epistemological labours seeks to delimit a domain of application in the qualities and properties, patterns and regularities, uses and potentials of traditional healing, including as these pertain to people for whom these qualities hold relevance or consequences (shamanic or traditional health practitioners, their clients, employers, other health professionals, and so on). Knowledge of this domain and its qualities enables choices and decisions about optimal arrangements that will ensure sovereign power is distributed continuously through its many forms, down to the grain of individuals. Transforming things into commodities and abilities into human capital is a particularly powerful form of epistemological practice. On the other side of the hinge, neoliberal *homo economicus* tends to deconstruct the sovereign's epistemological practice into embodied contingencies. Professional shamans and traditional health practitioners invest their embodied human capital and make an entrepreneur of the self. But although these practices partake of the same principle of economy, are a correlate of *raison d'état*, and may be amenable to epistemological mastery, to the extent that investing one's human capital references the range of practices related to working with spirits, these practices exceed epistemological circumscription and totalising representations (examples include reading bones, divining causes of ailments and afflictions, shamanic techniques of soul retrieval, conveying advice and instructions from ancestors, or, in the stripped-down Harnerian version, entering a shamanic state of consciousness to cultivate shamanic knowledge). More than that, they erode the imputed stability of shamanic practice as a knowledge domain. This is not to say that shamanic practice lacks an epistemological foundation or that neoliberal *homo economicus* escapes sovereign power. Rather, it suggests that no sooner is *homo economicus* circumscribed by *homo legalis* than a new contingency exceeds that circumscription and *homo economicus* is their own sovereign once again, relatively free to invest their human capital and transform ontological being into entrepreneurial enterprise. This constant oscillation between a subject of right and a subjectivity innervated with an economising principle that eludes epistemological circumscription indicates the dialectic, the perpetual motion dynamo, that animates and innervervates contemporary neoliberal society as much as it does neoliberal shamans.

Chapter 6

Imbrications

I have tried to represent the problems and issues considered in the preceding chapters in terms of processes. Rather than dependent and independent variables, we are dealing with interrelated events: things happen because other things have happened, are happening, or are anticipated to happen. An indigenist agenda became established at international forums such as the UN because the promise of a moral transcendence of politics contained in human rights utopianism produced political contexts more receptive to indigenist claims. In Bourdieusian terms, one could say the ascendancy of individual human rights discourse altered the stakes structuring the field of indigenous struggles at an international level and therewith the position of indigenists relative to other players competing for those stakes, mainly states but also non-government sectors and private-sector commercial interests too. These developments also increased the worth of symbolic capital cached in transnational indigenous identity and transformed indigeneity into an important mediator with respect to growing anxieties about the unsustainability of contemporary human development strategies and policies. The growing prominence of transnational indigenous identity has been imbricated with other global processes as well. Elaborations and consolidations of a specifically neoliberal *homo economicus* have incorporated signifiers of indigenous ontological alterity (for example, the unique cosmological bond between indigenous peoples and their ancestral lands, ecocentric disposition, indigenous knowledge, shamanic religiosity, and so on) into techniques of the self. But because this kind of self-conduct correlates with the principle of economy in the neoliberal art of government, these same signifiers are increasingly prominent in the constant adjustments between techniques that coerce the population and processes through which a self constructs and modifies its self. These imbricated processes have increased circulations of signs and bodies, broadened their range, intensified their local penetration, and brought about all kinds of new relations and exchanges (P. Johnson 2002; cf. Chidester 2006). They have, as Appadurai has said, brought us into altogether new conditions of neighbourliness, and therewith precipitated new kinds of problems and challenges (Appadurai 1996: 29). But what does all of this say about shamanism? What does shamanism mean in a world increasingly sensitive to indigenous peoples' practices of territoriality, increasingly concerned about humans' relationship with natural environments we all share, increasingly encouraged and coerced to adjust self-conduct to comport with and augment government conduct? Indeed, what does shamanism mean in a world increasingly integrated by digital communication technologies that not only extend the self in all kinds of novel ways, but also amplify polyvocality and intensify dialogism?

I have tried to show how shamanism is a form of discursive language variously utilised to articulate and represent a range of new and emerging concerns at a transnational level, along with debates and conflicts these concerns inevitably occasion. Examples presented in preceding chapters suggest shamanism supplies a discursive frame and thus language to an increasingly diverse array of interested parties. Indigenists, conservationists, jurists, bioprospectors, entrepreneurs, legislators, activists of various stripes, lawyers of various specialisations, state representatives and agencies, institutional agents, and innumerable related social actors, including academicians, all rely – in different ways – on shamanism's discursive language to articulate their concerns and interests and interpret the claims of others. For these agents, contemporary shamanism discourse variously articulates critiques of prevailing notions of universal human rights, anthropocentric mastery of nature, sovereignty and self-determination, and physiological, spiritual, personal and communal aspects of human health. This is as true for advocates of these critiques as for agents who are engaged by them, even if they disagree with their merits. These articulations and representations in terms of a discourse about shamans and shamanic religiosities have stimulated shamanism with more diverse applications and wider circulations, promoting its proliferation and dispersal to practical contexts in which historically people called 'shamans' and practices that may be described as 'shamanic' have been less prominent if not absent. In turn, the modalities, regularities and unities of discursive practices in these imbricated domains are conveyed back into shamanism's discursive language to inflect and modify representations of shamans and shamanic religiosities with the tropes, styles and themes of these practical domains.

I have also tried to show in the preceding chapters how shamanism is both a product and is productive of the modern limit attitude. Wherever shamanism's discursive language is instrumentalised to represent practical interests and concerns, perpetual oscillations between circumscription and contingency proliferate and disperse as well as intensify and condense a discourse about shamans and shamanic religiosities. These labours simultaneously expand the limits of knowledge about shamanic religiosity and multiply the surfaces of

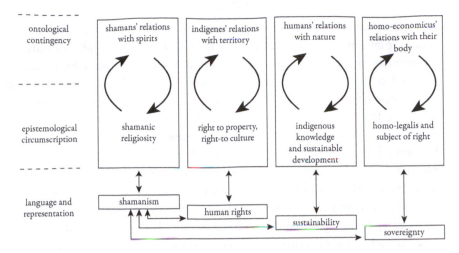

Figure 6.1   Contemporary shamanism. Diagram by the author.

appearance of a knowing, desiring self, as well as inflect knowledge about shamans with new concerns, generate more discursive iterations, and adjust shamanism's discursive regularities, modalities and unities. These two ideas – that shamanism is a product of the modern limit attitude, and supplies discursive language to related practical domains – are represented schematically in Figure 6.1.

This schematic representation encapsulates the basic argument: the emergence of modern subjectivity as a practical limit attitude inaugurated a discourse about shamans that has been elaborated over the course of three centuries via perpetual oscillations between epistemological labour's tendency towards universalism and ontological labour's tendency toward contingency. In recent decades, this discourse has supplied a discursive structuration for a diverse array of new interests and concerns, facilitating in turn proliferations and intensifications of shamanism discourse in new practical domains and at increasing scales of complexity and transnational distribution, and giving new prominence and visibility to people called 'shamans' and practices that may be described as 'shamanic'.

The two parts of this argument are perhaps most succinctly captured in the double meaning of 'articulate'. Various social actors use shamanism's discursive language to coherently express their concerns and cogently convey their interests. However, shamanism is itself an articulation, which is to say, it designates a hinged joint and range of movements. In this sense, shamanism as a form of discursive practice is an occasion for thinking about the operations of the modern limit attitude and the practical task this attitude obliges us to engage. Because contingencies of ontological labour will always exceed epistemological circumscription and totalising representations, this excess will always erode totalising circumscriptions and challenge the coherence and stability of universal representations. Epistemological circumscription therefore must be constantly adjusted to accommodate this endless surplus, while the bounded limits of what knowledge must renounce exceeding must be constantly renewed so that the edifice of the universal, or at least the possibility of universality, can be sustained. To some extent, this formulation resembles Derridean deconstruction. However, I am less concerned with a Derridean critique of the metaphysics of presence inhabiting language and more concerned with practical effects arising from instantiations of logos by discursive practice. I have sought to show how the animation and innervation of modern history via perpetual oscillations between epistemological and ontological labours have generated the kinds of relations and imbrications in relation to shamanism we have seen with reference to indigenism, environmentalism and neoliberalism, like a dynamo produces energy and nerves supply sensation to a body. Whether articulating indigenist claims to greater autonomy in relation to lands, territories and resources, or the anxieties of a transnational ecological imaginary about humans' destructive relationship with the planetary biosphere, or opportunities afforded professional shamanic practitioners by conversions of abilities and capacities to engage spirits into forms of embodied capital, or indeed challenges and opportunities posed to indigenous, traditional, or folk cultures by transformations of knowledge into asset and incorporations into transnational intellectual property regimes, these historical developments have drawn on shamanism to articulate their key concerns.

The various discussions in preceding chapters tend to confirm Adlam and Holyoak's analysis that future research will need to engage implications for shamanic religiosities of consumerism, commodification and late capitalism, along with impacts of new technologies, particularly as these stimulate new modes of cultural production and consumption, new patterns of circulation, and alter cultural profiles (Adlam and Holyoak 2005: 535). Although these problems are not exclusively relevant to shamanism research, and neither are they entirely new, they are increasingly salient under the new conditions of neighbourliness emerging in recent decades. From this perspective, shamanism increasingly adumbrates new kinds of problems in a widening range of practical domains with which shamanic religiosities are increasingly imbricated. I want to consider some of these imbrications by way of conclusion.

The frequency with which shamanism's discursive language is relied on to articulate concerns about degradations of the Earth's biosphere and to reimagine or modify humans' relations with nature indicates one such imbricated domain. The idea that notionally religious or spiritual subject positions offer useful and valuable perspectives on ethical problems implicated in anthropocentric mastery of nature is hardly novel, although the frequency of writings offering these perspectives arguably has increased in step with alarm at global warming and climate change. In this circumstance, shamanism and varieties of local indigenous religious traditions are for growing numbers of people around the planet important intellectual and cultural resources for critiquing humans' exploitative relationship with natural environments and for imagining alternatives (see, for example, contributions to Barnhill and Gottlied 2001, Burdon 2011 and Vaughan-Lee 2013; cf. Gagliano 2013, Orenstein 1993 and Sponsel 2012). In this sense, religion remains an important resource for eco-ethics.

Bron Taylor's research into the spiritual and religious dimensions of the environmental movement led him to coin the term 'dark green religion' to describe a range of religious or spiritual perspectives or dispositions mediating anxieties about humans' impacts on natural environments and the Earth's biosphere more generally (B. Taylor 2009, 2001a, 2001b; Taylor and Van Horn 2006). Dark green religion refers to a range of beliefs and practices 'flowing from a strong sense of belonging to and interconnectedness in nature, while perceiving the Earth and its living systems to be sacred and interconnected', and emerges from what Taylor calls the environmentalist milieu: 'contexts in which environmentally concerned officials, scientists, activists, and other citizens connect with and reciprocally influence each other' (B. Taylor 2009: 13–14). In this sense, Taylor's typology of dark green religion maps the spiritual and religious tendencies of the 'green' milieu. Although Taylor is not the first to distinguish varieties of concern about natural environment in terms of shades of green, his account is almost certainly the most thoroughly researched and historically situated. Taylor proposes a four-way typology of dark green religion (see Table 6.1). The rows and columns of this table indicate tendencies and the types themselves are highly permeable, indicated by the dotted lines distinguishing them. The tendency towards animism, in Taylor's analysis 'a shared perception that beings or entities in nature have their own integrity, ways of being, personhood, and even intelligence', leads to forms of ritualised action through which people develop relationships with these non-human beings, entities, or spirits. On the other hand, the tendency towards Gaian Earth Religion is informed by an organicist tradition that takes the whole, usually understood scientifically, as a model. The diverging tendencies between supernaturalism and naturalism in Taylor's analysis turns on differing attitudes towards non-human beings and entities, with the former tending to emphasise the factuality of spirits and agency of non-human beings, while the latter tends towards a more metaphorical and conceptual reference to non-human beings within an ecocentric view of the environment and people's place in it.

Table 6.1   Typology of Dark Green Religion (from Taylor 2009: 15)

	Animism	Gaian Earth Religion
Supernaturalism	Spiritual animism	Gaian spirituality
Naturalism	Naturalistic animism	Gaian naturalism

If one were to locate shamanic religiosities in relation to Taylor's typology, tendencies in much shamanism discourse towards what Taylor characterises as animism and supernaturalism suggests shamanic religiosities correspond with Taylor's spiritual animist type. However, if that was true in the past, it could be argued that shamanism's proliferations and dispersals into new practical domains have inflected shamanist discursive practice with tendencies towards Gaian Earth Religion and, to a lesser extent, naturalism. Harnerian core shamanism undoubtedly corresponds closest to spiritual animism as perhaps do indigenist representations of their cosmovisions in relation to indigenous self-determination. But the case is less clear when one considers indigenists' representations of their cosmovisions in the context of the indigenist-environmentalist alliance, or Gaia's Sacred Sites Network and Cormac Cullinan's 'wild law' (for examples of the latter, see contributions to Burdon 2011). It seems unlikely Gaian naturalists would have much use for shamanism and at present would likely have serious misgivings about the centrality of spirits and similar agentive forces in representing natural processes of the Earth's biosphere. Nevertheless, to the extent that shamanism is increasingly used to convey a critique of anthropocentric mastery of natural environments and ultimately the Earth's biosphere, it could be argued that enthusiasm for shamanic religiosities and hence for shamanism's discursive language in recent years is a creative response to the challenging difficulties of comprehending and responding to humans' impacts on the natural environments.

An essay by historian Dipesh Chakrabarty illustrates the problem. Chakrabarty is of course well known as a contributor to the Subaltern Studies collective and for his writings on history as an academic discipline. In his essay 'The Climate of History', he grapples with the profound and transformative implications that anthropogenic theories of climate change pose for thinking about human history. Referencing Alan Weisman's book *The World Without Us*, in which Weisman invites his readers to imagine a world left behind by humans who have become extinct, Chakrabarty suggests that going along with Weisman's thought experiment is profoundly difficult because it requires we insert ourselves into a future 'without us' in order to visualise it. Climate change disrupts the assumption underpinning the discipline of history – that our future, present, and past are connected by a continuity of human experience – by putting the future 'beyond the grasp of historical sensibility' and disconnecting future and past (Chakrabarty 2009: 197). Reflecting on this problem, Chakrabarty outlines four theses.

First, anthropogenic climate change collapses the time-honoured distinction between natural and human history. Whereas historians concern themselves with human affairs and perceive humans as agents of passing events, the events of nature are 'mere events'. Nature has no 'inside'; it is process without agency. Environmental historians have made some headway breaching this artificial distinction, but they too speak of humans as biological agents and operate within a disciplinary knowledge framework that prioritises the agency of humans above other kinds of agentive forces. This is precisely where the anthropogenic theory of climate change disturbs the historical sensibility: it challenges this artificial distinction between natural and human histories by positing humans not as individual biological agents, but as a collective geological force.

In geological periodisation, the last ice age or Pleistocene was followed by the warmer Holocene, our present period during which warmer conditions have enabled biological life to flourish. The notion that humans have become a geological agent on the planet has led some scientists to propose a new geological age, the Anthropocene. The key idea of this proposal, that humans are a geological force, posits a kind of agency that profoundly challenges the account of human agency familiar to professional historians like Chakrabarty, for whom the key concern for human histories since the eighteenth century to the present era of globalisation has been freedom, 'a blanket category for diverse imaginations of human autonomy and sovereignty'.[1] Certainly ideas about what constitutes freedom vary considerably with human cultural and historical diversity, but, Chakrabarty points out, this malleability only underlines this word's rhetorical

---

[1] 'Freedom, one could say, is a blanket category for diverse imaginations of human autonomy and sovereignty. Looking at the works of Kant, Hegel, or Marx; nineteenth-century ideas of progress and class struggle; the struggle against slavery; the Russian and Chinese revolutions; the resistance to Nazism and Fascism; the decolonization movements of the 1950s and 1960s and the revolutions in Cuba and Vietnam; the evolution and explosion of the rights discourse; the fight for civil rights for African Americans, indigenous peoples, Indian Dalits, and other minorities; down to the kind of arguments that, say, Amartya Sen put forward in his book *Development as Freedom*, one could say that freedom has been the most important motif of written accounts of human history of these two hundred and fifty years' (Chakrabarty 2009: 208).

power. He notes that in none of the humanist accounts of freedom has there been recognition that human beings have been acquiring geological agency 'at the same time as and through processes closely linked with their acquisition of freedom' (ibid.: 208). There are, of course, compelling (human) historical reasons why geological time and the chronology of human histories have been kept separate. Still, the anthropogenic theory of climate change is rapidly closing this distance, prompting Chakrabarty's second thesis: the Anthropocene severely qualifies humanist histories of modernity and globalisation. These qualifications create confusion. Is the period since the Enlightenment better conceived as one of freedom or the Anthropocene? Is the Anthropocene a critique of the narratives of freedom or is geological agency the price we pay for pursuing freedom? The problem is that, as Chakrabarty puts it, 'the geologic now of the Anthropocene has become entangled with the now of human history'. Although humans' acquisition of geological agency is deeply entangled with histories of capital, a critique of capital is insufficient for questioning that acquisition or its implications in the present time of rapid climate change (ibid.: 212).

The necessity of a different kind of historical perspective brings Chakrabarty to his third thesis: the hypothesis regarding humans' geological agency requires that global histories of capital be put in conversation with the species history of humans. These two kinds of histories begin differently. Geologists and climate scientists can give a historical account of why current trends in climate change are anthropogenic in nature. However, since it is not the geological planet that is threatened but rather the geological and biological conditions that have sustained human life during the Holocene, a particular kind of historical self-awareness is required to comprehend that climate change is a crisis for humans at a species level rather than for the planet as such. 'Species', a word Chakrabarty notes designates humans as a form of life among others, is used by biologists and geologists working in 'deep history', that is, hundreds of thousands of years beyond the horizon of the last few thousand years of 'recorded history'; it is never used in standard historical or political-economic critiques of globalisation by scholars on the Left. Some of the difficulties of bridging this distance and placing historically the crisis of climate change are suggested by the discomfort of bringing together the planetary and the global, deep and recorded histories, and species thinking and critiques of capital. It is uncomfortable because it entails unfamiliar arrangements, conjunctions, proximities and modes of thought, as if one were wearing clothes tailored for a body of different dimensions.

Chakrabarty's fourth thesis develops this idea: 'the cross-hatching of species history and the history of capital is a process of probing the limits of historical understanding' (ibid.: 220). This probing at the limits can be highly productive, but it is also profoundly challenging. Humanist histories produce meaning by appealing to our capacity to reconstruct events by drawing on our past experience. This capacity is not available to species histories because we humans never experience ourselves as a species: '[I]n species history, humans are only an instance of the concept species as indeed would be any other life form. But one never experiences being a concept' (ibid.: 220). We humans are challenged with a dilemma: we have developed sophisticated critiques with which we can understand ourselves as humans and locate ourselves in relation to the present crisis, but these are insufficient at the level of species history because we experience ourselves as so many instances of a human species rather than as the species itself. Summing up his essay, Chakrabarty concludes:

> Species may indeed be the name of a placeholder for an emergent, new universal history of humans that flashes up in the moment of the danger that is climate change. But we can never *understand* this universal ... climate change poses for us a question of a human collectivity, an us, pointing to a figure of the universal that escapes our capacity to experience the world. (ibid.: 221–2)

Chakrabarty's essay is not without problems (see, for example, Baucom 2012, Žižek 2010: 330–36). But that's the point too. His essay is perhaps better received as a prolegomenon, a sketch of a problematic that invites engagement and elaboration. From the perspective of shamanism studies, Chakrabarty's essay casts a different light on the analysis of shamanism presented in preceding chapters. I have argued that proliferations and intensifications of shamanism discourse in recent decades can be attributed at least in part to a conjuncture of historical processes that from around the 1970s onwards increasingly drew on shamanism's discursive language to articulate the concerns and interests of agents contesting stakes constituting corresponding practical fields. Could it be that proliferations and intensifications of shamanism discourse also have to do with this dilemma of bridging the distance between human and natural histories compelled to merge in the Anthropocene? Could it be that the various examples of discursive and embodied practice in relation to shamanism are also examples of experiments in bridging this distance? Is it plausible that at least some of shamanism's proliferations and intensifications in recent years are a consequence of attempts to fill this emerging lacuna in contemporary history? Can a case be made that shamanism discourse is better situated within and interpreted as part of a larger discussion about bridging this distance, or at least mediating it, by 'cross-hatching' diverse but interrelated perspectives in an interdisciplinary project that brings together radical ecology, economics, ethics, indigenism, history, philosophy and theology among other disciplinary perspectives, including shamanism studies? Are proliferations of shamanism discourse a correlate in non-academic contexts of emerging 'non-anthropocentric human sciences' (Domanska 2010: 118)?

I think there is something worthwhile in the suggestion that at least some of contemporary shamanism discourse is concerned with creatively experimenting with ways to articulate an emergent, new universal history of humans-as-species. The central motif of much shamanism discourse since the eighteenth century – that the shaman is a mediator between worlds – offers a suggestive metaphor for reorienting embodied dispositions from anthropocentric to ecocentric ones, no less than bridging the distance between species history and human history. Chapter 4 outlined a distinction between anthropocentric and ecocentric ways of perceiving the world, where the former refers to humans' mastery of nature, and the latter provides a critique disavowing a distinction between natural life and human life, along with a range of ethical implications and responsibilities this disavowal entails. Some of the examples mentioned in Chapter 4, notably Earth jurisprudence, 'wild law' and the Gaia Foundation's Sacred Sites Network, suggest something of the enthusiasm for resorting to a shamanic idiom in experimental modes of thinking about humans as a species among others and therewith our human species' part in the natural world. Growing interests in varieties of ecocriticism suggests there is room, enthusiasm and urgency for innovative research addressing these questions (Coupe 2000, Peterson and Peterson 1996, Zimmerman and Callicott 1998). A burgeoning field of research and practice in recent decades, ecocriticism has stimulated a range of more focused interdisciplinary studies, including literary ecocriticism, ecofeminism, ecotheology and ecological ethics.[2] It remains to be seen whether these experiments offer a route towards non-anthropocentric perspectives on humans' geological agency and species history. It is difficult to imagine what this labour at the limits of human understanding might look like, how it might proceed, or indeed the form of subjectivity from which it could proceed, if the premise of that labour disavows anthropocentrism. Ecocentrism implies taking leave of the practical limit attitude. Yet ecocentrism is difficult because it challenges us moderns to think *beyond* the limits, a task for which modern subjectivity is not geared. For some, shamanism provides an experimental mode

---

[2]   On literary ecocriticism, see Buell 2005, Garrard 2011, Goodbody and Rigby 2011, Glotfelty and Fromm 1996; on ecofeminism, see Kronlid 2003, Orenstein 1993, Ruether 2005, Sturgeon 1997, K.J. Warren 1997; on ecotheology, see Ashford 2012, Berry 2009, Berry 2006, Hallman 1994, McFague 2008, Neu 2002; on ecological ethics, see M. Smith 2001.

of language with which to respond to that difficulty, even if, as I have argued through these pages, these experiments overwhelmingly tend to proliferate and intensify an anthropocentric discourse about shamans.

One of the practical domains where these proliferations and intensifications are increasingly relevant and imbricated concerns commodifications of religiosity. This is hardly a new issue, least of all in relation to prosperity gospels (Coleman 2000), so-called 'eastern' religions (Kitiarsa 2007), or indeed indigenous religiosities (Ramos 2000). However, these examples are often located in relation to transnational circulations of commoditised culture and processes of globalisation and less so in relation to local economies and circulations. Some attention has been given to occult economies in postcolonial contexts, particularly where these are illicit (for example, J. Comaroff and Comaroff 1999, Whitehead and Wright 2004). However, illicit economies are also being targeted for incorporation into *raison d'état* as we saw with the South African government's development policies and legislative reforms in Chapter 5. Commoditisation raises problems of ownership, and therewith questions about who benefits and benefit sharing. This is a challenging problem in the context of reforming intellectual property law, both to guard against piracy and theft as well as to ensure communities are able to advance their socio-economic development by economic use of their culture, identity and local knowledge, as we saw in Chapter 5. Intellectual property law is part of a larger concern about ensuring local social and economic benefits are part of investment planning and are among measurable outcomes of business investment, particularly at a transnational level. For example, the Environmental and Social Sustainability Framework of the International Finance Corporation (hereafter IFC), a development finance institution and member of the World Bank Group, requires that clients establish ongoing relationships with communities affected by business investment and actively seek broader development opportunities, particularly where affected communities are indigenous. These requirements are outlined in the IFC's Performance Standard 7 with respect to indigenous peoples, and includes the following examples in the accompanying Guidance Notes: supporting indigenous peoples' development priorities; addressing gender and generational issues; documenting indigenous peoples' culture and society (including 'culture, demographic structure, gender and intergenerational relations and social organization, institutions, production systems, religious beliefs, and resource use patterns'); strengthening indigenous peoples' capacity to implement and monitor development programmes; protecting indigenous knowledge and safeguarding intellectual property rights, and facilitating indigenous peoples' partnerships with public, private and NGO sectors. As we saw in Chapter 3, international human rights law and jurisprudence is increasingly sensitive to these issues. Following the precedent set by the Awas Tingni case and the general trend in statutory requirements as well as new 'best practice' models such as promoted by the IFC, in future we should expect debates about indigenous development to be increasingly inflected by religious and cosmological aspects of indigenous peoples' development priorities, particularly concerning private-sector investments in their lands and territories as well as with regards partnerships with public, private and NGO sectors.

These issues are not only relevant for indigenous communities and private-sector corporations. Governments are embroiled too and compelled to mediate between the interests of national economies and local communities. The twin discussions in Chapter 5 demonstrated that while government is ordinarily thought of as an objective structure of authority, it is perhaps better conceived of as forms of practice that optimise a relation between scarce means and desired ends, and manages resources accordingly. The art of government refers to the conduct of governments as much as it does self-conduct, so that (neoliberal) governmentality extends sovereign power capillary-like into the bodies of sovereign subjects, connecting them into a kind of nervous system in which the whole is sensitive to self-conduct in the furthest parts. However, reading the discussion of governmentality in Chapter 5 with the indigenist critique of self-determination in Chapter 3, an important question arises. If government is better conceived as a form of reason that constitutes a sovereign power and a sovereign state (*raison d'état*), and secondly, if the principle of economy coordinating this practical reason is increasingly sensitive to religious cosmovisions, rituals, symbols, spiritual techniques and the like (whether entrepreneurial or territorial), then what does this intersection offer by way of a critical vantage on the changing relationship between religion and the state? Debates around post-secularism, public religions and public theologies have become increasingly topical and productive areas of research and scholarship in recent years. Much of this scholarship is stimulated by debates about the proper relationship between religion and the public sphere, and more generally the relationship between secularism and modernity, both in European and postcolonial contexts (for example, An-Na'im 2008, Asad 2003, Cady and Hurd 2010, Davis et al. 2005, De Vries and Sullivan 2006, Kaviraj 1995, Kalyvas 1996, Smith and Whistler 2010, Spivak 2007, C. Taylor 2007, Warner et al. 2010). However, the kind of state one has in mind makes a difference. In postcolonial societies like South Africa, indigenous religiosity is understood in terms of secular customary law and kingship, a legacy of indirect rule written into the Constitution of the post-apartheid state. Jason Myers (2008) has argued that indirect rule in South Africa was not, as Mamdani (1996) has argued, primarily or even merely concerned either with co-option of local elites or decentralised despotism. Rather, Myers argues, indirect rule operated as an ideological structure that legitimised racial segregation. Leatt's contention that colonialism in Africa was, among other things, a process of secularisation that segregated political and religious elements in order to rule more effectively extends Myers' argument. Where secular custom and tradition ends and religion begins is one aspect of a larger problematic that turns on theorising the location of religion in relation to the modern state, whether in the model of postcolony or European nation state. As Leatt has noted, 'the problem is that what is politics is shifting and what is religion is shifting. And we can no longer assume the naturalised distinctions between them' (Leatt 2009: 2; cf. Myers 1999). I would add that if this segregation between secular and religious domains is coming undone, it is not only because postcolonies like South Africa are grappling with the ambivalences and contradictions of their colonial legacies. They are grappling with them at the same time that a neoliberal art of government is innervating the body politic with an economising rationality for which segregations between secular and religious domains are increasingly more of a hindrance than an advantage to practicing sovereign power and *raison d'état*.

In light of the analyses pursued in preceding chapters and the questions these have raised and I have outlined above, we may well wonder who is this figure of an eponymous discourse that combines so many apparently disparate interests and concerns? I have tried to show throughout these pages that the figure of the shaman is in fact a figuration, a combination of an individual figure with the discourse that proceeds from, is imposed on, and then circles back to that figure, along the way acquiring new valuations that both expand and intensify this figure in relation to practical domains. As a figure in history, the shaman is a figuration of time, and we may recall the structural optics composing a chronophotograph to illustrate the point: the divisions of an object of perception into still smaller components; the framing of those divisions by the photographer's will; the relation in time this composition of time establishes with a viewer; and above all, the invitation this composition extends to a viewer to insert their self into this composition by (re)cognising the structural optics on which their perception and the coherence of the image relies. In this sense, the figure of the shaman is also a figuration of the practical limit attitude and therewith the double-hinged articulation of epistemological and ontological labour that constitutes modern subjectivity. Like a chronophotograph, the modern limit attitude has an internal logic that animates and innervates it, and holds out the possibility of critique. By directing us to query whatever is singular and contingent within what is given as universal, this practical limit attitude separates out from the contingencies that have made us the possibilities for saying, thinking and doing differently, and therewith gives impetus to the undefined work of freedom. However, no sooner has this will to freedom multiplied the surfaces of appearance of a desiring self than the transiency of desire's fulfilment inscribes new limits. Hence we have an enormous proliferation and intensification of a discourse about shamans as the limits of knowledge are pushed outwards and the limits of the desiring self are elaborated with ever-growing complexity and refinement. As a metonym for modernity's double-hinge, the shaman is an occasion for thinking about this endless alternation between a will to freedom and the temporalities and contingencies that enable it by constraining it, not only in relation to specific shamans (who they are, what they do, how and why they do it), but in relation to the diverse practical domains increasingly imbricated by a discourse about shamans.

References

Legal judgments

Community of Moiwana v. Suriname. [2005]. Series C No. 124, IACrtHR (15 June 2005).

Coulter et al. v. Brazil. [1985]. No. 7615, Report No. 12/85, IACHR (5 March 1985).

Indigenous Community of Sawhoyamaxa v. Paraguay. [2006]. Series C No. 146, IACrtHR (29 March).

Indigenous Community of Yakye Axa v. Paraguay. [2005]. Series C No. 125, IACrtHR (17 June).

Kayano et al. v. Hokkaido Expropriation Committee (Nibutani Dam Decision). [1997]. Unreported, Sapporo District Court (27 March).

Mabo v. Queensland (No. 2) ('Mabo case'). [1992]. HCA 23 (1992), 175 CLR 1 (3 June).

Maya Indigenous Communities of the Toledo District v. Belize. [2004]. Case 12.053, Report No. 40/04, IACHR (12 October).

Mayagna (Sumo) Awas Tingni Community v. Nicaragua. [2001]. Series C, No. 79, IACrtHR (31 August).

Saramaka People v. Suriname. [2007]. Series C No. 172, IACrtHR (28 November).

Tshavhungwe Nemarude et al. v. Tshivhase Development Corporation et al. [2010]. Case no. 360/2010, Limpopo High Court (7 July).

Tshavhungwe Nemarude et al. v. Tshivhase Development Foundation Trust et al. [2011]. Case no. 63/2011, Limpopo High Court (22 February).

Xákmok Kásek Indigenous Community v. Paraguay. [2010]. Series C No. 214, IACrtHR (24 August).

Legislation

Traditional Health Practitioners Act, no. 22 of 2007 (Republic of South Africa). Pretoria: Government Gazette.

Intellectual Property Laws Amendment Act, no. 28 of 2013 (Republic of South Africa). Pretoria: Government Gazette.
Alaska Native Claims Settlement Act, 1971 (43 USC 1601).

References

Adlam, Robert and Lorne Holyoak. 2005. Shamanism in the Postmodern World: A Review Essay. *Studies in Religion / Sciences Religieuses*, 34(3–4), pp. 517–68.

Aizelwood, Robin. 2000. Revisiting Russian Identity in Russian Thought: From Chaadaev to the Early Twentieth Century. *The Slavic and East European Journal*, 78(1), pp. 20–43.

Akwesasne Notes (ed.). 1991. *Basic Call to Consciousness*. Summertown, TN: Book Publishing Company.

Albanese, Catherine L. 1990. *Nature Religion in America: From the Algonkian Indians to the New Age*. Chicago, IL: University of Chicago Press.

—— 2007. *A Republic of Mind and Spirit: A Cultural History of American Metaphysical Religion*. New Haven, CT: Yale University Press.

Alberts, Thomas. 2008. Virtually Real: Fake Religions and Problems of Authenticity in Religion. *Culture and Religion*, 9(2), pp. 125–39.

Allen, Douglas. 1988. Eliade and History. *The Journal of Religion*, 68(4), pp. 545–65.

Alles, Gregory D. 1988. Wach, Eliade, and the Critique from Totality. *Numen*, 35(1), pp. 108–38.

An-Na'im, Abdullahi Ahmed. 2008. *Islam and the Secular State: Negotiating the Future of Shari'a*. Cambridge, MA: Harvard University Press.

Anagnost, Ann S. 1987. Politics and Magic in Contemporary China. *Modern China*, 13(1), pp. 40–61.

Anaya, S. James. 2004. *Indigenous Peoples in International Law*. Oxford: Oxford University Press.

Anon. 1868. Review: Lesley's Origin and Destiny of Man. *Anthropological Review*, 6(23), pp. 356–66.

Appadurai, Arjun. 1996. *Modernity at Large: Cultural Dimensions of Globalization*. Minneapolis, MN: University of Minnesota.

Arden, Nicky. 1996. *The Spirits Speak: One Woman's Mystical Journey into the African Spirit World*. New York: Henry Holt.

——. 1999. *African Spirits Speak: A White Woman's Journey into the Healing Tradition of the Sangoma*. Rochester: Destiny Books.

Asad, Talal. 2003. *Formations of the Secular: Christianity, Islam, Modernity.* Stanford, CA: Stanford University Press.

Ashford, Joan Anderson. 2012. *Ecocritical Theology: Neo-Pastoral Themes in American Fiction from 1960 to the Present.* Jefferson, MO: McFarland.

Ashforth, Adam. 2005. *Witchcraft, Violence and Democracy in South Africa.* Chicago, IL: University of Chicago Press.

Atkinson, Jane Monnig. 1992. Shamanisms Today. *Annual Review of Anthropology*, 21, pp. 307–30.

Balzer, Marjorie Mandelstam. 2008. Beyond Belief?: Social, Political, and Shamanic Power in Siberia. *Social Analysis*, 52(1), pp. 95–110.

———. 2003. Dynamic Ethnics: Socio-Religious Movements in Siberia. In *Extending the Borders of Russian History: Essays in Honour of Alfred J Reiber*, ed. M. Siefert. pp. 481–95. Budapest: CEU Press.

———. 1999. *The Tenacity of Ethnicity: A Siberian Saga in Global Perspective.* Princeton, NJ: Princeton University Press.

———. 1996. Changing Images of the Shaman: Folklore and Politics in the Sakha Republic (Yakutia). *Shaman*, 4(1&2), pp. 5–16.

——— and Uliana Alekseevna Vinokurova. 1996. Nationalism, Interethnic Relations and Federalism: The Case of the Sakha Republic (Yukutia). *Europe-Asia Studies*, 48(1), pp. 101–20.

Barnes, R.H., Andrew Gray and Benedict Kingsbury (eds). 1995. *Indigenous Peoples of Asia.* Ann Arbor: Association for Asian Studies.

Barnhill, David Landis and Roger S. Gottlieb (eds). 2001. *Deep Ecology and World Religions: New Essays on Sacred Grounds.* Albany: State University of New York.

Bassin, Mark. 1999. *Imperial Visions: Nationalist Imagination and Geographic Expansion in the Russian Far East, 1849–1917.* Cambridge: Cambridge University Press.

———. 1991. Inventing Siberia: Visions of the Russian East in the Early Nineteenth Century. *American Historical Review*, 96(3), pp. 763–94.

Baucom, Ian. 2012. Postcolonial Studies in an Age of Natural Science. *History of the Present*, 2(1), pp. 1–23.

Baudrillard, Jean. 1994. *Simulacra and Simulation* (trans. Sheila Faria Glasner). Ann Arbor: University of Michigan.

———. 1993. *Symbolic Exchange and Death* (trans. Iain H. Grant). London: Sage.

———. 1981. *For a Critique of the Political Economy of the Sign.* St. Louis, MO: Telos Press.

Baviskar, Amita. 2007. Indian Indigeneities: Adivasi Engagements with Hindu Nationalism in India. In *Indigenous Experience Today*, eds Marisol de la

Cadena, Orin Starn and Wenner-Gren Foundation for Anthropological Research. Oxford: Berg.

Beath, Andrew. 2005. *Consciousness in Action: The Power of Beauty, Love and Courage in a Violent Time*. New York: Lantern Books.

Becker, Gary S. 1964. *Human Capital: A Theoretical and Empirical Analysis, with Special Reference to Education*. New York: National Bureau of Economic Research.

Beckett, Jeremy. 1996. Contested Images: Perspectives on the Indigenous Terrain in the Late 20th Century. *Identities*, 3(1–2), pp. 1–13.

Benavides, Gustavo. 1998. Modernity. In *Critical Terms for Religious Studies*, ed. Mark C. Taylor. pp. 186–204. Chicago, IL: University of Chicago Press.

Benjamin, Walter. 1986a. Critique of Violence (trans. Edmund Jephcott). In *Reflections: Essays, Aphorisms, Autobiographical Writings*, ed. Peter Demetz. pp. 277–300. New York and London: Harcourt Brace Jovanovich.

———. 1986b. Surrealism: The Last Snapshot of the European Intelligentsia (trans. Edmund Jephcott). In *Reflections: Essays, Aphorisms, Autobiographical Writings*, ed. Peter Demetz. pp. 177–92. New York: Schocken Books.

Berry, Thomas. 2009. *The Sacred Universe: Earth, Spirituality, and Religion in the Twenty-First Century*. New York: Columbia University.

———. 2006. *Evening Thoughts : Reflecting on Earth as Sacred Community*. ed. Mary Evelyn Tucker. San Francisco, CA: Sierra Club Books.

Birch, Kean and Vlad Mykhnenko. 2010. Introduction: The World Turned Right Way Up. In *The Rise and Fall of Neoliberalism: The Collapse of an Economic Order?*, eds Kean Birch and Vlad Mykhnenko. pp. 1–20. London: Zed Books.

Black, J.L. 1989. J.-G. Gmelin and G.-F. Müller in Siberia, 1733–1743: A Comparison of Their Reports. In *The Development of Siberia: People and Resources*, eds A. Wood and R.A. French. London: MacMillan Press.

Boas, Franz. 1898. Traditions of the Tillamook Indians. *Journal of American Folklore*, 11(40), pp. 23–38.

———. 1895. Salishan Texts. *Proceedings of the American Philosophical Society*, 34(147), pp. 31–48.

———. 1893. Vocabulary of the Kwakiutl Language. *Proceedings of the American Philosophical Society*, 31(140), pp. 34–82.

———. 1891. Vocabularies of the Tlingit, Haida and Tsimshian Languages. *Proceedings of the American Philosophical Society*, 29(136), pp. 173–208.

———. 1889. Notes on the Snanaimuq. *American Anthropologist*, 2(4), pp. 321–28.

———. 1888. On Certain Songs and Dances of the Kwakiutl of British Columbia. *Journal of American Folklore*, 1(1), pp. 49–64.

———. 1887. A Year among the Eskimo. *Journal of the American Geographical Society of New York*, 19, pp. 383–402.

———. 1884. A Journey in Cumberland Sound and on the West Shore of Davis Strait in 1883 and 1894. *Journal of the American Geographical Society of New York*, 16, pp. 242–72.

Boekhoven, Jeroen W. 2011. *Genealogies of Shamanism: Struggles for Power, Charisma and Authority*. Groningen: Barkhuis.

Bogoras, Waldemar. 1974. *The Chukchee* (reprint of the 1909 edition). Publications of the Jesup North Pacific Expedition, v.7. ed. Franz Boas. New York: AMS.

Bourdieu, Pierre. 2001a. *Homo Academicus* (trans. Peter Collier). Cambridge: Polity Press.

———. 2001b. *Masculine Domination* (trans. Richard Nice). Cambridge: Polity Press.

———. 1997. The Forms of Capital. In *Education: Culture, Economy, and Society*, eds A.H. Halsey, Hugh Lauder, Phillip Brown and Amy Stuart Wells. pp. 46–58. Oxford: Oxford University Press.

———. 1991. *Language and Symbolic Power* (trans. Gino Raymond and Matthew Adamson). Cambridge, MA: Harvard University Press.

———. 1990a. *In Other Words: Essays Towards a Reflexive Sociology* (trans. Matthew Adamson). Cambridge: Polity.

———. 1990b. *The Logic of Practice* (trans. Richard Nice). Cambridge: Polity.

———. 1986. *Distinction: A Social Critique of the Judgement of Taste* (trans. Richard Nice). London: Routledge & Kegan Paul.

———. 1979. *Algeria 1960*. Cambridge: Cambridge University Press.

——— and Loic J.D. Wacquant. 1992. *An Invitation to Reflexive Sociology*. Chicago, IL: University of Chicago Press.

Boyer, L.B. 1962. Remarks on the Personality of Shamans with Special Reference to the Apache of the Mescalero Indian Reservation. *The Psychoanalytic Study of Society*, 2, pp. 233–54.

———. 1998. Can Culture Be Copyrighted? *Current Anthropology*, 39, pp. 193–222.

———. 1993. Facing the State, Facing the World: Amazonia's Native Leaders and the New Politics of Identity. *L'Homme*, 33, pp. 307–26.

Brunton, Bill. 1994. Tuva, Land of Eagles: The Foundation's 1993 Expedition to Tuva. *Shamanism*, 7(1). [online] Available at: <http://www.shamanism.org/articles/article08.html> [Accessed: 18 July 2011].

Brysk, Allison. 2000. *From Tribal Village to Global Village*. Stanford, CA: Stanford University Press.

———. 1994. Acting Globally: Indian Rights and International Politics in International Relations. In *Indigenous Peoples and Democracy in Latin America*, ed. Donna Lee van Cott. pp. 29–54. New York: St. Martins Press.

Buell, Lawrence. 2005. *The Future of Environmental Criticism : Environmental Crisis and Literary Imagination*. Malden: Blackwell.

Burdon, Peter (ed.). 2011. *Exploring Wild Law: The Philosophy of Earth Jurisprudence*. Kent Town: Wakefield Press.

Buyandelgeriyn, Manduhai. 2007. Dealing with Uncertainty: Shamans, Marginal Capitalism, and the Remaking of History in Postsocialist Mongolia. *American Ethnologist*, 34(1), pp. 127–47.

Cady, Linell E. and Elizabeth Shakman Hurd (eds). 2010. *Comparative Secularisms in a Global Age*. New York: Palgrave Macmillan.

Calhoun, Craig. 1993. Habitus, Field, and Capital: The Question of Historical Specificity (trans. Nicole Kaplan, Craig Calhoun and Leah Florence). In *Bourdieu: Critical Perspectives*, eds Craig Calhoun, Edward LiPuma and Moishe Postone. pp. 61–88. Cambridge: Polity.

———, Edward LiPuma and Moishe Postone (eds). 1993. *Bourdieu: Critical Perspectives*. Cambridge: Polity.

Campbell, Joseph. 2000. *The Masks of God: Primitive Mythology, v.1*. London: Souvenir Press.

Campbell, Susan Schuster. 2000. *Called to Heal: African Shamanic Healers*. Twin Lakes, WI: Lotus Press.

Canessa, Andrew. 2007. Who Is Indigenous? Self-Identification, Indigeneity, and Claims to Justice in Contemporary Bolivia. *Urban Anthropology and Studies of Cultural Systems*, 36(3), pp. 195–237.

Cape Cod Daré. 2012. About Cape Cod Community Daré. [online] Available at: <http://www.capecoddare.org/about.html> [Accessed: 16 May 2012].

Carver, Jonathan. 1781. *Travels through the Interior Parts of North America, in the Years 1766, 1767, and 1768*. London: J. Walter and S. Crowder.

Castaneda, Carlos. 1968. *The Teaching of Don Juan: A Yaqui Way of Knowledge*. Berkeley: University of California.

CERD. 1997. *General Recommendation 23, Rights of Indigenous Peoples, a/52/18, Annex V*. Geneva: Committee on the Elimination of Racial Discrimination.

Chaadaev, Petr. 1978. Philosophical Letters Addressed to a Lady. In *Russian Intellectual History: An Anthology*, ed. Marc Raeff. pp. 160–73. New York: Harcourt, Brace and World.

Chabal, Patrick and Jean-Pascal Daloz. 1999. *Africa Works: Disorder as Political Instrument*. Oxford: James Currey.

Chadwick, Nora Kershaw. 1936a. Shamanism among the Tartars of Central Asia. *Journal of the Royal Anthropological Institute of Great Britain and Ireland*, 66(June–July), pp. 75–112.

——. 1936b. The Spiritual Ideas and Experiences of the Tartars of Central Asia. *Journal of the Royal Anthropological Institute of Great Britain and Ireland*, 66, pp. 291–329.

—— and Victor Zhirmunsky. 1969. *Oral Epics of Central Asia*. Cambridge: Cambridge University Press.

Chakrabarty, Dipesh. 2009. The Climate of History. *Critical Inquiry*, 35(2), pp. 197–222.

——. 2002. *Habitations of Modernity: Essays in the Wake of Subaltern Studies*. Chicago, IL: University of Chicago Press.

——. 2000. *Provincializing Europe: Postcolonial Thought and Historical Difference*. Princeton, NJ and Oxford: Princeton University Press.

Chapin, Mac. 2004. A Challenge to Conservationists. *World Watch Magazine*, 17(6), pp. 17–31.

Chennels, Roger. 2012. Email correspondence with author. Received 7 and 17 January 2012.

——. 2008. The Ramunangi Claim of Rights to the Sacred Sites of Phiphidi Waterfall. [online] Available at: <http://www.sacredland.org/media/Ramunangi-Claim-of-Rights_15Nov08.pdf> [Accessed: 15 December 2011].

Chidester, David. 2012. *Wild Religion: Tracking the Sacred in South Africa*. Berkeley: University of California.

——. 2006. Indigenous Traditions, Alien Abductions: Creolized and Globalized Memory in South Africa. In *Religion, Violence, Memory, and Place*, eds O.B. Stier and J. Landres. pp. 181–97. Bloomington: Indiana University Press.

——. 2004. Credo Mutwa, Zulu Shaman: The Invention and Appropriation of Indigenous Authenticity in African Folk Religion. In *Religion, Politics and Identity in a Changing South Africa*, eds David Chidester, Abdulkader Tayob and Wolfram Weisse. pp. 69–87. Munster, Germany: Waxman Verlag.

——. 1996. *Savage Systems: Colonialism and Comparative Religion in Southern Africa*. Cape Town: University of Cape Town.

——, Chirevo Kwenda, Robert Petty, Judy Tobler and Darrel Wratten. 1997. *African Traditional Religion in South Africa: An Annotated Bibliography*. Westport, CT: Greenwood Press.

Choi, Chungmoo. 1997. Hegemony and Shamanism: The State, the Elite, and Shamans in Contemporary Korea. In *Religion and Society in Contemporary Korea*, eds Lewis R. Lancaster and Richard K. Payne. pp. 19–48. Berkeley: Institute for East Asian Studies.

Churchill, Ward. 2003. Spiritual Hucksterism: The Rise of the Plastic Medicine Men. In *Shamanism: A Reader*, ed. Graham Harvey. pp. 324–33. London and New York: Routledge.

CIPR. 2002. *Integrating Intellectual Property Rights and Development Policy*. London: Commission On Intellectual Property Rights.

Clapp, Roger Alex and Carolyn Crook. 2002. Drowning in the Magic Well: Shaman Pharmaceuticals and the Elusive Value of Traditional Knowledge. *Journal of Environment & Development*, 11(1), pp. 79–102.

Clifford, James. 1988. *The Predicament of Culture: Twentieth-Century Ethnography, Literature, and Art*. Cambridge, MA: Harvard University Press.

—— and George E. Marcus. 1986. *Writing Culture: The Poetics and Politics of Ethnography*. Berkeley: University of California Press.

Coates, Ken S. 2004. *A Global History of Indigenous Peoples: Struggle and Survival*. Basingstoke: Palgrave Macmillan.

Cohen, Rick. 2012. Vanishing Act: Activist Groups Say Donations Disappeared with Fiscal Sponsor. *Non-Profit Quarterly*. [online] Available at: <http://www.nonprofitquarterly.org/management/19616-vanishing-act-activist-groups-say-donations-disappeared-with-fiscal-sponsor.html> [Accessed: 14 May 2012].

COICA. 1990a. Declaration of Iquitos. *Cultural Survival Quarterly*, 14(4), p.82.

——. 1990b. First Summit Held between Indian Peoples and Environmentalists. *SAICC newsletter*, 5(3&4), pp. 10–11.

——. 1989. Two Agendas on Amazon Development. *Cultural Survival Quarterly*, 13(4), pp. 75–8.

Colchester, Marcus. 2003. *Salvaging Nature: Indigenous Peoples, Protected Areas and Biodoversity Conservation*. Uruguay: World Rainforest Movement.

Coleman, Mathew and Kevin Grove. 2009. Biopolitics, Biopower, and the Return of Sovereignty. *Environment and Planning D: Society and Space*, 27(3), pp. 489–507

Coleman, Simon. 2000. *The Globalisation of Charismatic Christianity: Spreading the Gospel of Prosperity*. Cambridge: Cambridge University Press.

Comaroff, Jean and John L. Comaroff (eds). 2006. *Law and Disorder in the Postcolony*. Chicago, IL: University of Chicago Press.

——. 2005. The Struggle between the Constitution and 'Things African'. *Interventions: The International Journal of Postcolonial Studies*, 7(3), pp. 299–303.

——. 2004. Criminal Obsessions, after Foucault: Postcoloniality, Policing, and the Metaphysics of Disorder. *Critical Inquiry*, 30(4), pp. 800–824.

——. 2000. Millennial Capitalism: First Thoughts on a Second Coming. *Public Culture*, 12(2), pp. 291–343.

——. 1999. Occult Economies and the Violence of Abstraction: Notes from the South African Postcolony. *American Ethnologist*, 26(2), pp. 279–303.

Comaroff, John L. and Jean Comaroff. 2009. *Ethnicity, Inc.* Chicago, IL: University of Chicago Press.

Conklin, Beth A. 2002. Shamans Versus Pirates in the Amazonian Treasure Chest. *American Anthropologist*, 104(4), pp. 1050–61.

——. 1997. Body Paint, Feathers, and VCRs: Aesthetics and Authenticity in Amazonian Activism. *American Ethnologist*, 24(4), pp. 711–37.

——. and Laura R. Graham. 1995. The Shifting Middle Ground: Amazonian Indians and Eco-Politics. *American Anthropologist*, 97(4), pp. 695–710.

Corless, Roger. 1993. After Eliade, What? *Religion*, 23, pp. 373–7.

Coronado, Jorge. 2009. *The Andes Reimagined: Indigenismo, Society and Modernity*. Pittsburgh, PA: University of Pittsburgh.

Coulter, Robert T. 2009. The U.N. Declaration on the Rights of Indigenous Peoples: A Historic Chance in International Law. *Idaho Law Review*, 45, pp. 539–53.

Coupe, Lawrence (ed.). 2000. *The Green Studies Reader: From Romanticism to Ecocriticism*. London: Routledge.

Cox, James L. 2010. *Introduction to the Phenomenology of Religion*. London: Continuum.

——. 2008. Community Mastery of the Spirits as an African Form of Shamanism. *Diskus*, 9. [online] Available at: <http://www.basr.ac.uk/diskus/diskus9/cox.htm> [Accessed: 9 April 2012].

——. 2003. Contemporary Shamanism in Global Contexts: 'Religious' Appeals to an Archaic Tradition? *Studies in World Christianity*, 9(1), pp. 69–87.

Craffert, Pieter F. 2008. *The Life of a Galilean Shaman: Jesus of Nazareth in Anthropological-Historical Perspective*. Cambridge: James Clarke.

Cullinan, Cormac. 1999. *Wild Law: A Manifesto for Earth Justice*. Totnes: Green Books and The Gaia Foundation.

Cumes, David. 2004. *Africa in My Bones: A Surgeon's Odyssey into the Spirit World of African Healing*. London: Global.

Czaplicka, Marie Antoinette. 1999. *The Collected Works of M.A. Czaplicka*. ed. David Collins. Richmond, Surrey (Britain): Curzon Press.

———. 1914. *Aboriginal Siberia: A Study in Social Anthropology*. Oxford: Clarendon Press.

Dahl, Jens. 2009. *IWGIA: A History*. Copenhagen: International Working Group on Indigenous Affairs.

Darnell, Regna. 2001. *Invisible Genealogies: A History of Americanist Anthropology*. Lincoln: University of Nebraska Press.

———. 1998. *And Along Came Boas: Continuity and Revolution in Americanist Anthropology*. Amsterdam and Philadelphia, PA: John Benjamins.

David-Fox, Michael, Peter Holquist and Alexander Martin (eds). 2006. *Orientalism and Empire in Russia*. Bloomington, IN: Slavica.

Davis, Creston, John Milbank and Slavoj Žižek. 2005. *Theology and the Political: The New Debate*. Durham, NC: Duke University.

Dawson, Andrew (ed.). 2011. *Summoning the Spirits: Possession and Invocation in Contemporary Religion* London: I.B. Tauris.

De la Cadena, Marisol. 2010. Indigenous Cosmopolitics in the Andes: Conceptual Reflections Beyond 'Politics'. *Cultural Anthropology*, 25(2), pp. 334–70.

De Man, Paul. 1970. Literary History and Literary Modernity. *Theory in Humanistic Studies*, 99(2), pp. 384–404.

De Vries, Hent and Lawrence E. Sullivan (eds). 2006. *Political Theologies: Public Religions in a Post-Secular World*. New York: Fordham University Press.

Deloria, Philip J. 1994. *Playing Indian*. Yale Historical Publications. New Haven, CT: Yale University.

Deloria, Vine. 1973. *God Is Red: A Native View of Religion*. New York: Putnam.

———. 1969. *Custer Died for Your Sins: An Indian Manifesto*. New York: Macmillan.

Derrida, Jacques. 2005a. Cogito and the History of Madness (trans. Alan Bass). In *Writing and Difference*. pp. 36–76. London: Routledge.

———. 2005b. Violence and Metaphysics: An Essay on the Thought of Emmanuel Levinas (trans. Alan Bass). In *Writing and Difference*. pp. 97–192. London: Routledge.

———. 2002a. Faith and Knowledge: The Two Sources Of 'Religion' At the Limits of Reason Alone. In *Acts of Religion*, ed. Gil Anidjar. pp. 40–101. New York: Routledge.

———. 2002b. Force of Law: The 'Mystical Foundation of Authority'. In *Acts of Religion*, ed. Gil Anidjar. pp. 228–98. New York: Routledge.

———. 1999. *Adieu to Emmanuel Levinas* (trans. Pascale-Anne Brault and Michael Naas). Stanford, CA: Stanford University Press.

———. 1976. *Of Grammatology* (trans. Gayatri Chakravorty Spivak). Baltimore, MD: John Hopkins University.

———. 1973. Differance. In *Speech and Phenomena: and Other Essays on Husserl's Theory of Signs*. Evanston, IL: Northwestern University Press.

Devereaux, George. 1969. *Mohave Ethnopsychiatry: The Psychic Disturbances of an Indian Tribe*. Washington, DC: Smithsonian Institution Press.

Dilts, Andrew. 2011. From 'Entrepreneur of the Self' to 'Care of the Self': Neo-Liberal Governmentality and Foucault's Ethics. *Foucault Studies*, 12, pp. 130–46.

Diment, Galya and Yuri Slezkine (eds). 1993. *Between Heaven and Hell: The Myth of Siberia in Russian Culture*. New York: St. Martin's Press.

Dixon, Roland B. 1908. Some Aspects of the American Shaman. *Journal of American Folklore*, 21(80), pp. 1–12.

Dmytryshyn, Basil. 1977. *A History of Russia*. Eaglewood Cliffs, NJ: Prentice-Hall.

Dodds, Eric R. 2004. The Greek Shamans and the Origin of Puritanism. In *Shamanism: Critical Concepts in Sociology*, v.2. pp. 245–74. London and New York: RoutledgeCurzon.

DOH. 1996. *National Drug Policy for South Africa*. Pretoria: Department of Health.

———, MRC and CSIR. n.d. *National Reference Centre for African Traditional Medicines: A South African Model*. Pretoria: Department of Health, Medical Research Council, Council for Scientific and Industrial Research.

Domanska, Ewa. 2010. Beyond Anthropocentrism in Historical Studies. *Historein*, 10, pp. 118–30.

Dove, Michael R. 2006. Indigenous People and Environmental Politics. *Annual Review of Anthropology*, 35(1), pp. 191–208.

Dressler, Markus and Arvind-pal S. Mandair (eds). 2011. *Secularism and Religion-Making*. London: Routledge.

DST. 2008. *Innovation Towards a Knowledge-Based Economy, 2008–2018: Ten-Year Plan for South Africa*. Pretoria: Department of Science and Technology.

———. 2004. *Indigenous Knowledge Systems Policy*. Pretoria: Department of Science and Technology.

DuBois, Thomas A. 2011. Trends in Contemporary Research on Shamanism. *Numen*, 58(1), pp. 100–128.

———. 2009. *An Introduction to Shamanism*. Cambridge: Cambridge University.

Duncan, Peter J.S. 2000. *Russian Messianism: Third Rome, Holy Revolution, Communism and After*. London: Routledge.

Dutfield, Graham. 2003. Bioprospecting: Legitimate Research or 'Biopiracy'? *Science and Development Network Policy Briefs*. [online] Available at: <http://www.scidev.net/en/policy-briefs/bioprospecting-legitimate-research-or-biopiracy--1.html> [Accessed: 22 May 2012].

Dworkin, Ronald. 1986. *Law's Empire*. Oxford: Hart Publishing.

Eaglewoman, Angelique. 2009. The Eagle and the Condor of the Western Hemisphere: Application of International Indigenous Principles to Halt the United States Border Wall. *Idaho Law Review*, 45, pp. 555–74.

Eliade, Mircea. 1973. *Australian Religions: An Introduction*. Ithaca, NY: Cornell University Press.

———. 1969. *The Quest: History and Meaning in Religion*. Chicago, IL: University of Chicago Press.

———. 1964. *Shamanism: Archaic Techniques of Ecstasy* (trans. Willard R. Trask). Bollingen Series, v.76. Princeton, NJ: Princeton University.

———. 1960. *Myths, Dreams, and Mysteries: The Encounter between Contemporary Faiths and Archaic Realities* (trans. Philip Mairet). London: Harvill Press.

———. 1959a. *The Sacred and the Profane: The Nature of Religion* (trans. Willard R. Trask). New York: Harcourt, Brace.

———. 1959b. The Yearning for Paradise in Primitive Religion. *Daedalus*, 88(2), pp. 255–67.

———. 1958. *Patterns in Comparative Religion* (trans. Rosemary Sheed). London: Sheed and Ward.

———. 1951. *Le Chamanisme et Les Techniques Archaïques de L'extase*. Paris: Payot.

Engle, Karen. 2010. *The Elusive Promise of Indigenous Development: Rights, Culture, Strategy*. Durham, NC: Duke University Press.

Englebert, Pierre. 2002. Patterns and Theories of Traditional Resurgence in Tropical Africa. *Mondes en développement*, 30(118), pp. 51–64.

Erni, Christian (ed.). 2008. *The Concept of Indigenous Peoples in Asia: A Resource Book*. Copenhagen: International Work Group for Indigenous Affairs, and Asia Indigenous Peoples Pact Foundation

Ertman, Martha M. and Joan C. Williams (eds). 2005. *Rethinking Commodification: Cases and Readings in Law and Culture*. New York: New York University Press.

Escobar, Arturo. 1998. Whose Knowledge, Whose Nature? Biodiversity, Conservation, and the Political Ecology of Social Movements. *Journal of Political Ecology*, 5, pp. 53–82.

Esposito, Roberto. 2008. *Bíos: Biopolitics and Philosophy* (trans. Timothy Campbell). Minneapolis, MN: University of Minnesota Press.

Ewen, Alexander (ed.). 1994. *Voice of Indigenous Peoples: Native People Address the United Nations*. Santa Fe, NM: Clear Light Publishers.

Fischer, Frank and Michael Black (eds). 1995. *Greening Environmental Policy: The Politics of a Sustainable Future*. London: Paul Chapman.

Fisher, William H. 1997. Doing Good?: The Politics and Antipolitics of NGO Practices. *Annual Review of Anthropology*, 26, pp. 439–64.

Fitzgerald, Timothy. 2000. *The Ideology of Religious Studies*. New York: Oxford University Press.

Flaherty, Gloria. 1992. *Shamanism and the Eighteenth Century*. Princeton, NJ: Princeton University Press.

———. 1988. The Performing Artist as the Shaman of Higher Civilization. *MLN*, 103(3), pp. 519–39.

Forsyth, James. 1992. *A History of the Peoples of Siberia: Russia's North Asian Colony, 1581–1990*. Cambridge: Cambridge University Press.

Foucault, Michel. 2009. *Security, Territory, Population: Lectures at the Collège de France, 1977–1978* (trans. Graham Burchell). Basingstoke: Palgrave Macmillan.

———. 2008. *The Birth of Biopolitics: Lectures at the Collège de France, 1978–1979* (trans. Graham Burchell). Basingstoke: Palgrave Macmillan.

———. 2006. *History of Madness* (trans. Jonathan Murphy and Jean Khalfa). London: Routledge.

———. 2003. What Is Enlightenment? (trans. Catherine Porter). In *The Essential Foucault: Selections from the Essential Works of Foucault 1954–1984*, eds Paul Rabinow and Nikolas Rose. pp. 43–57. London: The New Press.

———. 2002. *The Archaeology of Knowledge* (trans. A.M. Sheridan Smith). Oxon: Routledge.

———. 1993. About the Beginning of the Hermeneutics of the Self: Two Lectures at Dartmouth. *Political Theory*, 21(2), pp. 198–227.

———. 1980a. Prison Talk (trans. Colin Gordon). In *Power/Knowledge: Selected Interviews and Other Writings, 1972–1977*, ed. Colin Gordon. pp. 37–54. New York: Pantheon.

———. 1980b. Two Lectures (trans. Kate Soper). In *Power/Knowledge: Selected Interviews and Other Writings, 1972–1977*, ed. Colin Gordon. pp. 78–108. New York: Pantheon Books.

———. 1977a. *Discipline and Punish: The Birth of the Prison* (trans. Alan Sheridan). London: Penguin.

——. 1977b. Nietzsche, Genealogy, History (trans. Donald F. Bouchard and Sherry Simon). In *Language, Counter-Memory, Practice: Selected Interviews and Essays*, ed. Donald F. Bouchard. pp. 139–64. Ithaca, NY: Cornell University Press.

——. 1973. *The Birth of the Clinic: An Archaeology of Medical Perception* (trans. A.M. Sheridan Smith). London: Tavistock.

——. 1967. *Madness and Civilization: A History of Insanity in the Age of Reason* (trans. Richard Joseph Howard). London: Tavistock Publications.

Francfort, Henri-Paul and Roberte N. Hamayon (eds). 2001. *The Concept of Shamanism: Uses and Abuses*. Budapest: Akadémiai Kiadó.

Freeman, M.D.A. (ed.). 2008. *Lloyd's Introduction to Jurisprudence* (8th edition). London: Thomson Reuters.

FSS. 2010a. *FSS E-Newsletter*, 4(2).

——. 2010b. 'Baniwa Shamanic Revitalization', *FSS Mailing List*. [email] Available at: <http://www.shamanism.org> [Accessed: 5 May 2010].

——. 2012a. About the Foundation for Shamanic Studies. [online] Available at: <http://www.shamanism.org/fssinfo/index.html> [Accessed: 16 March 2014].

——. 2012b. Certificates. [online] Available at: <http://shamanism.org/workshops/certificates.html> [Accessed: 29 March 2012].

——. 2012c. Certified Shamanic Counselors. [online] Available at: <http://www.shamanism.org/resources/csc.html> [Accessed: 30 March 2012].

——. 2012d. Core Shamanism. [online] Available at: <http://www.shamanism.org/workshops/coreshamanism.html> [Accessed: 21 March 2012].

——. 2012e. Donate Today. [online] Available at: <https://www.shamanism.org/join/donation.php> [Accessed: 30 March 2012].

——. 2012f. Preservation and Revival of Indigenous Shamanism. [online] Available at: <http://www.shamanism.org/fssinfo/indigenousAssistance.html> [Accessed: 29 March 2012].

——. 2012g. Researching Shamanic Knowledge. [online] Available at: <http://www.shamanism.org/fssinfo/research.html> [Accessed: 21 March 2012].

——. 2012h. Shamanic Healing Questionnaire. [online] Available at: <http://www.shamanism.org/questionnaire.html> [Accessed: 21 March 2012].

——. 2012i. Urgent Indigenous Assistance Needed for Baniwa Shamanic Revitalization and Last Jaguar-Shaman. [online] Available at: <http://shamanism.org/news/2009/07/08/foundation-supports-last-jaguar-shaman/> [Accessed: 16 March 2014].

——. 2012j. What It Means If Someone Is a Harner Certified Shamanic Counselor (CSC). [online] Available at: <http://www.shamanism.org/resources/cscRequirements.html> [Accessed: 12 April 2012].

——. 2012k. Workshops. [online] Available at: <http://www.shamanism.org/workshops/index.php> [Accessed: 27 March 2012].

Gagliano, Monica. 2013. Persons as Plants: Ecopsychology and the Return to the Dream of Nature. *Landscapes*, 5(2). Available at: <http://ro.ecu.edu.au/landscapes/vol5/iss2/14> [Accessed: 2 May 2014].

Gaia Amazonas. 2012. Yaigojé Apaporis, Endangered by Gold. [online] Available at: <http://www.gaiaamazonas.org/en/yaigoje-apaporis-endangered-by-gold> [Accessed: 25 January 2012].

GAIA. 2012a. Mphatheleni – Mupo. [online] Available at: <http://www.gaiafoundation.org/mphatheleni-mupo> [Accessed: 15 January 2012].

——. 2012b. Sacred Sites Networks. [online] Available at: <http://www.gaiafoundation.org/sacred-sites-networks> [Accessed: 25 January 2012].

——. 2012c. The Altai – Gas Pipeline Threatens Sacred Land. *The Gaia Foundation*. [online] Available at: <http://www.gaiafoundation.org/altai-gas-pipeline-threatens-sacred-land> [Accessed: 17 April 2012].

——. 2010. Update on the Protection of the Phiphidi Falls Sacred Site, Venda, South Africa, 31 August. [online] Available at: <http://participatorygis.blogspot.com/2010/08/update-on-protection-of-phiphidi-fall.html> [Accessed: 17 August 2011].

Garrard, Greg. 2011. *Ecocriticism*. New York: Routledge.

Gatschet, Albert Samuel. 1883. The Shetimasha Indians of St. Mary's Parish, Southern Louisiana. *Transactions of the Anthropological Society of Washington*, 2, pp. 148–60.

——. 1880. The Timucua Language. *Proceedings of the American Philosophical Society*, 18(105), pp. 465–502.

——. 1877. The Timucua Language. *Proceedings of the American Philosophical Society*, 16(99), pp. 626–42.

Geertz, Armin W. 1993. Archaic Ontology and White Shamanism. *Religion*, 23, pp. 369–72.

Genel, Katia. 2006. The Question of Biopower: Foucault and Agamben. *Rethinking Marxism*, 18(1), pp. 43–62.

Ginzberg, Carlo. 1992. *The Cheese and the Worms: The Cosmos of a Sixteenth-Century Miller* (trans. John Tedeschi and Anne Tedeschi). Balimore, MD: Johns Hopkins.

Glotfelty, Cheryll and Harold Fromm (eds). 1996. *The Ecocriticism Reader: Landmarks in Literary Ecology*. Athens: University of Georgia.

Goodbody, Axel and Kate Rigby (eds). 2011. *Ecocritical Theory: New European Approaches*. Charlottesville: University of Virginia.

Goodman, Felicitas. 1990. *Where the Spirits Ride the Wind: Trance Journeys and Other Ecstatic Experiences*. Bloomington: Indiana University Press.

——. 1988. *Ecstasy, Ritual and Alternate Reality: Religion in a Pluralistic World*. Bloomington: Indiana University Press.

Gophe, Myolisi. 2000. Healer Goes into Battle for White Sangomas. *Cape Argus*, 1 November.

Gow, David G. and Joanne Rappaport. 2002. The Indigenous Public Voice: The Multiple Idioms of Modernity in Native Cauca. In *Indigenous Movements, Self-Representation and the State in South America*, eds Kay B. Warren and Jean Jackson. pp. 47–80. Austin: University of Texas Press.

Gqaleni, Nceba, Indres Moodley, Heidi Kruger, Abigail Ntuli and Heather McLeod. 2007. *South African Health Review: Traditional and Complementary Medicine*. Johannesburg: Health Systems Trust.

Graham, Laura R. 2002. How Should an Indian Speak? Amazonian Indians and the Symbolic Politics of Language in the Global Public Sphere. In *Indigenous Movements, Self-Representation and the State in Latin America*, eds Kay Warren and Jean E. Jackson. pp. 181–228. Austin: University of Texas Press.

——. 1987. Constitutional Lobbying in Brazil: Indians Seek Expanded Role. *Cultural Survival Quarterly*, 11(2), pp. 61–2.

Grant, Bruce. 1997. Empire and Savagery: The Politics of Primitivism in Late Imperial Russia. In *Russia's Orient: Imperial Borderlands, and Peoples, 1700–1917*, eds Daniel R. Brower and Edward J. Lazzerini. pp. 292–310. Bloomington & Indianapolis: Indiana University Press.

Green, Lesley J.F. 2008a. Anthropologies of Knowledge and South Africa's Indigenous Knowledge Systems Policy. *Anthropology Southern Africa*, 31(1&2), pp. 48–7.

——. 2008b. 'Indigenous Knowledge' and 'Science': Reframing the Debate on Knowledge Diversity. *Archaeologies: Journal of the World Archaeological Congress*, 4(1), pp. 144–63.

Greenfeld, Liah. 1992. *Nationalism: Five Roads to Modernity*. Cambridge, MA and London: Harvard University Press.

Grimaldi, Susan. 1997. Observations on Daniel Noel's 'The Soul of Shamanism': A Defense of Contemporary Shamanism and Michael Harner. *Shaman's Drum*, 46, pp. 4–9. [online] Available at: <www.susangrimaldi.com/docs/harner.pdf> [Accessed: 29 March 2012].

Grove, Richard. 1995. *Green Imperialism: Colonial Expansion, Tropical Island Edens and the Origins of Environmentalism, 1600–1860.* Cambridge: Cambridge University Press.

Guha, Ramachandra. 2000. *Environmentalism: A Global History.* New Delhi and New York: Oxford University Press.

Habermas, Jürgen. 1990. *The Philosophical Discourse of Modernity: Twelve Lectures* (trans. Frederick Lawrence). Cambridge: MIT Press.

Halifax, Joan. 1982. *Shaman: The Wounded Healer.* New York: Crossroad.

———. 1979. *Shamanic Voices: A Survey of Visionary Narratives.* New York: Dutton.

Hall, James. 1994. *Sangoma: My Odyssey into the Spirit World of Africa.* New York: GP Putnam's Sons.

Hallman, David G. (ed.). 1994. *Ecotheology: Voices from South and North.* Geneva: World Council of Churches.

Hamann, Trent H. 2009. Neoliberalism, Governmentality, and Ethics. *Foucault Studies*, 6, pp. 37–59.

Hamayon, Roberte N. 2001. Shamanism: Symbolic System, Human Capability and Western Ideology. In *The Concept of Shamanism: Uses and Abuses*, eds Henri-Paul Francfort and Roberte N. Hamayon. Budapest: Akadémiai Kiadó.

———. 1998. 'Ecstasy' or the West-Dreamt Siberian Shaman. In *Tribal Epistemologies: Essays in the Philosophy of Anthropology*, ed. Helmut Wautischer. pp. 175–87. Aldershot: Ashgate.

———. 1995. *Why Do Ritual Games Please Shamanic Spirits and Displease Transcendent Gods?: An Essay on 'Playing' as a Basic Type of Ritual Behaviour.* The Louis H. Jordan Lectures in Comparative Religion, SOAS, University of London.

———. 1993. Are 'Trace', 'Ecstasy', and Similar Concepts Appropriate in the Study of Shamanism? *Shaman*, 1(2), pp. 3–26.

Hames, Raymond. 2007. The Ecologically Noble Savage Debate. *Annual Review of Anthropology*, 36, pp. 177–90.

Harkin, Michael Eugene and David Rich Lewis (eds). 2007. *Native Americans and the Environment: Perspectives on the Ecological Indian.* Lincoln: University of Nebraska Press.

Harner, Michael. 2010. A Core Shamanic Theory of Dreams. *Shamanism Annual*, 23.

———. 2005a. The History and Work of the Foundation for Shamanic Studies. *Shamanism*, 18(1&2), pp. 5–10.

——. 2005b. Tribal Wisdom: The Shamanic Path. In *Higher Wisdom: Eminent Elders Explore the Continuing Impact of Psychedelics*, eds Roger N. Walsh and Charles S. Grob. pp. 159–78. Albany: State University of New York.

——. 1997. A Different Drummer. *Natural History*, 106(2), pp. 50–51.

——. 1990. Preface to the Third Edition. In *The Way of the Shaman*. pp. xi–xv. New York: HarperOne.

——. 1980. *The Way of the Shaman: A Guide to Power and Healing*. New York: Harper & Row.

——. 1973. *Hallucinogens and Shamanism*. New York: Oxford University Press.

——. 1972. *The Jívaro, People of the Sacred Waterfalls*. Garden City, NY: Doubleday.

Harvey, David. 2005. *A Brief History of Neoliberalism*. Oxford: Oxford University Press.

Harvey, Graham (ed.). 1999. *Indigenous Religions: A Companion*. London: Cassel.

Hathaway, Michael. 2010. The Emergence of Indigeneity: Public Intellectuals and an Indigenous Space in Southwest China. *Cultural Anthropology*, 25(2), pp. 301–33.

Havel, Václav. 1985. The Power of the Powerless. In *The Power of the Powerless: Citizens against the State in Central-Eastern Europe*, eds Václav Havel and John Keane. pp. 23–96. Armonk, NY: M.E. Sharpe.

Helleman, Wendy. 2004. *The Russian Idea: In Search of a New Identity*. Bloomington, IN: Slavica Publishers.

Hill, Michael Ortiz. 2012. Books, Essays, Poems. [online] Available at: <http://www.gatheringin.com/essays.html> [Accessed: 1 June 2012].

——. 2010. The Authors. [online] Available at: <http://www.gatheringin.com/the_author.html> [Accessed: 18 August 2010].

Hillman, James, Michael Meade and Malidoma Somé. 1992. *Images of Initiation*. Pacific Grove, CA: Oral Tradition Archives.

Hodgson, Dorothy L. 2002a. Introduction: Comparative Perspectives on the Indigenous Rights Movement in Africa and the Americas. *American Anthropologist*, 104(4), pp. 1037–49.

——. 2002b. Precarious Alliances: The Cultural Politics and Structural Predicaments of the Indigenous Rights Movement in Tanzania. *American Anthropologist*, 104(2), pp. 1086–97.

Hoffman, W.J. 1891. *The Midē'wiwin or 'Grand Medicine Society' of the Ojibwa*. Seventh Annual Report of the Bureau of Ethnology to the Secretary of the

Smithsonian Institution. ed. J.W. Powell. Washington: Government Printing Office.

——. 1888. Pictography and Shamanistic Rites of the Ojibwa. *American Anthropologist*, 1(3), pp. 209–30.

——. 1886a. Vocabulary of the Selish Language. *Proceedings of the American Philosophical Society*, 23(123), pp. 361–71.

——. 1886b. Vocabulary of the Waitshum'ni Dialect, of the Kawi'a Language. Tule Agency, Cal.. *Proceedings of the American Philosophical Society*, 23(123), pp. 372–9.

——. 1883. Comparison of Eskimo Pictographs with Those of Other American Aborigines. *Transactions of the Anthropological Society of Washington*, 2, pp. 128–46.

——. 1881. An Absaroka Myth. *Journal of the Anthropological Institute of Great Britain and Ireland*, 10, pp. 239–40.

Hogarth, Hyun-key Kim. 1999. *Korean Shamanism and Cultural Nationalism*. Korean Studies Series, v.14. Seoul: Jimoondang.

Hoppál, Mihály. 2004. Cosmic Symbolism in Siberian Shamanhood. In *Shamanism: Critical Concepts in Sociology, v.1*, ed. Andrei A. Znamenski. pp. 177–92. London: RoutledgeCurzon.

Hosken, Liz. 2011. Reflections on an Inter-Cultural Journey into Earth Jurisprudence. In *Exploring Wild Law: The Philosophy of Earth Jurisprudence*, ed. Peter Burdon. pp. 24–34. Kent Town: Wakefield Press.

Humphrey, Caroline. 1999. Shamans in the City. *Anthropology Today*, 15(3), pp. 3–10.

——. 1994. Shamanic Practices and the State in Northern Asia. In *Shamanism, History, and the State*, eds Nicholas Thomas and Caroline Humphrey. Ann Arbor: University of Michigan.

Hultkrantz, Åke. 1973. A Definition of Shamanism. *Temenos*, 9, pp. 25–37.

Husserl, Edmund. 1999. *The Idea of Phenomenology* (trans. Lee Hardy). Edmund Husserl Collected Works v.VIII. ed. Rudolf Bernet. Dordrecht: Kluwer Academic Publishers.

Hutton, Ronald. 2001. *Shamans: Siberian Spirituality and the Western Imagination*. London: Hambledon and London.

IACrtHR. 2002. Case of the Mayagna (Sumo) Awas Tingni: Transcripts. *Arizona Journal of International and Comparative Law (Special Issue)*, 19(1), pp. 1–456.

ILO. 1989. *Convention Concerning Indigenous and Tribal Peoples in Independent Countries (No. 169)*. Geneva: International Labour Organization.

Indie Shaman. 2012. Welcome to Indie Shaman. [online] Available at: <http://www.indieshaman.co.uk> [Accessed: 9 May 2012].

IOL. 2007. White Sangoma Dreams His Destiny. *Independent on Sunday*, 28 April.

IUCN, WWF and UNEP. 1980. *World Conservation Strategy: Living Resource Conservation for Sustainable Development*. Gland: International Union for Conservation of Nature.

Jackson, Jean E. 1995. Preserving Indian Culture: Shaman Schools and Ethno-Education in the Vaupes, Colombia. *Cultural Anthropology*, 10(3), pp. 302–29.

———. and Kay B. Warren. 2005. Indigenous Movements in Latin America, 1992–2004: Controversies, Ironies, New Directions. *Annual Review of Anthropology*, 34, pp. 549–73.

Jacobs, Cedric. 1981. Papers Presented by Rev. Cedric Jacobs, Deputy National Chairman, National Aboriginal Conference, at the International NGO Conference on Indigenous Peoples and the Land, Palais Du Nations, Geneva, 15–18 September 1981. [online] Available at: <http://www.aiatsis.gov.au/collections/exhibitions/treaty/docs/nac/m0015847_a.pdf> [Accessed: 5 March 2012].

Jacobs, Robert R. 1980. Indians as Ecologists and Other Environmental Themes in American Frontier History. In *American Indian Environments: Ecological Issues in Native American History*, eds Christopher Vecsey and Robert W. Venables. pp. 46–64. Syracuse, NY: Syracuse University Press.

Janelli, Roger L. 1986. The Origins of Korean Folklore Scholarship. *Journal of American Folklore*, 99(391), pp. 24–49.

Jenkins, Philip. 2004. *Dream Catchers: How Mainstream American Discovered Native Spirituality*. New York: Oxford University Press.

Jenkins, Richard. 2002. *Pierre Bourdieu*. London: Routledge.

Jochelson, Waldemar. 1975a. *The Koryak* (reprint of the 1908 edition). Publications of the Jesup North Pacific Expedition, v.6. ed. Franz Boas. New York: AMS Press.

———. 1975b. *The Yukaghir and the Yukaghirized Tungus* (reprint of the 1926 edition). Publications of the Jesup North Pacific Expedition, v.9. ed. Franz Boas. New York: AMS Press.

Jocks, Christopher. 1996. Spirituality for Sale: Sacred Knowledge in the Consumer Age. *American Indian Quarterly*, 20(3/4), pp. 415–32.

Johnson, Mike. 2000. *Winning the People Wars: Talent and the Battle for Human Capital*. London: Financial Times Prentice Hall.

Johnson, Paul C. 2002. Migrating Bodies, Circulating Signs: Brazilian Candomblé, the Garifuna of the Caribbean, and the Category of Indigenous Religions. *History of Religions*, 41(4), pp. 301–27.

—— and Mary Keller. 2006. The Work of Possession(s). *Culture and Religion*, 7(2), pp. 111–22.

Jones, Stokes. 2006. From Ancestors to Herbs: Innovation According to 'the Protestant Reformation' in African Medicine. *Ethnographic Praxis in Industry Conference Proceedings*, 1, pp. 177–97.

Jowitt, Juliette. 2007. Amazon Tribe Hits Back at Green 'Colonialism'. *The Observer*, 14 October. [online] Available at: <http://www.guardian.co.uk/environment/2007/oct/14/climatechange.brazil> [Accessed: 31 May 2011].

Kalyvas, Stathis N. 1996. *The Rise of Christian Democracy in Europe*. Ithaca, NY: Cornell University Press.

Kandemwa, Mandaza. 2012a. Daré. [online] Available at: <http://www.mandaza.org/Dare.html> [Accessed: 11 May 2012].

——. 2012b. Heart Wisdom. [online] Available at: <http://mandazaheartwisdom.ning.com/profiles/blogs/mandaza-augustine-kandemwa> [Accessed: 14 May 2012].

——. 2012c. Home. [online] Available at: <http://www.mandaza.org/index.html> [Accessed: 11 May 2012].

——. 2012d. Mandaza (Augustine) Kandemwa, Heart Wisdom. [online] Available at: <http://www.facebook.com/pages/Mandaza-Augustine-Kandemwa-Heart-Wisdom/124906470936250> [Accessed: 14 May 2012].

——. 2012e. Mandaza Heart Wisdom. [online] Available at: <http://www.peacevillages.com/group/mandazaheartwisdom> [Accessed: 14 May 2012].

——. 2012f. Mandaza's 2011 Calendar. [online] Available at: <http://www.mandaza.org/Calendar.html> [Accessed: 11 May 2012].

——. 2012g. Mission. [online] Available at: <http://www.mandaza.org/Mission.html> [Accessed: 11 May 2012].

——. 2010. Mandaza's 2010 International Tour Dates. [online] Available at: <http://www.mandaza.org/calendar.html> [Accessed: 20 August 2010].

Kant, Immanuel. 2009. *An Answer to the Question: What Is Enlightenment?* (trans. H.B. Nisbet). London: Penguin.

Kaviraj, Sudipta. 1995. Religion, Politics and Modernity. In *Crisis and Change in Contemporary India*, eds Upendra Baxi and Bhikhu C. Parekh. pp. 295–316. New Delhi: Thousand Oaks.

Keeney, Bradford. 2006. *Shamanic Christianity: The Direct Experience of Mystical Communion*. Rochester: Destiny Books.

—— (ed.). 2001. *Vusamazulu Credo Mutwa: Zulu High Sansusi*. Sedona: Ringing Rocks Press & Leet's Island Books.

Kehoe, Alice Beck. 2000. *Shamans and Religion: An Anthropological Exploration in Critical Thinking*. Long Grove, IL: Waveland Press.

——. 1990. Primal Gaia: Primitivists and Plastic Medicine Men. In *The Invented Indian: Cultural Fictions and Government Policies*, ed. James A. Clifton. pp. 193–209. New Brunswick, NJ and London: Transaction.

Kendall, Laurel. 1998. Who Speaks for Korean Shamans When Shamans Speak of the Nation? In *Making Majorities: Constituting the Nation in Japan, Korea, China, Malaysia, Fiji, Turkey and the United States*, ed. Dru C. Gladney. pp. 55–72. Stanford, CA: Stanford University Press.

——. 1985. *Shamans, Housewives, and Other Restless Spirits: Women in Korean Ritual Life*. Honolulu: University of Hawaii.

—— and Igor Krupnik (eds). 2003. *Constructing Cultures Then and Now: Celebrating Franz Boas and the Jesup North Pacific Expedition*. Washington, DC: Arctic Studies Center, National Museum of Natural History, Smithsonian Institution.

Kim, Andrew Eungi. 2005. Nonofficial Religion in South Korea: Prevalence of Fortunetelling and Other Forms of Divination. *Review of Religious Research*, 46(3), pp. 284–302.

Kimmel, Michael S. (ed.). 1995. *The Politics of Manhood: Profeminist Men Respond to the Mythopoetic Men's Movement (and the Mythopoetic Leaders Answer)*. Philadelphia, PA: Temple University Press.

King, Richard. 2011. Imagining Religions in India: Colonialism and the Mapping of South Asian History and Culture. In *Secularism and Religion-Making*, eds Markus Dressler and Arvind-pal Singh Mandair. pp. 37–61. London: Routledge.

——. 1999. *Orientalism and Religion: Post-Colonial Theory, India and the Mystic East*. London: Routledge.

Kingsbury, Benedict. 2001. Reconciling Five Competing Conceptual Structures of Indigenous Peoples' Claims in International and Comparative Law. *Journal of International Law and Politics*, 34(1), pp. 189–250.

——. 1998. 'Indigenous Peoples' in International Law: A Constructivist Approach to the Asian Controversy. *American Journal of International Law*, 92(3), pp. 414–57.

Kipuri, Naomi. 2009. Chapter 2: Culture. In *State of the World's Indigenous Peoples*. pp. 51–81. Geneva: United Nations Permanent Forum on Indigenous Issues.

Kirby, Ernest Theodore. 1975. *Ur-Drama: The Origins of Theatre*. New York: New York University.

———. 1974. The Shamanistic Origins of Popular Entertainments. *Drama Review*, 18, pp. 5–15.

Kitiarsa, Pattana (ed.). 2007. *Religious Commodifications in Asia: Marketing Gods*. London: Routledge.

Klein, Mickie, Stephen Polcari and Marc Restellini. 2008. *Jackson Pollock et le Chamanisme*. Paris: Pinacothèque de Paris.

Knight, Nathaniel. 2000. 'Salvage Biography' and Useable Pasts: Russian Ethnographers Confront the Legacy of Terror. *Kritika: Explorations in Russian and Eurasian History*, 1(2), pp. 365–75.

Koch, Eddie. 1995. South Africa's Cure Allure. *Mail & Guardian*, 25 August.

Köhler, Thomas and Kathrin Wessendorf (eds). 2002. *Towards a New Millennium: Ten Years of the Indigenous Movement in Russia*. Copenhagen: International Working Group for Indigenous Affairs, and Russian Association of Indigenous Peoples of the North.

Kohnert, Dirk. 2003. Witchcraft and Transnational Social Spaces: Witchcraft Violence, Reconciliation and Development in South Africa's Transition Process. *Journal of Modern African Studies*, 41, pp. 217–45.

Kottler, Jeffrey A., Jon Carlson and Bradford Keeney. 2004. *American Shaman: An Odyssey of Global Healing Traditions*. New York: Brunner-Routledge.

Kovalaschina, Elena. 2007. The Historical and Cultural Ideals of the Siberian *Oblastnichestvo* (trans. Alia A. Chaptykova). *Sibirica*, 6(2), pp. 87–119.

Kraus, R.F. 1972. A Psychoanalytical Interpretation of Shamanism. *The Psychoanalytic Review*, 59(1), pp. 19–32.

Krech, Shepard. 1999. *The Ecological Indian: Myth and History*. New York: W.W. Norton.

Kronlid, David. 2003. *Ecofeminism and Environmental Ethics: An Analysis of Ecofeminist Ethical Theory*. Uppsala: Academiae Ubsaliensis.

Laird, Sarah A. and Rachel P. Wynberg. 1996. Biodiversity Prospecting in South Africa: Towards the Development of Equitable Partnerships. In *Managing Access to Genetic Resources: Towards Strategies for Benefit-Sharing*, eds J. Mugabe, C. Barber, G. Henne, L. Glowka, and A. La Vina. pp. 143–85. African Centre for Technology Studies, Nairobi and World Resources Institute, Washington, DC.

Lang, Andrew. 1891. Apparitions. In *The Encyclopaedia Britannica: A Dictionary of Arts, Sciences, and General Literature. With New Maps, and Original American Articles by Eminent Writers. With American Revisions and*

Additions, Bringing Each Volume up to Date, v.2, ed. Thomas Spencer Baynes. pp. 202–8. Chicago, IL: R.S. Peale Company.

Langdon, E. Jean. 2006. Shamans and Shamanisms: Reflections on Anthropological Dilemmas of Modernity. *Vibrant*, 4(2). [online] Available at: <www.vibrant.org.br/downloads/v4n2_langdon.htm> [Accessed: 26 April 2012].

Larner, Wendy. 2000. Neo-Liberalism: Policy, Ideology, Governmentality. *Studies in Political Economy*, 63(1), pp. 5–25.

Laruelle, Marlène. 2007. Religious Revival, Nationalism and the 'Invention of Tradition': Political Tengrism in Central Asia and Tatarstan. *Central Asian Survey*, 26(2), pp. 203–16.

Latour, Bruno. 1993. *We Have Never Been Modern* (trans. Catherine Porter). Hemel Hempstead: Prentice Hall.

Laufer, Berthold. 1917. Origin of the Word Shaman. *American Anthropologist*, 19, pp. 361–71.

Leatt, Annie. 2009. Laws of Ambivalence: 'Religion' and 'Things African' in Post-Apartheid South Africa. Paper presented at the annual meeting of the American Academy of Religion, Montreal, Quebec, 7–10 November. Used with permission.

Ledyard, John. 1966. *John Ledyard's Journey through Russia and Siberia 1787–1788: The Journal and Selected Letters*. ed. Stephen D. Watrous. Madison: University of Wisconsin Press.

Lemke, Thomas. 2001. 'The Birth of Bio-politics': Michel Foucault's Lecture at the Collège de France on Neo-Liberal Governmentality. *Economy and Society*, 30(2), pp. 190–207.

Levi-Strauss, Claude. 1963. *Structural Anthropology, v.1* (trans. Clair Jacobson and Brooke G. Schnoepf). New York and London: Basic Books.

Lewis, Herbert S. 2001. Boas, Darwin, Science, and Anthropology. *Current Anthropology*, 42(3), pp. 381–406.

Lewis, Ioan M. 1981. What Is a Shaman? *Folk*, 23, pp. 23–35.

——. 1971. *Ecstatic Religion: An Anthropological Study of Shamanism and Spirit Possession*. Harmondsworth: Penguin.

Lewis-Williams, J.D. 1995. Perspectives and Traditions on Southern African Rock Art Research. In *Percieving Rock Art: Social and Political Perspectives*, eds Knut Helskog and Bjornar Olsen. pp. 65–86. Oslo: Instituttet for Sammenlignende Kulturforskning.

Li, Tania Murray. 2000. The Politics of Indigenism: Articulating Indigenous Identity in Indonesia: Resource Politics and the Tribal Slot. *Comparative Studies in Society and History*, 42(1), pp. 149–79.

Lindquist, Galina. 2005. Healers, Leaders and Entrepreneurs: Shamanic Revival in Southern Siberia. *Culture & Religion*, 6(2), pp. 263–85.

Linked-In. 2012. Shamanism Group. [online] Available at: <http://www.linkedin.com/groups?groupDashboard=&gid=1468817&trk=anet_about-an-rr-0> [Accessed: 22 March 2014].

Little, Paul 1995. Ritual, Power and Ethnography at the Rio Earth Summit. *Critique of Anthropology*, 15(3), pp. 265–88.

Lockley, John. 2010. The Sangoma's Apprentice. *Spirit and Destiny*, June, pp. 34–5.

Lopez, Donald S. 2011. *The Tibetan Book of the Dead: A Biography*. Princeton, NJ: Princeton University Press.

———. 1998. *Prisoners of Shangri-La: Tibetan Buddhism in the West*. Chicago, IL: University of Chicago Press.

———. (ed.). 1995. *Curators of the Buddha: The Study of Buddhism under Colonialism*. Chicago, IL: University of Chicago Press.

Lovelock, James. 1979. *Gaia, a New Look at Life on Earth*. Oxford: Oxford University Press.

Lucero, José Antonio. 2006. Representing 'Real Indians': The Challenges of Indigenous Authenticity and Strategic Constructivism in Ecuador and Bolivia. *Latin American Research Review*, 41(2), pp. 31–56.

Luke, Timothy W. 1995. Sustainable Development as a Power/Knowledge System: The Problem of 'Governmentality'. In *Greening Environmental Policy: The Politics of a Sustainable Future*, eds Frank Fischer and Michael Black. pp. 21–32. London: Paul Chapman.

Ma, Xisha and Huiying Meng (eds). 2011. *Popular Religion and Shamanism* (trans. Zhen Chi and Thomas David DuBois). Leiden: Brill.

Mamdani, Mahmood. 1996. *Citizen and Subject: Contemporary Africa and the Legacy of Colonialism*. Kampala, Uganda: Fountain Publishers.

Mandair, Arvind-pal S. and Markus Dressler. 2011. Introduction: Modernity, Religion-Making, and the Postsecular. In *Secularism and Religion-Making*, eds Markus Dressler and Arvind-pal Singh Mandair. pp. 3–36. London: Routledge.

Manouelian, Edward. 2006. Found Artefacts: Allegories of Salvage in the Siberian Fiction of Waclaw Sieroszewski. *Slavonic & East European Review*, 84(1), pp. 16–31.

Manuel, George and Michael Posluns. 1974. *The Fourth World: An Indian Reality*. Toronto: Collier-Macmillan.

Marcus, George E. 1986. Contemporary Problems of Ethnography in the Modern World System. In *Writing Culture: The Poetics and Politics of Ethnography*, eds James Clifford and George E. Marcus. pp. 165–93. Berkeley: University of California Press.

Marcy, Randolph Barnes. 1863. *Thirty Years of Army Life on the Border*. Philadelphia, PA: Lippincott.

—— and George Brinton McClellan. 1854. *Exploration of the Red River of Louisiana, in the Year 1852*. Washington, DC: A.O.P. Nicholson.

Marden, Emily. 1999. The Neem Tree Patent: International Conflict over the Commodification of Life. *Boston College International and Comparative Law Review*, 22, pp. 279–95.

Marketdata Enterprises. 2013. Press Release: $10.4 Billion Self-Improvement Market Survives Scandals & Recession, 2 January 2013. [online] Available at: <http://www.prweb.com/releases/2013/1/prweb10275905.htm> [Accessed: 22 March 2013].

——. 2012a. *The Market for Self-Improvement Products and Services* (9th edition). Tampa: Marketdata Enterprises.

——. 2012b. Press Release: Self-Improvement Market Has Unfilled Niches for Entrepreneurs, 26 March 2012. [online] Available at: <http://www.prweb.com/releases/2012/3/prweb9323729.htm> [Accessed: 22March 2013].

——. 2010. Press Release: $11 Billion Self-Improvement Market Moves Online, 1 December 2010. [online] Available at: <http://www.prweb.com/releases/2010/12/prweb4847314.htm> [Accessed: 22 March 2013].

Martinez, Dennis. 1998. First People - Firsthand Knowledge. *Winds of Change*, 13(3). [online] Available at: <http://www.ser.org/iprn/history.asp> [Accessed: 29 July 2011].

Masuzawa, Tomoko. 2005. *The Invention of World Religions: Or, How Universalism Was Preserved in the Language of Pluralism*. Chicago, IL and London: University of Chicago Press.

Mato, Daniel. 1997. On Global and Local Agents and the Social Making of Transnational Identities and Related Agendas in 'Latin' America. *Identities*, 4(2), pp. 167–212.

Matthews, Washington. 1897. *Navajo Legends, Collected and Translated by Washington Matthews, with Introduction, Notes, Illustrations, Texts, Interlinear Translations, and Melodies*. Boston, MA and New York: Houghton, Mifflin and Company.

——. 1894. Songs of Sequence of the Navajo. *Journal of American Folklore*, 7(26), pp. 185–94.

——. 1888. The Prayer of a Navajo Shaman. *American Anthropologist*, 1(2), pp. 148–71.

——. 1886. Some Deities and Demons of the Navajos. *The American Naturalist*, 20(10), pp. 841–50.

——. 1885. Ninety-Fourth Regular Meeting, April 7, 1885. *Transactions of the Anthropological Society of Washington*, 3, pp. 139–41.

Max Müller, Friedrich. 1868. *Chips from a German Workshop, v.1* (2nd edition). London: Longman, Green, and Co.

Mbembe, Achille. 2002. African Modes of Self-Writing. *Public Culture*, 14(1), pp. 239–73.

——. 2001. *On the Postcolony*. Berkeley: University of California.

McCutcheon, Russell T. 2003. Autonomy, Unity, and Crisis: Rhetoric and the Invention of a Discipline. In *The Discipline of Religion: Structure, Meaning, Rhetoric*. pp. 54–82. London and New York: Routledge.

—— (ed.). 1999. *The Insider/Outsider Problem in the Study of Religion: A Reader*. London: Cassell.

—— 1997. *Manufacturing Religion: The Discourse on Sui Generis Religion and the Politics of Nostalgia*. New York: Oxford University Press.

McFague, Sallie. 2008. *A New Climate for Theology: God, the World, and Global Warming*. Minneapolis, MN: Fortress.

McGee, W.J. 1901. Man's Place in Nature. *American Anthropologist*, 3(1), pp. 1–13.

McGown, Jay and Beth Elpern Burrows. 2006. *Out of Africa: Mysteries of Access and Benefit-Sharing*. Edmonds: Edmonds Institute and African Centre for Biosafety.

McIntosh, Ian. 2000. Are There Indigenous Peoples in Asia? *Cultural Survival Quarterly*, 24(1), pp. 4–7.

McKay, Gretchen Crilly. 2012a. Fees and Cancellation Policy. [online] Available at: <http://www.ancestralwisdom.com/fees_cancellation.html> [Accessed: 7 May 2012].

——. 2012b. Gretchen Crilly Mckay, Shamanic Practitioner at Ancestral Wisdom. [online] Available at: <http://www.linkedin.com/pub/gretchen-crilly-mckay/a/37b/73b> [Accessed: 3 May 2012].

——. 2012c. Links. [online] Available at: <http://www.ancestralwisdom.com/Links.html> [Accessed: 16 May 2012].

——. 2012d. Shamanic Services. [online] Available at: <http://www.ancestralwisdom.com/Shamanic-Services.html> [Accessed: 7 May 2012].

——. 2009. Journey of an American Sangoma. [online] Available at: <http://www.ancestralwisdom.com/American_Sangoma_Rev2011.pdf> [Accessed: 1 May 2012].

McNeely, Jeffrey A. and David C. Pitt. 1985. *Culture and Conservation: The Human Dimension in Environmental Planning*. London: Croom Helm.

McQuire, William. 1989. *Bollingen: An Adventure in Collecting the Past*. Princeton, NJ: Princeton University.

Metzger, Deena. 2012. Publications, Performances, Presentations and Projects (a Very Partial List). [online] Available at: <http://www.deenametzger. com> [Accessed: 1 June 2012].

Mhlabane, Jabu. 2002. Sangomas Are Doing It for Themselves. *Mail & Guardian*, 4 April. [online] Available at: <http://mg.co.za/article/2002-01-21-sangomas-are-doing-it-for-themselves> [Accessed: 1 October 2007].

Mikhailovskii, V.M. 1895. Shamanism in Siberia and European Russia, Being the Second Part of '*Shamanstvo*' (trans. Oliver Wardrop). *Journal of the Royal Anthropological Institute*, 24, pp. 62–100; 126–58.

Miller, Peter and Nikolas Rose. 1990. Governing Economic Life. *Economy and Society*, 19(1), pp. 1–31.

Miller, Thomas R. 1999. Mannequins and Spirits: Representation and Resistance of Siberian Shamans. *Anthropology of Consciousness*, 10(4), pp. 69–80.

Mironov, N. D. and Sergei M. Shirokogorov. 1924. Śramana-Shaman: Etymology of the Word 'Shaman'. *Journal of the North China Branch of the Royal Asiatic Society*, 55, pp. 105–30.

Mitchell, Gordon and Eve Mullen (eds). 2002. *Religion and the Political Imagination in a Changing South Africa*. Munster: Waxman Verlag.

Mitriani, P. 1992. A Critical Overview of the Psychiatric Approaches to Shamanism. *Diogenes*, 158, pp. 145–64.

Moagi, Lefatshe. 2009. Transformation of the South African Health Care System with Regard to African Traditional Healers: The Social Effects of Inclusion and Regulation. *International NGO Journal*, 4(4), pp. 116–26.

Mojo Doctors. 2012. The Mojo Doctors Bradford and Hillary Keeney: Publications. [online] Available at: <http://www.mojodoctors.com/publications.php> [Accessed: 31 July 2012].

Money, Mike. 2001. Deceit and Duality: Jacob's Shamanic Vision. *Shaman*, 9(1), pp. 19–33.

Mooney, James. 1891. *The Sacred Formulas of the Cherokees*. Seventh Annual Report of the Bureau of Ethnology to the Secretary of the Smithsonian Institution. ed. J.W. Powell. Washington, DC: Government Printing Office.

——. 1890. The Cherokee Ball Play. *American Anthropologist*, 3(2), pp. 105–32.

——. 1889a. Cherokee and Iroquois Parallels. *Journal of American Folklore*, 2(4), p.67.

————. 1889b. Cherokee Mound-Building. *American Anthropologist*, 2(2), pp. 167–71.

————. 1888. Myths of the Cherokees. *Journal of American Folklore*, 1(2), pp. 97–108.

Moore, Rachel. 1994. Marketing Alterity. In *Visualizing Theory: Selected Essays from V.A.R. 1990–1994*, ed. Lucien Taylor. pp. 127–39. New York: Routledge.

Moyn, Samuel. 2010. *The Last Utopia: Human Rights in History*. Cambridge, MA: Belknap.

Mtshali, P.H. 2004. *The Power of the Ancestors: The Life of a Zulu Traditional Healer*. Mbabane: Kamhlaba Publications.

Muehlebach, Andrea. 2003. What Self in Self-Determination? Notes from the Frontiers of Transnational Indigenous Activism. *Identities*, 10(2), pp. 241–68.

————. 2001. 'Making Place' at the United Nations: Indigenous Cultural Politics at the U.N. Working Group on Indigenous Populations. *Cultural Anthropology*, 16(3), pp. 415–48.

Muir, Stewart. 2007. The Good of New Age Goods. *Culture & Religion*, 8(3), pp. 233–53.

Multinational Monitor. 1992. Yanomani in Peril: An Interview with Davi Kopenawa Yanomami. *Multinational Monitor*, 13(9). [online] Available at: <http://www.multinationalmonitor.org/hyper/issues/1992/09/mm0992_01.html> [Accessed: 6 March 2012].

Musi, Carla Corradi. 1997. *Shamanism from East to West*. Budapest: Akadémiai Kiadó.

Mutume, Gumisai. 2007. 'Indigenous' People Fight for Inclusion. *Africa Renewal*, 21(1), pp. 6–8.

Mutwa, Vusamazulu Credo. 2003. *Zulu Shaman: Dreams, Prophecies, and Mysteries*. ed. Stephen Larsen. Rochester: Destiny Books.

————. 1999. *Indaba, My Children: African Folk Tales*. New York: Grove Press.

————. 1996. *Song of the Stars: The Lore of a Zulu Shaman*. ed. Stephen Larsen. Barrytown: Station Hill Openings.

————. 1969. *My People: The Incredible Writings of Credo Vusa'mazulu Mutwa*. Johannesburg: Blue Crane Books.

————. 1966. *Africa Is My Witness*. Johannesburg: Blue Crane Books.

————. 1964. *Indaba, My Children*. Johannesburg: Blue Crane Books.

Myers, Jason C. 2008. *Indirect Rule in South Africa: The Costuming of Political Power*. Rochester, NY: University of Rochester Press.

———. 1999. The Spontaneous Ideology of Tradition in Post-Apartheid South Africa. *Politikon*, 26(1), pp. 33–54.

Nadasdy, Paul. 2005. Transcending the Debate over the Ecologically Noble Indian: Indigenous Peoples and Environmentalism. *Ethnohistory*, 52(2), pp. 291–331.

Nadel, S.F. 1946. A Study of Shamanism in the Nuba Mountains. *Journal of the Royal Anthropological Institute of Great Britain and Ireland*, 76(1), pp. 25–37.

Næss, Arne. 1973. The Shallow and the Deep, Long-Range Ecology Movement. *Inquiry*, 16(1), pp. 95–100.

Narby, Jeremy and Francis Huxley (eds). 2001. *Shamans through Time: 500 Years on the Path to Knowledge*. New York: Jeremy P. Tarcher.

Ndlovu-Gatsheni, Sabelo J. 2007. *Tracking the Historical Roots of Post-Apartheid Citizenship Problems: The Native Club, Restless Natives, Panicking Settlers and the Politics of Nativism in South Africa*. Leiden: African Studies Centre.

Neddermeyer, Dorothy M. 2009. Holistic Health Care Facts and Statistics. [online] Available at: <http://www.disabled-world.com/medical/alternative/holistic/care-statistics.php> [Accessed: 23 April 2012].

Neihardt, John G. 1932. *Black Elk Speaks: Being the Life Story of a Holy Man of the Oglala Sioux*. Lincoln: University of Nebraska.

Neu, Diann L. 2002. *Return Blessings: Ecofeminist Liturgies Renewing the Earth*. Glasgow: Wild Goose Publications.

Ngubane, Harriet. 1977. *Body and Mind in Zulu Medicine: An Ethnography of Health and Disease in Nyuswa-Zulu Thought and Practice*. London: Academic Press.

Nicholson, Shirley J. (ed.). 1987. *Shamanism: An Expanded View of Reality*. Wheaton: Theosophical Publishing House.

Niezen, Ronald. 2009. *The Rediscovered Self: Indigenous Identity and Cultural Justice*. Montréa: McGill-Queen's University Press.

———. 2003. *The Origins of Indigenism: Human Rights and the Politics of Identity*. Berkeley: University of California.

Noel, Daniel C. 1997. *The Soul of Shamanism: Western Fantasies, Imaginal Realities*. New York: Continuum.

Norrgard, Lenore. 2012a. Lenore Norrgard, MA, Certified Shamanic Counselor. [online] Available at: <http://www.lenorenorrgard.com/about.html> [Accessed: 20 May 2012].

———. 2012b. Lenore Norrgard, Shamanic Healing Artist. [online] Available at: <http://www.linkedin.com/in/lenorenorrgard> [Accessed: 20 May 2012].

———. 2012c. Shamanic Healing Apprenticehip Program. [online] Available at: <http://www.shamanicapprenticeship.com/Curriculum.html> [Accessed: 20 May 2012].

Novakovsky, Stanislaus. 1924. Arctic or Siberian Hysteria as a Reflex of the Geographic Environment. *Ecology*, 5(2), pp. 113–27.

NPC. 2011. *National Development Plan: Vision for 2030*. Pretoria: National Planning Commission of South Africa.

———. 2012. *National Development Plan 2030: Our Future – Make It Work*. Pretoria: National Planning Commission of South Africa.

Nygren, Anja. 1999. Local Knowledge in the Environment-Development Discourse: From Dichotomies to Situated Knowledges. *Critique of Anthropology*, 19(3), pp. 267–88.

O'Malley, Lurana D. 1997. The Monarch and the Mystic: Catherine the Great's Strategy of Audience Enlightenment in 'The Siberian Shaman'. *Slavic and East European Journal*, 41(2), pp. 224–42.

Odora Hoppers, Catherine A. (ed.). 2002. *Indigenous Knowledge Systems and the Integration of Knowledge Systems: Towards a Philosophy of Articulation*. Cape Town: New Africa Books.

Ohlmarks, Åke 1939. *Studien Zum Problem Des Schamanismus*. Lund: C.W.K. Gleerup.

Okigbo, R.N. and E.C. Mmeka. 2006. An Appraisal of Phytomedicine in Africa. *KMITL Science and Technology Journal*, 6(2), pp. 83–94.

Olupona, Jacob K. 2004. Introduction. In *Beyond Primitivism: Indigenous Religious Traditions and Modernity*, ed. Jacob K. Olupona. pp. 1–19. New York: Routledge.

Orenstein, Gloria F. 1993. Towards an Eco-Feminist Ethic of Shamanism and the Sacred. In *Ecofeminism and the Sacred*, ed. Carol J. Adams. pp. 172–80. New York: Continuum.

Parkipuny, Moringe L. 1987. The Indigenous Peoples Rights Question in Africa, Statement before the United Nations Working Group on Indigenous Populations. [online] Available at: <http://cwis.org/GML/UnitedNationsDocuments> [Accessed: 24 April 2012].

Penrose, Jan. 2002. Nations, States and Homelands: Territory and Territoriality in Nationalist Thought. *Nations and Nationalism*, 8(3), pp. 277–97.

Peterson, M. and T. Peterson. 1996. Ecology: Scientific, Deep and Feminist. *Environmental Values*, 5(2), pp. 123–46.

Pika, Aleksandr and Bruce Grant. 1999. *Neotraditionalism in the Russian North: Indigenous Peoples and the Legacy of Perestroika*. Edmonton: Canadian Circumpolar Institute.

Povinelli, Elizabeth A. 2001. Radical Worlds: The Anthropology of Incommensurability and Inconceivability. *Annual Review of Anthropology*, 30, pp. 319–34.

Pratt, Christina. 2012. Why Shamanism Now. [online] Available at: <http://whyshamanismnow.com> [Accessed: 20 May 2012].

———. 2010. Ubuntu Means Humanity, Interview with John Lockley. [podcast] 21 September. Available at: <http://whyshamanismnow.com/2010/09/ubuntu-means-humanity> [Accessed: 20 May 2012].

Pritchard, Sarah and Charlotte Heindow-Dolman. 1998. Indigenous Peoples and International Law: A Critical Overview. *Australian Indigenous Law Reporter*, 3(4), pp. 473–509.

Rabinow, Paul and Nikolas Rose. 2006. Biopower Today. *BioSocieties*, 1(2), pp. 195–217.

Rachelatssp. 2011. SSP. [video online] Available at: <http://www.youtube.com/watch?v=UdRQvWVy3dE> [Accessed: 26 June 2014].

Radlov, Vasilii Vasilievich. 1884. *Aüs Sibirien: Lose Blatter aus dem Tagebuche eines reisenden Linguisten*. Leipzig: T.O. Weigel.

——— and (ed.) Arthur T. Hatto. 1990. *The Manas of Wilhelm Radloff*. Wiesbaden: Harrasowitz.

Raibmon, Paige Sylvia. 2005. *Authentic Indians: Episodes of Encounter from the Late-Nineteenth-Century Northwest Coast*. Durham, NC: Duke University Press.

Ramos, Alcida. 2003. Pulp Fictions of Indigenism. In *Race, Nature, and the Politics of Difference*, eds Donald S. Moore, Jake Kosek and Anand Pandian. pp. 356–379. Durham, NC: Duke University Press.

———. 2000. *The Commodification of the Indian*. Série Antropologia, no. 281. Brasília: Universidade de Brasília.

———. 1998. *Indigenism: Ethnic Politics in Brazil*. Madison: University of Wisconsin Press.

———. 1994. The Hyperreal Indian. *Critique of Anthropology*, 14(2), pp. 153–71.

Rautenbach, Christa. 2011. Institutionalisation of African Traditional Medicine in South Africa: Healing Powers of the Law? *Journal of Contemporary Roman-Dutch Law*, 74(1), pp. 28–46.

Redford, Kent H. 1991. The Ecologically Noble Savage. *Cultural Survival Quarterly*, 15(1), pp. 46–8.

——— and Allyn Maclean Stearman. 1993. Forest-Dwelling Native Amazonians and the Conservation of Biodiversity: Interests in Common or in Collision? *Conservation Biology*, 7(2), pp. 248–55.

Rennie, Bryan S. (ed.). 2006. *Mircea Eliade: A Critical Reader*. London: Equinox.

—— (ed.). 2001. *Changing Religious Worlds: The Meaning and End of Mircea Eliade*. Albany, NY: State University of New York Press.

Robins, Steven L. (ed.). 2005. *Limits to Liberation after Apartheid: Citizenship, Governance and Culture*. Cape Town: David Philip.

——. 2003. Whose Modernity? Indigenous Modernities and Land Claims after Apartheid. *Development and Change*, 34(2), pp. 265–85.

——. 2001. NGOs, 'Bushmen' and Double Vision: The ≠ khomani San Land Claim and the Cultural Politics of 'Community' and 'Development' in the Kalahari. *Journal of Southern African Studies*, 27(4), pp. 833–53.

Robinson, Daniel F. 2010. *Confronting Biopiracy: Challenges, Cases and International Debates*. London: Earthscan.

Rose, Brian. 1965. Indaba, My Children (Review). *The Journal of Modern African Studies*, 3(3), pp. 471–2.

Rothenberg, Jerome (ed.). 1967. *Technicians of the Sacred: A Range of Poetries from Africa, America, Asia, Europe, and Oceania*. Garden City, NY: Doubleday.

Rowley, David G. 1999. Redeemer Empire: Russian Millenarianism. *American Historical Review*, 104(5), pp. 1582–602.

RRF. 2010a. Profiles of Healing. [online] Available at: <http://www.ringingrocks.org/publications/poh/overview.php> [Accessed: 24 May 2010].

——. 2010b. Profiles of Healing: Vusamazulu Credo Mutwa: Zulu High Sansusi. [online] Available at: <http://ringingrocks.org/publications/poh/vusamazuluCredoMutwa.php > [Accessed: 6 November 2010].

——. 2010c. Regarding Dr. Keeney. [online] Available at: <http://www.ringingrocks.org/www/index.php?about_keeney_bio> [Accessed: 21 May 2010].

Ruether, Rosemary Radford. 2005. *Integrating Ecofeminism, Globalization, and World Religions*. Lanham, MD: Rowman & Littlefield.

Santasombat, Yos. 2004. Karen Cultural Capital and the Political Economy of Symbolic Power. *Asian Ethnicity*, 5(1), pp. 105–20.

Santos-Granero, Fernando. 2009. Hybrid Bodyscapes: A Visual History of Yanesha Patterns of Cultural Change. *Current Anthropology*, 50(4), pp. 477–512.

Satran, Shilo. 2012. About Shilo. [online] Available at: <http://www.sacredtoolmaker.com/about.html> [Accessed: 26 June 2014].

Saunders, David B. 1982. Historians and Concepts of Nationality in Early Nineteenth-Century Russia. *Slavonic & East European Review*, 60(1), pp. 44–62.

Sayce, A.H. 1880. *Introduction to the Science of Language, v.2.* London: C. Keegan Paul & Co.

Schultz, Theodore W. 1961. Investment in Human Capital. *The American Economic Review*, 51(1), pp. 1–17.

———. 1970. *Investment in Human Capital: The Role of Education and of Research.* New York: Free Press.

Schwab, Raymond. 1984. *The Oriental Renaissance: Europe's Discovery of India and the East, 1680–1880* (trans. Gene Patterson-Black and Victor Reinking). New York: Columbia University Press.

Scott, Colin and Monica Mulrennan. 2010. Reconfiguring *Mare Nullius*: Torres Strait Islanders, Indigenous Sea Rights, and the Divergence of Domestic and International Norms. In *Indigenous Peoples and Autonomy: Insights for a Global Age*, eds Mario Blaser, Ravi de Costa, Deborah McGregor and William D. Coleman. pp. 148–76. Vancouver and Toronto: UBC Press.

Settler, Federico. 2015. *Consensus and Coercion: Religion and the State in Post-Apartheid South Africa.*

———. 2010. Indigenous Authorities and the Post-Colonial State: The Domestication of Indigeneity and African Nationalism in South Africa. *Social Dynamics*, 36(1), pp. 52–64.

Shirokogorov, Sergei Mikhailovich. 1935. *Psychomental Complex of the Tungus.* London: K. Paul, Trench, Trubner.

Sieder, Rachel. 2002a. Introduction. In *Multiculturalism in Latin America: Indigenous Rights, Diversity and Democracy*. pp. 1–23. London: Palgrave Macmillan.

———. 2002b. Recognising Indigenous Law and the Politics of State Formation in Mesoamerica. In *Multiculturalism in Latin America: Indigenous Rights, Diversity and Democracy*. pp. 184–207. London: Palgrave Macmillan.

Siikala, Ann-Leena. 2004. Siberian and Inner Shamanism. In *Shamanism: Critical Concepts in Sociology, v.1*, ed. Andrei A. Znamenski. pp. 149–64. London and New York: RoutledgeCurzon.

Silverman, Julian. 1967. Shamans and Acute Schizophrenia. *American Anthropologist*, 69(1), pp. 21–31.

Slezkine, Yuri. 1994. *Arctic Mirrors: Russia and the Small Peoples of the North.* Ithaca and London: Cornell University Press.

SME. 2009. Listening to Our Hearts and Standing in Our Medicine. [online] Available at: <www.shamanismcanada.com/pdf/mandaza.pdf> [Accessed: 26 June 2014].

Smith, Anthony Paul and Daniel Whistler (eds). 2010. *After the Postsecular and the Postmodern: New Essays in Continental Philosophy of Religion*: Cambridge: Scholars Press.

Smith, Jonathan Z. 2004. *Relating Religion: Essays in the Study of Religion*. Chicago, IL: University of Chicago Press.

———. 1998. Religion, Religions, Religious. In *Critical Terms for Religious Studies*, ed. Mark C. Taylor. pp. 269–84. Chicago, IL: University of Chicago Press.

———. 1987. In Search of Place. In *To Take Place: Toward Theory in Ritual*. pp. 1–23. Chicago, IL: University of Chicago Press.

———. 1982. *Imagining Religion: From Babylon to Jonestown*. Chicago, IL: University of Chicago Press.

———. 1978. *Map Is Not Territory: Essays in the History of Religions*. Leiden: E.J. Brill.

Smith, Mark J. 1998. *Ecologism: Towards Ecological Citizenship*. Buckingham: Open University Press.

Smith, Mick. 2001. *An Ethics of Place: Radical Ecology, Postmodernity, and Social Theory*. Albany: State University of New York.

Somé, Malidoma Patrice. 2012. Malidoma Patrice Somé. [online] Available at: <http://malidoma.com> [Accessed: 14 May 2012].

———. 1995. *Of Water and the Spirit: Ritual, Magic, and Initiation in the Life of an African Shaman*. New York: Penguin.

———. 1993. *Creating a New Sense of Home: The Tribal Community of the Heart*. [audiobook on cassette] Pacific Grove, CA: Oral Tradition Archives.

——— and Sobonfu Somé. 1994. *We Have No Word for Sex*. [audiobook on cassette] Pacific Grove, CA: Oral Tradition Archives.

Sorensen, Clark W. 1995. Folk Religion and Political Commitment in South Korea in the 1980s. In *Render Unto Caesar: The Religious Sphere in World Politics*, eds Sabrina P. Ramet and Donald W. Treadgold. pp. 325–53. Washington, DC: American University Press.

Sponsel, Leslie E. 2012. *Spiritual Ecology: A Quiet Revolution*. Santa Barbara, CA: Praeger.

Spivak, Gayatri Chakravorty. 2007. Religion, Politics, Theology: A Conversation with Achille Mbembe. *Boundary 2*, 34(2), pp. 147–70.

———. 1999. *A Critique of Postcolonial Reason: Towards a History of the Vanishing Present*. Cambridge, MA: Harvard University Press.

———. 1988. Can the Subaltern Speak? In *Marxism and the Interpretation of Culture*, eds Cary Nelson and Lawrence Grossberg. pp. 271–313. London: Macmillan.

SSP. 2014. 'About the Society' and 'SSP History'. [online] Available at: <http:// www.shamansociety.org > [Accessed: 22 March 2014].

Stavenhagen, Rodolfo. 2002. Indigenous Peoples and the State in Latin America: An Ongoing Debate. In *Multiculturalism in Latin America: Indigenous Rights, Diversity and Democracy*, ed. Rachel Sieder. pp. 24–44. London: Palgrave Macmillan.

Sternberg, Leo. 2004. Extracts from 'Divine Election in Primitive Religion'. In *Shamanism: Critical Concepts in Sociology, v.1*, ed. Andrei A. Znamenski. pp. 124–48. London and New York: RoutledgeCurzon. Originally published in Congrès International des Américanistes (eds). 1925. *Compte-rendu de la XXIe session, Congrès International des Américanistes*, pp. 472–512. Göteborg: Göteborg Museum.

Stevens, Stan. 1997. New Alliances for Conservation. In *Conservation through Cultural Survival: Indigenous Peoples and Protected Areas*, ed. Stan Stevens. pp. 33–62. Washington, DC: Island Press.

Stolfo, Christin. 2009. Interview with Gretchen Crilly Mckay. *Luminous Living*. [audio blog] 17 September. Available at: <http://www.blogtalkradio.com/ illuminated/2009/09/17/luminous-living-interview-with-gretchen-crilly- mckay> [Accessed: 4 May 2012].

Sturgeon, Noel (ed.). 1997. Intersections of Feminisms and Environmentalisms. *Frontiers (special issue)*, 18(2).

Survival International. 2012. The Yanomami. [online] Available at: <http:// www.survivalinternational.org/tribes/yanomami> [Accessed: 18 March 2012].

Swartz, David. 1996. Bridging the Study of Culture and Religion: Pierre Bourdieu's Political Economy of Symbolic Power. *Sociology of Religion*, 57(1), pp. 71–85.

———. 1997. *Culture and Power: The Sociology of Pierre Bourdieu*. Chicago, IL: University of Chicago Press.

Sylvain, Renée. 2005. Disorderly Development: Globalization and the Idea of 'Culture' in the Kalahari. *American Ethnologist*, 32(3), pp. 354–70.

———. 2002. 'Land, Water, and Truth': San Identity and Global Indigenism. *American Anthropologist*, 104(4), pp. 1074–85.

Taber, Jay. 2011. Jay Taber. [online] Available at: <http://www.linkedin.com/ in/jaytaber> [Accessed: 15 December 2011].

Taussig, Michael. 1999. *Defacement: Public Secrecy and the Labour of the Negative*. Stanford, CA: Stanford University Press.

——. 1998. Viscerality, Faith, and Skepticism: Another Theory of Magic. In *In near Ruins: Cultural Theory at the End of the Century*, ed. Nicholas B. Dirks. pp. 221–56. Minneapolis, MN: University of Minnesota.

——. 1993. *Mimesis and Alterity: A Particular History of the Senses*. London: Routledge.

——. 1992. *The Nervous System*. London: Routledge.

——. 1989. The Nervous System Part 1: Homesickness and Dada. *Kroeber Anthropological Society Papers*, 69–70, pp. 32–61.

——. 1986. *Shamanism, Colonialism, and the Wild Man: A Study in Terror and Healing*. Chicago, IL: University of Chicago Press.

Taylor, Bron. 2009. *Dark Green Religion: Nature Spirituality and the Planetary Future*. Berkeley and Los Angeles: University of California Press.

——. 2001a. Earth and Nature-Based Spirituality (Part 1): From Deep Ecology to Radical Environmentalism. *Religion*, 31(2), pp. 175–93.

——. 2001b. Earth and Nature-Based Spirituality (Part 2): From Earth First! and Bioregionalism to Scientific Paganism and the New Age. *Religion*, 31(3), pp. 225–45.

—— and Gavin Van Horn. 2006. Nature Religion and Environmentalism in North America. In *Faith in America: Changes, Challenges, New Directions*, v.3, ed. Charles H. Lippy. pp. 165–90. Westport, CT: Praeger.

Taylor, Charles. 2007. *A Secular Age*. Cambridge, MA: Belknap.

Tennant, Chris. 1994. Indigenous Peoples, International Institutions, and the International Legal Literature from 1945–1993. *Human Rights Quarterly*, 16(1), pp. 1–57.

Theodoratus, Robert J. 1977. Waclaw Sieroszewski and the Yakut of Siberia. *Ethnohistory*, 24(2), pp. 103–15.

THO. 2012. 'About Us' and 'Documents'. [online] Available at: <http://www.traditionalhealth.org.za> [Accessed: 26 June 2014].

Thomas, Nicholas and Caroline Humphrey (eds). 1996. *Shamanism, History and the State*. Ann Arbor: University of Michigan Press.

Thorley, Anthony and Celia M. Gunn. 2007. *Sacred Sites: An Overview*. London: GAIA. [online]Available at: <http://www.sacredland.org/media/Sacred-Sites-an-Overview.pdf> [Accessed: 23 January 2012].

Thornton, Robert. 2009. The Transmission of Knowledge in South African Traditional Healing. *Africa*, 79, pp. 17–34.

TKDL. 2012. 'About TKDL' and 'TKDL in Media'. [online] Available at: <http://www.tkdl.res.in/tkdl/langdefault/common/Home.asp?GL=Eng> [Accessed: 26 June 2014].

Tolz, Vera. 2009. European, National, and (Anti-)Imperial: The Formation of Academic Oriental Studies in Late Tsarist and Early Soviet Russia. *Kritika: Explorations in Russian and Eurasian History*, 9(1), pp. 53–81.

Townsend, Joan B. 1997. Shamanism. In *Anthropology of Religion: A Handbook*, ed. Stephen D. Glazier. Westport, CT: Greenwood Press.

Tremlett, Paul-François. 2008. *Religion and the Discourse on Modernity*. London and New York: Continuum.

Turner, Rachel S. 2007. The 'Rebirth of Liberalism': The Origins of Neo-Liberal Ideology. *Journal of Political Ideologies*, 12(1), pp. 67–83.

Turner, Terence. 1997. Human Rights, Human Difference: Anthropology's Contribution to a Emancipatory Cultural Politics. *Journal of Anthropological Research*, 53(4), pp. 273–91.

——. 1995. An Indigenous Peoples Struggle for Socially Equitable and Ecologically Sustainable Production: The Kayapo Revolt against Extractivism. *Journal of Latin American Anthropology*, 1(1), pp. 98–121.

——. 1991. Representing, Resisting, Rethinking: Historical Transformations of Kayapo Culture and Anthropological Consciousness. In *Colonial Situations: Essays on the Contextualization of Ethnographic Knowledge*, ed. George W. Stocking. pp. 285–313. Madison: University of Wisconsin.

Uccusic, Paul. 2000. Shamanism Alive and Well: The 1999 Legacy of the First FSS Expedition to Tuva. *Shamanism*, 13(1&2). [online] Available at: <http://www.shamanism.org/articles/article11.html> [Accessed: 26 June 2014].

UN. 2009. *State of the World's Indigenous Peoples*. Geneva: United Nations Permanent Forum on Indigenous Issues, ST/ESA/328.

——. 2007. *Declaration on the Rights of Indigenous Peoples*. Geneva: United Nations Organisation.

——. 1960. *Declaration on the Granting of Independence to Colonial Countries and Peoples*. Geneva: United Nations Organisation.

——. 2001. *Prevention of Discrimination and Protection of Indigenous Peoples and Minorities: Indigenous Peoples and Their Relationship to Land, Final Working Paper Prepared by the Special Rapporteur, Mrs. Erica-Irene A. Daes, E/CN.4/Sub.2/2001/21*. Geneva: United Nations Commission on Human Rights.

——. 1999. *Study on Treaties, Agreements and Other Constructive Arrangements between States and Indigenous Populations, Final Report by Special Rapporteur Miguel Alfonso Martínez, E/CN.4/Sub.2/1999/20*. Geneva: United Nations Commission on Human Rights.

——. 1983a. *Study of the Problem of Discrimination against Indigenous Populations: Chapter 17: Land, E/CN.4/Sub.2/1983/21/Add.4.* New York: United Nations Economic and Social Council.

——. 1983b. *Study of the Problem of Discrimination against Indigenous Populations: Final Report (Last Part), E/CN.4/Sub.2/1983/21/Add.8.* New York: United Nations Economic and Social Council.

——. 1982. *Study of the Problem of Discrimination against Indigenous Populations: Chapter 19: Religious Rights and Practices, E/CN.4/Sub.2/1982/2/Add.7.* New York: United Nations Economic and Social Council.

——. 1981a. *Study of the Problem of Discrimination against Indigenous Populations: Chapter 4: Other International Action, E/CN.4/Sub.2/476/Add.5.* New York: United Nations Economic and Social Council.

——. 1981b. *Study of the Problem of Discrimination against Indigenous Populations: Introduction (Part 1), E/CN.4/Sub.2/476.* New York: United Nations Economic and Social Council.

UNEP. 2013. *A Toolkit to Support Conservation by Indigenous Peoples and Local Communities: Building Capacity and Sharing Knowledge for Indigenous Peoples' and Community Conserved Territories and Areas (ICCAS).* Cambridge, UK: United Nations Environment Programme World Conservation Monitoring Centre.

UNHRC. 2007. *Good Governance Practices for the Protection of Human Rights.* Geneva: Office of the United Nations High Commissioner for Human Rights.

——. 1994. *General Comment No. 23: The Rights of Minorities (Art. 27), CCPR/C/21/Rev.1/Add.5.* Geneva: Office of the United Nations High Commissioner for Human Rights.

Urban, Hugh B. 2003. Sacred Capital: Pierre Bourdieu and the Study of Religion. *Method and Theory in the Study of Religion*, 15(4), pp. 354–89.

Valentine, Lisa Philips and Regna Darnell (eds). 1999. *Theorizing the Americanist Tradition.* Toronto: University of Toronto.

Van Binsbergen, Wim M.J. 2005. 'We Are in This for the Money': Commodification and the Sangoma Cult of Southern Africa. In *Commodification: Things, Agency, and Identities (the Social Life of Things Revisited)*, eds Wim M.J. van Binsbergen and Peter Geschiere. pp. 319–48. Münster: Lit Verlag.

Van Cott, Donna Lee. 2006. Turning Crisis into Opportunity: Achievements of Excluded Groups in the Andes. In *State and Society in Conflict: Comparative*

Perspectives on Andean Crises, eds Paul W. Drake and Eric Hershberg. pp. 157–89. Pittsburgh, PA: Pittsburgh University Press.

———. 2002. *Constitutional Reform in the Andes: Redefining Indigenous-State Relations*. Basingstoke: Palgrave MacMillan.

———. 2000. Latin America: Constitutional Reform and Ethnic Right. *Parliamentary Affairs*, 53(1), pp. 41–54.

———. 1994. *Indigenous Peoples and Democracy in Latin America*. New York: St. Martin's Press.

Van der Oye, David S. 2010. *Russian Orientalism: Asia in the Russian Mind from Peter the Great to the Emigration*. New Haven, CT: Yale University Press.

Van Niekerk, J.P. de V. 2012. Traditional Healers Formalised? *South African Medical Journal*, 102(3), pp. 105–6.

Varese, Stefano. 1996. The New Environmentalist Movement of Latin American Indigenous People. In *Valuing Local Knowledge: Indigenous People and Intellectual Property Rights*, eds Stephen B. Brush and Doreen Stabinsky. pp. 122–42. Washington, DC: Island Press.

Vaughan-Lee, Llewellyn (ed.). 2013. *Spiritual Ecology: The Cry of the Earth*. Point Reyes, CA: The Golden Sufi Center.

Veber, Hannah. 1992. Why Indians Wear Clothes: Managing Identity across an Ethnic Boundary. *Ethnos*, 57(1–2), pp. 51–60.

———. 1996. External Inducement and Non-Westernization in the Uses of the Asheninka Cushma. *Journal of Material Culture*, 1(2), pp. 155–82.

Vecsey, Christopher and Robert W. Venables (eds). 1980. *American Indian Environments: Ecological Issues in Native American History*. Syracuse, NY: Syracuse University Press.

Vidal, John. 2009. When Davi Kopenawa Yanomami Leaves Home, You Know the World Is in Trouble. *Guardian*, 13 June.

Vitebsky, Piers. 1995. From Cosmology to Environmentalism: Shamanism as Local Knowledge in a Global Setting. In *Counterworks: Managing the Diversity of Knowledge*, ed. Richard Fardon. pp. 172–91. London: Routledge. Reprinted in Graham Harvey (ed.). 2003. *Shamanism: A Reader*. pp. 276–98. London: Routledge.

———. 2000. Shamanism. In *Indigenous Religions: A Companion*, ed. Graham Harvey. pp. 55–67. London: Cassell.

Voigt, Vilmos. 2008. Amban-Lai, a Siberian Shaman? The First Theatrical Representation of a Shaman: A Play by Empress Catherine II of Russia. *Shaman*, 16(1&2), pp. 115–36.

Von Strahlenberg, Philipp Johann. 1970. *Russia, Siberia and Great Tartary*. London: Arno Press and New York Times. Originally published in English in 1738 as *An Historico-Geographical Description of the North and Eastern Parts of Europe and Asia; But More Particularly of Russia, Siberia, and Great Tartary, translated from the original German edition of 1726.*

Von Stuckrad, Kocku. 2003. *Schamanismus Und Esoterik. Kultur- Und Wissenschaftsgeschichtliche Betrachtungen.* Leuven: Peeters.

——. 2002. Reenchanting Nature: Modern Western Shamanism and Nineteenth-Century Thought. *Journal of the American Academy of Religion*, 70(4), pp. 771–99.

Vuckovic, Nancy H., Christina M. Gullion, Louise A. Williams, Michelle Ramirez and Jennifer Schneider. 2007. Feasibility and Short-Term Outcomes of a Shamanic Treatment for Temporomandibular Joint Disorders. *Alternative Therapies in Health and Medicine*, 13(6), pp. 18–29.

Vuotto, Jonathan P. 2004. Awas Tingni v. Nicaragua: International Precedent for Indigenous Land Rights. *Boston University International Law Journal*, 22(1), pp. 219–43.

Walker, Andrew. 2001. The 'Karen Consensus', Ethnic Politics and Resource-Use Legitimacy in Northern Thailand. *Asian Ethnicity*, 2(2), pp. 145–62.

Wallis, Robert J. 2003. *Shamans / Neo-Shamans: Ecstasy, Alternative Archaeologies and Contemporary Pagans.* London and New York: Routledge.

——. 1998. Journeying the Politics of Ecstasy: Anthropological Perspectives on Neoshamanism. *Pomegranate: The International Journal of Pagan Studies*, 6, pp. 20–28.

Walters, Victoria. 2010. The Artist as Shaman: The Work of Joseph Beuys and Marcus Coates. In *Between Art and Anthropology : Contemporary Ethnographic Practice*, eds Arnd Schneider and Christopher Wright. Oxford: Berg.

Ward, Duren J.H. 1909. *The Classifications of Religions: Different Methods, Their Advantages and Disadvantages.* Chicago, IL: Open Court Publishing Company.

Warner, Michael, Jonathan Van Antwerpen and Craig Calhoun (eds). 2010. *Varieties of Secularism in a Secular Age.* Cambridge, MA: Harvard University Press.

Warren, Karen J. (ed.). 1997. *Ecofeminism: Women, Culture, Nature.* Indianapolis: Indiana University.

Warren, Kay B. 1998. *Indigenous Movements and Their Critics: Pan-Mayan Activism in Guatemala.* Princeton, NJ: Princeton University Press.

—— and Jean Jackson (eds). 2002a. *Indigenous Movements, Self-Representation and the State in South America.* Austin: University of Texas Press.

—— and Jean Jackson. 2002b. Introduction: Studying Indigenous Activism in Latin America. In *Indigenous Movements, Self-Representation and the*

State in South America, eds Kay Warren and Jean Jackson. pp. 1–46. Austin: University of Texas Press.

Watrous, Stephen. 1993. The Regionalist Conception of Siberia, 1860 to 1920. In *Between Heaven and Hell: The Myth of Siberia in Russian Culture*, eds Galya Diment and Yuri Slezkine. pp. 113–32. New York: St. Martin's Press.

Wax, Emily. 2010. 'Yoga Wars' Spoil Spirit of Ancient Practice, Indian Agency Says. *Washington Post*, 23 August.

WCC. 1971. *Declaration of Barbados*. Barbados: World Council of Churches, Programme to Combat Racism.

WCED. 1987. *Our Common Future*. Oxford: Oxford University Press.

WCIP. 1981. 'Some Reflections on Group Right Principles', and National Congress of American Indians' Annex 'Indigenous Ideology and Philosophy', Submission to Indigenous Ideology and Philosophy Workshop II by Secretariat of the National Aboriginal Conference, Canberra, Australian, 27 April–2 May. [online] Available at: <http://cwis.org/GML/TribalAndInter-TribalResolutionsAndPapers/WCIP.php> [Accessed: 24 April 2012].

——. 1979. Indigenous Peoples' Fishing Rights and Responsibilities: Draft Presentation before the International Conference on Fisheries, Sponsored by the Government of Mexico, 15 December 1979. [online] Available at: <http://cwis.org/GML/TribalAndInter-TribalResolutionsAndPapers/WCIP.php> [Accessed: 24 April 2012].

Wernitznig, Dagmar. 2003. *Going Native or Going Naive?: White Shamanism and the Neo-Noble Savage*. Lanham, MD: University Press of America.

Whitehead, Neil and Robin M. Wright (eds). 2004. *In Darkness and Secrecy: The Anthropology of Assault Sorcery and Witchcraft in Amazonia* Durham, NC: Duke University Press.

WHO. 2008. Traditional Medicine Fact Sheet. [online] Available at: <http://www.who.int/mediacentre/factsheets/fs134/en/> [Accessed: 24 April 2012].

Wiessner, Siegfried. 2011. The Cultural Rights of Indigenous Peoples: Achievements and Continuing Challenges. *European Journal of International Law*, 22(1), pp. 121–40.

Winkelman, Michael. 2010. *Shamanism: A Biopsychosocial Paradigm of Consciousness and Healing* (2nd edition). Santa Barbara, CA: Praeger.

——. 2006. Shamanism and Biological Origins of Religiosity. *Shaman*, 14(1&2), pp. 89–116.

——. 2004. Shamanism as the Original Neurotheology. *Zygon*, 39(1), pp. 193–217.

———. 2002a. Shamanism and Cognitive Evolution. *Cambridge Archaeological Journal*, 12(1), pp. 71–101.

———. 2002b. Shamanism as Neurotheology and Evolutionary Psychology. *American Behavioural Scientist*, 45(12), pp. 1875–87.

———. 2000. *Shamanism: The Neural Ecology of Consciousness and Healing*. Westport, CT: Bergin and Garvey.

———. 1992. *Shamans, Priests, and Witches: A Cross-Cultural Study of Magico-Religious Practitioners*. Tempe: Arizona State University.

———. 1990. Shamans and Other 'Magico-Religious' Healers: A Cross-Cultural Study of Their Origins, Nature, and Social Transformations. *Ethos*, 18(3), pp. 308–52.

———. 1986. Magico-Religious Practitioner Types and Socioeconomic Conditions. *Behavior Science Research*, 20(1), pp. 17–46.

World Bank. 2006. Biodiversity and Health Symposium Conclusions and Recommendations. *IK Notes*, 92.

Worobec, Catherine D. 2001. *Possessed: Women, Witches, and Demons in Imperial Russia*. Dekalb: Northern Illinois University Press.

Wreford, Jo Thobeka. 2008. *Working with Spirit: Experiencing Izangoma Healing in Contemporary South Africa*. Oxford: Berghahn Books.

———. 2007. 'Long-Nosed' Hybrids? Sharing the Experiences of White Izangoma in Contemporary South Africa. *Journal of Southern African Studies*, 33(4), pp. 829–43.

———. 2006. *Talking to the White: Sharing the Experiences of White Sangoma in Contemporary South Africa*. Cape Town: Centre for Social Science Research Working Papers.

Wright, Robin M. 2011. 'You Are Going to Save Many Lives': The Life Story of Mandu Da Silva, *Hohodene* Jaguar Shaman. *Shamanism Annual*, 24, pp. 30–36.

———. 2009. The Art of Being Crente: The Baniwa Protestant Ethic and the Spirit of Sustainable Development. *Identities*, 16, pp. 202–26.

———. 2007. Indigenous Moral Philosophies and Ontologies and Their Implications for Sustainable Development. *Journal for the Study of Religion, Nature and Culture*, 1(1), pp. 92–108.

———. 1998. *Cosmos, Self, and History in Baniwa Religion: For Those Unborn*. Austin: University of Texas.

———. 1988. Anthropological Presuppositions of Indigenous Advocacy. *Annual Review of Anthropology*, 17, pp. 365–90.

Xanthaki, Alexandra. 2004. Indigenous Rights in the Russian Federation: The Case of Numerically Small Peoples of the Russian North, Siberia, and Far East. *Human Rights Quarterly*, 26(1), pp. 74–105.

Zhukovskaya, N. L. 2000. Neo-Shamanism in the Context of the Contemporary Ethno-Cultural Situation in the Republic of Buryatia. *Inner Asia*, 2, pp. 25–36.

Zimmerman, Michael E., J. Baird Callicott, George Sessions, Karen J. Warren and John Clark (eds). 1998. *Environmental Philosophy: From Animal Rights to Radical Ecology*. Englewood Cliffs, NJ: Prentice-Hall.

Žižek, Slavoj. 2010. *Living in the End Times*. London: Verso.

Znamenski, Andrei A. 2007. *The Beauty of the Primitive: Shamanism and the Western Imagination*. Oxford and New York: Oxford University Press.

———. 2005. Power of Myth: Popular Ethnonationalism and Nationality Building in Mountain Altai, 1904–1922. *Acta Slavica Iaponica*, 22, pp. 25–52.

———. 2004a. General Introduction: Adventures of a Metaphor: Shamanism and Shamanism Studies. In *Shamanism: Critical Concepts in Sociology*, *v.1*, ed. Andrei A. Znamenski. pp. xix–lxxxvi. London and New York: RoutledgeCurzon.

———. 2004b. The Beauty of the Primitive: Native Shamanism in Siberian Regionalist Imagination, 1860s–1920. *Shaman*, 12(1&2), pp. 145–71.

———. 2003a. *Shamanism in Siberia: Russian Records of Indigenous Spirituality*. Dordrecht, Boston, MA and London: Kluwer Academic Publishers.

———. 2003b. *Through Orthodox Eyes: Russian Missionary Narratives of Travels to the Dena'ina and Ahtna, 1850s–1930s* (trans. Andrei A. Znamenski). Fairbanks: University of Alaska Press.

———. 1999. *Shamanism and Christianity: Native Encounters with Russian Orthodox Missions in Siberia and Alaska, 1821–1917*. Westport, CA: Greenwood Press.

Index